Communications
in Computer and Information Science 478

T0212910

Sissi Closs   Rudi Studer
Emmanouel Garoufallou
Miguel-Angel Sicilia (Eds.)

Metadata and Semantics Research

8th Research Conference, MTSR 2014
Karlsruhe, Germany, November 27-29, 2014
Proceedings

 Springer

Volume Editors

Sissi Closs
Hochschule Karlsruhe
Technik und Wirtschaft, Fakultät IMM
Amalienstr. 81-87, 76133 Karlsruhe, Germany
E-mail: closs@ctopic.de, sissi.closs@hs-karlsruhe.de

Rudi Studer
Karlsruhe Institute of Technology (KIT)
Institute AIFB
76128 Karlsruhe, Germany
E-mail: studer@kit.edu

Emmanouel Garoufallou
Alexander Technological Educational Institute of Thessaloniki
Department of Library Science and Information Systems
57400 Thessaloniki, Greece
E-mail: mgarou@libd.teithe.gr

Miguel-Angel Sicilia
University of Alcalá
Computer Science Department, Polytechnic School
Ctra. Barcelona km. 33.6, 28871 Alcalá de Henares, Madrid, Spain
E-mail: msicilia@uah.es

ISSN 1865-0929   e-ISSN 1865-0937
ISBN 978-3-319-13673-8   e-ISBN 978-3-319-13674-5
DOI 10.1007/978-3-319-13674-5
Springer Cham Heidelberg New York Dordrecht London

Library of Congress Control Number: 2014955465

Typesetting: Camera-ready by author, data conversion by Scientific Publishing Services, Chennai, India

Printed on acid-free paper

Springer is part of Springer Science+Business Media (www.springer.com)

Preface

Metadata and semantics are integral to any information system and significant to the sphere of Web data. Research focusing on metadata and semantics is crucial to advancing our understanding and knowledge of metadata; and, more profoundly, for being able to effectively discover, use, archive, and repurpose information. In response to this need, researchers are actively examining methods for generating, reusing, and interchanging metadata. Integrated with these developments is research on the application of computational methods, linked data, and data analytics. A growing body of work also targets conceptual and theoretical designs providing foundational frameworks for metadata and semantic applications. There is no doubt that metadata weaves its way nearly through every aspect of our information ecosystem, and there is great motivation for advancing the current state of metadata and semantic. To this end, it is vital that scholars and practitioners convene and share their work.

Since 2005, the Metadata and Semantics Research Conference (MTSR) has served as a significant venue for dissemination and sharing of metadata and semantic-driven research and practices. This year, 2014, marked the eighth MTSR—Metadata and Semantics Research Conference, drawing scholars and researchers investigating and advancing our knowledge on a wide range of metadata and semantic-driven topics. MTSR has grown in numbers and submission rates over the last decade, marking it as a leading, international research conference. Continuing the successful mission of previous MTSR conferences (MTSR 2005, MTSR 2007, MTSR 2009, MTSR 2010, MTSR 2011, MTSR 2012, and MTSR 2013), MTSR 2014 aimed to bring together scholars and practitioners that share a common interest in the interdisciplinary field of metadata, linked data, and ontologies.

The MTSR 2014 program and the contents of the following proceeding show a rich diversity of research and practices from metadata and semantically focused tools and technologies, linked data, cross language semantics, ontologies, metadata models, semantic systems, and metadata standards. The general session of the conference included 13 papers covering a broad spectrum of topics, proving the interdisciplinary field of metadata, and was divided into three main themes: Metadata and Linked Data: Tools and Models; (Meta)Data Quality Assessment and Curation; and Semantic Interoperability, Ontology-Based Data Access, and Representation. Metadata as a research topic is maturing, and the conference also supported the following four tracks: Metadata and Semantics for Open Repositories; Research Information Systems and Data Infrastructures;

Big Data and Digital Libraries in Health, Science, and Technology; Metadata and Semantics for Cultural Collections and Applications; Metadata and Semantics for Agriculture, Food, and Environment. Each of these tracks had a rich selection of papers, in total 19, giving broader diversity to MTSR, and enabling deeper exploration of significant topics.

All the papers underwent a thorough and rigorous peer-review process. The review and selection this year was highly competitive and only papers containing significant research results, innovative methods, or novel and best practices were accepted for publication. Only 23 of 57 submissions were accepted as full papers, representing 40.35% of the total number of submissions. Additional contributions covering noteworthy and important results in project reports were accepted, totaling 32 accepted contributions.

This year's conference included two outstanding keynote speakers. Dr. Philipp Slusallek, Professor for Computer Graphics at Saarland University and Scientific Director at the German Research Center for Artificial Intelligence (DFKI), presented an outstanding keynote "Simulated Reality: Intelligent and Efficient Use of Semantics in 3D Environments" in which he addressed his main current research activities that include 3D visualization with semantic content, semantic reasoning for SW agents in these environments, and semantic middleware in the context of ARVIDA.

The second keynote speaker was Dr. H.C. Peter Wittenburg, Senior Advisor Data Systems at Max Planck Compute and Data Center and Senior Advisor "The Language Archive" at Max Planck Institute for Psycholinguistics. The title of his presentation was "Principles for Proper Data Stewardship and Re-use – An RDA View."

This year's conference also offered two tutorials for Semantic MediaWiki. Tobias Noeske, a Wiki expert, gave an introduction into Semantic MediaWiki, and Jonas Wäckerle, a Semantic MediaWiki professional, showed in detail how to set up Semantic MediaWiki for special purposes.

It is fitting that MTSR 2014 was in Karlsruhe, the second-largest city in the state of Baden-Württemberg, in southwest Germany, near the Franco-German border. Karlsruhe is a city that can be referred to as a "knowledge factory with savoir vivre." The Karlsruhe University of Applied Sciences, the largest university of technology in the state of Baden-Württemberg, was both honored and inspired to host MTSR. The conference organizers were committed to supporting an engaging conference environment enabling thoughtful discussion and advancing approaches to addressing metadata challenges.

We conclude this preface by thanking the many people who contributed their time and energy to MTSR 2014, and made possible this year's conference. We thank, also, all the organizations that supported the conference.

We extend a sincere thank you to members of the Program Committees (track committees included), the Steering Committee and the Organizing Committees (both general and local), and the conference reviewers. A special thank you to our colleagues D. Koutsomiha and P. Gaitanou, who assisted us with the proceedings.

September 2014   Sissi Closs
                                                                Rudi Studer
                                                        Emmanouel Garoufallou
                                                        Miguel-Angel Sicilia

Organization

General Chairs

Sissi Closs, (Chair) Karlsruhe University of Applied Sciences, Germany

Rudi Studer, (Co-chair) Karlsruhe Institute of Technology (KIT), Germany

Program Chair

Garoufallou, Emmanouel Alexander Technological Educational Institute of Thessaloniki, Greece

Organization Chair

Miriam Geppert, Karlsruhe University of Applied Science, Germany

Special Track Chairs

Imma Subirats Food and Agriculture Organization of the United Nations, Italy

Nikos Houssos National Documentation Centre, Greece

Michalis Sfakakis Ionian University, Corfu, Greece

Lina Bountouri Ionian University, Corfu, Greece, and General State Archives, Greece

Juliette Dibie AgroParisTech and INRA, France

Liliana Ibanescu AgroParisTech and INRA, France

Lydie Soler INRA, France

Miguel-Ángel Sicilia University of Alcalá, Spain

Garoufallou, Emmanouel Alexander Technological Educational Institute of Thessaloniki, Greece

Hartley, R.J. Manchester Metropolitan University, UK

Conference Steering Committee

Sicilia, Miguel-Angel University of Alcalá, Spain

Manouselis, Nikos Agro-Know Technologies, Greece

Sartori, Fabio Università degli Studi di Milano-Bicocca, Italy

Dodero, Juan Manuel University of Cádiz, Spain

Garoufallou, Emmanouel Alexander Technological Educational Institute of Thessaloniki, Greece

Organizing Committee

Gaitanou, Panorea	Ionian University, Greece
Koutsomiha, Damiana	American Farm School, Greece
Siatri, Rania	Alexander Technological Educational Institute of Thessaloniki, Greece
Dani, Anxhela	Alexander Technological Educational Institute of Thessaloniki, Greece

Technical Support Staff

Christianoudis, Ioannis	Alexander Technological Educational Institute of Thessaloniki, Greece
Noulas, Nikolaos	Alexander Technological Educational Institute of Thessaloniki, Greece
Paraskeuopoulos, Kostas	Alexander Technological Educational Institute of Thessaloniki, Greece

Program Committee

Akerkar, Rajendra	Western Norway Research Institute, Norway
Altun, Arif	Hacetepe University, Turkey
Athanasiadis, Ioannis N.	Democritus University of Thrace, Greece
Balatsoukas, Panos	University of Manchester, UK
Bartol, Tomaz	University of Ljubljana, Slovenia
Bluemel, Ina	German National Library of Science and Technology TIBm, Germany
Caracciolo, Caterina	Food and Agriculture Organization of the United Nations, Italy
Cechinel, Christian	Federal University of Pampa, Brazil
Chebotko, Artem	University of Texas - Pan American, USA
Closs, Sissi Karlsruhe	University of Applied Sciences, Germany
Costopoulou, Constantina	Agricultural University of Athens, Greece
Cunningham, Sally Jo	Waikato University, New Zealand
Escribano Otero, Juan José	Universidad Europea de Madrid, Spain
Dodero, Juan Manuel	University of Cádiz, Spain
Dogdu, Erdogan	TOBB Teknoloji ve Ekonomi University, Turkey
Foulonneau, Muriel	Tudor Public Research Centre, Luxemburg
Gaitanou, Panorea	Ionian University, Greece
Garoufallou, Emmanouel	Alexander Technological Educational Institute of Thessaloniki, Greece
Gergatsoulis, Manolis	Ionian University, Greece
Greenberg, Jane	Drexel University, USA
Hartley, R.J.	Manchester Metropolitan University, UK
Houssos, Nikos	National Documentation Center (EKT), Greece

Iglesias, Carlos A.   Universidad Politecnica de Madrid, Spain
Jaiswal, Pankaj   Oregon State University, USA
Jorg, Brigitte   UKOLN, UK
Kanellopoulos, Dimitris   University of Patras, Greece
Kapidakis, Sarantos   Ionian University, Greece
Kop, Christian   University of Klagenfurt, Austria
Luzi, Daniela   National Research Council, Italy
Manghi, Paolo   Institute of Information Science and
                                 Technologies (ISTI), National Research
                                 Council (CNR), Italy
Manouselis, Nikos   Agro-Know Technologies, Greece
Moen, William   University of North Texas, USA
Ochoa, Xavier   Centro de Tecnologias de Informacion
                                 Guayaquil, Ecuador
Okur, Mehmet C. Yaşar   University, Turkey
Colomo-Palacios, Ricardo   Universidad Carlos III, Spain
Palmonari, Matteo   University of Milano-Bicocca, Italy
Papaleo, Laura   University of Genoa, Italy
Papatheodorou, Christos   Ionian University, Greece
Poulos, Marios   Ionian University, Greece
Prabhakar, T. V.   Indian Institute of Technology Kanpur, India
Sanchez, Salvador   University of Alcalá, Spain
Sartori, Fabio   Università degli Studi di Milano-Bicocca, Italy
Senkul, Pinar   METU, Turkey
Sgouropoulou, Cleo   Technological Educational Institute, Athens,
                                 Greece
Sicilia, Miguel-Ángel   University of Alcalá, Spain
Subirats, Imma   Food and Agriculture Organization (FAO),
                                 Italy
Sugimoto, Shigeo   University of Tsukuba, Japan
Ternier, Stefaan   Open University of the Netherlands,
                                 The Netherlands
Tonkin, Emma   University of Bath, UK
Zschocke, Thomas   United Nations University, Germany

Additional Reviewers

Rousidis, Dimitris   Vassilakaki, Evgenia
Koskela, Rebecca   Rayabi, Enayat
Yilmaz, Ozgun   Vlachidis, Andreas
Ünalir, Murat   Osman Antonopoulou Stavroula
Helou, Mamoun   Abu Siatri Rania
Bursa, Okan   Zafeiriou Georgia

Track on Big Data and Digital Libraries in Health, Science and Technology

Special Track Chairs

Garoufallou, Emmanouel (Chair)	Alexander Technological Educational Institute of Thessaloniki, Greece
Hartley, R. J. (Co-chair)	Manchester Metropolitan University, UK
Siatri, Rania (Co-chair)	Alexander Technological Educational Institute of Thessaloniki, Greece

Program Committee

Balatsoukas, Panos	University of Manchester, UK
Can, Ozgu	Ege University, Turkey
Closs, Sissi	Karlsruhe University of Applied Sciences, Germany
Conway, Mike	University of North Carolina at Chapel Hill, USA
Emrouznejad, Ali	Aston University, UK
Gaitanou, Panorea	Ionian University, Greece
Greenberg, Jane	Drexel University, USA
Hartley, R.J.	Manchester Metropolitan University, UK
Korfiatis, Nikos	University of East Anglia, UK and Goethe University Frankfurt, Germany
Koskela, Rebecca	University of New Mexico, USA
Moniarou-Papaconstantinou, Valentini	Technological Educational Institute of Athens, Greece
Rousidis, Dimitris	University of Alcalá, Spain
Sicilia, Miguel-Angel	University of Alcalá, Spain
Vassilakaki, Evgenia	Technological Educational Institute of Athens, Greece
Virkus, Sirje	Tallinn University, Estonia
Zafeiriou, Georgia	University of Macedonia, Greece

Track on Metadata and Semantics for Open Repositories, Research Information Systems and Data Infrastructures

Special Track Chairs

Subirats, Imma	Food and Agriculture Organization of the United Nations, Italy
Houssos, Nikos	National Documentation Centre, Greece

Program Committee

Aubin, Sophie	Institut National de la Recherche Agronomique, France
Baker, Thomas	Sungkyunkwan University, Korea
Besemer, Hugo	Wageningen UR Library, The Netherlands
Dunshire, Gordon	University of Strathclyde, UK
Greenberg, Jane	Drexel University, USA
Guru, Siddeswara	University of Queensland, Australia
Jack, Kris	Mendeley, UK
Jeffery, Keith	Keith G. Jeffery Consultants, UK
Koskela, Rebecca	University of New Mexico, USA
Lindholm, Jessica	Malmö University, Sweden
Luzi, Daniela	Institute for Research on Population and Social Policies - Italian National Research Council (IRPPS-CNR), Italy
Madalli, Devika P.	Indian Statistical Institute, India
Manghi, Paolo	Institute of Information Science and Technologies - Italian National Research Council (ISTI-CNR), Italy
Manola, Natalia	University of Athens, Greece
Matthews, Brian	Science and Technology Facilities Council, UK
Mendez, Eva	Carlos III University, Spain
Schirrwagen, Jochen	University of Bielefeld, Germany
Schmidt, Birgit	University of Göttingen, Germany
Schöpfel, Joachim	University of Lille, France
Stathopoulos, Panagiotis	National Documentation Center (EKT), Greece
Tsinaraki, Chrisa	European Commission, Joint Research Centre, Italy
Tzitzikas, Yannis	University of Crete and ICS-FORTH, Greece
Vila, Daniel	Polytechnic University of Madrid, Spain
Wang, Zhong	Sun-Yat-Sen University, China
Wittenburg, Peter	Max Planck Institute for Psycholinguistics, The Netherlands
Zeng, Marcia	Kent State University, USA

Track on Metadata and Semantics for Cultural Collections and Applications

Special Track Chairs

Sfakakis, Michalis	Ionian University, Greece
Bountouri, Lina	Ionian University, Greece, and General State Archives, Greece

Program Committee

Aalberg, Trond	Norwegian University of Science and Technology (NTNU), Norway
Angjeli, Anila	Bibliotheque National de France, France
Bredenberg, Karin	The National Archives of Sweden, Sweden
Dallas, Costis	Faculty of Information, University of Toronto, Canada
Gergatsoulis, Manolis	Ionian University, Greece
Isaac, Antoine	Vrije Universiteit Amsterdam, The Netherlands
Kapidakis, Sarantos	Ionian University, Greece
Lourdi, Irene	Libraries Computer Centre, National and Kapodistrian University of Athens, Greece
Masci, Maria Emilia	Scuola Normale Superiore di Pisa, Italy
Meghini, Carlo	National Research Council of Italy (ISTI-CNR), Italy
Ore, Christian-Emile	University of Oslo, Norway
Papatheodorou, Christos	Ionian University and Digital Curation Unit, IMIS, Athena RC, Greece
Pitti, Daniel	Institute for Advanced Technology in the Humanities, University of Virginia, USA
Stead, Stephen	Paveprime Ltd., UK
Tsinaraki, Chrisa	Joint Research Centre, European Commission, Italy
Vlachidis, Andreas	University of South Wales, UK
Wisser, Katherine	Graduate School of Library and Information Science, Simmons College, USA
Žumer, Maja	University of Ljubljana, Slovenia

Track on Metadata and Semantics for Agriculture, Food and Environment

Program Chairs

Dibie, Juliette	AgroParisTech and INRA, France
Ibanescu, Liliana	AgroParisTech and INRA, France
Sicilia, Miguel-Ángel	University of Alcalá, Spain
Soler, Lydie	INRA, France

Special Track Steering Committee

Athanasiadis, Ioannis	Democritus University of Thrace, Greece
Janssen, Sander	Alterra, Wageningen UR, The Netherlands

Caracciolo, Caterina	FAO of the United Nations, Italy
Manouselis, Nikos	Agro-Know Technologies, Greece
Pane, Juan	Universidad Nacional de Asunción, Paraguay and Universidad de Trento, Italy

Program Committee

Baez, Marcos	University of Trento, Italy
Bernardi, Ansgar	German Research Center for Artificial Intelligence (DFKI), Germany
Brewster, Christopher	Aston Business School, Aston University, UK
Buche, Patrice	INRA, France
Drakos, Andreas	Agro-Know Technologies, Greece
Ebner, Hannes	Metasolutions, Sweden
Houssos, Nikos	National Documentation Center, Greece
Konstantopoulos, Stasinos	NCSR Demokritos, Greece
Le Hénaff, Diane	INRA RD 10, France
Lezcano, Leonardo	University of Alcalá, Spain
Nedellec, Claire	INRA, France
Palavitsinis, Nikos	Agro-Know Technologies, Greece
Pane, Juan	Universidad Nacional de Asunción, Paraguay and Universidad de Trento, Italy
Pierozzi, Ivo, Jr.	Embrapa Agricultural Informatics, Brazil
Protonotarios, Vassilis	Agro-Know Technologies, Greece
Rizzoli, Andrea E.	IDSIA, Switzerland
Roche, Mathieu	CIRAD, France
Rodriguez, Carlos	University of Trento, Italy
Roussey, Catherine	IRSTEA, France
Stellado, Armando	University of Tor Vergata, Italy
Top, Jan Vrije	Universiteit, Faculty of Sciences, The Netherlands
Vaccari, Lorenzino	Autonomous Province of Trento, Italy
Verhelst, Elisabeth (Lieke)	Informagic, The Netherlands
Vignare, Karen	University of Maryland, University College, USA

Table of Contents

General Session

Metadata and Linked Data: Tools and Models

(Meta)Data Quality Assessment and Curation

Semantic Interoperability, Ontology-Based Data Access and Representation

Track on Big Data and Digital Libraries in Health, Science and Technology

Track on Metadata and Semantics for Open Repositories, Research Information Systems and Data Infrastructures

Track on Metadata and Semantics for Cultural Collections and Applications

Track on Metadata and Semantics for Agriculture, Food and Environment

Metadata Capital: Automating Metadata Workflows in the NIEHS Viral Vector Core Laboratory

Jane Greenberg[1], Angela Murillo[2], Adrian Ogletree[1], Rebecca Boyles[3], Negin Martin[4], and Charles Romeo[4]

[1] Metadata Research Center <MRC>, College of Computing & Informatics (CCI), Drexel University, Philadelphia, PA, USA
{janeg,aogletree}@drexel.edu
[2] SILS-University of North Carolina at Chapel Hill, NC, USA and <MRC>/CCI/Drexel University, Philadelphia, PA, USA
amurillo@email.unc.edu
[3] Office of Scientific Information Management, National Institute of Environmental Health Sciences, NIH/DHHS, Research Triangle Park, NC, USA
rebecca.boyles@nih.gov
[4] Laboratory of Neurobiology, National Institute of Environmental Health Sciences, NIH/DHHS, Research Triangle Park, NC, USA
{romeoc,martin}@niehs.nih.gov

Abstract. This paper presents research examining metadata capital in the context of the Viral Vector Core Laboratory at the National Institute of Environmental Health Sciences (NIEHS). Methods include collaborative workflow modeling and a metadata analysis. Models of the laboratory's workflow and metadata activity are generated to identify potential opportunities for defining microservices that may be supported by iRODS rules. Generic iRODS rules are also shared along with images of the iRODS prototype. The discussion includes an exploration of a modified capital sigma equation to understand metadata as an asset. The work aims to raise awareness of metadata as an asset and to incentivize investment in metadata R&D.

Keywords: Metadata Capital, Viral Vector Core Laboratory, qPCR data, Workflows, E-Science, iRODS.

1   Introduction

Digital technologies and networking capacities are dramatically changing scientific processes across many disciplines. This change has had a positive impact, helping to motivate national and global data sharing efforts. Enthusiasm for change aside, the reality is that a significant amount of science still relies heavily on manual activity and paper-based applications, simply because state-of-the-art technology cannot adequately support the full research plan. Even software solutions, such as spreadsheet applications used for data management (e.g., Excel) often require intensive, repetitive human

S. Closs et al. (Eds.): MTSR 2014, CCIS 478, pp. 1–13, 2014.

interaction for data input and analyses. These shortcomings contribute to the high cost of data management [1].

Automating scientific processes and workflows will help address these challenges, and give scientists more time to 'do their science.' Investigating metadata workflows is crucial for developing robust, machine-driven data management [2]. To this end, metadata researchers need to provide convincing arguments and show the concrete benefits of metadata R&D. One potential research hook is to examine metadata as a financial asset. Cost is a significant economic factor in any domain, and can provide an angle for obtaining research resources and advancing metadata operations.

This paper reports on an investigation exploring metadata cost and aspects of metadata value. The research presented is currently being pursued via the Metadata Capital Initiative (MetaDataCAPT'L) [3], an ongoing project spearheaded by the Metadata Research Center (MRC) [4] with support from the National Consortium for Data Science (NCDS) [5]. The test case is the Viral Vector Core Laboratory (VVCL) at the National Institute of Environmental Health Sciences (NIEHS) [6], which is an ideal setting, given the lab's small size and a demonstrated need for data workflow automation.

The remainder of this paper is organized as follows: Section 2 reviews selected research relating to metadata cost and value; Section 3 links metadata capital to workflow needs in the VVCL at the NIEHS; Section 4 states the research objectives; Section 5 reviews the research methods and processes; Section 6 presents research results; Section 7 discusses current activity and illustrates the modified capital sigma equation as a means for quantifying metadata capital. Finally, Section 8 summarizes the work presented and offers several concluding remarks.

2   Metadata as an Asset: Studying Cost and Value

An asset is something of value, either tangible or intangible. Metadata experts emphasize the value of *metadata* for data lifecycle management (e.g., data capture, use/reuse, provenance tracking, etc.) [7, 8, 9]. Lytras and Sicilia [9] have conducted one of the more extensive investigations in this area and confirm a connection between the cost of metadata creation and effective resource management. These researchers demonstrate how metadata is both a 'product' and an asset; in addition, they suggest using parametric models for estimating metadata cost.

Work exploring information as an economic asset is fundamental to the study of metadata value. Machlup's *The Production and Distribution of Knowledge in the United States* [10] is a classic, providing a solid foundation in this area. Taylor's [11] work on the *value of information*, specifically on categories, types, and the notion of 'value added,' provides further groundwork. One may anticipate cataloging and metadata cost analyses providing further insight into the topic of cost/value; however, cataloging cost studies merely acknowledge metadata value (e.g., discovery and access), and primarily focus on staff costs and productivity. A key factor limiting measurement of long-term cataloging/metadata value is the research challenge associated with gathering the necessary longitudinal data. Breaking the mold is

Stalberg and Cronin's [12] award-winning investigation, which stands out as an important contribution providing evidence on the cost and impact of bibliographic work, and offering insight into metadata cost/value relationships.

Reuse of good quality metadata underscores the value of a 'good' initial investment. To this end, metadata/cataloging quality is also germane to the study of metadata capital. Garoufallou and Papatheodorou's [8] introduction to an e-science/e-research special issue of the *International Journal of Metadata, Semantics, and Ontologies* highlights data complexity; the sheer and growing amount of data; and provenance among factors impacting metadata quality. In the larger digital arena, Bruce and Hillman [13] have produced one of the most useful and well-known frameworks shaped by a set of criteria, such as *completeness*, *accuracy*, and *conformance to expectations*. Park [14] uses the Bruce and Hillmann framework to measure metadata quality via functional perspectives; she also maps Bruce and Hillman's work to Gasser and Stvilia's [15] more granular framework. The body of research targeting metadata quality, together with the other research studies identified in this section, all fold into the study of metadata capital.

3 MetaDataCAPT'L and NIEHS Viral Vector Core Laboratory

3.1 Metadata Capital and the MetaDataCAPT'L Initiative

Metadata capital targets metadata as an asset, or a valued resource. The term 'metadata capital' was first introduced in the context of the Dryad Digital Repository [16, 17], with an emphasis on *metadata reuse*. The argument put forth is that reuse of high-quality metadata over time and across systems increases the value of this asset (metadata). In other words, there is a greater return on the initial metadata investment when metadata is reused. A more recent articulation of metadata capital in the 2014 April/May *ASIST Bulletin* (2014) [18] further expounds on the metadata cost/value paradigm and explores *capital* as both a 'good' and as a 'service.' This work is inspired by classic, theoretical groundwork in economics [19, 20], as well as broader interpretations, such as intellectual capital [21] and social capital [22].

Viewing metadata as an asset helps advance both the day-to-day activity and the philosophical positing of metadata-related practices for data. Targeting metadata in this context may even elevate the importance of metadata research. All of these goals combined underlie the MetaDataCAPT'L Initiative, a project spearheaded by the Metadata Research Center <MRC> in partnership with the National Institute of Environmental Health Sciences (NIEHS), and supported by the National Consortium for Data Science (NCDS).

3.2 The NIEHS Viral Vector Core Laboratory (VVCL)

The NIEHS Viral Vector Core Laboratory (VVCL) provided the test case for this paper. NIEHS is a research institution of the U.S. National Institutes of Health, providing research infrastructure for, arguably, the world's most important toxicology- and environmental health-related research. The VVCL aids NIEHS researchers by specializing in the design, production, and validation of viral gene delivery. NIEHS scientists employ adenoviruses, adeno-associated viruses, lentiviruses, retroviruses, and sindbis viruses so that scientists can pursue their work. A viral vector is a commonly-used and effective tool for gene transfer to modify specific cell types or tissues [23]. The VVCL's operation supports and trains the NIEHS community, specifically scientists studying genes and looking for cures to various diseases.

As highlighted in the introduction of this paper, many scientific workflows lack fully automated functions. The VVCL is indicative of this current state, with VVCL scientists using a number of paper-based applications and relying heavily on human labor for data management. This predicament makes the NIEHS/VVCL an ideal case for exploring metadata-driven ROI (return on investment). In particular, the VVCL is exploring the Integrated Rule-Oriented Data System (iRODS) [24] technology for developing automated pathways. iRODS uses machine-based actionable rules to automate and expedite data processes—and metadata is crucial for such operations. The need to understand metadata cost and value in this context aligns with the MetaDataCAPT'L research program and informed the research objectives pursued in this study.

4   Research Objectives

Researchers engaged in the MetaDataCAPT'L project, including NIEHS VVCL scientists, have identified initial steps for understanding metadata capital. The research objectives guiding the work reported in this paper were to:

1. Understand the Viral Vector Core Laboratory (VVCL) workflow.
2. Map the VVCL metadata lifecycle.
3. Explore machine-actionable rules that can support the VVCL metadata lifecycle.
4. Create an iRODS prototype for the VVCL workflow, and explore the application of machine-actionable rules.

These objectives were defined to gather foundational data toward studying metadata cost, and aspects of value. A larger unifying goal was to further scientific study of 'metadata capital.'

5   Methods

A series of methods were used to address the above objectives.

- *Objective 1*. Collaborative workflow modeling was used to capture the day-to-day workflow.
- *Objective 2*. A metadata analysis was conducted to identify basic metadata generated and automatically propagated during each workflow stage in the VVCL process.

- *Objectives 3 and 4.* The collaborative workflow and metadata analysis methods (conducted to address objectives 1 and 2) also provided textual data describing workflow steps. This text can be parsed for microservices to aid the VVCL workflow via an iRODS implementation.

6   Results

6.1   NIEHS Viral Vector Core Lab (VVCL) Workflow

Capturing a generic scenario can be a valuable first step to understanding a workflow. In spring 2014, the MetaDataCAPT'L research team worked with a generic scenario template to capture both qPCR and Flow Cytometry workflows [25]. A graphical representation for the general VVCL workflow is presented in Figure 1, followed by an outline of the key steps. The textual descriptions for each step can help in identifying microservices that may be supported by iRODS rules.

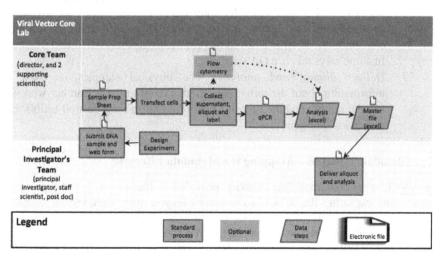

Fig. 1. Viral Vector Core Laboratory Workflow

Viral Vector Core Laboratory Workflow
The VVCL workflow involves the following seven key steps:

VVCL Workflow
1. *Design experiment:* A researcher needs to express a particular gene, for example GFP, to make particular cells fluoresce under a microscope. The researcher communicates this need to the VVCL staff who suggest a particular virus based on the need.
2. *Submit DNA sample and web form:* The researcher submits a formal request form to the VVCL and drops off a physical sample of the DNA they need to be incorporated into the virus.

3. *Transfect cells:* VVCL staff perform transfection to get the DNA into the viral cells. This is a physical process where the reagents are added to growing cells and allowed to incubate for 48 hrs.
4. *Collect the supernatant, aliquot, and label:* If the transfection has been successful the liquid (supernatant) contains liver virus with the specific DNA (e.g., GFP). The liquid is manually extracted from the cells and aliquoted into small tubes. VVCL staff handle many experiments at one time, and manually label the tubes. Accurate metadata for the sample is critical.
5. *Present the qPCR:* A small sample is taken from the supernatant to quantify the amount of virus that was made by the cells. The qPCR machine produces a readout that can be exported as a txt file. VVCL staff open the txt file in Excel and perform a few statistical calculations to estimate the concentration of virus DNA in the sample (this gets translated into the titer). In some ways this is a QA (quality assurance) step.
6. *Flow cytometry:* This is another method for calculating the concentration of virus in the sample. The flow cytometry machine produces a print-to-file pdf. VVCL staff manually enter the results from the flow cytometer into an Excel sheet, where statistical calculations estimating the sample's concentration of virus DNA in recorded (this gets translated into the titer). In some ways this is a QA step.
7. *Deliver aliquot and analysis:* The physical samples, as well as information about the virus titer, are delivered to the researcher who will use the sample and the titer information to infect their desired cell(s) with their particular gene.

6.2   Metadata Analysis – Mapping the Metadata Lifecycle

The VVCL workflow modeling activity provided a framework for the metadata analysis, and capturing the VVCL's metadata lifecycle (this includes the metadata lifecycle for VVCL work, not metadata that may be reused over time—beyond the lab). Metadata analysis results are presented in Tables 1, 2, and 3. Table 1 presents metadata captured by the scientists' VVCL request form. Asterisks represent "required" metadata, and the shading indicates automatically generated metadata derived from the scientist's profile.

Table 1. Web form submission metadata

* = required, ■ = scientific/lab profile, automatic generated

REQUESTER INFORMATION	PROJECT INFORMATION	SAMPLE INFORMATION
Requester Name*	Is this a repeat project?	Sample Name*
Requester email*	Have you published using these vectors?	Vector Type*
Building/Room	Will the virus be shipped	Vector Backbone*
Phone	Will the virus be used at the NIEHS facility?	Drug Selection*
Mail drop	Will the virus be administered to animals?	Concentration*
Lab/branch*		Vol. Virus Request*
PI*		Aliquot Volume*
		# of Aliquots*

Next, metadata is captured through the VVCL request web form prompts the viral request form. Table 2 shows the metadata properties for this step. Metadata automatically propagated from the request web is shaded.

Table 2. Viral Vector request form metadata

Prep Data	Sample Name	Contact Name	PI Name	Branch	Core Prepared?	Prepared By	Virus Type
Vector Name	Insert Name	Reporter Gene	Drug Selection	DNA Conc	Prep Size	Aliquot number & size	Prep Time

Metadata from the two forms (captured in Table 1 and 2) transfers to a master spreadsheet. As part of this step, several metadata values are calculated and manually added by the VVCL scientists. Table 3 presents the full collection of metadata captured in the master spreadsheet. The transferring of metadata to the master spreadsheet is, at best, semi-automatic, and requires a fair amount of time-consuming tasks, including cutting-and-pasting and manual input. iRODS supports automatic replication and transfer of metadata properties and associated values, and could expedite the VVCL metadata workflow.

Table 3. Master spreadsheet

Entry number	Prep name	Sample name	Contact name	Pi name	Branch	Core prepared?	Prepared by
Virus Type	Vector Name	Insert Name	Reporter Gene	Drug Selection	DNA Conc	Prep Size	Aliquot Number & Size
Prep Time	Titer FLOW (TU/ml)	Conc. Titer FLOW	Titer Colonies	Titer QPCR (TU/ml)	Conc. Titer QPCR TU/ml	Titer QPCR (GC/ml)	Titer p24 (PP/ml)
Infectivity Index (PP/TU flow)	Infectivity Index (PP/TU QPCR)	Comments					

The collaborative workflow and metadata analysis methods provided a set of textual data from which rule-based microservices can be generated. Rule based microservice form a significant part of anyiRODS implementation. The following section presents example rules and provides a glimpse of the iRODS prototype that is under development.

6.3   Microservices, Rules, and an iRODS Prototype

The third objective of this work was to explore microservices. Microservices are the iRODS units invoked by rules. A data policy microservice may address:

- Access, approval
- Archiving

- Assessment criteria
- Authentication, authorization
- Deletion, trash cans, versioning
- Integrity, replication, synchronization
- IRB, audit trails
- Provenance tracking
- Retention, distribution, arrangement

The VVCL is at an early stage of defining desired microservices for a potential iRODS implementation. A generic rule in Example 1 demonstrates the basic structure of an iRODS rule, where A and B are workflow variables.

Example 1. iRODS generic rule

```
Rule_name{
microservice1(…,*A,…,*B);
microservice2(*A,…);
}
```

Example 2 shows a rule counting metadata properties associated with a collection, and could apply to a data collection. This rule counts the number of unique metadata properties and associated values.

Example 2. iRODS metadata count/association rule

```
myTestRule {
#Rule available as rule-list-metadata.r in shared Rules
directory
#Input parameters are:
# none
#Output parameter is:
# Result string
 *Coll = "/$rodsZoneClient/home/$userNameClient%";
 *Query = select COLL_NAME where COLL_NAME like '*Coll';
 foreach(*Row in *Query) {
 *Col = *Row.COLL_NAME;
 *Q1 = select count(DATA_NAME) where COLL_NAME = '*Col';
 foreach (*R1 in *Q1) {*Nfiles = *R1.DATA_NAME;}
 *Q2 = select order_asc(META_DATA_ATTR_NAME),
count(META_DATA_ATTR_ID) where COLL_NAME = '*Col';
 writeLine("stdout","Collection *Col has *Nfiles files,
metadata attributes:");
 foreach(*R2 in *Q2) {
 *Meta = *R2.META_DATA_ATTR_NAME;
 *Nmeta = *R2.META_DATA_ATTR_ID;
 writeLine("stdout"," *Meta is used *Nmeta times");
 }
 }
}
INPUT null
OUTPUT ruleExecOut
```

iRODS rules are written in a modified C programming language and can be shared across other iRODS instances. An iRODS instance can reduce the labor-intensive task of checking metadata capture and transmission, which is burdensome for VVCL scientists and keeps takes time away from conducting science.

Sandbox (VVCL iRODS prototype)

The last objective of the work reported on in this paper was to build a VVCL iRODS prototype. To this end, the MetaDataCAPT'L team has focused on the qPCR data. For context, qPCR data is polymerase chain reaction (PCR) data, which is used to identify and measure DNA molecules. This process is significant for studying genes and researching cures to genetic diseases. Figure 2 shows metadata associated with an Excel data set archived in iRODS; and Figure 3 presents a metadata template for attribute-value-units (AVUs). AVUs are basic metadata statements akin to the Resource Description Format (RDF) statements. iRODS provides a form that enables automatic propagation and modification of AVUs.

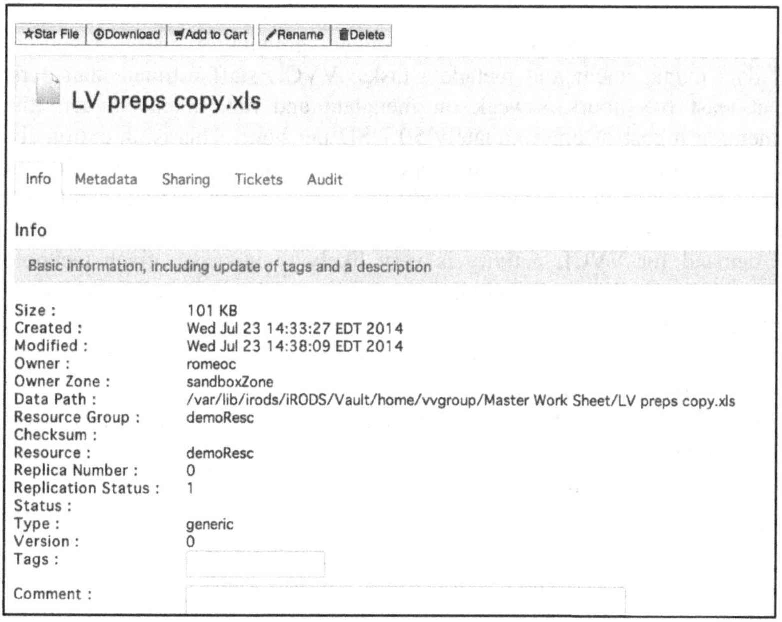

| ☆Star File | ⊕Download | ☙Add to Cart | ✎Rename | 🗑Delete |

LV preps copy.xls

Info   Metadata   Sharing   Tickets   Audit

Info

Basic information, including update of tags and a description

Size :	101 KB
Created :	Wed Jul 23 14:33:27 EDT 2014
Modified :	Wed Jul 23 14:38:09 EDT 2014
Owner :	romeoc
Owner Zone :	sandboxZone
Data Path :	/var/lib/irods/iRODS/Vault/home/vvgroup/Master Work Sheet/LV preps copy.xls
Resource Group :	demoResc
Checksum :	
Resource :	demoResc
Replica Number :	0
Replication Status :	1
Status :	
Type :	generic
Version :	0
Tags :	
Comment :	

Fig. 2. Screenshot of a dataset in iRODS

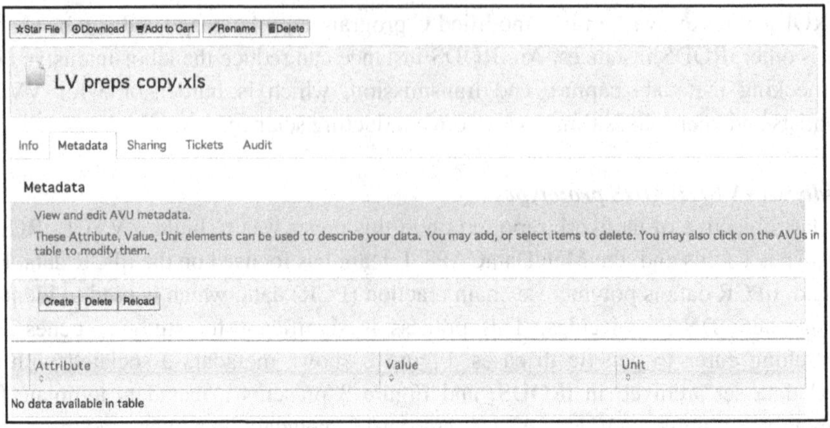

Fig. 3. iRODS AVU metadata tab

7   Discussion: VVCL and Metadata Capital

Currently, VVCL scientists devote a significant amount of human resource time toward data management and metadata tasks. VVCL staff estimate that personnel spend at least 6-8 hours a week on metadata and data intensive activities per experiment, at a cost of approximately 50 USD per hour. This is an extremely high cost, when considering that basic data input hourly costs range from 5 to 20 USD per hour [26]. The cost escalates very quickly too, given that the VVCL can be running on order of 35+ experiments at any one time.

The demand for VVCL activity is very likely to increase, given technological innovation and affordances in genomic engineering. Clearly, VVCL's current mode of operation is not sustainable, and it is imperative to pursue a more automated metadata workflow. The R&D challenge is not simply in streamlining a workflow, but in conveying a need for metadata R&D investment.

The work presented in this paper is predicated on a need for metadata investment to yield a better ROI, that is a ROI is seen with reuse of high quality metadata. Metadata capital has implications in this context, and is explored here via a modified capital gains equation.

$$R + \sum_{i=1}^{N} a_i = R + a_1 + a_2 + a_3 + \cdots a_n$$

R = value of the metadata record
i = number of usages
a = incremental increase in value
n = maximum number of reuse

If we consider the VVCL's cost estimate via a time sequence (Figure 4), we can begin with data entry and management activities estimated at 50 USD per hour for an experiment. Next, we can theoretically utilize the modified capital gains equation to calculate the increased value of metadata over time, as it is re-used. Here, we assume that a = 20 USD, representing the cost of metadata reuse per instance. We may then hypothesize metadata automatically re-used 18 times at this current cost, resulting in a total value of 410 USD. We may also anticipate that the interest in qPCR decreases over time. At this stage in time, only the basic citation metadata is reused, not the full metadata; and the cost of reuse is lowered to a =10 USD per instance. This change is graphed in the below example extending from a_{19} through a_{29}. Finally, it may be that the value of the metadata record will eventually max out when a = 29, with no further metadata reuse. It's important to point out the use of 'cost' and 'value' in this equation are illustrative, and we are aware that cost is not always equated with value. A case in point is a product or service that is purchased at an inflated value. Even so, cost is a measure of value, and provides a way to examine metadata as an asset; and can motivate further research in this area.

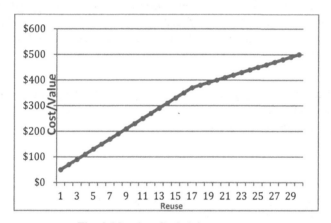

Fig. 4. Metadata Capital time sequence

Scientists need to do their science, and there are many actions that scientists simply neglect relating to long-term quality control and resource management because current systems are too labor-intensive [27]. Scientific data management workflows, such as the workflow utilized by the VVCL, are serving more and more scientists. Solutions can be sought via partnering with metadata researchers and through metadata investment. The MetaDataCAPT'L Initiative is making this apparent by joining the efforts of scientists and metadata researchers. The solutions developed may impact other NIEHS labs over time. Finally, this work has much broader implications; and, already parallels are emerging in addressing significant challenges interconnected with heightened awareness of biosecurity and infectious agents [28].

8   Conclusion

This paper presented baseline research examining metadata capital at the Viral Vector Core Laboratory and the National Institute of Environmental Health Sciences

(VVCL/NIEHS). Specific objectives met and reported on here include the VVCL workflow and metadata early stages of the metadata lifecycle. These steps provide data that can be used to identify microservices. This work is necessary to identify machine-actionable rules that could support the VVCL metadata lifecycle. The paper includes generic examples of iRODS rules for microservices and presents images from the VVCL iRODS prototype. Finally, the discussion explores the modified capital sigma equation to understand metadata as an asset.

Metadata plays a vital role in the scientific mission, and although it is cliché to say "your data is only as good as your metadata," this phrase underscores the significance of metadata for data management [18]. Investigating cost and value is a complex and requires longitudinal data, and this takes time and resources. As noted, investment in metadata R&D is limited, because it is seen as a practical matter—not necessarily worth of rigorous study. There are grand challenges to address, such as curing of disease and reversing climate change [29]. Resources must be allocated to metadata R&D if we are to aid scientists in pursuing their work and address grand challenges. The work being pursued at the VVCL/NIEHS serves as a model here by examining cost/value, contributing to a sustainable metadata infrastructure, and demonstrating metadata capital.

Acknowledgements. We are grateful for the support of the National Consortium for Data Science (NCDS) (http://data2discovery.org/), and the NCDS Faculty Fellows Program supporting of this research.

References

1. Rubin, H.: Technology Economics: The Cost of Data. Wall Street & Technology (2011), http://www.wallstreetandtech.com/data-management/technology-economics-the-cost-of-data/d/d-id/1265161
2. Ogletree, A.: Metadata Workflows Across Research Domains: Challenges and Opportunities for Supporting the DFC Cyberinfrastructure. In: 14th International Conference on Dublin Core and Metadata Applications (forthcoming, 2014)
3. The Metadata Capital Initiative, http://cci.drexel.edu/mrc/metadatacaptl/
4. Metadata Research Center, http://cci.drexel.edu/mrc/
5. National Consortium for Data Science (NCDS), http://data2discovery.org/
6. National Institute of Environmental Health Sciences (NIEHS), http://www.niehs.nih.gov/
7. Ball, A.: Review of Data Management Lifecycle Models. University of Bath, Bath (2012), http://opus.bath.ac.uk/28587/1/redm1rep120110ab10.pdf
8. Garoufallou, E., Papatheodorou, C.: A Critical Introduction to Metadata for E-Science and E-Research. Int. J. of Metadata, Semantics and Ontologies 9(1), 1–4 (2014)
9. Lytras, M.D., Sicilia, M.-A.: Where is the Value in Metadata? International Journal of Metadata, Semantics, and Ontologies 2, 235–241 (2007)
10. Machlup, F.: The Production and Distribution of Knowledge in the United States. Princeton University Press, Princeton (1962)
11. Taylor, R.S.: Value-Added Processes in Information Systems. Ablex, Norwood (1986)

12. Stalberg, E., Cronin, C.: Assessing the Cost and Value of Bibliographic Control. Library Resources and Technical Services 55, 124–137 (2011)

13. Bruce, T.R., Hillmann, D.I.: The Continuum of Metadata Quality: Defining, Expressing, Exploiting. In: Hillmann, D.I., Westbrooks, E.L. (eds.) Metadata in Practice. ALA, Chicago (2004)

14. Park, J.-R.: Metadata Quality in Digital Repositories: A Survey of the Current State of the Art. Cataloging & Classification Quarterly 47, 213–228 (2009)

15. Gasser, L., Stvilia, B.: A New Framework for Information Quality. Technical Report. University of Illinois at Urbana Champaign, Champaign (2001)

16. Greenberg, J., Swauger, S., Feinstein, E.M.: Metadata Capital in a Data Repository. In: Proc. Int'l Conf. on Dublin Core and Metadata Applications, Lisbon, Portugal, September, 3-6, pp. 140–150 (2013)

17. Dryad Digital Repository, http://datadryad.org/

18. Greenberg, J.: Metadata Capital: Raising Awareness, Exploring a New Concept. Bulletin of the Association for Information Science and Technology 40(4), 30–33 (2014), https://www.asis.org/Bulletin/Apr-14/AprMay14_Greenberg.pdf

19. Weber, M.: The Protestant Ethic and the Spirit of Capitalism. In: Berhr, P., Wells, G.C. (eds.) Penguin Books, New York (2001)

20. Smith, A.: The Wealth of Nations. Modern Library, New York (2000)

21. Stewart, T.A.: The Wealth of Knowledge: Intellectual Capital and the Twenty-First Century Organization. Doubleday/Currency, New York (2001)

22. Burt, R.S.: Structural Holes: The Social Structure of Competition. Harvard University, Cambridge (1992)

23. Warnock, J.N., Daigre, C., Al-Rubeai, M.: Introduction to Viral Vectors. Methods in Molecular Biology 737, 1–25 (2011), doi:10.1007/978-1-61779-095-9

24. iRODS, http://irods.org/

25. Greenberg, J.: Metadata Capital 2: The Metaphor Extended. iORG Lecture Series. School of Information Studies. University of Wisconsin, Milwaukee (April 22, 2014), http://www4.uwm.edu/sois/news/events/iorg-greenberg-20140422.cfm

26. Dyer, M.: What Is the Pay Scale for Entry-Level Data Entry Positions? Chron, Demand Media (2014), http://work.chron.com/pay-scale-entrylevel-data-entry-positions-1360.html

27. Akmon, D., Zimmerman, A., Daniels, M., Hedstrom, M.: The Application of Archival Concepts to a Data-Intensive Environment: Working with Scientists to Understand Data Management and Preservation Needs. Archival Science 11(3-4), 329–348 (2011)

28. Barthold, S.W.: Hidden costs of biodefense research. ILAR Journal 46(1), 1–3 (2005)

29. Greenberg, J., Garoufallou, E.: Change and a Future for Metadata. In: Garoufallou, E., Greenberg, J. (eds.) MTSR 2013. CCIS, vol. 390, pp. 1–5. Springer, Heidelberg (2013)

Research Objects Interlinking: The Case of Dryad Repository

Enayat Rajabi, Miguel-Angel Sicilia, and Salvador Sanchez-Alonso

Information Engineering Research Unit, Computer Science Department,
University of Alcalá, 28805, Spain
{enayat.rajabi,msicilia,salvador.sanchez}@uah.es

Abstract. Interlinking research objects using the RDF links facilitates sharing and data discovery on the Web of Data. This works toward enriching the research repositories by linking their research artifacts to various scientific or even general data on the Web. In this paper, we experiment on an interlinking approach over Dryad, a research object repository, to a digital library dataset in the Linked Open Data cloud. We fetch data from both targets in different steps, run an interlinking tool and report as well as analyze the results. The generated outputs and assessed matched links show that interlinking a research dataset like Dryad to Web of Data brings an added value to the repository, as it connects its research artefacts to scientific objects of other datasets.

Keywords: Research object, Linked Data, Interlinking, Dryad.

1   Introduction

Nowadays, there is a rapid move towards exposing, sharing and reusing research data on the Web [1] using various data sharing platforms and software. Researchers, research funding organizations, and research institutions began to discuss the possibilities of sharing and reusing the research data. Dealing with a wide variety of research objects motivates the data providers to interconnect all these artifacts to make them discoverable and reusable through the Web. On the other hand, Linked Data [2] provides an innovative approach for integrating any kinds of data on the Web as it establishes links between arbitrary objects and facilitates their sharing and reusability. Given that providing the RDF links between research objects offers a flexible solution for resource interlinking, the Linked Data approach is a good candidate to tackle the question "how the research objects in different repositories can be enriched?". There exist several research data environments applying Linked Data to expose their artifacts. Notably, Figshare[1] is a research data repository that "allows researchers to publish all of their data in a citable, searchable and sharable manner". In this paper, we interlink a research data repository, Dryad [3] to a scientific dataset in the Linked Open Data cloud and report on the results and benefits of such interlinking in detail.

---

[1] http://figshare.com

S. Closs et al. (Eds.): MTSR 2014, CCIS 478, pp. 14–21, 2014.

The rest of this study is organized as follows. Section 2 briefly describes the Dryad repository and the related studies in regard with interlinking. In Section 3, we discuss our methodology for accessing and interlinking the both datasets. This is followed by a report on the interlinking results and its evaluation (Section 4). Conclusions and outlooks are also provided in Section 5.

2   Background

The Dryad repository, as an open access dataset in the research context, allows scientists mostly in fundamental science to explore, share and reuse research data related to scholarly publications. Most of the data, which are available in scientific and medical literature, provide benefits to individual researchers, educators, students, and to a diversity of stakeholder organizations. Data in this repository are stored as files identified by DOIs along with metadata that include information about the digital objects i.e. authors, title, contributor, publication year and publisher. At the time of this research, Dryad has published around 24,000 metadata records which are available as part of the dataCite research repository[4]. DataCite also comprises millions of research data and makes them accessible through an API at http://search.datacite.org/. Apart from publishing research metadata, one of the main goals addressed by Dryad repository, is supporting of the resource discovery, and reusing heterogeneous digital data mentioned by Greenberg [5]. One of the strong and appealing characteristics of Dryad according to Peer [6] is that its curatorial team "works to enforce quality control on existing content". In another study, Rousidis et al. [7] analyzed and evaluated the quality of data in Dryad and proposed a set of ideas to improve the quality in some of its metadata elements. In regard with research artifacts, Guéret [1] investigated the relation between digital research objects and Linked Data. Furthermore, the author discussed how Digital Archives can support and share the research objects leveraging the Linked Data principles. However, an interlinking approach in research data repositories was not investigated in the mentioned studies.

As mentioned earlier, a dataset is enriched when its contents are linked to the several related datasets on the Web. Connecting various datasets to each other can be done manually which is a laborious and time-consuming task. Therefore, it is mostly agreed amongst dataset owners that the interlinking tools are very useful in terms of matching concepts to the LOD cloud [8][9], as they connect different kinds of resources by finding links between them in a semi-aromatically approach. Data providers are also motivated to apply the interlinking tools to enrich their contents. These tools help them to find the relationships between different datasets and discover similarities by leveraging a number of matching techniques. To this aim, several studies and projects (e.g., [10][11][12]) have used various interlinking tools to not only do their researches [10], but also integrate them into their works [11].

3   Methodology

As data in the Dryad repository, were available in JSON format[2] through the DataCite API[3], we wrote a Java program to first obtain the Dryad's records and then convert them to the Linked Data format (RDF) according to the Dublin Core schema. In this program, we could download around 24,000 research data records and parse them to get the research data items such as title, author, and publication date. Eventually, we could map the data items to Dublin Core schema and generate an RDF dump with around 230,000 triples which the following elements and specification:

- Identifier (DOI) exposed → dc:identifier
- Article title   exposed → dc:title
- Creator of article exposed → dc:creator
- Data publisher exposed → dc:publisher
- Publication date exposed → dc:date

Analyzing the records, the total number of authors of research papers in Dryad was 111,576 (average 4.6 authors per publication) and the publication year ranged from 2007 to 2014 (see Table 1). The number of publications per year is an increasing number with the exception of the current year given that this study was performed in July 2014. Also, 540 publications did not include information about the date.

Table 1. The publication year of Dryad research data

Date	Publication#
2007	7
2008	192
2009	485
2010	719
2011	2709
2012	5030
2013	8886
2014	5256
Unspecified	540

After exposing the Dryad data, we explored several LOD datasets to find an appropriate target for interlinking. In this study, we considered that the target dataset should pass the following criteria to be interlinked to Dryad:

- The dataset includes an available SPARQL endpoint or RDF dump
- The context of the dataset is related to science, research and publication

---

[2] http://json.org/
[3] http://search.datacite.org/ui?q=*&fq=publisher_facet:
%22Dryad+Digital+Repository%22

Finally, we selected the British National Bibliography[4] (BNB) dataset that publishes its books and digital objects as Linked Data by the British Library, and is linked to external sources including GeoNames[5] and RDF Book Mashup[6]. Currently, BNB includes approximately 2.8 million descriptions (more than 93 million triples) of books and serials published in the UK over the last 60 years.

As a consequence of the interlinking process, we applied LIMES, a promising tool in this context [13], to perform the interlinking between Dryad and BNB. It is important to remark that before running LIMES, the user must set it up by shaping an input configuration file that specifies the criteria under which concepts in both datasets are matched. The source dataset, the target dataset, the entities that should be considered in both targets, and the criteria under which two entities are compared, are parts of the configuration file. There also exists a threshold in the setting that can be set by the user and it means two instances are considered as matched and linked via a relation such as "owl:sameAs", when the text similarity between them exceeds the defined threshold. Eventually, a number of links are generated by the tool and written in an output file to be later reviewed by experts. Once the interlinking process is finished, the user can evaluate the accuracy of generated links. Figure 1 depicts the process we followed to perform the interlinking and evaluate the result.

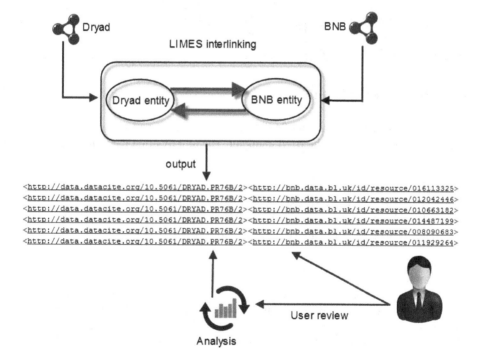

Fig. 1. Interlinking process for matching between Dryad and BNB

---

[4] http://bnb.bl.uk/

[5] http://www.geonames.org/

[6] http://wifo5-03.informatik.uni-mannheim.de/bizer/bookmashup/

For the purpose of this research, we configured LIMES with the following specifications to interlink the Dryad and BNB datasets. According to the setting mentioned in Table 2, we performed the interlinking process between the titles of research objects. Particularly, if a title in the Dryad repository had more than 95% similarity with a title of book in the BNB dataset using "trigrams" matching algorithm[7], those records were considered as matched. We focused on the title element as the other elements either did not yield any useful results or were not applicable semantically for the interlinking. For example, the research objects in the Dryad repository had identifiers which were originally different from each other. Moreover, the interlinking output over e.g., publication year includes a lot of matched research objects in one year without knowing their similarities in title or subject. Having this in mind, the authors believe that the "title" of research objects was the most appropriate element for the interlinking purpose.

Table 2. LIMES configuration

Setting	Value
Source data type	Dryad RDF dump
Target data type	SPARQL endpoint (http://bnb.data.bl.uk/sparql)
Source and target entity	Research data title (dcterms:title)
Matching algorithm	Trigrams
Threshold of acceptance	95%

4   Interlinking Result

As a result, LIMES read around 24,000 titles from the Dryad repository and more than 2.9 million titles from the BNB endpoint. The tool reported the following figures as output:

- Reading time from Dryad RDF dump: 3 seconds
- Reading time from BNB SPARQL endpoint: 11495 seconds (> 3 hours)
- Number of matched links above 95% similarity: 790 links
- Number of matched links above 75% similarity: 127 links

Total number of matched links between Dryad and BNB dataset was 790 records linked through owl:sameAs relationship which means that their values had more than 95% similarity to each other. In another step, we imported the results into a spreadsheet tool to manually analyze the number of resources matched in each dataset. Finally, 109 articles in Dryad were linked to 630 books and scientific digital objects in BNB. Appendix 1 also shows a sample of matched titles in Dryad linked to the BNB dataset.

---

[7] http://ii.nlm.nih.gov/MTI/Details/trigram.shtml

To examine the results in the BNB dataset, we wrote a program that allowed us to retrieve the following information about the matched resources from its endpoint.

• The type of resources (rdf:type): 587 resources were books (93%), 37 BNB objects were periodical publications(general magazines, newspapers, etc.) and the rest (6 records) were Multi-volume books.
• Language (dcterms:language): The language of research objects was the next predicate that we retrieved from the BNB target. Almost all of matched records in BNB (629 resources) were in English language and only one resource was in Japanese.

As the content reviewing the books and articles in both targets was not accessible due to the unavailability of the actual resources, we could not assess the relatedness of contents in both resources. Nevertheless; most of titles matched between two datasets include scientific terminologies (e.g., Fecundity, Boraginaceae) which reinforce the idea that the majority of matched resources in Dryad and BNB were related. A set of the matched terms, which were the titles of research objects in the Dryad repository, have been outlined in the annex. To take some examples regarding the matched resources, a paper in Dryad repository about "Descriptive statistics" (http://data.datacite.org/10.5061/DRYAD.37B28/2) was linked to a book with the same title in BNB dataset (http://bnb.data.bl.uk/doc/resource/006999841) or an article about "Morphology" published in an organic journal (http://data.datacite.org/10.5061/DRYAD.RH686/1) was identified as a similar object to a book in the BNB library collection with the same name (http://bnb.data.bl.uk/doc/resource/010979718). However, we found a number of resources with implicit titles which made the assessment difficult for a human expert. For instance, some cases[8] pointed to a title named "Data" and only reading their research abstracts could clarify the context of those resources. The foregoing discussion implies that data enrichment has been carried out by making use of an automatic interlinking tool, as many research objects were interconnected to another published dataset in the Web of Data. However, the quality of output is significantly improved if a domain expert reviews the generated results by the tool.

5   Conclusion

With the rapid number of research objects, accurately interconnecting them is a key issue. One of the goals of interlinking is to make the research data enriched by other useful information on the Web. To this aim, in this paper we interlinked a research data repository (Dryad) to a digital library dataset (BNB) which recently exposed its books and periodical collections as Linked Data. After identifying the type of information they exposed, we used LIMES, as the selected interlinking tool, to interconnect the Dryad repository to the BNB dataset. To sum up and according to our findings, 109 research papers in Dryad were linked to 630 BNB books or periodical

---

[8] http://bnb.data.bl.uk/doc/resource/008428773 and
http://data.datacite.org/10.5061/DRYAD.2024G/1

publications on the Web and this number definitely is increased when we interlink Dryad (or any other research repository) to other related datasets on the Web of Data and leads to have more useful knowledge in the source dataset. This study is just a proof of how using an interlinking tool can enrich a research object dataset after publishing its resources as Linked Data. Although configuring a linking tool and identifying appropriate entities in two targets requires time and technical expertise, it is fair to conclude that the verification of matched resources generated by the tools takes much less effort than comparing and connecting them manually by data publishers.

Acknowledgements. The work presented in this paper has been part-funded by the European Commission under the ICT Policy Support Programme CIP-ICT-PSP.2011.2.4-e-learning with project No. 297229 "Open Discovery Space (ODS)", and INFRA-2011-1.2.2-Data infrastructures for e-Science with project No. 283770 "AGINFRA".

References

1. Guéret, C.: Digital Archives As Versatile Platforms for Sharing and Interlinking Research Artefacts. In: Proceedings of the 1st International Workshop on Digital Preservation of Research Methods and Artefacts, pp. 1–7. ACM, New York (2013), http://doi.acm.org/10.1145/2499583.2499588
2. Bizer, C., Heath, T., Berners-Lee, T.: Linked Data - The Story So Far. International Journal on Semantic Web and Information Systems 5(3), 1–22 (2009)
3. Dryad, a general-purposed research data repository, http://datadryad.org/ (accessed July 4, 2014)
4. DataCite, research data repository, https://www.datacite.org/ (accessed July 4, 2014)
5. Greenberg, J.: Theoretical Considerations of Lifecycle Modeling: An Analysis of the Dryad Repository Demonstrating Automatic Metadata Propagation, Inheritance, and Value System Adoption. Cataloging & Classification Quarterly 47(3-4), 380–402 (2009)
6. Limor, P.: The Role of Data Repositories in Reproducible Research (2013), http://isps.yale.edu/news/blog/2013/07/the-role-of-data-repositories-in-reproducible-research#.U7aAp_mSzQI
7. Rousidis, D.G.: Data Quality Issues and Content Analysis for Research Data Repositories: The Case of Dryad. In: Let's Put Data to Use: Digital Scholarship for the Next Generation, 18th International Conference on Electronic Publishing, Thessaloniki, Greece, June 19-20 (2014), http://elpub.scix.net/cgi-bin/works/Show?106_elpub2014
8. Rajabi, E., Sicilia, M.-A., Sanchez-Alonso, S.: Interlinking Educational Data: an Experiment with GLOBE Resources, Salamanca, Spain (2013)
9. Dietze, S., Yu, H.Q., Giordano, D., Kaldoudi, E., Dovrolis, N., Taibi, D.: Linked education: interlinking educational resources and the Web of data. In: Proceedings of the 27th Annual ACM Symposium on Applied Computing (Internet), pp. 366–371. ACM, New York (2012), http://doi.acm.org/10.1145/2245276.2245347
10. Scharffe, F., Euzenat, J.: MeLinDa: an interlinking framework for the web of data. Report No.: 1107.4502 (July 2011), http://arxiv.org/abs/1107.4502

11. The Datalift project, a catalyser for the Web of data. The Datalift project, a catalyser for the Web of data, http://datalift.org (accessed July 4, 2014)
12. Ferrara, A., Nikolov, A., Noessner, J., Scharffe, F.: Evaluation of instance matching tools: The experience of OAEI. Web Semantics: Science, Services and Agents on the World Wide Web 21, 49–60 (2013)
13. Rajabi, E., Sicilia, M.-A., Sanchez-Alonso, S.: An empirical study on the evaluation of interlinking tools on the Web of Data. Journal of Information Science (June 11, 2014), http://jis.sagepub.com/content/early/2014/06/10/016551514538151.abstract

Annex: a sample of interlinking results between Dryad and BNB datasets

Title	Dryad resource	BNB resource
"Emergence"	http://data.datacite.org/10.5061/DRYAD.2320N/1	http://bnb.data.bl.uk/id/resource/010047461
"Survival"	http://data.datacite.org/10.5061/DRYAD.PR76B/2	http://bnb.data.bl.uk/id/resource/012213547
"Data"	http://data.datacite.org/10.5061/DRYAD.Q4F09SR3/1	http://bnb.data.bl.uk/id/resource/008428773
"Aphids"	http://data.datacite.org/10.5061/DRYAD.T815G/1	http://bnb.data.bl.uk/id/resource/012633269
"Simulations"	http://data.datacite.org/10.5061/DRYAD.J3R20/4	http://bnb.data.bl.uk/id/resource/009460240
"Productivity"	http://data.datacite.org/10.5061/DRYAD.4PD30/3	http://bnb.data.bl.uk/id/resource/006975537
"Archive"	http://data.datacite.org/10.5061/DRYAD.QR3T2/1	http://bnb.data.bl.uk/id/resource/008825701
"Risk"	http://data.datacite.org/10.5061/DRYAD.HM690/1	http://bnb.data.bl.uk/id/resource/009749329
"Behaviour"	http://data.datacite.org/10.5061/DRYAD.5FC56/2	http://bnb.data.bl.uk/id/resource/009412520
"Assemblies"	http://data.datacite.org/10.5061/DRYAD.7C99F/1	http://bnb.data.bl.uk/id/resource/012268844
"Predation"	http://data.datacite.org/10.5061/DRYAD.82C67/3	http://bnb.data.bl.uk/id/resource/009086948
"Pipeline"	http://data.datacite.org/10.5061/DRYAD.7C99F/2	http://bnb.data.bl.uk/id/resource/009934222
"Rattlesnakes"	http://data.datacite.org/10.5061/DRYAD.2H4N301T/1	http://bnb.data.bl.uk/id/resource/009013404

String Similarity in CBR Platforms:
A Preliminary Study

Alice Mazzucchelli[2] and Fabio Sartori[1]

[1] Department of Informatics, Systems and Communication,
University of Milano-Bicocca,
Viale Sarca 336/14, 20126, Milano, Italy
sartori@disco.unimib.it

[2] Department of Business Administration, Finance, Management and Law,
University of Milano-Bicocca,
Via Bicocca degli Arcimboldi 8, 20126, Milano, Italy
alice.mazzucchelli@unimib.it

Abstract. Case Based Reasoning is a very important research trend in Artificial Intelligence and can be a powerful approach in the solution of complex problems characterized by heterogeneous knowledge. In this paper we present an ongoing research project where CBR is exploited to support the identification of enterprises potentially going to bankruptcy, through a comparison of their balance indexes with the ones of similar and already closed firms. In particular, the paper focuses on how developing similarity measures for strings can be profitably supported by metadata models of case structures and semantic methods like Query Expansion.

Keywords: Case Based Reasoning, XML, Bankruptcy Prediction.

1 Introduction

During the last twenty years, the Case Based Reasoning (CBR) paradigm [1] has become one of the most important research areas in Artificial Intelligence: it is a four–steps process which uses past experiences to understand new situations, in order to suggest a suitable way to solve new problems or to criticize the proposed solutions. This kind of approach has immediately been adopted in Knowledge Management applications, as in the case of chemistry [2], diagnosis and troubleshooting [3, 4], and many other domains, as well as in the design and implementation of general-purpose platforms [5–7].

In this paper, we present a recent development of CRePERIE platform, about the development of similarity functions to compare alphanumerical attributes (i.e. strings of characters) to support the identification of enterprises to be potentially bankrupting. A library of metrics based on both syntactic and semantic approaches has been developed, with the aim to compare enterprises on the basis of their business sector. The rest of the paper is organized as follows: Section 2 briefly introduces the metadata model adopted in the development

S. Closs et al. (Eds.): MTSR 2014, CCIS 478, pp. 22–29, 2014.
© Springer International Publishing Switzerland 2014

of CRePERIE. Section 3 describes the five similarity functions implemented to take care of strings. The case study and the results obtained from the tests are provided in Section 4. The paper ends with final considerations about future developments of this work in the context of CRePERIE.

2   CRePERIE: Case Retrieval Platform Extended to RevIsE

In our approach, a case is a collection of *case elements* which correspond to nodes of a tree-structure [8]. Formally, a *case element ce* is a member of the *CaseElement* set: $\forall ce \in CaseElement$, $ce = (id, t, n)$ where: $id \in Z^+ - \{0\}$ is the identifier of the case element; $t \in T$ identifies the range of values associated to *ce* (i.e. String, Integer, Double); $n \in String$ is the name used to refer to the case element.

A *case base* $C = \{c_1, .., c_n\}$, $1 \leq n < \infty$, is a finite and not empty collection of cases and every case is defined as a set of couples $(ce_1, v_1), .., (ce_m, v_m)$, $1 \leq m < \infty$, where $\forall (ce_i, v_i)$, $ce_i \in CaseElement$ and $t(ce_i) = t$ and $v_i \in t \cup \{\bot\}$ (i.e. v_i is the value associated to ce_i).

Considering a case base, each case has to be organized following a particular tree-structure: In this structure, *inner nodes* and *outer nodes* can be identified: outer nodes, also named *attributes* overlap with leaves whereas inner nodes represent *categories* which the attributes belong to. In our approach, only one structure can be defined for each case base so every case belonging to a particular case base has the same structure. The structure defines the three parts of a generic case according to literature: $\forall x \in StructBase$, $x = (d, sol, o)$, where *StructBase* is a finite and not empty collection of case structures; $d(x) = d$ denotes the problem description part; $sol(x) = sol$ denotes the solution part; $o(x) = o$ denotes the outcome part. The following code describes the XML schema adopted to represent the case structure in CRePERIE (further details can be found in [9]):

```
<CREPeRIE:struct name="StructName.xml" id="1">
<CREPeRIE:caseDescription>
        <CREPeRIE:aggregationFunctionName>avgMatRoot
            </CREPeRIE:aggregationFunctionName>
        <CREPeRIE:innerNode>
        <CREPeRIE:similarityFunctionName>simCaseSenString
                </CREP:similarityFunctionName>
        <CREPeRIE:aggregationFunctionName>avgMatNoRoot
                </CREP:aggregationFunctionName>
        <CREPeRIE:caseElementId>1</CREPeRIE:caseElementId>
                <CREPeRIE:innerNode>
                <CREPeRIE:similarityFunctionName>simCaseSenString
                    </CREPeRIE:similarityFunctionName>
                <CREPeRIE:aggregationFunctionName>avgMatNoRoot
                    </CREPeRIE:aggregationFunctionName>
                <CREPeRIE:caseElementId>2</CREPeRIE:caseElementId>
                <CREPeRIE:outerNode>
                <CREPeRIE:similarityFunctionName>simCaseInString
                    </CREPeRIE:similarityFunctionName>
                <CREPeRIE:caseElementId>3</CREPeRIE:caseElementId>
                </CREPeRIE:outerNode>
```

```
        </CRePeRIE:innerNode>
        </CRePeRIE:innerNode>
        ...
</CRePeRIE:caseDescription>
<CRePeRIE:caseSolution> </CRePeRIE:caseSolution>
<CRePeRIE:caseOutcome> </CRePeRIE:caseOutcome>
</CRePeRIE:struct>
```

In the structure, each node (namely inner and outer) overlaps with a particular $ce \in CaseElement$. Moreover, in order to support the fundamental methodology of CBR approach based on comparison among cases, every node is coupled with a similarity function sf, defined as $sf : C_c \times C_r \longrightarrow [0..1]$, where C_c and C_r denote the case descriptions of the *current* (i.e. the description of the new problem to solve) and *retrieved* (i.e. the most similar problem to the current one, already solved in the past) cases respectively.

A set of similarity functions is available in the system; considering a tree-structure in which sub-trees can be identified, in order to obtain a single similarity value for each sub-tree, we introduce the concept of aggregation function af, that works on similarity degrees of child nodes and of the parent node. In our approach, two kinds of aggregation functions are implemented: average functions and weighted average function. Both of them consider the similarity degrees of inner nodes (if the root is included in calculation by means of the *Root* modality) or not (if the root is included in calculation by means of the *NoRoot* modality). A first type works on number intervals (both integer and double); it is necessary to define minimum and maximum values of the range allowed for every node. The similarity value on a node n corresponding to case element ce between two cases x and y is defined as follows:

$$sf(n)(v_{ce}(x), v_{ce}(y)) = 1 - \frac{|v_{ce}(x) - v_{ce}(y)|}{max - min}$$

A second type of similarity functions works on *strings*: they compare strings in case–sensitive or case–no–sensitive ways and produce as result 1 (if the strings are equal) or 0 (otherwise): since this way of comparing strings is very poor, in order to improve the quality of CRePERIE answers we have extended the similarity calculus by means of new functions, as described in the next section.

3 Similarity Measures for Strings in CRePERIE

As reported above, a similarity function is an instance of the case element class in CRePERIE. Similarity is calculated attribute by attribute, given that attributes' nature can be both numerical and textual. This section describes the evolution of the CRePERIE platform in ranking cases from the textual attribute similarity point of view. Given that the main aim of CRePERIE is providing the user with collections of similarity functions, the study has focused on the design and implementation of different kinds of metrics in order to transform them into similarity functions. The metrics have been divided into two categories: *syntactic functions* and *semantic functions*.

Three syntactic methods [10] to calculate similarity between two strings have been considered: the *Jaro distance*, the *Cosine similarity* and the *Jaccard similarity*. The first method is one of the most used in literature, thanks to the good results obtained in record–linkage domain, and it is based on the number and order of the common characters between two strings. Given strings $s = a_1, a_2, ..., a_k$ and $t = b_1, b_2, ..., b_l$, a character a_i in s is said to be *common with t* if there is a character b_j in t such that $i - H \leq j \leq i + H$, where $H = \frac{min(|s|, |t|)}{2}$. Let $s' = a'_1, a'_2, ..., a'_{k'}$ be the characters in s which are common with t, in the same order they appear in s, and let $t' = b'_1, b'_2, ..., b'_{l'}$ be the characters in t which are common with s, in the same order they appear in t: a *transposition* for s', t' is a position i such that $a'_i \neq b'_i$. Let $T_{s', t'}$ be half the number of transpositions for s' and t'. The *Jaro similarity metric* for s and t is

$$Jaro(s, t) = \frac{1}{3} \cdot \left(\frac{|s'|}{|s|} + \frac{|t'|}{|t|} + \frac{|s'| - T_{s', t'}}{|s'|} \right)$$

The *Cosine similarity* is based on the evaluation of the angle θ between two vectors, and it is necessary to convert strings into vectors before proceeding; given two strings $s = a_1, a_2, ..., a_k$ and $t = b_1, b_2, ..., b_l$, let $U = s \bigcup t = u_1, u_2, ..., u_n$ be the union between the set of characters in s and the set of characters in t; let $vect_{s,U}$ and $vect_{t,U}$ be two vectors counting how many times each character $u \in U$ occurs in s and t respectively; the Cosine similarity between s and t is defined as

$$SIM_{Cos} = \cos(\theta) = \frac{vect_{s,U} \cdot vect_{t,U}}{\|vect_{s,U}\| \|vect_{t,U}\|}$$

where $\|vect_{s,U}\| = \sqrt{\sum_{i=1}^{n} (vect_{s,U_i})^2}$ and $\|vect_{t,U}\| = \sqrt{\sum_{i=1}^{n} (vect_{t,U_i})^2}$

Finally, the *Jaccard similarity* beween two strings $s = a_1, a_2, ..., a_k$ and $t = b_1, b_2, ..., b_l$, given S and T the sets of characters occurring in s and t respectively, is computed as

$$Jaccard(s, t) = \frac{|S \bigcap T|}{|S \bigcup T|}$$

Different from syntactic methods, semantic metrics work on string meaning to evaluate the similarity. In other words, the similarity between two strings doesn't depend on the number of operation necessary to transform the first word into the second one, but on the calculus of the distance between them: to this scope, strings should be organized in an opportune structure that allows to relate them. In CRePERIE, two different methods have been implemented, namely *TreeSearch* and *Dictionary* based on *search trees* and *thesauri* respectively.

The *TreeSearch* method is applicable when strings are related the one to each other by means of *is-a* and *part-of* relationships. The method fully meets the design requirements of CRePERIE, in which the case structure is hierarchical as described in Section 2. Given strings $s = a_1, a_2, ..., a_k$ and $t = b_1, b_2, ..., b_l$ belonging to a n–ary search tree T, the first step to calculate their similarity is determining their Lowest Common Ancestor [11] in T $LCA_{s,t}^T$. If $LCA_{s,t}^T =$

$Root^T$, the similarity between s and t is zero, since they are in different subtrees. Otherwise, the similarity value is returned by the following formula

$$SIM_{TreeSearch}(s,t) = \frac{1}{2} * (sim(s, LCA_{s,t}^T) + sim(t, LCA_{s,t}^T))$$

where $sim(s, LCA_{s,t}^T) = 1 - \dfrac{Path_{LCA_{s,t}^T,s}}{h_T}$ and $sim(t, LCA_{s,t}^T) = 1 - \dfrac{Path_{LCA_{s,t}^T,t}}{h_T}$.

The *Dictionary* approach is based on the exploitation of *thesauri*, sort of ontologies where terms are bounded by means of semantic relationships like *hyponimy, hypernimy, holonimy* and *meronimy*. In particular, an existing tool named *QueryExpander* [12] is invoked to perform query expansion on each string to compare. In this way, each string is evaluated according to the underlying thesaurus (that is imported by QueryExpander) producing a query expansion set for each term composing it; QueryExpander calculates also a ranking similarity value between the term to be expanded and its query expansion set, such that the final similarity value between the original string and the adopted thesaurus is the mean of all the values returned by QueryExpander; the last step of the algorithm is to calculate the mean between the two values; summarizing, given two strings $s = a_1, a_2, ..., a_k$ and $t = b_1, b_2, ..., b_l$ and the QueryExpander (QE) tool

$$SIM_{Dictionary}(s,t) = \frac{1}{2} * (sim_{s,QE} + sim_{t,QE})$$

where $sim_{s,QE} = \frac{\sum_{i=1}^{k} QE(a_i)}{k}$ and $sim_{t,QE} = \frac{\sum_{i=1}^{l} QE(b_i)}{l}$. The Dictionary algorithm is useful when CRePERIE must compare strings not characterized by the existence of *a priori* relationships between them.

4 Case Study

The chosen case study is an ongoing collaboration between the Department of Computer Science, Systems and Communication and the Department of Business Administration, Finance, Management and Law of the University of Milano–Bicocca, that aims at the development of a complete methodology to identify Italian enterprises close to bankruptcy. The challenge of this project is to demonstrate the suitability of CBR in bankruptcy forecasting, although the previous results are contradictory (see e.g. [13]). By choosing objective numerical attributes to describe enterprises (e.g. *Return on Investement, Return on Equity, Leverage,* and so on), it would be possible to define a proper case structure (see Section 2) and a case base composed of failed enterprises; in this way, it could be possible to understand if a currently sane enterprise will be close to bankruptcy in the next future comparing its case description with the case base.

It has been recently decided to include in the analysis a textual parameter, namely the *ATECO 2007 Code*: it is an index composed of one to three fields, elaborated by ISTAT[1], useful to understand which category an Italian enterprise

---

[1] Acronym of *The National Insitute of Statistics*, see http://www.istat.it/en/ for further information.

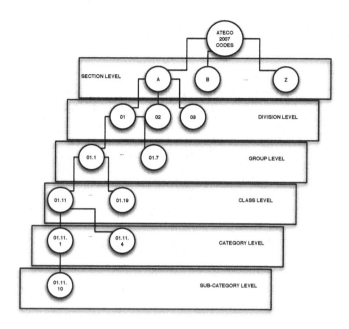

Fig. 1. Representation of a ATECO 2007 Codes as a Tree

belongs to. The codes are clustered into a hierarchical structure made of 21 *Sections* (dividing it into 21 sub–trees), 88 *Divisions*, 272 *Groups*, 615 *Classes*, 918 *Categories* and 1224 *Sub-categories*. Figure 1 shows a sketch of Section A sub–tree. Each code is completed by a description that specifies the business typology of the enterprise. This code is very useful in comparing enterprises in a more objective way: depending on the sector, it could be possible that numerical indexes count differently in the decision if an enterprises is close to bankruptcy or not. For this reason, it is very important to compare homogeneous enterprises: the original similarity function for textual attributes in CRePERIE was only able to understand if a word was equal to another one (similarity equal to 1) or not (similarity equal to 0), by comparing them character by character (with the possibility of case–sensitive matching). Doing so, the pruning of the case base resulted too deep, and the retrieval phase of CRePERIE could not be considered satisfying. On the other hand, ignoring the ATECO Code comparison would lead to misunderstanding results.

5   Results and Future Works

The implementation of the library of similarity functions for strings described above has provided the CRePERIE platform with the possibility to compare enterprises with similar ones from the business sector point of view (i.e. two enterprises are comparable if they belong to the same subtree), allowing the user to adopt the most suitable technique according to the specific problem domain.

Table 1. ATECO 2007 Codes used in the test and their descriptions, in Italian

ATECO Code	Description
A	AGRICOLTURA, SILVICOLTURA E PESCA
01	COLTIVAZIONI AGRICOLE E PRODUZIONE DI PRODOTTI ANIMALI, CACCIA E SERVIZI CONNESSI
01.11.10	Coltivazione di cereali (escluso il riso)
01.49.3	Apicoltura
02	SILVICOLTURA ED UTILIZZO DI AREE FORESTALI
02.2	UTILIZZO DI AREE FORESTALI
02.20.00	Utilizzo di aree forestali
03.1	PESCA
03.2	ACQUACOLTURA
01.12	Coltivazione di riso
01.26	Coltivazione di frutti oleosi

Table 1 shows an extract of the Ateco 2007 Codes tree, where samples from both equal (e.g. codes 01 and 01.11.10 or 02 and 02.2) and different (e.g. 01.12 and 03.1) subtrees are taken. Descriptions are in Italian language because of the project nature, but this is not a limitation from the result analysis standpoint. While the first four methods work on codes, Dictionary starts from their descriptions to calculate the similarity value. Table 2 reports the similarity value obtained in some tests on the codes above. As a first consideration, it is important to notice that all the functions always return values in the range $[0...1]$. Then, they are capable to evaluate the full similarity (i.e. the test on $s = A$ and $t = A$). The third important point is that all the methods except the Cosine one can detect null similarity (i.e. codes belonging to different subtrees). The best results are obtained from the application of Jaro, TreeSearch and Dictionary, but the last two methods are more precise since they take care of string semantics. On the other hand, Jaro is faster than other two (in particular, Dictionary can result very slow due to the Internet connection) approaches.

Summarizing, the syntactic methods performance seems to decade when strings to compare are long, because of the error margin concerning the matching

Table 2. Similarity values for strings s and t extracted from Table 1

String s	String t	$Jaro(s, t)$	SIM_{Cos}	$Jaccard(s, t)$	$TreeSearch(s, t)$	$Dictionary(s, t)$
A	A	1.0	1.0	1.0	1.0	1.0
01	01.11.10	0.7	0.9	0.2	0.6	0.6
01	02	0.0	0.9	0.1	0.0	0.0
01.11.10	02.20.00	0.0	0.9	0.0	0.0	0.0
02.2	03.1	0.0	0.3	0.0	0.0	0.0
A	03.1	0.4	0.6	0.1	0.8	0.7
01.49.3	03.2	0.0	0.9	0.4	0.0	0.0
01.12	01.26	0.0	1.0	0.4	0.6	0.7

between characters growing up. The two semantic methods can be considered more reliable. In particular, the Dictionary method will be further explored in the future, to improve its performance: the current impossibility to choose which terms are more relevant within the query is a problem, since the expansion is carried out on all the description words. The research and evaluation process can take a long time in lot of cases and the results can be affected by mistakes. This disadvantage could be solved by loading a dedicated thesaurus within the platform in the future: it would be necessary to build a specific thesaurus of concepts within ATECO sections and to develop all the relationships between the various terms.

References

1. Kolodner, J.: Case Based Reasoning. Morgan Kaufmann Pu., San Mateo (1993)
2. Craw, S., Wiratunga, N., Rowe, R.: Case-Based Design for Tablet Formulation. In: Smyth, B., Cunningham, P. (eds.) EWCBR 1998. LNCS (LNAI), vol. 1488, pp. 358–369. Springer, Heidelberg (1998)
3. Montani, S., Portinale, L., Leonardi, G., Bellazzi, R., Bellazzi, R.: Case-based retrieval to support the treatment of end stage renal failure patients. Artificial Intelligence in Medicine 37(1), 31–42 (2006)
4. Bandini, S., Colombo, E., Frisoni, G., Sartori, F., Svensson, J.: Case-Based Troubleshooting in the Automotive Context: the SMMART Project. In: Althoff, K.-D., Bergmann, R., Minor, M., Hanft, A. (eds.) ECCBR 2008. LNCS (LNAI), vol. 5239, pp. 600–614. Springer, Heidelberg (2008)
5. Wilke, W., Bergmann, R.: Incremental Adaptation with the INRECA-System. In: ECAI 1996 Workshop on Adaptation in Case-Based Reasoning (1996)
6. Plaza, E., Arcos, J.L.: Constructive Adaptation. In: Craw, S., Preece, A.D. (eds.) ECCBR 2002. LNCS (LNAI), vol. 2416, pp. 306–320. Springer, Heidelberg (2002)
7. Díaz-Agudo, B., González-Calero, P.A., Recio-García, J.A., Sánchez-Ruiz, A.A.: Building CBR systems with jCOLIBRI. Journal Science of Computer Programming 69, 1–3 (2007)
8. Bergmann, R., Stahl, A.: Similarity Measures for Object-Oriented Case Representations. In: Smyth, B., Cunningham, P. (eds.) EWCBR 1998. LNCS (LNAI), vol. 1488, pp. 25–36. Springer, Heidelberg (1998)
9. Manenti, L., Sartori, F.: Metadata support to retrieve and revise solutions in case-based reasoning. IJMSO 6(3/4), 185–194 (2011)
10. Cohen, W.W., Ravikumar, P.D., Fienberg, S.E.: A Comparison of String Distance Metrics for Name-Matching Tasks. In: IIWeb 2003, pp. 73–78 (2003)
11. Aho, A.V., Hopcroft, J.E., Ullman, J.D.: On Finding Lowest Common Ancestors in Trees. SIAM J. Comput. 5(1), 115–132 (1976)
12. Fersini, E., Sartori, F.: Semantic storyboard of judicial debates: a novel multimedia summarization environment. Program: Electronic Library and Information Systems 46(2), 199–219 (2012)
13. Bryant, S.M.: A case-based reasoning approach to bankruptcy prediction modeling. Int. Syst. in Accounting, Finance and Management 6(3), 195–214 (1997)

Automating Technical Reviews in Software Forges and Repositories Based on Linked Data

Juan Manuel Dodero[1], Iván Ruiz-Rube[1], and Ignacio Traverso[2]

[1] Informatics Engineering Department
University of Cadiz, Spain
`{juanma.dodero,ivan.ruiz}@uca.es`
[2] FZI Research Center for Information Technologies, Karlsruhe, Germany
`{traverso}@fzi.de`

Abstract. Automating the evaluation of a software process is complex due to the absence of interoperability mechanisms between the tools that are used to manage, develop or maintain software projects. This work presents an approach to facilitate the construction of mechanisms to evaluate software projects. Based on information integration principles and Linked Open Data techniques, project management and development tools can expose their data using a set of shared models, thereby facilitating the development of integration solutions intended for software process evaluation. A practical application of the approach is here described in order to facilitate automated technical reviews of projects in software forges and repositories.

Keywords: Software Quality, Software Process Engineering, Information Integration, Linked Open Data.

1 Introduction

Evaluation of software processes is essential for continuous quality improvement [7]. In order to make improvements, it is necessary to measure and analyse the errors, deficiencies or deviations in the actual process execution. Analyzing metrics and indicators enables improving the management of software processes, providing ways to predict and control the execution of the projects and to assess the quality of the developed products [6].

Technical reviews are a relevant set of control activities in software engineering. These activities are usually quite repetitive and require a significant allocation of human resources, as they are often manual activities. Reviews are usually completed at certain checkpoints throughout the software lifecycle, such as at the end of certain phases, milestones, activities, or iterations (in incremental life cycles) or just before delivery to the client [1]. During the review processes, evidence of the good use or misuse of the organization's methodology and software engineering practices are checked, usually by using checklists defined for this purpose. These lists typically include checking the completion of activities of production and management, the correct format of work products

S. Closs et al. (Eds.): MTSR 2014, CCIS 478, pp. 30–41, 2014.
© Springer International Publishing Switzerland 2014

and deliverables, checking for the evidences of using a certain technique, tool or method, etc.

It is common that organizations cannot allocate sufficient effort and human resources to make this work. This is because software quality activities are not traditionally considered as productive labor, in the sense that they do not directly generate new software assets. Therefore, some mechanisms to automate technical reviews are needed.

This paper explains how to use the SPDEF *framework*[14] to automate technical reviews during the development of software projects. The solution uses the RDF data exposed from each of the support tools. It enables the launch of SPARQL queries in order to automate the collection of evidences required by technical reviews. These tools must be previously endowed with some of the mechanisms of data exposition and configured with a set of vocabularies suitable for the specific tools.

The rest of this paper is organized as follows: the conceptual models designed for the different supporting tools, the RDFs vocabularies implemented and the mechanisms of data exposition required are presented in Section 2. Section 3 presents a detailed scenario of data integration for automating technical reviews. Finally, some conclusions and other research related to our approach is included in Section 4.

2   Models of Software Tools

Although there are no complete tools for evaluating software processes, a lot of open source software development and management tools or *software forges* [3] have wide spread in recent years. Software forges usually store a large amount of information that can be useful for evaluating software processes. However, the analysis of that information is difficult because of the discrepancy of the data models used in different tools. Publishing such data under a shared information model is essential to facilitate subsequent processes of mapping the information contained in the different tools. As long as the different support tools publish their data in a common and standardized way, and one easily processed by machines, the construction of new tools focused on the evaluation of the quality of processes and the calculation of metrics can be simplified.

With the aim of describing the structure of the information managed by such support tools, we have designed a number of models corresponding to several families of tools.

- *Visual Modeling tool Model (VMM).* From the characterization and analysis of several UML tools, such as *Enterprise Architect*[1], *Visual Paradigm for UML*[2] and *Rational Rose*[3], the model shown in Figure 1 has been

---

[1] http://www.sparxsystems.com/

[2] http://www.visual-paradigm.com/

[3] www.ibm.com/software/awdtools/developer/rose/

designed. This model enables representing the basic information structure of these UML tools, but without excluding other tools commonly used to model software systems or other entities by using other visual languages.

- *Wiki Tool Model (WIKIM)*. From the analysis of various systems, such as *MediaWiki*, *Confluence*[4], and *DokuWiki*[5], the model depicted in Figure 2 was designed.
- *Issue Tracking Tool Model (ITM)*. This model (see Figure 3) was designed from the analysis of the features of task management tools and issue tracking systems, such as *Redmine*[6], *Jira*[7], and *Trac*[8].

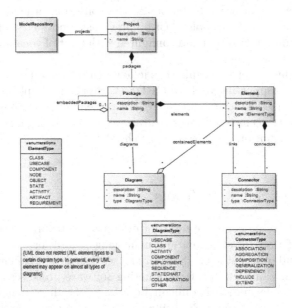

Fig. 1. Visual Modeling tool Model

Usually, work team members use different types of tools to manage the work products elaborated during the development of software projects. For instance, the non-code work products of the projects can be managed both in visual modeling tools either in wiki systems. In order to uniformly access to the data of the work products, regardless of the tool used, a model to define work products with a flexible structure and types of its artifacts is also defined, as we can see in Figure 4.

---

[4] https://www.atlassian.com/en/software/confluence
[5] https://www.dokuwiki.org/dokuwiki
[6] http://www.redmine.org/
[7] https://www.atlassian.com/en/software/jira
[8] http://trac.edgewall.org/

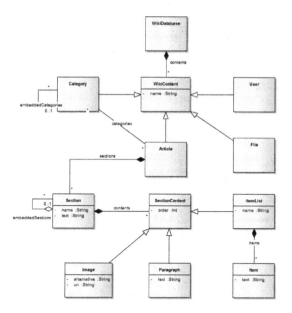

Fig. 2. Wiki Tool Model

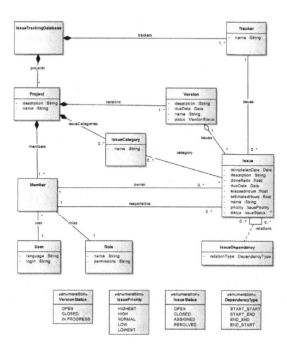

Fig. 3. Issue Tracking Tool Model

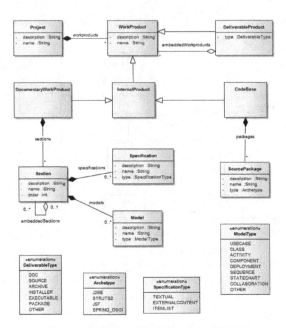

Fig. 4. Software Work Product Model

2.1 Vocabularies and Equivalence Rules

According to the LOD approach, reusing vocabularies rather than reinventing them increases the probability of LOD datasets to be re-used without further modifications for new applications [8]. Hence the DOAP vocabulary[9] was used as a starting point to describe the basic project data that can be managed by a software forge or repository. Since DOAP does not consider certain aspects of software processes (e.g. versions and tasks), new vocabularies were defined for the above generic tools models (VMM, WIKIM and ITM). All the new vocabularies have been published on the Web, using the *Neologism* tool, and indexed in the LOD directory[10]. The enumerated types existing in the conceptual models described above have been implemented as instances of the SKOS standard vocabulary [11].

There are defined relationships between the SWPM and the vocabulary terms of specific forge tools. For example, the forge provide a simple wiki (i.e. consisting of formatted text articles with embedded images) to describe any software model, or the issue tracking tool might not define milestones. For this purpose, the equivalence and specialization axioms *owl:equivalentClass*, *owl:equivalentProperty*, *rdfs: subClassOf* and *rdfs:subPropertyOf* were used. However, an univocal correspondence between the elements of the models at the different levels does not always

---

[9] https://github.com/edumbill/doap/wiki

[10] http://lov.okfn.org/dataset/lov/

[11] http://www.w3.org/2004/02/skos/

exist. For example, a *Software Product Model* of the SWPM model can be mapped to a different elements of the WIKIM model. A rule engine is needed to implement the inference needed from the RDF triples that describe a concrete deployment scenario.

2.2   Mechanisms for Opening Data

A set of components to expose data (using the above vocabularies from the software process support tools is needed. Thus, the tools provide interfaces that enable managing HTTP requests on resources identified by URIs, as well as SPARQL queries. These interfaces return the requested information in any of the serialization formats available for RDF.

First, we implemented a tool, called *Abreforjas* [15], to provide a single access mechanism and a common format for software project data hosted on different task management tools. This tool extracts and normalizes the information stored in the software forges, such as *Assembla* or *Redmine. Abreforjas* enables a LOD interface for publishing RDF data using the ITM vocabulary with the information of the projects.

Furthermore, a data adapter for publishing LOD from the UML-based editing tool Enterprise Architect has been implemented. For that, we opted for using *D2R Server*, a linked data-relational mapper [2]. In that way, this adapter exposes RDF data conforming to the VMM vocabulary.

3   Automating Technical Reviews

Figure 5 depicts the overall integration solution. It is implemented using the LMF[12] platform, which includes data storing, caching, versioning, reasoning, indexing, and querying capabilities, among others.

LMF has a triple local repository in which the vocabularies of the supporting tools (VMM, WIKIM and ITM) and the upper vocabulary of work products (SWPM) included in this work were loaded. In addition, the inference rules were also included in the semantic reasoner provided by the platform, joint with the common rules of reasoning about the axioms of equivalence and specialization of *RDF Schema* and OWL. LMF offers a module for transparently fetching and loading RDF resources on demand from a previously registered set of datasets. Therefore, we set the SPARQL endpoint for *Enterprise Architect* and the *Abreforjas* endpoint for *Redmine*, which allows us to extract the required data.

Next, it is essential to make links between each of the resource identifiers (URIs) that the projects have in the several support tools. In Listing 1, a registry of projects of a given fictional organization, implemented as a set of RDF triples, is presented.

The code snippet above shows how a given sample project is linked, using an equivalence axiom, with the corresponding projects hosted in the datasets of

---

[12] https://code.google.com/p/lmf/

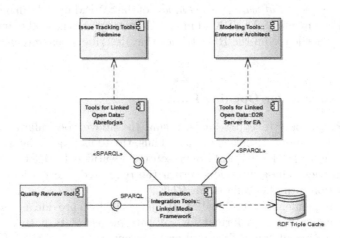

Fig. 5. EII solution for automating technical reviews

```
@prefix rdf:
  <http://www.w3.org/1999/02/22-rdf-syntax-ns#> .
@prefix doap:
  <http://usefulinc.com/ns/doap#> .
@prefix dc:
  <http://purl.org/dc/elements/1.1/> .
@prefix owl:
  <http://www.w3.org/2002/07/owl#> .

<http://integration.my.org/resource/projects/foobar>
  rdf:type doap:Project ;
  dc:name "JAVA Web App" ;
  owl:sameAs <http://ea.my.org/resource/projects/foo> ;
  owl:sameAs <http://abreforjas.my.org/resource/projects/bar> .

<http://integration.my.org/resource/projects/openupTemplate>
  rdf:type doap:Project ;
  dc:name "Template Project for OpenUp Methodology" ;
  owl:sameAs <http://ea.my.org/resource/projects/openUp> ;
  owl:sameAs <http://abreforjas.my.org/resource/projects/openUp> .
```

Listing 1. RDF implementation of a registry of internal projects

```
PREFIX vmm:
  <http://spi-fm.uca.es/spdef/models/genericTools/vmm/1.0#>
SELECT ?actorId ?actorName
WHERE{
  <http://integration.my.org/resource/projects/foobar>
    vmm:packages/vmm:embeddedPackages*/ vmm:elements* ?actorId .
  ?actorId vmm:type "Actor" .
  ?actorId vmm:name ?actorName .

  MINUS {
    ?connId vmm:type "UseCase" .
    ?actorId vmm:connectors ?connId
  } .
  MINUS {
    ?connId vmm:type "UseCase" .
    ?connId vmm:target ?actorId
  } .
  MINUS {
    ?connId vmm:type "Association".
    ?cduId vmm:type "UseCase" .
    ?actorId vmm:connectors ?connId .
    ?connId vmm:target ?cduId
  } .
  MINUS {
    ?connId vmm:type "Association" .
    ?cduId vmm:type "UseCase" .
    ?connId vmm:target ?actorId .
    ?cduId vmm:connectors ?connId
  }
}
ORDER BY ?actorName
```

Listing 2. SPARQL query for getting the actors who are not associated with any use case

Enterprise Architect and *Abreforjas*. Furthermore, the project template resulting from the previous deployment of the *OpenUP* methodology on the support tools is also registered. With the data integration solution described above, developers will be able to build new applications intended for conducting quality reviews of software projects. Below, a number of SPARQL queries illustrating the quality check rules are included.

In order to check the correct application of some practices of Software Engineering, such as the UML modeling techniques, or agile project management, a series of SPARQL queries are issued. For instance, with the query in Listing 2, we can retrieve the actors of the system, which are identified during the phase of analysis of a project, that are not associated with any use case. Another example is the query in Listing 3 aimed at knowing if there are unresolved tasks that have been planned for project milestones whose deadline has already expired.

```
PREFIX itm: <http://spi-fm.uca.es/spdef/models/genericTools/itm/1.0#>
SELECT ?versionName ?versionDueDate ?issueName ?issueCompletedDate
WHERE{
    <http://integration.my.org/resource/projects/foobar>
        itm:versions ?versionId .
    ?versionId a itm:Version .
    ?versionId itm:name  ?versionName .
    ?versionId itm:dueDate ?versionDueDate.
    ?versionId itm:issues ?issueId .
    ?issueId itm:name  ?issueName .
    ?issueId itm:completedDate ?issueCompletedDate .
    FILTER (?issueCompletedDate > ?versionDueDate)
}
ORDER BY ?issueDueDate
```

Listing 3. SPARQL query to check whether all the tasks belonging to a completed milestone are closed

```
PREFIX swpm: <http://spi-fm.uca.es/spdef/models/deployment/swpm/1.0#>
SELECT ?productName
WHERE{
    <http://integration.my.org/resource/projects/openupTemplate>
        swpm:workproducts ?productId .
    ?productId swpm:name ?productName .
    MINUS {
        <http://integration.my.org/resource/projects/foobar>
            swpm:workproducts ?productId .
        ?productId swpm:name ?productName
    }
}
ORDER BY ?productName
```

Listing 4. SPARQL query to check which work products have not been elaborated as specified in the process

In addition to the above checks, it is possible to verify the adherence of the projects with respect to the procedures deployed in the organization. Since in our integration solution, the data of project templates are also exposed from the support tools, it is easy to check whether the work products expected for a given project or the UML models required in any of the technical documents have been developed. The query in Listing 4 allows the user to know whether the documentary products expected for the project have been elaborated, by comparing the product names of the process base template with those in the set of products generated in the project under analysis.

The above queries illustrate some of the opportunities offered by the LOD approach for evaluating software processes. Choosing a vocabulary or others when designing SPARQL queries depends on the desired level of detail for collecting evidence. In the first examples, we used the generic tools vocabularies, VMM and ITM, for retrieving evidence about the use of UML modeling techniques and the tracking of project tasks, respectively.

In order to check whether the work products were elaborated, the SWPM vocabulary was used. Using this vocabulary for queries is especially recommended in contexts where the work products of the projects are managed both in visual modeling tools and in wiki systems. In this way, regardless of the tool used, the way of access to the data will always be uniform.

4   Related Work

A related research to the work of this paper, but targeted to the field of scientific information systems, is presented in [10]. Some other works related to the evaluation of software processes can be found, such as: an approach to collecting and analyzing metrics collected from different data sources [4]; the detection of inconsistencies between the definition of the processes and the data collected from the projects, by using semantic web technologies [13], and the use of techniques of model relaxing and model changing for dynamically adapting process models [11]. Other authors have used large amounts of information about projects managed in popular software forges, as an empirical database for experimentation in Software Engineering [9][12]. Also, some authors have proposed using semantic technologies in the field of Software Engineering, such as a framework to represent testing processes in distributed development projects [5]. More recently, several software provider companies, led by IBM, have been developing a set of open specifications aimed at simplifying the integration of software development tools by using LOD technologies and REST web services [16].

5   Conclusions and Further Work

This paper presents an approach aimed at tackling the high complexity of conducting automated evaluation procedures of processes, based on the application of the principles and technologies of LOD. The main objective of this work is to ease the development of data integration solutions for process evaluation, by using the LOD approach. Our approach comes with a series of models, implemented as *RDF Schema* vocabularies, and a set of relationships between models, implemented as RDF axioms and inference rules.

Achieving a global and complete view of the information managed by the support tools would enable automating the quality evaluation in software processes. To validate this hypothesis, a detailed description of a data integration scenario for automating quality reviews on software projects, by issuing SPARQL queries, was described. This integration solution uses two software components (Abreforjas and D2R Server) for opening RDF data from some issue-tracking systems and visual modeling tools, such as *Redmine* and *Enterprise Architect*.

Designing models for tools targeted at other aspects of the Software Engineering, as configuration management or people management are proposed as future lines of work. In addition, we are exploring the techniques of natural language processing and OLAP cubes for enhancing the mechanisms for opening data from the support tools and the automated evaluation procedures.

Acknowledgements. This work has been sponsored by grants from the *Plataforma para el modelado, personalización y benchmarking en la mejora de procesos normalizados (BESTMARK)* project (TSI-020100-2011-396) of the Spanish Ministry of Industry, Tourism and Trade.

References

1. Aurum, A., Petersson, H., Wohlin, C.: State-of-the-art: software inspections after 25 years. Software Testing, Verification and Reliability 12(3), 133–154 (2002)
2. Bizer, C., Cyganiak, R.: D2r server-publishing relational databases on the semantic web. In: Poster at the 5th International Semantic Web Conference (2006)
3. Cabot, J., Wilson, G., et al.: Tools for teams: A survey of web-based software project portals. Dr. Dobb's, 1–14 (2009)
4. Colombo, A., Damiani, E., Frati, F., Oltolina, S., Reed, K., Ruffatti, G.: The Use of a Meta-Model to Support Multi-Project Process Measurement. In: 2008 15th Asia-Pacific Software Engineering Conference, pp. 503–510. IEEE (2008)
5. Colomo-Palacios, R., López-Cuadrado, L.J., González-Carrasco, I., García-Peñalvo, J.F.: Sabumo-dtest: Design and evaluation of an intelligent collaborative distributed testing framework. Computer Science and Information Systems 11(11), 29–45 (2014)
6. DeMarco, T.: Controlling software projects: Management, measurement, and estimates. Prentice Hall PTR, Upper Saddle River (1986)
7. Emami, M.S., Ithnin, N.B., Ibrahim, O.: Software process engineering: Strengths, weaknesses, opportunities and threats. In: 2010 6th International Conference on Networked Computing (INC), pp. 1–5. IEEE, Gyeongju (2010)
8. Heath, T., Bizer, C.: Linked data: Evolving the web into a global data space. Synthesis Lectures on the Semantic Web: Theory and Technology 1(1), 1–136 (2011)
9. Herraiz, I., Gonzalez-Barahona, J.M., Robles, G., German, D.M.: On the prediction of the evolution of libre software projects. In: 2007 IEEE International Conference on Software Maintenance, pp. 405–414 (October 2007)
10. Joerg, B., Ruiz-Rube, I., Sicilia, M.A., Dvořvoák, J., Jeffery, K., Hoellrigl, T., Rasmussen, H.S., Engfer, A., Vestdam, T., Barriocanal, E.G.: Connecting closed world research information systems through the linked open data web. International Journal of Software Engineering and Knowledge Engineering 22(03), 345–364 (2012)
11. Mohammed, K., Redouane, L., Bernard, C.: A deviation-tolerant approach to software process evolution. In: Ninth International Workshop on Principles of Software Evolution in Conjunction with the 6th ESEC/FSE Joint Meeting, IWPSE 2007, p. 75. ACM Press, New York (2007)
12. Robles, G., González-Barahona, J.M.: A comprehensive study of software forks: Dates, reasons and outcomes. In: Hammouda, I., Lundell, B., Mikkonen, T., Scacchi, W. (eds.) OSS 2012. IFIP AICT, vol. 378, pp. 1–14. Springer, Heidelberg (2012)
13. Rodríguez, D., García, E., Sánchez, S.: Defining Software Process Model Constraints with rules using OWL and SWRL. Int. J. Soft. Eng. Knowl. 20, 533–548 (2010)

14. Ruiz-Rube, I., Dodero, J.M.: Un framework para el despliegue y evaluación de procesos software. Ph.D. thesis, University of Cádiz, Spain (December 2013)
15. Traverso-Ribón, I., Ruíz-Rube, I., Dodero, J.M., Palomo-Duarte, M.: Open data framework for sustainable assessment in software forges. In: Proceedings of the 3rd International Conference on Web Intelligence, Mining and Semantics, WIMS 2013, pp. 20:1–20:8. ACM, New York (2013)
16. Workgroup, O.C.S.: Oslc core specification version 3.0 draft. Tech. rep., OSLC (2013)

Representing Statistical Indexes as Linked Data Including Metadata about Their Computation Process

Jose Emilio Labra Gayo[1], Hania Farham[2],
Juan Castro Fernández[1], and Jose María Álvarez Rodríguez[3]

[1] WESO Research Group
{jelabra,juan.castro}@weso.es
[2] The Web Foundation
hania@webfoundation.org
[3] Dept. Computer Science
Carlos III University
josemaria.alvarez@uc3m.es

Abstract. In this paper we describe the development of the Web Index linked data portal that represents statistical index data and the computations from which it has been obtained.

The Web Index is a multi-dimensional measure of the World Wide Web's contribution to development and human rights globally. It covers 81 countries and incorporates indicators that assess several areas like universal access; freedom and openness; relevant content; and empowerment.

In order to empower the Web Index transparency, we established as an internal requirement that every published data could be externally verified. The verification could be that it was just raw data obtained from a secondary source, in which case, the system must provide a link to that data source or that the value has been internally computed, in which case, the system provides links to the values from which it has been calculated. The resulting portal contains data that can be tracked to its sources so an external agent can validate the whole index computation process.

We describe the different aspects involved in the development of the WebIndex data portal that also offers new linked data visualization tools. Although in this paper we concentrate on the Web Index development, this approach can be generalized to other projects which involve the publication of externally verifiable computations.

1 Introduction

Statistical indexes are a widely accepted practice that have been applied to numerous domains like economics and Bibliometrics (Impact factor), research and academic performance (H-Index or Shanghai rankings), cloud computing (Global Cloud Index, by CISCO), etc. Those indexes will benefit from a Linked Data approach where the rankings can be seen, tracked and verified by their users linking each rank to the original values and observations from which it has been computed.

As a motivating example, we will employ the Web Index project (http://thewebindex.org), which created an index to measure the World Wide

S. Closs et al. (Eds.): MTSR 2014, CCIS 478, pp. 42–53, 2014.
© Springer International Publishing Switzerland 2014

Web's contribution to development and human rights globally. Scores are given in the areas of access; freedom and openness; relevant content; and empowerment. First released in 2012, the 2013 Index has been expanded and refined to include 20 new countries and features an enhanced data set, particularly in the areas of gender, Open Data, privacy rights and security.

The 2012 version offered a data portal[1] whose data was obtained by transforming raw observations and precomputed values from Excel sheets to RDF. The technical description of that process was described in [2] where we followed the methodology presented in [5].

In this paper, we describe the development of the 2013 version of that data portal, where we employ a new validation and computation approach that enables the publication of a verifiable linked data version of WebIndex results.

We defined a generic vocabulary of computational index structures called *Computex* which could be applied to compute and validate any other kind of index and can be seen as an specialization of the RDF Data Cube vocabulary [9].

Given that the most important part of a data portal about statistical indexes are the numeric values of each observation we established the internal requirement that any value published should be justified either declaring from where it had been obtained or linking it to the values of other observations from which it had been computed.

The validation process employs a combination of SPARQL [10] queries and Shape Expressions [3] to check the different integrity constraints and computation steps in a declarative way. The resulting data portal http://data.webfoundation.org/webindex/2013 contains not only a linked data view about the statistical data but also a machine verifiable justification of the index ranks.

In the rest of the paper we will use Turtle and SPARQL notation and assume that the namespaces have been declared using the most common prefixes found in http://prefix.cc.

2 WebIndex Computation Process

The Web Index is a composite measure that summarizes in a single (average) number the impact and value derived from the Web in various countries. There are serious challenges when attempting to measure and quantify some of the dimensions the Index covers (e.g. the social and political), and suitable proxies were used instead.

Two types of data were used in the construction of the Index: existing data from other data providers (*secondary data*), and new data gathered via a multi-country questionnaire (*primary data*) which was specifically designed by the Web Foundation and its advisers. These primary data will begin to fill in some of the gaps in measurement of the utility and impact of the Web in various countries.

As the Web Index covers a large number of countries, some of which have serious data deficiencies or were not covered by the data providers, some missing data had to be imputed.

---

[1] http://data.webfoundation.org

The following steps summarise the computation process of the Index:

1. Take the data for each indicator from the data source for the 81 countries covered by the Index for the 2007-2012 time period (or 2013, in the case of the Web Index expert assessment survey).
2. Impute missing data for every secondary indicator for the sample of 81 countries over the period 2007-2012. Broadly, the imputation of missing data was done using two methods: country-mean substitution if the missing number is in the middle year (e.g. have 2008 and 2010 but not 2009), or taking arithmetic growth rates on a year-by-year basis.
3. Normalise the full (imputed) dataset using z-scores, making sure that for all indicators, a high value is *good* and a low value is *bad*.
4. Cluster some of the variables, taking the average of the clustered indicators post-normalisation. For the clustered indicators, this clustered value is the one to be used in the computation of the Index components.
5. Compute the component scores using arithmetic means, using the clustered values where relevant.
6. Compute the min-max values for each z-score value of the components, as this is what will be shown in the visualisation tool and other publications containing the component values (generally, it is easier to understand a min-max number in the range of $0 - 100$ rather than a standard deviation-based number). The formula for this is: $\frac{x-min}{max-min} \times 100$
7. Compute sub-index scores by calculating the weighted averages of the relevant components for each sub-Index and the min-max values for each z-score value of the sub-Indexes.
8. Compute overall composite scores by calculating the weighted average of the sub-indexes and the min-max values.

The computation process was originally done by human experts using an Excel file although once the process was established, the computation was automated to validate the whole process.

3   WebIndex Workflow

The WebIndex workflow has been depicted in figure 1. The Excel file was comprised of 184 Excel sheets and contained a combination of raw, imputed and normalized data created by the statistical experts.

That external data was filtered and converted to RDF by means of an specialized web service called *wiFetcher*[2].

Although some of the imported values had been pre-computed in Excel by human experts, we collected only the raw values, so we could automatically compute and validate the results.

---

[2] https://github.com/weso/wiFetcher

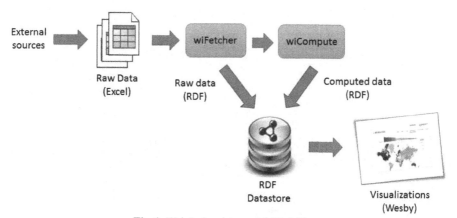

Fig. 1. Web Index data portal WorkFlow

In this way, another application called *wiCompute*[3] took the raw values and computed the index following the computation steps defined by the experts. *wiCompute* carried out the computations generating RDF datasets for the intermediary results and linking the generated values to the values from which they had been computed.

Finally, the RDF data generated was published to a SPARQL endpoint from which we created a specialized visualization tool called *Wesby*[4].

4   WebIndex Data Model

Given the statistical nature of the data, the WebIndex data model is based on the RDF Data Cube vocabulary. Figure 4 represents the main concepts of the data model

As can be seen, the main concept are observations of type `qb:Observation`, which can be raw observations, obtained from an external source, or computed observations derived from other observations. Each observation has a float value `cex:value` and is related to a country, a year, a dataset and an indicator.

A dataset contains a number of slices, each of which also contains a number of observations.

Indicators are provided by an organization of type `org:Organization` from the Organization ontology[18]. Datasets are also published by organizations.

As a sample of some data, an observation can be that Italy has -0.80 as the normalized value using Z-Scores in 2007 for the indicator WEF_L (*Impact of ICT on organizational models*) provided by the World Economic Forum. This information can be represented in RDF using Turtle syntax as[5]:

---

[3] `https://github.com/weso/wiCompute`

[4] `https://github.com/weso/wesby`

[5] The real observation is `http://data.webfoundation.org/webindex/v2013/observation/computed_2007_1386752461095_26549`. The real URIs also include an internal long number to uniquely identify each entity

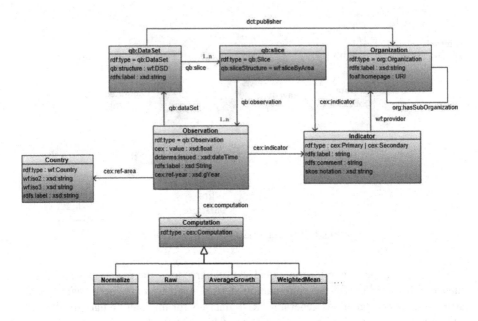

Fig. 2. WebIndex data model

```
obs:computed_26549 a qb:Observation ;
 cex:indicator indicator:WEF_L ;
 qb:dataSet dataset:d_52 ;
 cex:value "-0.80"^^xsd:double ;
 cex:ref-area country:Italy ;
 cex:ref-year 2007 ;
 sdmx-concept:obsStatus cex:Normalized ;
 cex:computation computation:c26550
 ...other properties omitted for brevity
 .
```

Notice that the WebIndex data model contains data that is completely interrelated. Observations are linked to indicators, datasets and computations. Datasets contain also links to slices and slices have links to indicators and observations again. Both datasets and indicators are linked to the organizations that publish or provide them.

The following example contains a sample of interrelated data for this domain.

```
dataset:d_52 a qb:DataSet ;
 qb:structure wf:DSD ;
 qb:slice slice:computed_54 , slice:computed_55, ...
 ...
slice:computed_54 a qb:Slice ;
 qb:sliceStructure wf:sliceByArea ;
 qb:observation obs:computed_26549, obs:computed_26941, ... ;
 ...
```

```
indicator:WEF_L a cex:SecondaryIndicator ;
 rdfs:label "Impact of ICT on organizational models"@en ;
 wf:provider-link org:WEF ;
 ...
org:WEF a org:Organization ;
 rdfs:label "World Economic Forum" ;
 foaf:homepage <http://www.weforum.org/>
 .
country:ITA a wf:Country ;
 wf:iso2 "IT" ; wf:iso2 "ITA" ;
 rdfs:label "Italy" .
 ...
computation:c26550 a cex:Normalize ;
 cex:slice slice:WEF_L2007-Imputed ;
 cex:stdDesv "0.75"^^xsd:double ;
 cex:mean "4.39"^^xsd:double ;
 cex:observation obs:obs29761
 .
```

Computed observations and datasets contain a property cex:computation that associate them to a node of type cex:Computation which links the computed observation to the observations from which it has been obtained. In the above example, the computation c26550 indicates that it is a normalization of the observation obs:obs29761 using the observations in slice slice:WEF_L2007-Imputed which has a standard deviation of 0.75 and a mean of 4.39. Including these declarations, an external agent can verify if the value of the observation has been well computed or if it has been tampered. We also noticed that these declarations had another positive effect to debug the computation process in the development phase of the data portal.

5   Computex Vocabulary

The *Computex*[6] vocabulary defines terms related to the computation of statistical index data and can be seen as a specialization of the RDF Data Cube vocabulary for this kind of statistical computations. Some terms defined in the vocabulary are:

- **cex:Concept** represents the entities that we are indexing. In the case of the Web Index project, the concepts are the different countries. In other applications it could be Universities, journals, services, etc.
- **cex:Indicator**. A dimension whose values add information to the Index. Indicators can be simple dimensions, for example: the mobile phone suscriptions per 100 population, or can be composed from other indicators.
- **cex:Computation**. It represents a computation. We included the main computation types that we needed for the WebIndex project, which have been summarized in Table 1. That list of computation types is non-exhaustive and can be further extended in the future.

---

[6] http://purl.org/weso/ontology/computex

Table 1. Some types of statistical computations

Computation	Description	Properties
Raw	No computation. Raw value obtained from external source.	
Mean	Mean of a set of observations	cex:observation cex:slice
Increment	Increment an observation by a given amount	cex:observation cex:amount
Copy	A copy of another observation	cex:observation
Z-score	A normalization of an observation using the values from a Slice.	cex:observation cex:slice
Ranking	Position in the ranking of a slice of observations.	cex:observation cex:slice
AverageGrowth	Expected average growth of N observations	cex:observations[7]
WeightedMean	Weighted mean of an observation	cex:observation cex:slice cex:weightSchema

- **cex:WeightSchema** a weight schema for a list of indicators. It consists of a weight associated for each indicator which can be used to compute an aggregated observation.

6   Development and Validation Approach

The validation approach employed in the 2012 WebIndex project was based on ad-hoc resource templates and a MD5 checksum field. Apart from that, we did not verify that the precomputed values imported from the Excel sheets really matched the value that could be obtained by following the declared computation process.

In the 2013 version, we did a step forward on the validation approach. The goal was not only to check that a resource contained a given set of fields and values, but also that those values really matched the values that can be obtained by following the declared computations.

The proposed approach was inspired by the integrity constraint specification proposed by the RDF Data Cube vocabulary, which employs a set of SPARQL ASK queries to check the integrity of RDF Data Cube data. Although ASK queries provide a good means to check integrity, in practice their boolean nature does not offer too much help when a dataset does not accomplish with the data model.

We decided to use CONSTRUCT queries which, in case of error, contain an error message and a list of error parameters that can help to spot the problematic data.

We transformed the ASK queries defined in the RDF Data Cube specification to CONSTRUCT queries. In order to make our error messages compatible with EARL [1], we have defined cex:Error as a subclass of earl:TestResult and declared it to have the value earl:failed for the property earl:outcome.

---

[7] This is in plural because the value of this property is an ordered list of observations

We have also created our own set of SPARQL CONSTRUCT queries to validate the
Computex vocabulary terms, specially the computation of index data. For example, the
following query validates whether every observation has at most one value.

```
CONSTRUCT { [ a cex:Error ; cex:errorParam # ... omitted
             cex:msg "Observation has two different values" . ]
} WHERE { ?obs a qb:Observation .
?obs cex:value ?value1 . ?obs cex:value ?value2 .
FILTER ( ?value1 != ?value2 ) }
```

Using this approach, it is possible to define more expressive validations. For example, we are able to validate whether an observation has been obtained as the mean of
other observations.

```
CONSTRUCT { [ a cex:Error ; cex:errorParam # ...omitted
   cex:msg "Mean value does not match" ] .
} WHERE { ?obs a qb:Observation ;
          cex:computation ?comp ;
          cex:value ?val .
          ?comp a cex:Mean .
   { SELECT (AVG(?value) as ?mean) ?comp WHERE {
     ?comp cex:observation ?obs1 .
     ?obs1 cex:value ?value ;
     } GROUP BY ?comp }
FILTER( abs(?mean - ?val) > 0.0001) }
```

Validating statistical computations using SPARQL queries offered a good exercise to
check SPARQL expressiveness. Although we were able to express most of the computation types, some of them had to employ functions that were not part of SPARQL 1.1
or had to be defined in a limited way. We described these limits in [13].

We implemented an online validation tool called *Computex*[8] which takes as input an
RDF graph and checks if it follows the integrity constraints defined by Computex. The
validation tool can also check if the RDF graph follows the RDF Data Cube integrity
constraints and it can also do the index computation for RDF Graphs. Although this
declarative approach was very elegant, computing the webindex using only SPARQL
queries was not practical (it took around 15 minutes for a small subset), so the computation process was finally done by a specialized program implemented in Scala [9].

7   Visualizing the Data Portal

We developed a visualization tool called Wesby [10] which takes as input an SPARQL
endpoint and offers a linked data browsing experience. Wesby was inspired by
Pubby [8] and was developed in Scala using the Play! Framework. Wesby combines
the visualization with a set of templates to offer specialized views for different types of

---

[8] http://computex.herokuapp.com/
[9] Source code is available here: https://github.com/weso/wiCompute
[10] http://wesby.weso.es

resources. For example, figure 3 contains the WebIndex visualization of Italy[11]. The interactive visualization graphics use a javascript library called WesCountry that we have also developed [12].

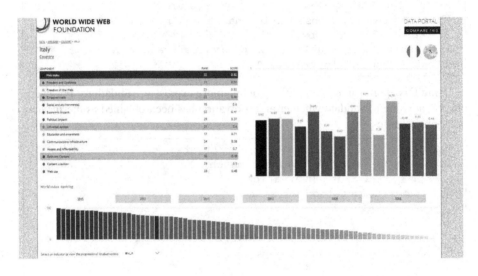

Fig. 3. Web Index visualization of country Italy

When there is no template for a given type of node, Wesby shows a table of properties and values similar to Pubby. Wesby also handles content negotiation so it can return different representations depending on the ACCEPT header.

In order to document the resulting data portal we created a set of templates using Shape Expressions [13]. We consider that this approach offers a good balance between human readability and machine processable specification.

8   Related Work

There is a growing interest in developing solutions to improve the quality of linked data [11, 15, 12]. We consider that it is very important to publish linked data that is not only of high quality, but also that can automatically be validated. Validating RDF has also attracted a number of approaches. Most of them were presented at the W3c Workshop on RDF Validation [17] and can be classified as inference based, SPARQL queries or grammar based.

Inference based approaches try to adapt OWL for validation proposes. However, the use of Open World and Non-unique name assumption limits the validation possibilities.

---

[11] It can be seen here:
http://data.webfoundation.org/webindex/v2013/country/ITA
[12] http://weso.github.io/wesCountry/
[13] http://weso.github.io/wiDoc/

A variation of OWL semantics using Closed World Assumption to express integrity constraints has been proposed in [6, 20, 16]. SPARQL queries can also express validation constraints and offer a great level of expressiveness [13]. Grammar based approaches like OSLC Resource Shapes [19] and Dublic Core Application Profiles [7] define a domain specific language to declare the validation rules. Recently, Shape Expressions [3] have been proposed as a new technology to describe and validate RDF data portals.

Representing statistical linked data has also seen an increasing interest. SDMX [14] is the primary format of the main statistical data organizations. The transformation of SDMX-ML to RDF/XML has been described in [4]. The RDF Data Cube vocabulary [9] has been accepted as a W3c Recommendation technology to publish multidimensional statistical data and to link it with other concepts and data. We have opted to follow the RDF Data Cube vocabulary and in fact, we consider that Computex can be seen as a further specialization of RDF Data Cube to represent statistical index computations.

Another line of related work is the representation of mathematical expressions as linked data. Lange [14] gives an overview of the different approaches. OpenMath was proposed as an extensible standard that can represent the semantic meaning of mathematical objects. Wenzel and Reinhardt [21] propose an approach to integrate OpenMath with RDF data for the representation of mathematical relationships and the integration of mathematical computations into reasoning systems. We consider *Computex* as a first step in that direction to represent statistical computations and we expect more future work to appear about how to represent statistical computations as linked data.

9   Conclusions

In this paper, we described how we were able to represent statistical index computations as linked data which include information to track the origin of any published observation. Although the number of triples were around 3,5 million, we consider that the data portal is of medium size, so we were able to play with different validation possibilities.

Although we have been able to express most of the computations using SPARQL queries, we have found some limitations in current SPARQL 1.1 expressiveness with regards to built-in functions on maths, strings, RDF Collections and performance. In fact, although we initially wanted to do the whole computation process using SPARQL CONSTRUCT queries, we found that it took longer than expected and was difficult to debug, so we opted to develop an independent program that did all the computation process in a few seconds.

After participating in the W3c RDF Validation workshop we were attracted by the Shape Expressions formalism so we developed the documentation of the WebIndex data portal using Shape Expressions. We consider that some structural parts of the data portal can be better expressed in Shape Expressions.

Our future work is to automate the declarative computation of index data from the raw observations and to check the performance using the Web Index data. We are also

---

[14] http://sdmx.org/

improving the Wesby visualization tool and the WesCountry library for statistical graphics. We are even considering to relate visualization templates with Shape Expressions offering a better separation of concerns in the development process.

Acknowledgements. We would like to thank Jules Clements, Karin Alexander, César Luis Alvargonzález, Ignacio Fuertes Bernardo and Alejandro Montes for their collaboration in the development of the WebIndex project.

References

1. Abou-Zahra, S.: Evaluation and Report Language EARL 1.0 schema. W3C Working Draft (2011), http://www.w3.org/TR/EARL10-Schema/
2. Alvarez Rodríguez, J.M., Clement, J., Labra Gayo, J.E., Farhan, H., Ordoñez, P.: Publishing Statistical Data following the Linked Open Data Principles: The Web Index Project. In: Cases on Open-Linked Data and Semantic Web Applications, pp. 199–226. IGI Global (2013), doi:10.4018/978-1-4666-2827-4.ch011
3. Boneva, I., Labra, J.E., Hym, S., Prud'hommeau, E.G., Solbrig, H., Staworko, S.: Validating RDF with Shape Expressions. ArXiv e-prints (April 2014)
4. Capadisli, S., Auer, S., Ngonga Ngomo, A.-C.: Linked sdmx data. Semantic Web Journal, 1–8 (2013)
5. Cifuentes Silva, F.A., Sifaqui, C., Labra Gayo, J.E.: Towards an architecture and adoption process for linked data technologies in open government contexts: a case study for the library of congress of chile. In: Ghidini, C., Ngomo, A.-C.N., Lindstaedt, S.N., Pellegrini, T. (eds.) I-SEMANTICS. ACM International Conference Proceeding Series, pp. 79–86. ACM (2011)
6. Clark, K., Sirin, E.: On RDF validation, stardog ICV, and assorted remarks. In: RDF Validation Workshop. Practical Assurances for Quality RDF Data, Cambridge, Ma, Boston (September 2013), W3c, http://www.w3.org/2012/12/rdf-val
7. Coyle, K., Baker, T.: Dublin core application profiles. separating validation from semantics. In: RDF Validation Workshop. Practical Assurances for Quality RDF Data, Cambridge, Ma, Boston (September 2013), W3c, http://www.w3.org/2012/12/rdf-val
8. Cyganiak, R., Bizer, C.: Pubby: A linked data frontend for sparql endpoints, http://www4.wiwiss.fu-berlin.de/pubby/
9. Cyganiak, R., Reynolds, D.: The RDF Data Cube Vocabulary, W3c Candidate Recommendation (2013), http://www.w3.org/TR/vocab-data-cube/
10. Harris, S., Seaborne, A.: SPARQL 1.1 Query Language (2013), http://www.w3.org/TR/sparql11-query/
11. Hogan, A., Harth, A., Passant, A., Decker, S., Polleres, A.: Weaving the pedantic web. In: Linked Data on the Web Workshop (LDOW 2010) at WWW 2010. CEUR Workshop Proceedings, vol. 628, pp. 30–34 (2010)
12. Kontokostas, D., Westphal, P., Auer, S., Hellmann, S., Lehmann, J., Cornelissen, R., Zaveri, A.: Test-driven evaluation of linked data quality. In: Proceedings of the 23rd International Conference on World Wide Web, WWW 2014, Republic and Canton of Geneva, Switzerland, pp. 747–758 (2014), International World Wide Web Conferences Steering Committee
13. Labra, J.E., Alvarez Rodríguez, J.M.: Validating statistical index data represented in RDF using SPARQL queries. In: RDF Validation Workshop. Practical Assurances for Quality RDF Data, Cambridge, Ma, Boston (September 2013), http://www.w3.org/2012/12/rdf-val, W3c
14. Lange, C.: Ontologies and languages for representing mathematical knowledge on the semantic web. Semantic Web 4(2), 119–158 (2013)

15. Mendes, P.N., Mühleisen, H., Bizer, C.: Sieve: Linked data quality assessment and fusion. In: Proceedings of the 2012 Joint EDBT/ICDT Workshops, EDBT-ICDT 2012, pp. 116–123. ACM, New York (2012)

16. Motik, B., Horrocks, I., Sattler, U.: Adding Integrity Constraints to OWL. In: Golbreich, C., Kalyanpur, A., Parsia, B. (eds.) OWL: Experiences and Directions 2007 (OWLED 2007), Innsbruck, Austria, June 6-7 (2007)

17. RDF Working Group W3c. W3c validation workshop. practical assurances for quality rdf data (September 2013)

18. Reynolds, D.: The Organization Ontology (2014),
    http://www.w3.org/TR/vocab-org/

19. Ryman, A.G., Hors, A.L., Speicher, S.: OSLC resource shape: A language for defining constraints on linked data. In: Bizer, C., Heath, T., Berners-Lee, T., Hausenblas, M., Auer, S. (eds.) Linked Data on the Web. CEUR Workshop Proceedings, vol. 996. CEUR-WS.org (2013)

20. Tao, J., Sirin, E., Bao, J., McGuinness, D.L.: Integrity constraints in OWL. In: Proceedings of the 24th AAAI Conference on Artificial Intelligence (AAAI 2010). AAAI (2010)

21. Wenzel, K., Reinhardt, H.: Mathematical computations for linked data applications with openmath. In: Conferences on Intelligent Computer Mathematics, CICM 2012 (2012)

rdfedit: User Supporting Web Application for Creating and Manipulating RDF Instance Data

Oliver Pohl

Berlin School of Library and Information Science, Humboldt-Universität zu Berlin
oliverpohl@ibi.hu-berlin.de

Abstract. rdfedit is a web application running on Django, rdflib and jQuery DataTables that supports novices in the field of Semantic Web technologies with the creation of RDF instance metadata. By utilizing the Semantic Web search engine Sindice, rdfedit can transform literals into URIs, fetch triples from external resources and import them into the user's local graph. Metadata experts can easily configure these features of rdfedit to fit their preferences regarding metadata schemata, so metadata creators with few knowledge about Semantic Web technologies can create RDF data in a fast and consistent manner while also following the Linked Data principles.

Keywords: RDF Editor, Metadata, Sindice.

1   Introduction

More than a decade has passed since [3] has shared his ideas of the Semantic Web. Since then, the Semantic Web has grown and evolved [5, 12, 19]but it is still is not living up to its potential. When analyzing the application of RDFa throughout the Web in 2012, [13] only determined 4.7 per cent of all websites inside the Bing corpus made use of that technology. A year later, [4] conducted a similar study, this time analyzing websites within the Common Crawl Index[1], receiving only slightly higher percentage of 5.6.

The reasons on why Semantic Web technologies are not used more thoroughly are diverse. For once, businesses do not see a valid reason for adopting such technologies [21]. Moreover, these technologies require background knowledge regarding the Semantic Web, but underlying concepts are hard to explain and hard to understand for non-experts [1, 18]. [16] predicted that the adoption of the Semantic Web will slowly rise by 2014 and finally be accepted as a mainstream technology by 2019. Hence Semantic Web technologies seem to be on the verge of the innovators phase to the early adopters phase when grouping the Semantic Web user base into [17]'s diffusion model of innovations.

The opinions on how to get more people to use Semantic Web technologies vary. [11] suggests to make the generation of Semantic Web metadata completely invisible for users, since it should be "a by-product of everyday computer use".

---

[1] http://commoncrawl.org/common-crawl-url-index/

S. Closs et al. (Eds.): MTSR 2014, CCIS 478, pp. 54–59, 2014.

Following this approach, a toolkit that generates RDFa when users create new content was added to the content management software Drupal [6, 10]. Other opinions state that such technologies should provide an additional value to the user [22] and should be founded on features that users are already acquainted with, such as relational database tables [14].

With the intention of supporting the growth of the Semantic Web by helping novices in that field access related technologies, I programmed the web application *rdfedit*[2] to helpt users create and edit RDF data. The core idea behind *rdfedit* is to make the creation of RDF instance data easier for people who know little to nothing about Semantic Web and associated technologies. The responsibility of creating good quality RDF data is distributed among Semantic Web or metadata experts and the users who create the actual RDF data, thus only having a few expert users who maintain and manage the system and many novice users who feed it with data.

A target audience for this application are cultural heritage institutions who want to create or enrich RDF metadata. Only a few experts will suffice to configure *rdfedit* in a way so it can be used by non-experts in order to produce data in a schema of their institution's preference.

2   Impelementation and Features

rdfedit is running on Django while heavily making use of rdflib[3], a python library to process RDF data, and jQuery DataTables[4] for displaying the tabular interface. Users currently can upload already existing RDF/XML [9] files for further editing or simply start with a new, empty graph. When uploading a graph, Django/rdflib receives the file, extracts all triples and parses it to the RDF table so the users can start working with their graphs in their web browser. The table consists of three columns: subject – predicate – object, showing the simple triple like structure of RDF.

On upload of an already existing graph, all triples are analyzed and preprocessed for later auto-completion. Since many subject and predicate URIs will be used multiple times, full URIs are being suggested to the user when they start typing them during a triple addition. This way, users do not have to re-type or re-paste URIs, thus saving time and adding valid and consistent data.

In general, *rdfedit* offers basic functionalities like adding, editing and deleting single triples and more complex features like bulk editing, literal-to-URI conversion and aggregation of RDF data from external resources. To make these processes work, an RDF/JSON [7] is being kept in the background and invisible to the user. New jQuery functions were written in order to synchronize the changes made to the table by the user with the RDF/JSON object, hence intertwining the DataTables powered RDF table and the RDF/JSON object with

---

[2] rdfedit can be accessed at: http://141.20.126.167/rdfedit/index

 Source code repository available at: https://github.com/suchmaske/rdfedit

[3] https://github.com/RDFLib

[4] http://www.datatables.net/

Django and rdflib. When users are done editing their graph, *rdfedit* submits the altered RDF/JSON object back to Django, where rdflib transforms that object to a RDF/XML file and serves it as a download to the user.

Since *rdfedit* aims towards helping the creation of valid and consistent RDF data, users can apply changes made to a single triple to all other affected triples within the same graph. When applying a bulk edit, *rdfedit* looks for all triples containing the old, unaltered URIs in the subject and object column and substitutes all matching cells with the new URI.

rdfedit also utilizes the API of the Semantic Web search engine Sindice[5] to offer the user a literal-to-URI conversion and fetch data from external graphs. Administrators (Semantic Web experts) of *rdfedit* can determine centrally what kind of URIs are appropriate, what data to fetch from where and how imported data should be mapped into the local graph. Hence they ease the burden of good quality metadata creation off the metadata creators (Semantic Web novices), since the latter no longer need to think about what vocabularies to use or what knowledge base might be the most appropriate for their current task. All the experts have to do is to edit two *rdfedit* configuration files (see Table 1). These files influence the outcome of the literal-to-URI conversion and triple aggregation from external resources.

Table 1. Example configurations for fetching graphs and triples from Sindice.com

Query Configuration	Mapping configuration

```{```
 ``` "foaf:person": {```
 ```   "fq=domain": "dbpedia",```
 ```   "fq=class": "foaf:person"```
 ``` },```
 ``` "dcterms:spatial": {```
 ```   "fq=domain": "geonames",```
 ```   "fq=format": "RDF"```
 ``` }```
 ```}```
	```{```
	 ``` "foaf:person": {```
	 ``` "dbpprop:author": "dc:creator",```
	 ``` "foaf:name": "foaf:name"```
	 ``` },```
	 ``` "dcterms:spatial": {```
	 ``` "rdfs:isDefinedBy": "dcterms:spatial"```
	 ``` }```
	 ```}```

When the user adds a single new triple, *rdfedit* checks the `query-config.json` file (see Table 1, left) and checks whether the predicate of that new triple exists as a JSON-key in the configuration file. If that is the case, Django composes a query for Sindice accordingly. For example, a user wants to add a new triple about the actor Wil Wheaton. Since he or she knows that Mr. Wheaton is a person, the user chooses to use `foaf:person` as the predicate. The new triple would consist of a literal object: `:subject foaf:person ''Wil Wheaton'' ..` *rdfedit* then queries Sindice with the parameters given by the configuration file: a) only include graphs from the DBPedia, b) only show graphs that are of the class `foaf:person`. The results of that query are being forwarded into the object

---

[5] http://sindice.com/developers/searchapiv3

cell, where the user then can choose one of the result URIs. In this case, he picks `dbpedia:Wil_Wheaton` and the literal `''Wil Wheaton''` is then replaced by the aforementioned URI, following the principle of using "Things, not Strings" [20].

Fig. 1. Screenshot of rdfedit showing the imported triples from `dbpedia:Wil_Wheaton`

Fetching triples from external resources happens in a similar fashion. Relying on the JSON-keys in the `query-config.json` file, *rdfedit* renders a dropdown menu in the browser, which the user can select predefined classes from. In combination with the chosen class, the user enters some keywords and *rdfedit* composes and submits a query to Sindice, where relevant graphs are being looked up. This time, the user wants to import a set of triples about Wil Wheaton rather than adding them one by one. He chooses the class `foaf:person`, enters the keywords "Wil Wheaton" and *rdfedit* interacts with Sindice in the same way as described in the literal-to-URIs conversion example. Again, Sindice returns a list of URIs from which the user can choose one that fits his or her intentions best.

When having decided for a URI, *rdfedit* loads the graph behind that URI. At this point, *rdfedit* compares the `mapping-config.json` file (see Table 1, right) with the fetched graph and extracts all triples that have the same value, as the JSON-keys for the user picked class of the configuration file. Since the user in our example has chosen the class `foaf:person` the triples with the predicates `dbpprop:author` and `foaf:name` will be extracted from the graph. Additionally, *rdfedit* transforms the original predicates to the values of those JSON-keys. Here, `dbpprop:author` would be remapped to `dc:creator` (see Fig. 2). This feature encourages the reuse of already existing data and supports the Linked Data principles as described by [2].

3   Discussion and Outlook

It is unclear whether the features relying on Sindice will continue to work in the future, since the team behind the Semantic Web search engine announced the termination of support for their product [8]. Therefore alternate solutions for the tasks described have to be evaluated and implemented. It might be necessary to use SPARQL queries instead of utilizing the Sindice API to ensure a better longevity of *rdfedit*. For *rdfedit* the application of SPARQL is controversial, because its original intention was to not bother users with SPARQL's complexity, whether they are Semantic Web experts or newcomers. Still, users should be able to create RDF data in a semi-automatic way: while the application fetches and inserts the data automatically, the user should still maintain in control and check whether the imported data is actually useful.

At the moment, empirical usability tests are planned but have not been conducted yet. In the near future, *rdfedit* will be evaluated by researchers of the Berlin Brandenburg Academy of Science (BBAW), whose disciplinary background, technical affinity and Semantic Web expertise vary heavily. It is expected that most of the participating BBAW members will fall into [15]'s user cube category of novice users since they have a background in the (Digital) Humanities rather than Computer or Information Science related fields.

With the results of the evaluation, *rdfedit* will further try to make the creation of RDF instance data easier for people new to Semantic Web technologies. It will continue trying to lessen the responsibility for those newcomers for creating good quality data, for instance by implementing interoperability with metadata crosswalks for the expert side. Furthermore, the jQuery written for the manipulation of RDF/JSON are planned to be extracted and published separately under an Open Source license, in order to contribute the growth and application of Semantic Web technologies.

References

[1] Benjamins, D.V.R., Radoff, M., Davis, M., Greaves, M., Lockwood, R., Contreras, D.J.: Semantic Technology Adoption: A Business Perspective. In: Domingue, J., Fensel, D., Hendler, J.A. (eds.) Handbook of Semantic Web Technologies, pp. 619–657. Springer, Heidelberg (2011), http://link.springer.com/referenceworkentry/10.1007/978-3-540-92913-0_15

[2] Berners-Lee, T.: Linked Data - Design Issues (2006), http://www.w3.org/DesignIssues/LinkedData.html

[3] Berners-Lee, T., Hendler, J., Lassila, O.: The Semantic Web. The Scientific American (May 2001), http://www.scientificamerican.com/article/the-semantic-web/

[4] Bizer, C., Eckert, K., Meusel, R., Mühleisen, H., Schuhmacher, M., Völker, J.: Deployment of RDFa, Microdata, and Microformats on the Web – A Quantitative Analysis. In: Alani, H., et al. (eds.) ISWC 2013, Part II. LNCS, vol. 8219, pp. 17–32. Springer, Heidelberg (2013), http://link.springer.com/chapter/10.1007/978-3-642-41338-4_2

[5] Bizer, C., Heath, T., Berners-Lee, T.: Linked Data - The Story So Far. International Journal on Semantic Web and Information Systems 5(3), 1–22 (2009), http://www.igi-global.com/article/linked-data-story-far/37496

[6] Corlosquet, S., Delbru, R., Clark, T., Polleres, A., Decker, S.: Produce and Consume Linked Data with Drupal! In: Bernstein, A., Karger, D.R., Heath, T., Feigenbaum, L., Maynard, D., Motta, E., Thirunarayan, K. (eds.) ISWC 2009. LNCS, vol. 5823, pp. 763–778. Springer, Heidelberg (2009), http://link.springer.com/chapter/10.1007/978-3-642-04930-9_48

[7] Davis, I., Steiner, T., Le Hors, A.J.: RDF 1.1 JSON Alternate Serialization (RDF/JSON): W3C Working Group Note 07. Tech. rep., W3 (November 2013), http://www.w3.org/TR/rdf-json/

[8] Franzon, E.: End of Support for the Sindice.com search engine: history, lessons learned, and legacy (May 2014), http://semanticweb.com/end-support-sindice-com-search-engine-history-lessons-learned-legacy-guest-post_b42797

[9] Gandon, F., Schreiber, G.: RDF 1.1 XML Syntax: W3C Recommendation 25 February 2014. Tech. rep., W3 (2014), http://www.w3.org/TR/2014/REC-rdf-syntax-grammar-20140225/

[10] Havlik, D.: Building Environmental Semantic Web Applications with Drupal. In: Hřebíček, J., Schimak, G., Denzer, R. (eds.) ISESS 2011. IFIP AICT, vol. 359, pp. 385–397. Springer, Heidelberg (2011), http://link.springer.com/chapter/10.1007/978-3-642-22285-6_42

[11] Hendler, J.: Agents and the semantic web. IEEE Intelligent Systems 16(2), 30–37 (2001)

[12] Jentzsch, A., Cyganiak, R., Bizer, C.: State of the LOD Cloud. Tech. rep. (2011), http://lod-cloud.net/state/

[13] Mika, P., Potter, T.: Metadata Statistics for a Large Web Corpus. LDOW 937 (2012)

[14] Newman, A.: A Relational View of the Semantic Web (March 2007), http://www.xml.com/pub/a/2007/03/14/a-relational-view-of-the-semantic-web.html

[15] Nielsen, J.: Interactive Technologies: Usability Engineering. Morgan Kaufmann, Saint Louis (1994), http://site.ebrary.com/lib/alltitles/docDetail.action?docID=10712933

[16] Nixon, L., Volz, D.R., Ciravegna, F., Studer, R.: Future Trends. In: Domingue, J., Fensel, D., Hendler, J.A. (eds.) Handbook of Semantic Web Technologies, pp. 581–618. Springer, Heidelberg (2011), http://link.springer.com/referenceworkentry/10.1007/978-3-540-92913-0_14

[17] Rogers, E.M.: Innovativeness and Adopter Categories. In: Diffusion of Innovations, pp. 267–299. Free Press, New York (2003)

[18] Salo, D.: Soylent Semantic Web Is People! In: SWIB 2013, Hamburg, Germany (November 2013), http://www.slideshare.net/cavlec/soylent-semantic-web-is-people-with-notes?utm_source=slideshow&utm_medium=ssemail&utm_campaign=upload_digest

[19] Schmachtenberg, M., Bizer, C., Paulheim, H.: Adoption of the Linked Data Best Practices in Different Topical Domains. In: Janowicz, K. (ed.) ISWC 2014, Part I. LNCS, vol. 8796, pp. 245–260. Springer, Heidelberg (2014), http://dws.informatik.uni-mannheim.de/fileadmin/lehrstuehle/ki/pub/SchmachtenbergBizerPaulheim-AdoptionOfLinkedDataBestPractices.pdf

[20] Singhal, A.: Introducing the Knowledge Graph: things, not strings (February 2012), http://googleblog.blogspot.de/2012/05/introducing-knowledge-graph-things-not.html

[21] Sletten, B.: Keep on Keeping on (January 2014), http://semanticweb.com/keep-on-keepin-on_b41339

[22] Stuart, D.: Facilitating access to the web of data: a guide for librarians, 1st publ. edn. Facet Publ., London (2011)

Metadata Guiding Knowledge Engineering: A Practical Approach

Fabio Sartori and Luca Grazioli

Department of Informatics, Systems and Communication,
University of Milano-Bicocca,
Viale Sarca 336/14, 20126, Milano, Italy
sartori@disco.unimib.it,
l.grazioli3@campus.unimib.it

Abstract. This paper presents an approach to the analysis, design and development of Knowledge Based Systems based on the Knowledge Artifact concept. Knowledge Artifacts can be meant as means to acquire, represent and maintain knowledge involved in complex problem solving activities. A complex problem is typically made of a huge number of parts that are put together according to a first set of constraints (i.e. the *procedural knowledge*), dependable on the functional properties it must satisfy, and a second set of rules, dependable on what the expert thinks about the problem and how he/she would represent it. The paper illustrates a way to unify both types of knowledge into a Knowledge Artifact, exploiting Ontologies, Influence Nets and Task Structures formalisms and metadata paradigm.

Keywords: Knowledge Artifact, ANDROID, Rule–Based Systems.

1 Introduction

The process of acquiring and modeling core knowledge concerning a specific domain is a very important research topic. Many Knowledge Based Systems (KBS) have been developed to deal with several knowledge fields [1], but the phase of knowledge acquisition and representation is still the main problem of this type of tools [2].

Knowledge engineering methodologies, such as CommonKads [3] and MIKE [4], have been proposed as standard and generalized solutions to satisfy enterprize needs. Another possible approach to knowledge engineering consists in the development of dedicated knowledge based systems providing specific solutions to each problem; in this case, domain specific knowledge acquisition and representation tools should be adopted.

The aim of the paper is the creation of a CAKE environment (Computer-Aided Knowledge Engineering) based on the integration of tools for the representation and the use of procedural and experiential knowledge, similar to existing platforms for the development of software projects. As presented in [5], the development of Knowledge Based Systems should be based on the acquisition and representation of at least three kinds of knowledge:

S. Closs et al. (Eds.): MTSR 2014, CCIS 478, pp. 60–67, 2014.
© Springer International Publishing Switzerland 2014

1. Ontological Knowledge, related to the definition of functional and structural properties of an object or problem;
2. Procedural Knowledge, concerning the description of the main steps to solve the problem, as well as which factors influence the different steps of the process;
3. Experiential Knowledge, devoted to represent into a homogeneous conceptual framework the heuristic rules adopted by the different kinds of expert involved.

For these reasons, the implementation of KBSs has been always conceived as a very specific activity, which can be only conducted by knowledge engineers with the support of domain experts. The main aim of this paper is to show an ongoing project to build up frameworks that make able everyone to develop a KBS. To this aim the Knowledge Artifact (KA) model has been adopted: Ontologies are exploited to represent structural and functional knowledge, Influence Nets [6] are used to deal with procedural knowledge and Task Structures [7] to represent experiential knowledge. An XML schema for each component of the Knowledge Artifact has allowed to transform it into a practical and usable framework, making a user with very few specific competencies and skills able to design and implement a complete Knowledge Based System: the reference language to implement the KBS is JESS[1].

The rest of the paper is organized as follows: next section will introduce the conceptual model of Knowledge Artifact. Then, a metadata–based description of this model implementation will be provided, through the adoption of XML language. Finally, conclusions and future work will be briefly pointed out.

2   The KA Approach: Components and Relationships Among Them

In our approach, the Knowledge Artifact is described as a 3–tuple $\langle O, IN, TS \rangle$, where O is an Ontology of the investigated domain, IN is an Influence Net to represent the causal dependencies among the Ontology elements and TS are Task Structures to represent how one or more outputs can be produced by the system according to a rule–based system strategy.

Figure 1 shows the KA elements and relationships among them: each element is modeled on a three-level architecture: *inputs* (i.e. the observations necessary to initialize the under-construction system), *partial outputs* (i.e. the results of elaborations made by the system to reach its goals, starting from inputs) and *outputs* (i.e. the goals of the system).

In the KA model, the underlying Ontology is a taxonomy: the root is the description of the problem to be solved, the inner nodes are system inputs or partial outputs and the leaves of the hierarchy are effective outputs of the system.

---

[1] Acronym of Java Expert System Shell,
   http://http://herzberg.ca.sandia.gov/

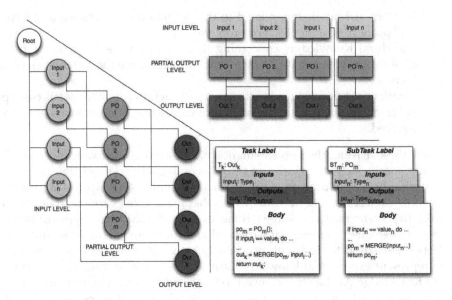

Fig. 1. The relationship existing among Ontology (on the left), Influence Net (on the top) and Task/Subtask Structures (on the bottom) in the KA model.

The Influence Net model is a structured process that allows to analyze complex problems of cause-effect type in order to determine an optimal strategy for the execution of certain actions, to obtain an optimal result. The Influence Net is a graphical model that describes the events and their causal relationships. Using information based on facts and experience of the expert, it is possible to analyze the uncertainties created by the environment in which we operate. This analysis helps the developer to identify the events and relationships that can improve or worsen the desired result. In this way you can determine the best strategy. The Influence Net can be defined as a 4–tuple $\langle I, P, O, A \rangle$, where

- I is the set of *input nodes*, i.e. the information needed to the KBS to work properly;
- P is the set or *partial output nodes*, i.e. the collection of new pieces of knowledge and information elaborated by the system to reach the desired output;
- O is the set of *output nodes*, i.e. the effective answers of the system to the described problem; outputs are values that can be returned to the user;
- A is the set of *arcs* among the nodes: an arc between two nodes specifies that a causal relationship exists between them; an arc can go from an input to a partial node or an output, as well as from partial node to another one or an output. Moreover, an arc can go from an output to another output. Every other kind of arcs is not permitted.

Finally, Task Structures allow to describe in a rule–based system way how the causal process defined by a given IN can be modeled. Each Task is devoted to define computationally a portion of an Influence Net: in particular, *Subtasks* are procedures to specify how a partial output is obtained, while *Tasks* are used to explain how an output can be derived from one or more influencing partial outputs and inputs. A Task cannot be completed until all the Subtasks influencing it have been finished. In this way, the TS modeling allows to clearly identify all the levels of the system. The Task and Subtask bodies are a sequence of rules, i.e. $LHS(LeftHandSide) -> RHS(RightHandSide)$ constructs.

Each LHS contains the conditions that must be verified so that the rule can be applied: it is a logic clause, which turns out to be a sufficient condition for the execution of the action indicated in the RHS. Each RHS contains the description of the actions to conduct as a result of the rule execution. The last step of our model is the translation of all the Task and Subtask bodies into production rules of a specific language (JESS in our case).

3   Metadata Implementation

The implementation of the different elements composing the knowledge engineering framework has exploited the XML language. A proper schema has been developed for each of them, as well as dedicated parsers to allow the user to interact with them. Following the conceptual model briefly introduced in the previous section, the first schema is the ontological one, as presented below.

The schema presents opportune tags to specify *inputs*, where the name of the input can be put (i.e. the ⟨*name*⟩ tag in the code below) together with a value for it (the ⟨*value*⟩ tag). Morevoer, it is possible to define an ⟨*affects*⟩ relationship for each input, in order to explain how it is involved in the next steps of the elaboration (i.e. which output it or partial output does it contribute to state?).

```
<ontology>
    <name> ... </name>
    <description> ... </description>
    <input>
        <name> ... </name>
        <value> ... </value>
        ...
        <affects> ... </affects>
        ...
    </input>
    <partialOutput>
        <name> ... </name>
        <value> ... </value>
        ...
        <affects> ... </affects>
        ...
         <influencedBy> ... </influencedBy>
        ...
    </partialOutput>
    <output>
        <name> ... </name>
        <value> ... </value>
        ...
        <influencedBy> ... </influencedBy>
        ...
    </output>
</ontology>
```

A *partialOutput* (i.e. an inner node between an input and a leaf of the taxonomy) is limited by the ⟨*partialOutput*⟩ and ⟨*/partialOtuput*⟩ pair of tags. The fields are the same as the input case, with the difference that a partial output can be influenced by other entities too: this is the sense of the ⟨*influencedBy*⟩ tag. Finally, the ⟨*output*⟩ tag allows to describe completely an effective output of the system, i.e. a leaf of the taxonomy developed to represent the problem domain. Output can be influenced by other elements of the Ontology, i.e. inputs and partial outputs, but the vice-versa is not valid (i.e. the ⟨*affects*⟩ relationship is not defined on outputs).

The following code illustrates an example of how an Influence Net is produced. The taxonomy is bottom–up parsed, in order to identify the right flow from inputs to outputs by navigating the *influenced by* relationships designed by the user. In this way, different portions of the under development system can be described. Outputs, partial outputs and inputs are bounded by arcs which specify the *source* and the *target* nodes (the source and target attribute respectively).

```
<influenceNet>
    <name> ... </name>
    <description> ... </description>
    <root>
        -------------------- Start Output List--------------------
        <output id = "id" value = "output from ontology">
        </output>
        ...
        <output id = "id" value = "output from ontology">
        </output>
        -------------------- End Output List --------------------
        ---------------- Start partialOutput List ----------------
        <partialOutput id = "id" value = "partialOutput from ontology">
        </partialOutput>
        ...
         <partialOutput id = "id" value = "partialOutput from ontology">
          </partialOutput>
        ---------------- End partialOutput List ----------------
        ---------------------- Start Input List --------------------
        <input id = "id" value = "output from ontology">
        </input>
        ...
        <input id = "id" value = "output from ontology">
        </input>
        ---------------------- End Input List --------------------
        ----------------------  Start Arc List   --------------------
        <arc id = "id" value = "name of the arc" source = "id input or partialOutput"
            target =  "id output or    partialOutput">
        </arc>
        ...
        <arc id = "id" value = "name of the arc" source = "id input or partialOutput"
            target =  "id output or    partialOutput">
        </arc>
    </root>
</influenceNet>
```

Finally, an XML schema for the *Task* (*Subtask* elements of the framework are defined in the same way) can be produced as follows. The parser composes a XML file for each output considered in the Influence Net. The *input* and *subtask* tags allow to define which inputs and partial outputs are needed to the output represented by the Task to be produced. The *body* tag is adopted to model the sequence of rules necessary to process inputs and results returned by influencing Subtasks: a rule is composed of an $\langle if \rangle$ ... $\langle do \rangle$ construct, where the if statement permits to represent the LHS part of the rule, while the do statement concerns the RHS part of the rule.

```
<task>
    <name> ... </name>
    <description> ... </description>
    <input>
        <element> Input from the ontology </element>
        ...
        <element> Input from the ontology </element>
    </input>
    <body>
        <subtask> subtask name </subtask>
        ...
        <subtask> subtask name </subtask>
        <if> rule LHS  </if>
        <do> rule RHS </do>
        ...
        <if> rule LHS  </if>
        <do> rule RHS </do>
    </body>
    <output>
        <value> ... </value>
        ...
         <value> ... </value>
    </output>
</task>
```

The XML files introduced above can be incorporated into dedicated decision support systems to guide the user in the design of the underlying taxonomy, Influence Net and Tasks/Subtasks. Moreover, it is possible to transform the Task into a collection of files containing rules written for instance in the JESS language.

4   Conclusion and Future Works

This paper has presented an ongoing research project aiming to design and implement tools for supporting the user in the development of knowledge based systems. As described above, the metadata approach is very useful to this scope. The framework has been initially tested thanks to the support of the students attending the *Knowledge Engineering and Expert Systems* course at the Computer Science Department of the University of Milano-Bicocca. The students have been asked to design and implement their projects without the framework support and with the framework support: the JESS files produced in both cases were similar, and this has been interpreted as a very encouraging result.

In order to extend the framework beyond the academic world, the first step would be to create a multi-language environment, expanding it to other rule-based languages, such as Drools. Furthermore, it could be possible to improve the rule encoding by supporting a complete definition and interpretation of *facts* in the knowledge base. From the definition point of view, it would be necessary to extend the syntax inherent to the incorporation of conditions. In this way it could be possible to define *unordered facts* too. From the interpretation

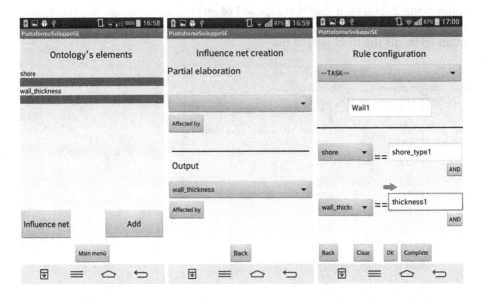

Fig. 2. The GUI for supporting user in the creation of rule–based system from Ontology, Influence Net and Task/Subtask Structures.

point of view, it would be necessary to generate all the files to load the facts in the knowledge base. The possibility to save the project and then reopen it at a later time, it is a vital function for the user, but it has been neglected during the implementation of the framework since it was not the main objective of the study.

Moreover, the project is going to allow the user to design and implement his/her own KBSs remotely exploiting the potentialities of Android OS: in this way, the framework could be executed from every kind of PDAs, like smart-phones and tablets, with the possibility to create an ad–hoc KBS when neces-sary. Figure 2 shows a sketch of the supporting tool for this scope, where an Android client interacts with a Java server to develop the three steps of the framework. In this sense, a potential collaboration with the Italian Fire Corps has started, to provide each firemen with tools to understand how to operate in critical situations, like geographically distributed fires and earthquakes man-agement. A prototype of the system is described in [8].

Acknowledgements. The author wishes to thank the students of the Knowl-edge Engineering and Expert Systems course for their support in the develop-ment of this project. Special thanks to *Daniele Asnaghi* for his active part in the design and implementation of the framework.

References

1. Hayes-Roth, F., Jacobstein, N.: The State of Knowledge Based Systems. Communications of the ACM 37(3), 27–39 (1994)
2. Cairó, O.: The KAMET Methodology: Contents, Usage and Knowledge Modeling. In: Gaines, B., Mussen, M. (eds.) Proceedings of the 11th Banff Knowledge Acquisition for Knowledge-Based Systems Workshop (KAW 1998), vol. 1, pp. 1–20. SRGD Publications, Department of Computer Science, University of Calgary, Proc.-1 (1998)
3. Akkermans, H., de Hoog, R., Shreiber, A., van de Velde, W., Wielinga, B.: CommonKADS: A Comprehensive Methodology for KBS Development. IEEE Expert, 28–37 (1994)
4. Angele, J., Fensel, D., Studer, R.: Developing Knowledge-Based Systems with MIKE. Journal of Automated Software Engineering (1998)
5. Bandini, S., Sartori, F.: From handicraft prototypes to limited serial productions: Exploiting knowledge artifacts to support the industrial design of high quality products. AIEDAM 24(1), 17–34 (2010)
6. Rosen, J.A., Smith, W.L.: Influence Net Modeling with Causal Strengths: An Evolutionary Approach, Virginia (1996)
7. Chandrasekaran, B., Johnson, T.R., Smith, J.W.: Task-Structure Analysis for Knowledge Modeling. Commun. ACM 35(9), 124–137 (1992)
8. Sartori, F., Manenti, L., Grazioli, L.: A Conceptual and Computational Model for Knowledge-based Agents in ANDROID. In: WOA@AI*IA 2013, pp. 41–46 (2013)

Application Profile for Earth Observation Images

Jean-Christophe Desconnets[1], Hatim Chahdi[1], and Isabelle Mougenot[2]

[1] Espace Dev IRD site de Lavalette, Montpellier, France
{Jean-Christophe.Desconnets,Hatim.Chahdi}@ird.fr
[2] Espace-Dev, Université de Montpellier 2, Bâtiment 21, CC083
F-91405 Montpellier Cedex 5, France
Isabelle.Mougenot@univ-montp2.fr

Abstract. Based on the concept of an application profile as proposed by the Dublin Core initiative, the work presented in this manuscript attempts to propose an application profile for the Earth Observation images. This approach aims to provide an open and extensible model facilitating the sharing and management of distributed images within decentralized architectures. It is intended to eventually cover the needs of discovery, localization, consulting, preservation and processing of data for decision support. We are using the Singapore framework recommendations to build the application profile. A particular focus on the formalization and representation of Description Set Profile (DSP) in RDF is proposed.

Keywords: metadata, metadata standards, data interoperability, Dublin Core application profile, Earth observation.

1 Introduction

The satellite image has become an essential source of information to address and analyze environmental issues quickly, repeatedly and in a reliable way. Available technologies for Earth observation satellite, offer a wide range of tools to address the needs of scientists and territory managers more accurately. To facilitate their sharing and access, many initiatives are emerging from the community of Earth observation (space agencies, industry) or the broader environmental community, whether they are national (THEIA[1].), European(INSPIRE[2], COPERNICUS[3]) or global (GEOSS[4]). In most cases, access to the images is made possible by the deployment of a spatial data infrastructure that provides access to distributed and heterogeneous data [3]. It provides access to images through web services discovery, viewing and downloading, as well as online processing. These facilities require the implementation of an interoperability framework. The latter relies primarily on the adoption of a specific metadata standard from the user community or its variation. It is the basis for the implementation of image access

---

[1] THEIA : French Land Data Center
[2] INSPIRE : Infrastructure for Spatial Information in the European Community.
[3] The European Earth Observation Program.
[4] Global Earth Observation System of Systems.

S. Closs et al. (Eds.): MTSR 2014, CCIS 478, pp. 68–82, 2014.

services. However, these systems are weakly interconnected and do not provide an as comprehensive view of available images as end-users could expect. Indeed, the process that led to these achievements is domain-specific and produces heterogeneous metadata schemes. That renders the implementation of common tools for image discovery difficult.

In addition, various interoperability frameworks are defined in the field of Earth observation. They offer metadata schemes that take the common needs of multiple users from various communities into account. The resulting scheme usually corresponds to the core elements of a standard. It provides general information about the resource to meet the needs of discovery and location. Those involving spatial characteristics (projection, resolution), acquisition parameters or quality (lineage, precision) are often absent from the proposed metadata. It will be difficult to foresee the extension of the functionality delivered by such a system without challenging underlying models or interoperability. To manage large sets of heterogeneous and distributed resources, this analysis leads us to propose a new approach to support the interconnection of geospatial resources from various communities. Many studies [6] have been conducted for several years to make different metadata standards interoperable and allow the conversion of various metadata sets from one standard to another and to ensure an efficient federated management.

Based on the concept of application profile as proposed by the Dublin Core initiative [7,8], the work presented in this manuscript endeavor to propose an application profile for the Earth observation images. Focused communities are those of earth observation and environment. This approach aims to provide an open model, extensible and usable, facilitating the sharing and management of distributed images within decentralized architectures. It is intended to eventually cover the needs of discovery, localization, consulting, preservation and processing of data for decision support. As a first step, our approach proposes a state of the art, which introduces the concept of satellite image and the analysis of appropriate standards for the description of geospatial resources. We also provide a brief overview on the role of metadata in the sharing of resources in the area studied. The notion of application profile will also be introduced. The following section presents the application profile through the various stages of its building. We identify functional requirements, describe the domain model and illustrate by examples, the formal constraint model named DSP (Description Set Profile) associated with the definition of our application profile.

2   State of the Art

2.1   Earth Observation Image

In the context of our work, the resources[5] that we want to describe are images from the Earth observation. These resources are acquired by artificial earth satellites, equipped with various sensors. They ensure the acquisition of an image of

---

[5] The term resource is taken in its broadest sense, as any concrete or abstract entity, which may be identified, named, manipulated across multiple representations.

a part of the Earth. This acquisition is performed according to an acquisition characteristic for each sensor, which that will depend on the nature of the acquired image, such as spatial resolution. It is noted that an image is a large digital resource. For example, a very high resolution[6] image on an area of 20 km by 20 km has a volume of several gigabytes.

Fig. 1. SPOT 5 image representing a portion of the mediteranean sea (East zone of Marseille city), 10 meters of resolution. (source : équipex-Geosud project)

2.2　Metadata Standards for Earth Observation

Different standards, general or dedicated to a particular discipline, play essential roles facilitating the distributed resource management in decentralized architectures. After specifying the content and the added value of the standard Dublin Core, the section presents current standards dedicated to the description of both geospatial resources and Earth observations.

Dublin Core. The Dublin Core standard has a general scope that goes well beyond the sharing of satellite images. Indeed, it has been proposed to provide evidence to generically describe any type of resource. Thus, it provides efficient ways to help discovery in the context of the web for any communities. For this purpose, Dublin Core has a fifteen elements description, which constitutes the core of standard. In our context, Dublin Core is used by the Discovery Service OGC CSW [19] to define the searchable elements (queryable elements) of the service in a generic way and could provide also a simplified view of retrieved results.

---

[6] the basic unit of the image represents a portion of space less than 1 meter on Earth.

ISO 19115 and ISO 19115-2. ISO 19115 standard [1], enacted by ISO TC/211 is the metadata standard for geospatial resources. It proposes a conceptual framework for describing these resources. It was designed to cover very large geographic community needs that extend from the data management to dissemination through their processing. Represented with the UML object formalism it includes twelve main packages, nine of which are common to all geospatial resources. Several packages are dedicated to the description of the spatial dimension of the resources, such as Extent Information, Spatial Representation or Reference System Information.

The ISO 19115 standard defines core elements. It corresponds to a minimum set of elements considered essential to meet the needs of discovery and location of a resource. Most of time, these core elements are used to provide metadata interoperability in information systems, which are pooling geospatial resources. The ISO 19115 standard has been extended by the ISO standard 19115-2 [12] to support the description of spatial gridded resources, such as satellite images. It provides new elements of description, such as the information on the platform and acquisition sensors. It defines some other to complete existing descriptions, especially to clarify the characteristics of processing performed on an image (Lineage Information package). Thus, it expands the scope of the ISO 19115 standard to meet the specific needs of image producers. The operationalization of the standards is guided by the ISO 19139 specification [10] which gives the transformation rules for serialization of metadata in XML format.

Earth Observation Metadata Profile of Observations & Measurements. Focused on the specific needs of the Earth Observation community, the metadata profile Observation and Measurement (O & M) [13] was built [14]. It is part of the HMA interoperability framework defined by the ESA[7]. It aims to facilitate the sharing of Earth observation products, whatever the mission and the sensor from which they come. In this context, the concept of metadata profile is the one proposed by ISO [11] and is quite different in these principles to the one presented in section3. It describes a metadata scheme and writing rules in XML, needed to describe the metadata of Earth observation products. More specifically, the metadata scheme is designed for the products from the general description to the more detailed observation mission (e.g SENTINEL) features provided with the acquisition of the image by one of these platforms. For this the model defines three levels of description: a "general" level on main characteristics of the products, a "thematic" one, which extends the previous one to describe the specific characteristic thematic products, such as optical, radar or atmospheric. The last one, the "mission" level, extending the previous one, describes the specific products of a mission, like those of the European mission SENTINEL ensuring the acquisition of radar images. Thus, this metadata scheme provides new metadata descriptions, related among others to acquisition parameters of an image, such as *pitch, roll, yaw* of the acquisition platform. They are essential to the geometric corrections made on the images after their acquisition.

---

[7] ESA : European Spatial Agency.

2.3   Role of Metadata for Sharing and Access to Earth Observation Data

Scientific, institutional and community initiatives for implementation of information systems to facilitate the discovery and access to the images are numerous. In Earth observation domain, the most emblematic is the system of the Group of Earth Observation Systems: GEOSS. On a global scale, GEOSS aims to provide decision support tools for a very wide range of users. The system of systems interconnects different observing systems, production or dissemination of data from satellite imagery.

The interconnection of different systems is based on a common set of standards including ISO 19115 [5]. It is used to provide a common metadata scheme for the description of resources aggregated by the systems of the system. The ISO 19115 scheme is used as a switch-across model for processing different metadata formats. It is also used to allow a uniform query of all descriptions via a discovery service OGC CSW [19]. It is based on the ISO19115 standard core elements. They are extended to describe the data access services, such as Web Map Service. If this model is relevant to the expected functional requirements, it offers a very limited capability to filter the large amount of data referenced by GEOSS. The heterogeneity of vocabularies, such as keywords which are used to annote the nature of the resource, from different descriptions is not considered and often leads to unsatisfactory accuracy of results. The THEIA Land Data Center provides geospatial resources from images at high and very high resolution for scientific community and public actors at the French national scale. It consists of a federation of data centers and processing units that diffuse their data via web services. The metadata have a similar role. At federation level, a specific abstract model inspired by the OGC specification called EO OpenSearch [20], is used to harmonize the harvested metadata records and represents them in a uniform manner to perform homogenous queries. Minimalistic, in order to simplify the operations of metadata harmonization and to meet the needs of image location, this abstract model focuses mainly on describing the context of data production and the main features of the image. Information about the data content and quality are not considered. A query on the content of the original image (spectral bands, spectral resolution) or on elements of his lineage can not be achieved.

European project GENESI-DR[8] and GENESI-DEC[9] could be considered relevant for our goals. Similar to the others, but with a clear focus on multidisciplinary issue, the objectives are also to facilitate access to Earth observation data. For this purpose the project has implemented a spatial data infrastructure federating many heterogeneous databases. In addition, the infrastructure provides a set of customizable services that offers users the opportunity to compose their own processing [4]. Moreover, metadata play as the role of descriptors for

---

[8] GENESI-DR: Ground European Network for Earth Science interoperations - Digital Repositories.

[9] GENESI-DEC: Ground European Network for Earth Science interoperations Digital Earth Community.

the purposes of discovery and data processing services. In this multi-disciplinary context, the description of resources is not domain-specific but addressed by the use of the Dublin Core vocabulary. It extended to specific geospatial data descriptors, such as dclite4g : resolution, dclite4g : projection. Indeed, the metadata scheme DCLite4G [15] are built on the recommendations of the Dublin Core Metadata Initiative, namely on application profile principles [9]. Thus, the proposed model overcomes the community standards as they are from the geographical, the biodiversity and climate change community. The achievements of these projects address in part our goals. We want to extend the functional scope and take advantage of the use of the interoperability framework provided by RDF, including associated RDF vocabularies of geospatial domain.

2.4   Notion of Application Profile

General Notions. A potential reproach to metadata standards is that they have been designed independently of each other and thus are not able to meet all the information needs. For this purpose, application profiles reuse metadata standards to respond either to new requirements, or to more specific ones, for example to combine information from different sources to deliver new interpretations or to apply different filters on information. The principle is an open approach, by taking different elements of different metadata standards and combining them in a "mix and match" manner [7] to generate a new organization of metadata elements particularly suitable for the target application. The construction of an application profile is expected to meet the needs of discovery, characterization and consultation of distributed and heterogeneous resources, to cater to the application needs of a specific community.

Building Principles. The definition of an application profile is subject to different rules: a first principle is to rely on existing metadata standards, or to maintain an open and long term a new metadata standard, which covers the newly introduced metadata elements. The following principles relate to the publication of enrichment approaches and use of model entities from metadata elements. We use the work developed around the Singapore framework and application profile named DCAP (Dublin Core Application Profile) by the Dublin Core community.

Methodological recommendations [18] and the specification of UML conceptual models facilitate construction activities of an application profile. A first structural model called DCAM (Dublin Core Abstract Model) [23], emphasizes the notion of resource. Its specialization on described resources is a collection of property-value pairs. The value is sometimes envisaged as a labeled resource and can be taken from controlled vocabularies.

A second structural model named DSP (Description Set Profile) [18] complements the DCAM model to provide a prescriptive framework for the construction of the application profile. An application profile is then considered as a set of descriptions, and described through the concept of `DescriptionSetTemplate`. Each description is called `DescriptionTemplate`. It enriches a resource

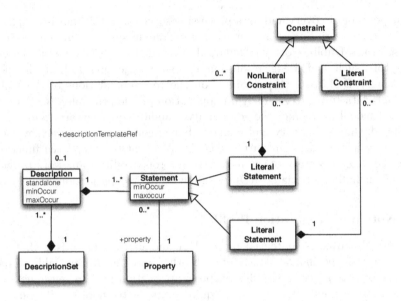

Fig. 2. Simplified UML Class Diagram of Description Set Profile

of interest in a decentralized manner and documents it through metadata elements from appropriate standards. These elements, as well as
the different syntactic and/or semantics constraints that apply, are structured in statements called `StatementTemplate`. Statements are either
`LiteralStatementTemplate`, when metadata elements relate to literals or
`NonLiteralStatementTemplate` when metadata elements relate to URI labeled resources. Constraints are explained through the concept of `Constraint`,
which specialize in `LiteralConstraint` and `NonLiteralConstraint`.

Figure 2 shows a simplified structural diagram for the DSP, largely inspired
by diagrams described in [18,24].

3   Earth Observation Application Profile

3.1   Background

Our work takes place in the context of a project distribution of satellite images,
the Equipex Geosud project [16]. Developed under the observation of use of spatial data by public French actors working on the management of natural areas
and their resources, one of the objectives of this project is to set up a *technical device* to make high resolution satellite images accessible to users of heterogeneous
skills, from non-specialist to remote sensing expert. These images come from
different platforms and acquisition instruments. They are delivered in specific
formats, whether the image itself, or the associated metadata. Furthermore, the
spatial data infrastructure is part of the French national data center, the THEIA
pole (cf. section 2.3), with which it has to interconnect. The figure 3 shows an

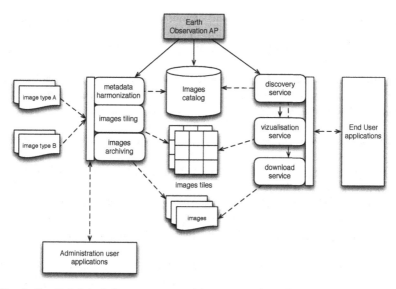

Fig. 3. Spatial data infrastructure architecture and *application profile position*

overview of the architecture of our system. It is based on components ensuring harmonization of image metadata, their tiles and their archives. The web user services : discovery, viewing and downloading are based on the image catalog. It provides the descriptions to search available images to invoke their visualization and consultation of their detailed characteristics. It also gives information to locate and download them. The application profile is a core element of our system. It provides descriptions which the metadata transformations rely on. It has a central role in the image catalog by structuring stored metadata. Finally, image access services build their queries on descriptions of images formalized through the application profile.

In a second step, it is planned to lean against user applications, designed to generate environmental indicator maps for the monitoring of natural resources. In this context, the application profile will also provide the descriptions required for running business processes.

3.2   Approach

The methodological approach proposed by Dublin Core metadata initiative finds its justification to overcome the heterogeneity of images from different providers. One of the main objectives is to offer uniform and semantically accessible image metadata to the target community. In addition, the ability to reuse different existing standards allows taking over the broad functional spectrum that we want to meet. Following the recommendations of the Dublin Core community, and particularly those encouraged by the Singapore framework, we present in this section the functional requirements on which our profile is based. Then, we describe the domain model related to context dissemination and processing of satellite images. Finally, we give some elements of the Description Set Profile (DSP) that ensures the implementation of the application profile in our infrastructure and a part of a DSP is proposed.

Identifying Functional Requirements. According to the goals of our infrastructure and the user community, which it addressed, the main functional requirements are the following:

- Carry out a decentralized data description management to mobilize images only for download,
- Solve the heterogeneity of metadata schemes and terminologies to ensure a uniform query of an image catalog,
- Have a comprehensive model for describing images that can be used by the different access and processing services, but also for the administration of data (management life cycle, permanent archiving, monitoring data consumption by users, ...),
- Enrich vocabulary metadata to be accessible to non-specialist users, including adding new descriptions about the content of the image (*e.g land cover range in the image*),
- Offer a discovery service for images at different levels of granularity (collection, feature) to facilitate the discovery in a large amount of data,
- Search and processing of the images within the infrastructure,
- Provide indicators of image quality (e.g geometric accuracy) to allow the user to evaluate the image quality himself.

Domain Model. A domain model is a conceptual model that identifies the entities that we want to describe and the relationships between them, according to functional requirements. Its object representation using UML formalism allows to share our point of view with the different participants in your system, whether they are information system specialists or not. The proposed model generalizes and extends the existing models within the geographical community, including the one proposed by the Public Geospatial Data Project FGDC [21] and its specialization by GENESI-DEC (cf. section 2.3) to establish an application profile: DCLite4G [22].

Our model is shown in figure 4. The core entity *Resource* refers to the concept of *Resource* as proposed by the DCAM (Dublin Core Abstract Model). This is an abstract entity that represents all the resources that are shared. It generalizes the two types of specific domain resources, namely the entities *Process* and *EarthImage*. The reflexive relationship *isPartOf* the *Resource* entity can represent, for EarthImage resource type, aggregation relationship between a collection of images, all images having common properties, and an image. Semantically equivalent to the Class dcmi:Agent, the *Agent* entity is an abstract entity, which is specialized in *Organization* and *Sensor*. The first describes the institutions involved in the creation of a resource or its distribution within the community through relationships *isCreatedBy, isDistributedBy*.

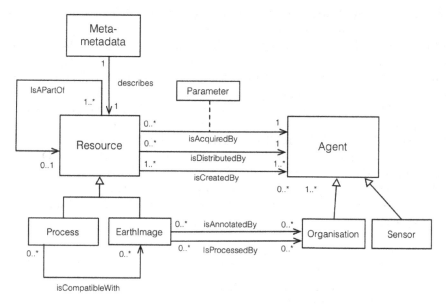

Fig. 4. Domain model for Earth Observation (UML Class diagram)

The second *Sensor*, describes the instruments used to acquire a satellite image. The *isAcquiredBy* association allows to describe the characteristics of the sensor used to acquire an image or set of images, as well as the parameters for the acquisition of an image (association class *Parameter*).

The entity *EarthImage* represents the Earth observation images that we want to make accessible or process. It provides the intrinsic characteristics of the image including information on the temporal and spatial extent, its spatial and spectral resolutions and information to ensure its distribution, such as size and conditions of use. Its characteristics are completed by semantic annotations relating, for example, administrative entities covered by the image or the land cover classes identified on its spatial extent. These annotations are intended to facilitate the discovery process by non-expert users.

The entity *Process* represents unit processing or processing chains applicable to Earth observation images. They correspond to basic operation support, for instance, to extract a portion of an image, to calculate a vegetation index or to more complex processing leading to the creation of a new resource, such as a map indicator of natural resources. The relationship *isCompatibleWith* to associate an image or collection of images to processing and specifying the compatibility of a processing to a collection of images. Finally, *Meta-metadata* entity provides the information required for the management of metadata records (e.g modification date, description language, etc..).

Description Set Profile. According to the proposal of Singapore Dublin Core framework and formalization of description constraints language proposed by [17,18], each of the entities identified in the domain model are divided into sets of description. In a first stage, we have focused our efforts on describing a few features of interest to cover the needs of discovery and location. Description of the Template *EarthImage* and *Organization* classes are available at this address: http://purl.org/eoap/. For clarity they are serialized using the RDF N3 syntax [2]. The properties that describe our interest entities refine elements from basic description of DCMI Metadata Terms. They are refined to describe the characteristics of spatial data, such as spatial footprint of an image by the ISO 19115 metadata standard.

We provide an extract from Template Description *EarthImage_T* on the refinement of the element dcterms : coverage by iso19115 : EX_GeographicBoundingBox coverage class.

```
eoap:EarthImage_T
        a       dsp:DescriptionTemplate ;
        dsp:maxOccur "1"^^xsd:nonNegativeInteger ;
        dsp:minOccur "1"^^xsd:nonNegativeInteger ;
        dsp:resourceClass eoap:EarthImage ;
        dsp:standalone "true"^^xsd:boolean ;
        [...]
        dsp:statementTemplate
                [ a       dsp:NonLiteralStatementTemplate ;
                        dsp:maxOccur "infinity" ;
                        dsp:minOccur "1"^^xsd:nonNegativeInteger ;
                        dsp:NonliteralConstraint
                                [ a       dsp:NonLiteralConstraint ;
                        dsp:DescriptionTemplate
                                <eoap:GeographicExtent_T>;
                        dsp:valueStringOccurence
                                "disallowed"^^<dsp:Occurence>;
                        dsp:VocabularyEncodingSchemeOccurence
                                "disallowed"^^<dsp:Occurence>;
                                ] ;
                        dsp:property dcterms:coverage
                ] .
eoap:GeographicalExtent_T
        a       dsp:DescriptionTemplate ;
        dsp:maxOccur "infinite" ;
        dsp:minOccur "1"^^xsd:nonNegativeInteger ;
        dsp:resourceClass iso19115:EX_GeographicalBoundingBox ;
        dsp:standalone "false"^^xsd:boolean .
[...]
```

Listing 1.1. code 1 : Statement template coverage. Description Template EarthImage_T sample

Furthermore, the appropriate description of the entity *EarthImage* relies on properties only available in the ISO 19115 standard. Such is the case, for example, to describe the spatial resolution of an image or the hierarchical level of the resource described.

```
[...]
dsp:statementTemplate
        [ a        dsp:NonLiteralStatementTemplate ;
          dsp:maxOccur "infinity" ;
          dsp:minOccur "1"^^xsd:nonNegativeInteger ;
          dsp:nonliteralConstraint
              [ a        dsp:NonLiteralConstraint ;
                dsp:descriptionTemplateRef
                    eoap:Resolution_T ;
                dsp:valueURIOccurrence
                    "mandatatory" ;
                dsp:vocabularyEncodingSchemeOccurrence
                    "disallowed"
              ] ;
          dsp:property iso19115:MD_DataIdentificationInfo:spatialResolution
        ] ;
eoap:Resolution_T
        a        dsp:DescriptionTemplate ;
        dsp:maxOccur "1"^^xsd:nonNegativeInteger ;
        dsp:minOccur "1"^^xsd:nonNegativeInteger ;
        dsp:resourceClass iso19115:MD_Resolution ;
        dsp:standalone "false"^^xsd:boolean .
```

Listing 1.2. code 2 : Statement template *spatialResolution.* Description Template *EarthImage_T* extract

```
dsp:statementTemplate
        [ a        dsp:NonLiteralStatementTemplate ;
          dsp:maxOccur "1"^^xsd:nonNegativeInteger ;
          dsp:minOccur "0"^^xsd:nonNegativeInteger ;
          dsp:nonliteralConstraint
              [ a        dsp:NonLiteralConstraint ;
                dsp:valueURIOccurrence
                    "mandatatory" ;
                dsp:vocabularyEncodingSchemeOccurrence
                    "mandatatory" ;
                dsp:vocabularyEncodingSchemeURI
                    iso19115:MD_ScopeCode
              ] ;
          dsp:property iso19115:MD_Metadata:hierarchyLevel
        ] ;
```

Listing 1.3. code 3 : Statement template *hierarchyLevel.* Description Template *EarthImage_T* extract

We present in Table 5 an extract from the documentation of our Description Set Profile, the Statement Template hierarchyLevel described therein.

User Scenario. We propose to illustrate the use of the application profile in our system. This scenario that focuses on the discovery of images having properties suitable to meet the demand of a user: a geographer wants to follow the evolution of the urbanization of the city of Montpellier by quantifying the change of the outskirts of the eastern zone, including the passage of land under agricultural influence to a residential area. To identify images that allow him to distinguish different land uses and on which he will conduct his spatial analysis, he needs to ask a question via the discovery service, such as: I'm searching images with a spatial resolution of less than 5 meters, which are located within the bounding rectangle between the coordinates longitude 3,71° ; latitude: 43.72°

NAME OF TERM	hierarchyLevel
TERM URI	iso19115:MD_Metadata.hierarchyLevel
DEFINED BY	http://www.tc211.org/
SOURCE DEFINITION	scope to which the metadata applies
EOAP COMMENTS	For satellite image, dataset level and feature [...]
VOCAB. ENCODING SCHEME URI	iso19115:MD_ScopeCode
OBLIGATION	Optional
OCCURRENCE	Not repeatable

Fig. 5. Extract of Description Template EarthImage_T - Statement Template hierarchyLevel

and coordinates longitude: 4.04° ; latitude: 43.53°. The request of the image catalog will be based on properties dcterms:coverage for the spatial extent and iso19115:spatialResolution for spatial resolution written in our DSP. The response provides a set of metadata for images corresponding to the value of these two criteria. We present above, an extract from a DSP instance describing one of the identified images.

```
geosud:geographicExtent_1
      iso19115:EX_GeographicBoundingBox.eastBoundLongitude
            "4.04" ;
      iso19115:EX_GeographicBoundingBox.northBoundLatitude
            "43,72" ;
      iso19115:EX_GeographicBoundingBox.southBoundLatitude
            "43,53" ;
      iso19115:EX_GeographicBoundingBox.westBoundLongitude
            "3,71" .

geosud:earthImage_1
      iso19115:MD_DataIdentification.spatialResolution
            geosud:resolution_1 ;
      iso19115:MD_Metadata.hierarchyLevel
            iso19115:MD_Scope.feature ;
      dcterms:coverage geosud:geographicExtent_1 ;
      dcterms:identifier "2900423f−7aee−478b−ab20−fe932d4adb" .

geosud:resolution_1
      iso19115:MD_Resolution.distance
            "5" .
```

Listing 1.4. Instantiation of Earth Observation DSP

4   Conclusion and Prospects

This manuscript presents an application profile for Earth observation data. It aims to facilitate sharing of distributed data within a decentralized architecture to various user communities. We have retained guidelines from the Singapore Framework to build an open and expandable model reusing existing metadata standards. Therefore the Earth Observation application profile is critical to cover the application requirements such as discovery, location, access, preservation and processing of images underpinning decision activities. The application profile is the core element of the data catalog component within the spatial data infrastructure. In a short-term perspective it is planned to implement the transformation of metadata sets describing the resource from the Earth observation in collections of metadata records compliant to DSP. Likewise, web components are under development using Java EE technologies and will facilitate the building and the management of DSP models. Additionally, they will provide some capabilities to edit, transform and visualize pre-existing or even new metadata records that will enrich newly acquired resources.

Prospects to longer term include:

– Definition of model-based constraints to develop control mechanisms (especially validity) based on the elements of metadata records,
– Harmonization of metadata standards to take advantage of all the metadata sets regardless of their pre-existing format,
– Use of the application profile as an ontology in order to run reasoning on metadata records.

Acknowledgement. This work was supported by public funds received in the framework of GEOSUD, a project (ANR-10-EQPX-20) of the program "Investissements d'Avenir" managed by the French National Research Agency.

References

1. Geographic Information – Metadata. ISO 19115:2003 (May 2003)
2. Berners-Lee, T., Connolly, D., KagalL, L., Scharf, Y., Hendler, J.: N3Logic: A logical framework for the World Wide Web. Theory and Practice of Logic Programming 8, 249–269 (2008)
3. Granell, C., Gould, M., Manso, M.A., Bernabé, M.A.: V: Spatial Data Infrastructures. In: Handbook of Research on Geoinformatics, pp. 36–41. Idea Group Publishing (2009)
4. Cossu, R., Pacini, F., Brito, F., Fusco, L., Li Santi, E., Parrini, A.: GENESI-DEC: a federative e-infrastructure for Earth Science data discovery, access, and on-demand processing. In: 24th International Conference on Informatics for Environmental Protection (2010)
5. GEO Architecture and Data Committee (version 1.0). GEOSS Core Architecture Implementation Report (2007)
6. Haslhofer, B., Klas, W.: A survey of techniques for achieving metadata interoperability. ACM Computing Surveys (CSUR) 42(2), 7 (2010)
7. Heery, R., Patel, M.: Application profiles: mixing and matching metadata schemas. Ariadne 25 (2000)
8. Hillman, D.I., Phipps, J., Coyle, K.: Introduction to Application Profiles (2010)
9. Hillmann, D.I., Phipps, J.: Application Profiles: Exposing and Enforcing Metadata Quality. In: Proceedings of the 2007 International Conference on Dublin Core and Metadata Applications: Application Profiles: Theory and Practice, DCMI 2007, pp. 53–62. Dublin Core Metadata Initiative (2007)
10. International Organization for Standardization. ISO 19139 (2007)
11. International Organization for Standardization. Geographic Information – Metadata. ISO 19106:2004 (2004)

12. International Organization for Standardization. ISO 19115:2009 (2009)
13. International Organization for Standardization. Geographic information – Observations and measurements. ISO 19156:2011 (2014)
14. Gasperi, J., Houbie, F., Woolf, A.: Earth Observation Metadata profile of Observations & Measurements. OGC Document Number: 10-157r3 (2012)
15. Walsh, J., Goncalves, P.: DCLite4G Vocabulary (2008)
16. Kazmierski, M., Desconnets, J.-C., Guerrero, B., Briand, D.: GEOSUD SDI: Accessing Earth Observation data collections with semantic-based services. In: Proceedings of the 17th AGILE Conference on Geographic Information Science, Connecting a Digital Europe through Location and Place, Castellon, Spain (June 2014)
17. Nilsson, M.: Description Set Profiles: A constraint language for Dublin Core Application Profiles. DCMI Working Draft (2008)
18. Nilsson, M., Miles, A., Johnston, P., Enoksson, F.: Formalizing Dublin Core Application Profiles - Description Set Profiles and Graph Constraints. In: Sicilia, M.-A., Lytras, M.D. (eds.) Metadata and Semantics, pp. 101–111. Springer US (2009)
19. OGC 07-045. OpenGIS Catalogue Services Specification 2.0.2 - ISO Metadata Application Profile (2007)
20. OGC 10-032r7. OGC® OpenSearch Geo and Time Extensions (2013)
21. OSGEO. Geodata metadata model (2007)
22. OSGEO. Dublin Core Lightweight Profile for Geospatial (2008)
23. Powell, A., Nilsson, M., Naeve, A., Johnston, P., Baker, T.: DCMI Abstract Model. DCMI Recommendation (June 2007)
24. Pulis, S., Nevile, L.: Using the DC Abstract Model to support application profile developers. In: International Conference on Dublin Core and Metadata Applications (2006)

The Errors of Our Ways: Using Metadata Quality Research to Understand Common Error Patterns in the Application of Name Headings

Katherine M. Wisser

School of Library and Information Science, Simmons College, Boston, Massachusetts, USA
wiser@simmons.edu

Abstract. Using data culled during a metadata quality research project for the Social Network and Archival Context (SNAC) project, this article discusses common errors and problems in the use of standardized languages, specifically unambiguous names for persons and corporate bodies. Errors such as misspelling, qualifiers, format, and miss-encoding point to several areas where quality control measures can improve aggregation of data. Results from a large data set indicate that there are predictable problems that can be retrospectively corrected before aggregation. This research looked specifically at name formation and expression in metadata records, but the errors detected could be extended to other controlled vocabularies as well.

Keywords: Metadata, Quality assessment, Authority control, Data utilization, MARC, Encoded Archival Description, Encoded Archival Context – Corporate Bodies, Persons and Families.

1   Introduction

The dream of aggregating data and providing seamless access to metadata has been realized. That dream, though, illustrates very real issues of data quality that confront the library and archival professions. Incomplete or inaccurate metadata have been a topic of conversation in the bibliographic cataloging world for many years. As early as 1987, aggregating services such as OCLC's World Cat and the former aggregation, RLIN, were assessed for data quality.[1] Efforts to improve the overall quality of the metadata being added to these aggregations were made and overall quality was improved. More recently, large-scale research on the use of content designation in the MARC environment exposed the actual use of specific fields and subfields to open up discussions for extending that functionality. [5] In contrast to the focus on metadata code, though, a large-scale analysis on controlled vocabulary application provides different perspectives on metadata quality.

Research on metadata quality is not new. With the introduction of integrated library systems and the use of digital technologies to represent materials in collections, the quality of metadata has been scrutinized and analyzed and further identified as a problem space that requires attention. As Yasser notes, much recent research has examined various aspects of metadata quality, primarily in the digital

S. Closs et al. (Eds.): MTSR 2014, CCIS 478, pp. 83–94, 2014.

libraries arena. Yasser identifies five categories of metadata problems, including incorrect values, elements, missing information, information loss and inconsistent value representation. Yasser goes on to assert that the identification of problem areas provides metadata projects with the ammunition for preventive and/or corrective measures to enhance their metadata quality. [9] Aggregating data outside of local implementation has exacerbated these issues. Shreeves, Riley and Milewicz coined a new term – "shareable metadata" – to deal with the very real problems associated with aggregating metadata from multiple local implementations. [7] The concept of shareable metadata came from the significant aggregation in the IMLS-funded Illinois Digital Collection and Content project, which explored the use of OAI Metadata Harvesting Protocol to bring together disparate digital collections. [1]

The importance of accuracy in authority data cannot be overstated. Without accuracy, the purpose of authority work is undermined. As Jeng notes in discussing the purpose of authority control, "to be full, useful, and best is to be accurate." [4] Authority control does not operate in a vacuum, however. As Hearn notes, authority records are dynamic as information and perception evolves. [3]

The large data set produced through the Social Network and Archival Context (SNAC) project allows for in-depth analysis of metadata quality, particularly regarding common errors in name formation. Errors such as misspelling, qualifiers, format, and miss-encoding point to several areas where quality control measures can improve aggregation of data. These common error patterns can also be applied to other uses of controlled vocabularies.

2 Sample Description

The Social Network and Archival Context (SNAC) project "aims to not only make the records more easily discovered and accessed but also, and at the same time, build an unprecedented resource that provides access to the socio-historical contexts (which includes people, families, and corporate bodies) in which the records were created." [8] SNAC uses automated extraction and merging to generate records to describe corporate bodies, persons, and families. It extracts names from encoded documents provided by large-scale repositories and aggregators. These records are provided in Encoded Archival Description and MARC formats and generally comply with the use of controlled vocabularies. The advantage of this process is that the data can be predictable in form and format. SNAC targeted specific areas of these records for extraction, including those that would most likely use a controlled form of the name (<origination> and <controlaccess> in EAD, 1xx and 7xx fields in MARC) but also other areas where name references would be more freeform (e.g., names within the <dsc>). SNAC stores the information in records using Encoded Archival Context – Corporate Bodies, Persons and Families (EAC-CPF) and creates relationship structures between entities and other entities and entities and resources.

As part of this work, SNAC relies on algorithms and n-gram matching techniques to decrease the number of duplicative records for the same entity. To test the effectiveness of these techniques, two phases of research were conducted. The first phase examined the success of extraction techniques for targeted names and the accuracy of merging records that represent the same entity. The results showed a high success in extraction and some problem areas for merging (reported in an unpublished technical paper for the project). The second phase, conducted in late 2013, reexamined the merging protocols to see if adjustments improved the merging process. Additionally, new strategies were employed to examine the undermatching of names. One of these strategies entailed the examination of more than 26,000 names in browsing lists.

3   Methodology

A visual scan (and count for descriptive statistical purposes) of alphabetically organized lists of headings provided a specific view of the names in the SNAC data. Recording headings that appeared to represent the same entities illustrated some common patterns to name formation. Figure 1 demonstrates the view of the data as collected to create the sample.

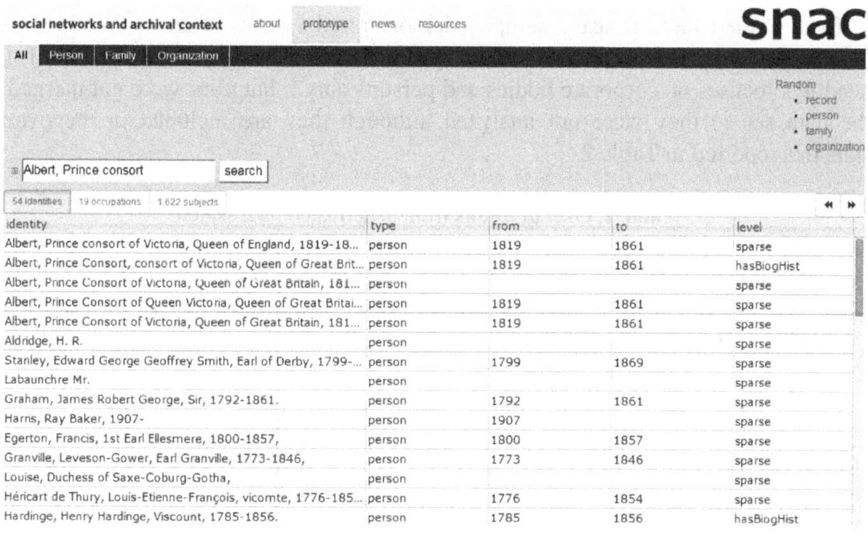

Fig. 1. Example of undermatching browsing approach, Albert, Prince Consort...

Figure 1 illustrates the way in which the data was collected. In this browse screen, there are several entries for "Albert, Prince Consort of ..." and within them several variations of Queen Victoria. This indicates that there is the potential for multiple records for the same entity (although this example is perhaps more obvious than others encountered). For the purposes of the quality metrics for the SNAC project, this result constituted "undermatching." Over 26,000 headings for records in different initial character strings were examined. The different sets examined were determined based on initial character strings (symbol, A-Adams, Col-Cole, T., Gle, University, and US). Some of those were based on random selection while others were based on the researcher's curiosity. Table 1 indicates the breakdown of those samplings and its percentage as compared to the sample of the whole letter.

Table 1. Sample details

Grouping	Sample size	Whole letter size	Percentage: sample to whole letter
Initial character: symbol	922	922	100%
A-Adams	10,143	84,488	12.0%
Col-Cole, T.	1,525	160,830	0.9%
Gle	1,122	90,319	1.2%
University	12,020	44,756	26.9%
US	455	44,756	1.0%
Total sample	26,187	381,315	6.9%*

* This number, 381,315 of the total set (19.8%), represents the percentage of the total sample of headings examined against the total number of records in the specific letters examined. If this were broadened to the entire data set, which includes 1,922,345 data records, the percentage examined constitutes 1.4% of the data set.

Each of the character string samples demonstrated a series of errors. While SNAC handles records for corporate bodies, persons and families, the analysis of the headings focuses on corporate bodies and persons only. Families were not merged in the data set so they were not analyzed although they are included in the overall statistics reported in Table 2.

Table 2. Overall results from undermatching research

Sample range	Corporate bodies	Persons	Families	Total	
				Groupings	Headings
Symbol	19 (100.0%)	0	0	19	40
A-Adams	90 (34.0%)	174 (65.7%)	1 (0.4%)	265	746
Col – Cole, T.	11 (16.2%)	57 (83.8%)	0 (0.0%)	68	149
Gle	17 (43.6%)	22 (56.4%)	1 (2.6%)	39	106
University	107 (100.0%)	0 (0.0%)	0 (0.0%)	107	222
Us	2 (22.2%)	7 (77.8%)	0	9	20
Total	245 (48.3%)	260 (51.3%)	2 (0.4%)	507	1,283**

** Note: This sample accounts for an average of 2.5 headings in each grouping. This average has little meaning, though, given that the two family names constitute 161 headings. If the families are removed from the total number of groupings and their corresponding headings (505 and 1,122 respectively), the average drops to 2.2.

Personal name headings "groupings" outnumber corporate body headings by fifteen records. When examined more closely, though, two ranges represent only corporate body headings (Symbol and University) and when those two ranges are removed, rather than constituting nearly 48.3% of the potential errors, the number of corporate bodies drops to 31.4%. Correspondingly, personal name errors move from just over half (51.1%) to over two-thirds (67.8%). These results would indicate that while on the surface it appears that the issues were evenly spread across entity types, the issues of consistent name formation are more centered on personal names than on corporate bodies. These results are surprising given that corporate body name formation constitutes very complex rules.

Within the 507 groupings discovered in the analysis of the heading for matching, 35 pairs were exact matches. Exact matches are identical character strings. These pairs were removed from the sample before the analysis on error types was conducted. The results outlined below are based on a sample of 472 groupings and 1,213 headings.

Once the sample was established, the headings were examined for differentiations. Thirty difference types were detected. These types ranged from miss-encoding, spelling and punctuation, the presence or absence of qualifiers, abbreviations, and so forth. Groupings were examined for all instances of difference; therefore, a grouping could exhibit more than one type of difference. Multiple errors occurred in 136 groupings where between two and five differences were identified. In contrast, 336 groupings exhibited only one type of difference.

4   Results

The difference types were first examined as categories and percentages calculated (see Table 3). Encoding errors constituted the smallest percentage of differences at almost 5%; typographical problems and format problem appeared at rates over 10% and 15% respectively. Content differences constituted the largest number of errors at just over 68%. This ratio could indicate that either the actual content is the center of the problem in name formation consistency or that the categorization of problems encountered was overly oriented toward content differences.

Table 3. Differences by categories

Category	Number of occurrences	Percentage of whole sample (n=639)
Encoding	31	4.9%
Possible typographical errors	71	11.1%
Content differences	439	68.7%
Format differences	98	15.3%
Total	638	100.0%

When each category is examined more closely, some surprising issues comes to light. For instance, in encoding errors (see Table 4), MARC encoding problems within the content of the heading are prevalent, such as the presence of subfield letters. These errors indicate that the subfield and delimiter syntax was problematic in the data. The MARC encoding issues are significantly less of a problem, however, than the miss-assignment of the heading type. In the sample, nearly 90% of the encoding errors are attributed to a personal name being coded as a corporate body or vice versa. In addition, the single group that consisted of headings that were neither personal name nor corporate body name entities were encoded as corporate bodies (i.e., Account book, Account books, Account journal, and Accounts).

Table 4. Encoding errors

Specific Error	Number of occurrences	Percentage within category	Percentage of whole sample (n=639)
Erroneous encoding persname/corpname or 100/110	27	87.1%	4.2%
MARC subfield as part of heading	3	9.7%	0.5%
Not a personal name or corporate body	1	3.2%	0.2%
Total	31	100.0%	4.9%

The next category is a set of possible typographical errors, such as punctuation and spelling differences (see Table 5). In this category, there is a differentiation made between misspelled words and spelling differences. With misspelled words, it is clear that a typographical error has taken place. This is particularly true with the corporate body names, where such words as dentistry, information and veterinary are all examples of misspellings, appearing as "dentsitry," "informtion," and "veternary," respectively.

Other spelling issues were less clear. For example, these two headings are part of a group:

"Abbott, John Stephens Cabaot, 1805-1877"
"Abbott, John Stevens Cabet, 1805-1877"

In this example, two of the four names are spelled differently but it cannot be automatically assumed that the names are misspelled, although Cabaot in comparison to Cabet is a little more clear than Stephens and Stevens. Despite these differences, when examined in the light of other evidence it is suspected that these represent the same entity.

Table 5. Possible typographical errors

Specific Error	Number of occurrences	Percentage within class	Percentage of whole sample (n=639)
Punctuation differences	17	23.9%	2.7%
Spelling differences	3	4.2%	0.5%
Spacing	13	18.3%	2.0%
Misspelling	38	53.5%	5.9%
Total	71	100.0%	11.1%

Content differences constitute the largest percentage of issues within this sample (see Table 6). The content differences identified included additional parts to the name, including the inclusion of specific information such as Ltd., LLC, and Inc., and the use of different words that have similar meaning (such as University of Alabama in Birmingham and University of Alabama at Birmingham). Many of the content differences are focused on various kinds of qualifiers and the syntax of those qualifiers as they are included in the heading. In Table 6, the use of the term "qualifier" refers to those expressions in parentheses, such as (Firm) or (Ship). Other additions include the fuller form of name (as expressed in the MARC subfield $q) and dates (as expressed in the MARC subfield $d). Finally, a large number of issues involve geographic qualifiers.

Table 6. Content differences

Specific Error	Number of occurrences	Percentage within category	Percentage of whole sample (n=639)
Additional parts to the name (MARC $a)	33	7.5%	5.2%
Different dates for same entity (data discrepancies)	41	9.3%	6.4%
Presence of dates (MARC $d)	73	16.6%	11.4%
Inclusion of Inc., LLC, Ltd., etc.	21	4.8%	3.3%
Addition of geographic qualifier	37	8.4%	5.8%
Addition of other qualifier	20	4.6%	3.1%
Additional words in the name	28	6.4%	4.4%

Table 6. (*continued*)

Specific Error	Number of occurrences	Percentage within category	Percentage of whole sample (n=639)
Geographic term as part of heading rather than qualifier	6	1.4%	0.9%
Different words, similar meaning	7	1.6%	1.1%
Completeness of geographic qualifier	13	3.0%	2.0%
Co. versus & Co.	1	0.2%	0.2%
Different words	7	1.6%	1.1%
Different non-geographic qualifiers	8	1.8%	1.3%
Fuller form of name (MARC $q)	51	11.6%	8.0%
Initials/abbreviations versus spelled out name	29	6.6%	4.5%
Amount of completion of date different	43	9.8%	6.7%
Non-geographic qualifier term as part of the name (e.g., inclusion of title)	15	3.4%	2.3%
Abbreviations in geographic qualifier	4	0.9%	0.6%
Subordinate corporate body	2	0.5%	0.3%
Total	439	100.0%	68.7%

There is a broad distribution of difference types within the content differences category. The presence or absence of dates is the most common issue in this category, but it still only accounts for just under 17%. Other more common issues include the presence or absence of the fuller form of name and date completion discrepancies. These issues indicate that there is significant misunderstanding or lack of agreement on the rules for the formation of headings rather than careless application. Another explanation for these differences could result from the sources of information from which the headings are formed. Tables 8 and 9 explore in more depth the issues with geographic terms and dates respectively. They are discussed below.

Table 7 illustrates the differences in the format of the heading. The largest group of differences is the application of established abbreviations for relatively common words such as company, department, or street. Date formats constitute over 10% of the problems in this category. This refers to the use of, for example, "b. 1876" versus "1876-". Descriptive standards sanction both formats to express date information, meaning that either heading is not technically an error. Enhanced guidelines would help headings creators understand when one format is appropriate over another and help with the consistency of application.

Table 7. Format differences

Specific Error	Number of occurrences	Percentage within category	Percentage of whole sample (n=639)
Format of dates	12	12.2%	1.9%
Same word, plural/singular	13	13.3%	2.0%
Co. vs. Company, St. vs. Street, Dept. vs. Department	50	51.0%	7.8%
And vs. &	23	23.5%	3.6%
Total	98	100.0%	15.3%

Nearly a quarter of the format differences were identified as the difference between an ampersand and the word "and." Logically, these concepts are exactly equivalent and should be automatically recognized as equivalent. The number of times this issue occurs, therefore, is surprising. Particularly surprising is that 13 of the 23 instances (56.5%) of this issue constitute the only difference detected between the two headings.

Table 8. Differences within geographic terms as part of a heading

Specific Error	Number of occurrences	Percentage within errors with geographic terms	Percentage within class (content differences)	Percentage of whole sample (n=639)
Addition of geographic qualifier	37	61.7%	8.4%	5.8%
Geographic term as part of the heading rather than as a qualifier	6	10.0%	1.4%	0.9%
Completeness of geographic qualifiers	13	22.7%	3.0%	2.0%
Abbreviations in geographic qualifiers	4	6.7%	0.9%	0.6%
Total	60	100.0%	13.7%	9.4%

Geographic term issues account for nearly 10% of all the issues found in the sample. The breakdown, while skewed to the presence or absence of a geographical qualifier, demonstrates a relatively even breakdown of problems. The issue least present, the use of abbreviations in geographic qualifiers (e.g., Tenn. or Tennessee), only appears four times in the sample but is indicative of the other content problems that center on the application of rules to form headings.

Table 9. Differences relating to dates

Specific Error	Number of occurrences	Percentage within errors relating to dates	Percentage within class	Percentage of whole sample (n=639)
Different dates for the same entity, data discrepancies	41	24.3%	9.3% (n=439, content differences)	6.4%
Presence of dates	73	43.2%	16.6% (n=439, content differences)	11.4%
Amount of completion of date different	43	25.4%	9.8% (n=439, content differences)	6.7%
Total for content differences	157	92.9%	35.8% (n=439, content differences)	24.6%
Date formats different	12	7.1%	12.4% (n=97, format differences)	1.9%
Total	169	100.0%	NA	26.4%

Date differences focus more on the actual content rather than the ways in which that content is expressed. Data discrepancies and completion constitute nearly one half of the data issues found. The presence or absence of dates constitutes over 40% and the rest of the date issues are in the ways in which they are formatted for expression. It is clear that aside from accuracy issues (e.g., clear typographical errors such as 100-1993, 1900-1993) are bound to occur and are accounted for as a data discrepancy, but some discrepancies are surprising. For example, John Quincy Adams appears with four different headings, and the dates that appear are listed as: 1767-1848, 1767-1848, 1787-1848, 1797-1848. Given how much is known about the sixth President of the United States, it is hard to reconcile these discrepancies.

5   Discussion

Assessing metadata quality is a challenge for researchers. As Hearn suggests, much metadata quality research is done through the analysis of individual records. [2] Large-scale aggregated data provides an alternative view of data. That view allows for the assessment of common issues. Once those issues are brought to light, data providers can employ local preventive measures before sharing their data in an aggregation. Human error will always be a factor in metadata creation, whether it is through carelessness or lack of standards application. Nonetheless, understanding the nature of errors does provide insight that can help improve the overall quality of the data.

Highlighting error patterns can point to corrective measures that can be taken at a local level to benefit the quality of the data sent to the aggregator, such as better standards adherence, better education of standards, and quality control measures. There are, though, issues that can handled by the aggregator. The latter category includes recognizing equivalences such as "&" and "and." These issues could be resolved automatically in the aggregation. If visual integrity to the original source is a desire in the aggregation, behind-the-scenes equivalence can take place. The same could be said for equivalences between abbreviations and fully spelled-out words (such as Dept. and Department). This approach can be overused, however. Recent justifications in descriptive standard rules, for instance, demonstrate the danger in making assumptions about abbreviations: in the English language, "St." can and does stand for multiple words, such as street and saint. Careful consideration of any automated corrective measures should take place to mitigate the possibilities of erroneous equivalences.

More problematic are the issues that cannot be easily corrected through automated means post-aggregation. There are a myriad of content rules that provide conflicting guidelines on the addition and format of dates, geographic qualifiers, or other types of information. In order to ensure that aggregators are cognizant of the guidelines followed by a particular data provider, it would be useful to know which rules were being followed to establish a particular heading. While many current metadata standard implementations provide this specificity at a record level, the implementation of data components such as the second indicator (and possible corresponding subfield 2) in a MARC 6xx field or the source attribute in Encoded Archival Description can be leveraged to lessen the impact of data that accurately follows disparate guidelines. The use of these data components, while not new to data structure standards, would enhance the possibilities for recognizing that differently structured headings according to different rules belong to the same entity.

6   Conclusion

Aggregating data is one way to address the dispersion of information resources through technological means. But the success of aggregation is dependent on the quality of the data being aggregated. Complicating this process is the very human element of data creation, standards adherence and the myriad of standards currently in use. These notions are not new. As noted in Shreeves, Riley, and Mileczek, conformance to standards, including descriptive content standards, enhances the shareability of that information. [7] Often, though, this advice is only part of a larger critique of metadata quality rather than the center of it. As data sets get larger, more and more work needs to go into quality control mechanisms and more information needs to be attached to smaller data units. Tools have been developed to assist repositories in the use of standardized vocabularies, but tools alone cannot mitigate against the errors that can occur when data is considered outside of its initial context. A better understanding of the sources of data and the decisions that go into the creation of that data will empower the reuse of that information in multiple contexts.

References

[1] Cole, T.W., Shreeves, S.L.: Search and Discovery Across Collections: the IMLS Digital Collections and Content Project. Library Hi Tech 22(3), 307–322 (2004)

[2] Hearn, S.: Comparing Catalogs: Currency and Consistency of Controlled Headings. LRTS 53(1), 25–40 (2009)

[3] Intner, S.S.: Much ado about nothing: OCLC and RLIN cataloging quality. Library Journal 114(2), 38–40 (1989)

[4] Jeng, L.H.: Why authority? Why control? Cataloging & Classification Quarterly 34(4), 91–97 (2002)

[5] Moen, W.E., Benardino, P.: Assessing Metadata Utilization: An Analysis of MARC Content Designation Use. In: 2003 Dublin Core Conference: Supporting Communities of Discourse and Practice – Metadata Research and Application, Seattle, Wash. (2003), http://www.unt.edu/wmoen/publications/MARCPaper_Final2003.pdf

[6] Moen, W.E.: Examining MARC records as Artifacts that Reflect Metadata Utilization Decisions. First Monday 11(8) (2006), http://www.firstmonday.org/issues/issue11_8/moen/index.html

[7] Shreeves, S.L., Riley, J., Milewicz, L.: Moving towards Shareable Metadata. First Monday 11(8) (2006), http://www.firstmonday.org/issues/issue11_8/shreeves/index.html

[8] Social Network and Archival Context, http://socialarchive.iath.virginia.edu/index.html

[9] Yasser, C.M.: An Analysis of Problems in Metadata Records. Journal of Library Metadata 11, 51–62 (2011)

Enhancing Data Curation of Cultural Heritage for Information Sharing: A Case Study Using Open Government Data

Hyoungjoo Park and Richard P. Smiraglia

School of Information Studies, University of Wisconsin Milwaukee,
Northwest Quad Building B, 2025 E Newport, Milwaukee, WI 53211, USA
{park32,smiragli}@uwm.edu

Abstract. The purpose of this paper is to enhance cultural heritage data curation. A core research question of this study is how to share cultural heritage data by using ontologies. A case study was conducted using open government data mapped with the CIDOC-CRM (Conceptual Reference Model). Twelve library-related files in unstructured data format were collected from an open government website, Seoul Metropolitan Government of Korea (http://data.seoul.go.kr). By using the ontologies of the CIDOC CRM 5.1.2, we conducted a mapping process as a way of enhancing cultural heritage information to share information as a data component. We graphed each file then mapped each file in tables. Implications of this study are both the enhanced discoverability of unstructured data and the reusability of mapped information. Issues emerging from this study involve verification of detail for complete compatibility without further input from domain experts.

Keywords: Cultural heritage metadata models standards interoperability mappings and integration, Ontologies and knowledge representation for the cultural heritage domain, Integration of intra or inter disciplinary heterogeneous resources, Infrastructures for sharing content, Digital Curation workflows and models

1 Introduction: Enhancing Cultural Heritage Data Curation

The purpose of this paper is to enhance cultural heritage data curation. The specific problem for this study begins from the current situation that much of cultural heritage data cannot be sharable because those data are "stuck," which is to say restricted, or isolated in siloed, proprietary datasets. Relatively recently, the publication of open data by governments for their citizens has been growing steadily. Recently the publication of open government data has become an important communication channel (DiFranzo et al. 2011). A primary research question is how to share cultural heritage data by using ontologies.

For the present case study, cultural heritage data records were downloaded from the Seoul Metropolitan Government of Korea (http://data.seoul.go.kr) website, without

S. Closs et al. (Eds.): MTSR 2014, CCIS 478, pp. 95–106, 2014.
© Springer International Publishing Switzerland 2014

researcher intervention. Twelve files related to libraries located in the region of the Seoul Metropolitan Government of Korea were selected. Each data record in Microsoft Excel format was translated from Korean to English. Direct language translation was been conducted to prevent confusion due to subtle differences in meaning. Two distinct records were selected from each file for ontology mapping using CIDOC CRM. CIDOC CRM, ISO (International Standard Organization) 21127:2006, is a standard for knowledge sharing in cultural heritage. The CRM is a model developed empirically by an interdisciplinary team, based on real world cultural heritage information sources (What is the CIDOC CRM 2014). This study is expected to show practical approaches to enhancing cultural heritage data curation.

2   Background: Data Curation, Cultural Heritage and the CIDOC CRM

Data curation is to maintain, preserve and add value to research data for its lifecycle (IDCC 2014). Cultural heritage refers to the means by which cultural knowledge that brings universal value from the perspectives of history, art or science is transmitted (Buckland 1997). Cultural heritage institutions are libraries, museums, archives, and galleries. There are few published studies addressing means to enhance data curation in cultural heritage from open government data for knowledge sharing. However, a few studies were conducted by using the CIDOC CRM to summarize structure and combine existing data for a generic ontological model and to map and formalize existing knowledge for interoperability with other data sets (Bountouri and Gergatsoulis 2011; Doerr and Iorizzo 2008; González-Pérez and Parcero-Oubiña 2011; Koutsomitropoulos, Solomou and Papatheodorou 2009; Lin, Hong and Doerr 2008; Stasinopoulou et al. 2007; Theodoridou et al. 2010). Bountouri and Gergatsoulis semantically mapped Encoded Archival Description (EAD) to the CIDOC CRM ontology. Koutsomitropoulos et al. conducted a case study to implement a prototype with Dublin Core in digital object collections. Lin, Hong and Doerr studied inference platforms by using OWL for using CIDOC CRM in cultural heritage digital libraries. Stasinopoulou et al. investigated ontology-based metadata using the CIDOC CRM ontology for knowledge-integration in the cultural heritage domain. Theodoridou et al. studied CRMdig in RDF/S for modeling and querying provenance. Doerr and Iorizzo discussed how heterogeneous cultural heritage information can be enhanced by using the CIDOC CRM due to its flexibility for integration, mediation, and interchange. They presented a case study using core ontologies of the CIDOC CRM. This study demonstrated the difficulties of linking documents and knowledge. For that reason, semi-automatic co-reference detection and correction were needed to match between identifiers and resources because direct data input into a semantic network showed ineffectiveness (see also Dionissiadou and Doerr 1994). The values of these studies is in that both theoretical and practical issues are applied to face challenges in knowledge-sharing and studies to enhance discoverabilities of cultural heritage are conducted by using CIDOC CRM.

3   The Case Study: Mapping with the CRM

Specifically, twelve files related to libraries selected from among sixty files (as of May 1, 2014) in Seoul city were retrieved from the Seoul Open Data website (http://data.seoul.go.kr/). Each file was translated from Korean to English. After ana-lyzing all of the records in the twelve files (Table 1), two distinctive records were selected from each of these files. An attempt was made to select records with data representing each value to provide the fullest mapping experience. The ontologies of the CIDOC CRM version 5.1.2 (CIDOC CRM 2013), which is the most recently re-leased version, were used to interpret and construct a specific mapping format.

Attributes of distinctive records from each file and CIDOC CRM were compared. Several values of each attribute were null values. Null values might be due to the nature of open government data, which is unstructured in a heterogeneous data format.

CIDOC CRM core ontologies were used to map cultural heritage data in the select-ed records. The twelve files used for the case study were:

> Adolescent Libraries/Reading Rooms in Seoul City
> School Library Hours in Seoul City
> Geographic Information of libraries in Seoul City
> Geographic Information of Small Libraries in Seoul City
> Libraries' Events in Seoul City
> Libraries for the Disabled in Seoul City
> Library Hours (Closing Day) in Seoul City
> Library Hours (Event) in Seoul City
> Library Schedule in Seoul City
> Location and Book holdings at Guro-gu District in Seoul City
> Small Library Information in Seoul City
> Total numbers of book holdings at Guro-gu District in Seoul City.

In order to prevent confusion due to subtle differences in meaning, direct language translation was conducted. For example, both 'facility name' and 'library name' have equivalent meaning although those attributes could be represented in different attributes. Also, the Korean government recently changed its address system in order to make the address simpler. Equivalent addresses might be written differently de-pending on the creation date of data.

Table 1 displays geographic information of small libraries in Seoul City, which in-volved 775 libraries, as mapped to the CRM. Table 1 shows characteristics of the Korean address system: address-dong, address-mountain, address-master, address-slave, and address.

Table 1. Mapping results of 'Geographic Information of Small Libraries in Seoul City' by using CIDOC CRM

	Entity	Subclass of:	Property	Value
Library ID	E42 Identifier	E41 Appellation	P87 is identified by (identifies)	89
District Name	E44 Place Appellation	E41 Appellation	-	Jongno-gu
Address-Dong	E45 Address	E44 Place Appellation	-	Nooha-dong
Address-Mountain	E45 Address	E44 Place Appellation	-	1
Address-Master	E45 Address	E44 Place Appellation	-	64
Address-Slave	E45 Address	E44 Place Appellation	-	-
Address	E45 Address	E44 Place Appellation	-	Taepydong town #402, 64 Nooha-dong, Jongno-gu
Facility Name	E19 Physical Object	E18 Physical Thing	has former or current location (is former or current location of)	Braille Library of Korean students
Operating Agency	E40 Legal Body	E74 Group	-	Welfare for the Blind Siloam Presbyterian Church
Principal Establishment	E40 Legal Body	E74 Group	-	-
Characteristics of Facility	-	-	-	Library for the Disabled
Establishment	E50 Date	E49 Time Appellation	-	12/11/2009

Table 1. (*Continued*)

Total Area	E54 Dimension	E1 CRM Entity	-	140
Website	E51 Contact Point	E41 Appellation	-	-
Telephone Number	E51 Contact Point	E41 Appellation	-	-
Data Creation Date	E50 Date	E49 Time Appellation	-	-
Longitude	E47 Spatial Coordinates	E44 Place Appellation	P87 is identified by (identifies)	197217.146
Latitude	E47 Spatial Coordinates	E44 Place Appellation	P87 is identified by (identifies)	453373.479

4   Mapping with the CIDOC CRM

Here we explore some specific issues arising from mapping open government data records concerning Korean public libraries using the CIDOC CRM. In this section we look at four of the twelve specific mappings and the data interpretation problems that arose.

Table 2. Mapping results of "Geographic Information of libraries in Seoul City"

	Entity	Subclass of:	Property	Value 1	Value 2
District Name	E44 Place Appellation	E41 Appellation	-	Jongno-gu	Jongno-gu
Address-Dong	E45 Address	E44 Place Appellation	-	Sajik-dong	Pilun-dong
Address-Mountain	E45 Address	E44 Place Appellation	-	1	1
Address-Master	E45 Address	E44 Place Appellation	-	1	287
Address-Slave	E45 Address	E44 Place Appellation	-	28	
Address	E45 Address	E44 Place Appellation	-	1-28 Sajik-dong, Jongno-gu	96 Sajijk-ro, Jongno-gu

Table 2. (*Continued*)

Facility Name	E19 Physical Object	E18 Physical Thing	has former or current location (is former or current location of):	Jongno library	Children"s Library
Operation Organization	E40 Legal Body	E74 Group	-	-	-
Establishment	E40 Legal Body	E74 Group	-	--	
Characteristics of Facility	E40 Legal Body	E74 Group	-	Department of Education Library	Department of Education Library
Opening Date	E50 Date	E49 Time Appellation	-	11/17/1998	5/4/1979
Total Areas	E54 Dimension	E1 CRM Entity	-	0	0
Website	E51 Contact Point	E41 Appellation	-	lib.sen.go.kr/lib_index.jsp	lib.sen.go.kr/lib_index.jsp
Telephone Number	E51 Contact Point	E41 Appellation	-	-	-
Data Creation Date	E50 Date	E49 Time Appellation	-	-	-
Longitude	E47 Spatial Coordinates	E44 Place Appellation	P87 is identified by (identifies)	197109.533	197299.357
Latitude	E47 Spatial Coordinates	E44 Place Appellation	P87 is identified by (identifies)	452932.916	452895.106

Table 2 displays information about geographic information in Seoul City. This record did not use "library name" but rather used "facility name," which could be confusing. However, confusion can be alleviated through linkage using the CIDOC CRM. This record was mainly populated with address information, which was very challenging to map. The CIDOC CRM seems to be developed based on western systems. In Eastern countries, original address systems are in use.

Table 3. Mapping results of "Library Hours (Event) in Seoul City"

	Entity	Subclass of:	Property	Value 1	Value 2
Event ID	E42 Identifier	E41 Appellation	P42 assigned (was assigned by)	3705	5575
Event Name	E5 Event	E7 Activity	-	Psychological journey in life	Financial Planning
Library Number	E42 Identifier	E41 Appellation	P1 is identified by (identifies)	24	15
Library Name	E19 Physical Object	E18 Physical Thing	P54 has current permanent location (is current permanent location of)	Gangdong Public Lilbrary	Yangcheon Library
District Code	E42 Identifier	E41 Appellation	P1 is identified by (identifies)	10	2
District Name	E44 Place Appellation	E41 Appellation	P1 is identified by (identifies)	Gangdong-gu	Yangcheon-gu
Beginning date of the event	E52 Time-Span	E1 CRM Entity	P83 had at least duration (was minimum duration of):	7/12/2011	1/8/2014
Last date of the event	E52 Time-Span	E1 CRM Entity	P84 had at most duration (was maximum duration of):	10/4/2011	1/22/2014
Detail	E3 Condition State	E2 Temporal Entity	P5 consists of (forms part of)	Tuesday, 19:00 ~ 21:00	
Beginning date of the registration	E52 Time-Span	E1 CRM Entity	P83 had at least duration (was minimum duration of):	6/15/2011	12/28/2013

Table 3. (*Continued*)

Last date of the Registration	E52 Time-Span	E1 CRM Entity	P84 had at most duration (was maximum duration of):	7/8/2011	1/22/2014
Users	E39 Actor	E77 Persistent Item	P131 is identified by (identifies)	Adults - 40 people	Anyone
Place	E44 Place Appellation	E41 Appellation	P1 is identified by (identifies)	4 floor, 2 cultural room	Damoabang
Price	E54 Dimension	E1 CRM Entity	-	Free	-
Telephone Number	E51 Contact Point	E41 Appellation	P76 has contact point (provides access to)	02-483-0728	02-2062-3955
Longitude	E47 Spatial Coordinates	E44 Place Appellation	P87 is identified by (identifies)	37.538576	37.533389
Latitude	E47 Spatial Coordinates	E44 Place Appellation	P87 is identified by (identifies)	127.143788	126.876088

Table 3 displays "Library Hours (Event) in Seoul City." Due to the nature of event information, this file included very specific information. "Price" included "KRW (Korean Won)" rather than a simple number. "Price" also had many string values, such as "Free" rather than "KRW 0" or "0." These records did not give address information, but provided longitude and latitude instead.

Table 4. Mapping results of "Total numbers of book holdings at Guro-gu District in Seoul City"

	Entity	Subclass of:	Property	Value 1	Value 2
Registration Number	E42 Identifier	E41 Appellation	P1 is identified by (identifies)	28910	28912
Book Title	E35 Title	E41 Appellation	-	Newspaper	Traditional Liquor
Author	E21 Person	E20 Biological Object	-	Chaebak	Rokdam Park
Publisher	E40 Legal Body	E74 Group	-	Daewonsa	Daewonsa

Table 4. (*Continued*)

Year of Publication	E50 Date	E49 Time Appellation	-	2003	2008
Call Number	E42 Identifier	E41 Appellation	P1 is identified by (identifies)	608 빛11 252 v. 252	608 빛11 254 v. 254
ISBN	E42 Identifier	E41 Appellation	P1 is identified by (identifies)	9.78894E+12	9.78894E+12
Description of Book Status	-	-	-	Not available	Not available
Branch ID	E42 Identifier	E41 Appellation	P1 is identified by (identifies)	24	24
Branch Name	E44 Place Appellation	E41 Appellation	-	Wooshin Godo Library	Wooshin Godo Library
Archives	E46 Section Definition	E44 Place Appellation	-	Room	Evaluation Room

Table 4 displays "Total numbers of book holdings at Guro-gu District in Seoul City." This is standard library information regarding books: ISBN, author, publisher, and call number. "Archives" field displays where the book is currently located so that library users might learn whether they can check out books or not.

5   Discussion

It might be essential to work with domain or knowledge experts because accurate ontological mapping based on CIDOC CRM demands thorough knowledge of CIDOC CRM ontology. For good conceptual modeling, domain experts might need to accumulate of factual and categorical knowledge. Another limitation that might be encountered arises from the subtle differences of meaning when each term is translated from Korean to English. The potential solution of this issue might be improved with the knowledge of the meaning of a term and the domain for the improvement of the usage and mapping process to discover knowledge and or information.

Some problems arose during the mapping process. When an attribute was related to a description, there appeared to be no instructions for using the CIDOC CRM ontology. This might be because the CRM is an event-centered ontology. Cultural heritage in open government data did not emphasize temporal entities such as events on a timeline. Also, open government data in the case study had many null values: the most frequently occurring null values were 'E3 Condition State' and 'E51 Contact Point.' 'E45 Address' and 'E50 Date' also had null values. The absence of concepts in the ontology presented challenges for creating semantically equivalent mappings (see Stasinopoulou et al. 2007).

Data curation means to maintain, preserve and add value to research data over its lifecycle (IDCC, 2014) to enable data reuse to support new user needs. Appropriate data curation with the CIDOC CRM might enhance data discoverability, maintenance and reusability. When the original data are not sharable, translating those data into the CIDOC CRM core ontologies might make those original data sharable and storable to enhance discoverability and interoperability among different datasets, especially those from cultural heritage and open government repositories containing diverse knowledge resources. The CIDOC CRM is RDF (Resource Description Framework) compliant because the graph of CIDOC CRM is usually represented in the form of subject-predicate-object expressions, which describe its relationships in RDF. To implement an RDF-compliant database in information systems, open government data that might otherwise be in messy and or unstructured original form can be mapped into the extensions of CIDOC CRM ontologies to offer new approaches to cultural heritage data curation. Following RDF-compliant examples of CIDOC CRM descriptive relationships through actual cases can provide guidance for the fundamental work of data curation.

Table 5. RDF-compliant examples of CIDOC CRM relationships

Subject	Predicate	Object
E22 Man-Made Object	P1 *is identified by*	E41 Appellation
E22 Man-Made Object	P48 *has preferred identifier*	E42 Identifier
E40 Legal Body	P131 *is identified by*	E82 Actor Appellation
E52 Time-Span	P78 *is identified by*	E50 Date
E53 Place	P2 *has type*	E55 Type
E53 Place	P87 *is identified by*	E45 Address

Scalability is an essential consideration for data curation because cultural heritage data in open government websites can be huge in quantity and can be rapidly increasing. In the present case study, of course, we did not use large scale data but rather explored a small set of cases to explore processes that might be involved in data curation. When original data are extracted from open government websites, appropriate scalability might need to be considered carefully. Small amounts of cultural heritage data using the CIDOC CRM for data curation can be effective and efficient when those datasets are discovered and shared with appropriate scalability.

Data reuse over the data curation lifecycle might support new needs by adding potential values to current data. Geospatial data reuse might be an essential way to share information. Park (2014) studied data curation by reusing open government data to support new needs for users in Seoul, Korea who might want to find cultural heritage information at a glance on a familiar visual map. She reused open government data with geographic data such as latitude and longitude to display integrated cultural heritage information at a glance by turning and plugging geographic data into Google Maps™ to display the location of each cultural heritage dataset with icons. The map can be visually enlarged or shrunk and when a user clicks any icon a pop-up menu opens showing integrated cultural heritage information as a whole—library name, district name, address, library size, web address, closing date, operation hours, and reading room hours.

6   Conclusion

One contribution of this study is that open government data, which is unstructured in a heterogeneous data format, was studied for mapping to the CIDOC CRM. The majority of studies in cultural heritage were conducted using structured metadata. This case study revealed the complexity of mapping open government data in which many attributes with identical and or similar meaning were represented differently. A future study might be conducted enhancing the methodology from this study with the RDF and RDFS (RDF Schema), which might be meaningful for enabling discoverability of open government data over distributed knowledge resources. Another goal for future study will be to address the problems of scalability by mapping a larger data-set.

Information sharing among currently distributed resources or heterogeneous data structures might enhance the understanding of the cultural heritage domain. The discovery of information might be facilitated with the process of mapping between cultural heritage information in heterogeneous resources and the CIDOC CRM Domain experts and systematic understanding might help to enhance semantic interoperability. Mapping consistency might lead to more successful resource discovery and exchange over distributed sources.

Acknowledgement. Patrick Le Boeuf at the Bibliotheque Nationale de France was immensely helpful in constructing CRM mapping as a graph.

Works Cited

Bountouri, L., Gergatsoulis, M.: The Semantic Mapping of Archival Metadata to the CIDOC CRM Ontology. Journal of Archival Organization 9(3-4), 174–207 (2011)

Buckland, M.: So What is Cultural Heritage? UC Berkeley iSchool (1997),
   http://courses.ischool.berkeley.edu/i142ac/f97/what.html
   (accessed February 26, 2014)

CIDOC CRM. Definition of the CIDOC Conceptual Reference Model, International Council of Museums, International Committee for Documentation (CIDOC) Conceptual Reference Model (CRM) (2013), ICOM CIDOC CRM SIG, http://www.cidoc-crm.org/docs/cidoc_crm_version_5.1.2.pdf (accessed February 20, 2014)

DiFranzo, D., Ding, L., Erickson, J.S., Li, X., Lebo, T., Michaelis, J., Graves, A., Williams, G.T., Zheng, J.G., Flores, J., Shangguan, Z., Gervasio, G., McGuinness, D.L., Hendler, J.: TWC LOGD: A portal for linked open government data.Semantic Web Challenge 2010 (2011), http://challenge.semanticweb.org/submissions/swc2010_submission_16.pdf (accessed February 20, 2014)

Dionissiadou, I., Doerr, M.: Mapping of material culture to a semantic network. Paper presented at Automating Museums in the Americas and Beyond, Sourcebook, ICOM-MCN Joint Annual Meeting (1994)

Doerr, M., Iorizzo, D.: The dream of a global knowledge network—A new approach. Journal on Computing and Cultural Heritage (JOCCH) 1(1), 5 (2008)

González-Pérez, C., Parcero-Oubiña, C.: A conceptual model for cultural heritage definition and motivation. Paper presented at Revive the Past: Proceeding of the 39th Conference on Computer Applications and Quantitative Methods in Archaeology (2011)

9th International Digital Curation Conference, IDCC 2014, San Francisco, California, pp. 24–27 (February 2014), http://www.dcc.ac.uk/digital-curation/what-digital-curation (accessed February 3, 2014)

Koutsomitropoulos, D.A., Solomou, G.D., Papatheodorou, T.S.: Metadata and semantics in digital object collections: A case-study on CIDOC-CRM and Dublin Core and a prototype implementation. Journal of Digital Information 10(6) (2009)

Lin, C.-H., Hong, J.-S., Doerr, M.: Issues in an inference platform for generating deductive knowledge: case study in cultural heritage digital libraries using the CIDOC CRM. International Journal on Digital Libraries 8(2), 115–132 (2008)

Park, H.: Integrated Geographic Data Visualization with Open Government Data – Seoul Metropolitan Government of Korea. In: 9th International Digital Curation Conference (2014), http://www.dcc.ac.uk/sites/default/files/documents/IDCC14/225Hyoungjoo_Park_idcc_14.pdf (accessed July 14, 2014)

Stasinopoulou, T., Bountouri, L., Kakali, C., Lourdi, I., Papatheodorou, C., Doerr, M., Gergatsoulis, M.: Ontology-based Metadata Integration in the Cultural Heritage Domain. In: Goh, D.H.-L., Cao, T.H., Sølvberg, I.T., Rasmussen, E. (eds.) ICADL 2007. LNCS, vol. 4822, pp. 165–175. Springer, Heidelberg (2007)

Theodoridou, M., Tzitzikas, Y., Doerr, M., Marketakis, Y., Melessanakis, V.: Modeling and querying provenance by extending CIDOC CRM. Distributed and Parallel Databases 27(2), 169–210 (2010)

What is the CIDOC CRM. The CIDOC CRM, http://www.cidoc-crm.org/index.html# (accessed February 12, 2014)

Towards Exploiting Query History for Adaptive Ontology-Based Visual Query Formulation

Ahmet Soylu[1], Martin Giese[1], Ernesto Jimenez-Ruiz[2], Evgeny Kharlamov[2], Dmitriy Zheleznyakov[2], and Ian Horrocks[2]

[1] Department of Informatics, University of Oslo, Norway
{ahmets,martingi}@ifi.uio.no
[2] Department of Computer Science, University of Oxford, United Kingdom
{name.surname}@cs.ox.ac.uk

Abstract. Grounded on real industrial use cases, we recently proposed an ontology-based visual query system for SPARQL, named OptiqueVQS. Ontology-based visual query systems employ ontologies and visual representations to depict the domain of interest and queries, and are promising to enable end users without any technical background to access data on their own. However, even with considerably small ontologies, the number of ontology elements to choose from increases drastically, and hence hinders usability. Therefore, in this paper, we propose a method using the log of past queries for ranking and suggesting query extensions as a user types a query, and identify emerging issues to be addressed.

Keywords: Visual Query Formulation, Ontology-based Data Access, SPARQL, Ranking, Recommendation.

1 Introduction

In data-intensive organisations, *domain experts* usually meet their *information needs* either by operating a set of predefined *queries* embedded into applications or by involving *IT experts* to translate their information needs into queries. This is because domain experts often lack necessary *technical knowledge* and *skills* pertaining to query languages and databases. This man-in-the-middle approach for extracting data introduces a bottleneck in *data access* and consequently delays in *value creation* processes (cf. [1]).

Visual query formulation (cf. [2]) is a longstanding research endeavour and, though oriented towards a wide spectrum of users, a particularly prominent approach to mitigate the data access problem of users without any technical skills (i.e., *end users* – cf. [3]). This is due to fact that visual query formulation tools rely on *recognition*, rather than *recall*, and *direct manipulation* of objects, rather than a *command language syntax*, by using *visual representations* to depict the domain of interest and queries. In this context, we have recently introduced an ontology-based *visual query system* (*VQS*) for end users, named *OptiqueVQS* [4,5]. It is built on a scalable data access platform for *Big Data* developed within an EU project called *Optique*[1] [1]. *Ontologies* provide reasoning support and a

---

[1] http://www.optique-project.eu/

S. Closs et al. (Eds.): MTSR 2014, CCIS 478, pp. 107–119, 2014.
© Springer International Publishing Switzerland 2014

domain representation closer to end users' understanding, compared to earlier approaches built on low-level domain models (e.g., relational schemas) (cf. [6,2]). Besides, Optique employs an *ontology-based data access* (*OBDA*) (cf. [7,8]) technology that extends the platform's data access capabilities to traditional *relational data sources*, which store a significant amount of the world's enterprise data today.

One of the main problems that OptiqueVQS and typically any other VQS face is *scalability* against large ontologies (cf. [9]). A VQS has to provide its users with the elements of ontology (e.g., *concepts* and *properties*) continuously, so that users can select relevant ontology elements and iteratively construct their queries. However, even with considerably small ontologies, the number of concepts and properties to choose from increases drastically due to the propagative effect of ontological reasoning (cf. [10]). In turn, the high number of ontology elements overloads the user interface and hinders *usability*.

We approach the aforementioned problem with *adaptivity* (cf. [11]) by exploiting a *query history* to *rank* and *suggest* ontology elements with respect to an incomplete query that a user has constructed so far (i.e., *context-aware*). The approach is specifically devised for *SPARQL* [12], takes semantics into account with reasoning support, and uses SPARQL, as a programming language, for the implementation. In the rest of paper, we first describe OptiqueVQS, present our ranking proposal, and then discuss the related work. Finally, we provide a discussion on the proposal and emerging issues and conclude the paper.

2   OptiqueVQS

OptiqueVQS is built on multiple and coordinated *representation* and *interaction paradigms* (cf. [2]) and enables end users to formulate comparatively complex queries. OptiqueVQS has a *widget-based* architecture, which underpins its multi-paradigm approach and provides extensibility and flexibility. In the followings, we describe the interface and the formal aspects of SPARQL generation.

2.1   Interface

OptiqueVQS currently has three widgets, see Fig. 1: *W1* (see the top part of Fig. 1) employs a *diagram-based* representation paradigm, gives an overview of the constructed query, and allows further manipulation of it; *W2* (see the bottom-left part of Fig. 1) employs a *menu-based* representation paradigm along with *query by navigation* interaction style (cf. [13]) to let users join concepts via relationships connecting them; *W3* (see the bottom-right part of Fig. 1) is *form-based* and presents the attributes of a selected concept for *selection* and *projection* operations. W3 also has a *faceted search* flavour (cf. [14]), as it uses several natural interaction mechanisms, such as range sliders.

Query construction process in OptiqueVQS works as follows [4,5] – a demo is available[2]. The user begins with selecting a starting concept in W2, i.e., a

---

[2] http://youtu.be/ks5tcPZVHp0

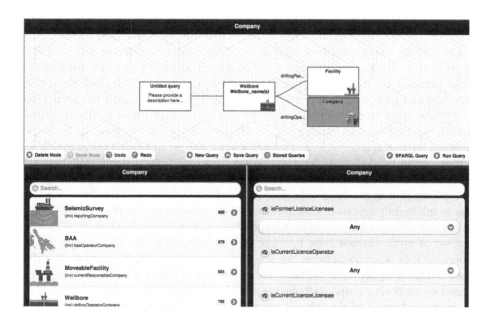

Fig. 1. OptiqueVQS – an example query is depicted

kernel concept, the selected concept appears in W1 as a typed *variable-node*, and becomes *active* (aka *focus, pivot* etc.). Then, the user can extend the query either by selecting one of the offered concept-property pairs in W2, i.e., concepts reachable from the pivot via some *object property*, or by setting constraints on *data type properties* or selecting output variables in W3, i.e., by restricting the data properties of the objects belonging to the pivot. W3 also handles *subclass* selection, as it presents direct subclasses of the pivot concept as a multi-select form element. The user can change the pivot by clicking on any variable-node in W1 and continue extending the query by selecting a concept-property pair in W2. OptiqueVQS automatically extends the list of concept-property pairs and data properties in W2 and W3 via the *HermiT reasoner* [15] (e.g., a concept inherits all the properties of its parent concept). The user can delete nodes, access query catalogue, save/load queries, undo/redo actions, or continue query construction in the textual SPARQL mode.

2.2 Formal Description

OptiqueVQS currently supports *linear* and *tree-shaped conjunctive* queries. The OBDA framework behind OptiqueVQS supports *OWL 2 QL* [16] and a conjunctive fragment of *SPARQL 1.1* [12]. OWL 2 QL is a *profile* of *OWL 2* and in this profile query answering can be implemented by rewriting queries into a standard relational query language [17].

The way the ontology controls the behaviour of OptiqueVQS should be seen from two perspectives: from a *knowledge representation (KR)* perspective, Optique exploits the graph-based organisation of ontological elements and data for representing the domain and query structures (cf. query by navigation); from a *logic* perspective, it uses ontological *axioms* to constrain the behaviour of the interface and to extend the available knowledge. On a purely structural level, OptiqueVQS could be controlled directly by a graph G that captures the concepts and the properties of an ontology O. An OWL ontology can be viewed as a *labeled directed* RDF graph $G = (N, E)$, where N is a finite set of labeled *nodes* and E is a finite set of labeled *edges* (cf. [17]). We consider pairwise disjoint alphabets U, a set of *URIs*, L, a set of *terminal literals*, and B, a set of *blank nodes*. An edge is a *triple* written in the form of $\langle s, p, o \rangle \in (U \cup B) \times U \times (U \cup L \cup B)$. The nodes of the graph mainly represent concepts and edges represent properties. A SPARQL query is formally represented by a tuple defined as $Q = (A, V, D, P, M, R)$. A is the set of *prefix declarations*, V is the *output form*, D is the *RDF graph* being queried, P is a *graph pattern*, M are *query modifiers*, which allow to modify the results by applying *projection, order, limit*, and *offset* options. SPARQL is based on matching graph patterns against RDF graphs. P is composed of a set of *triple patterns* and describes a *subgraph* of D. The main difference between a triple pattern and RDF triple comes from the fact that the former may have each of *subject, predicate* and *object* as a variable. However, once we substitute variables in triple patterns with constants or blank nodes, we reach an RDF graph $P'(N', E')$ that could be considered as a subgraph of the actual RDF data graph.

Every query generated by OptiqueVQS has a graph pattern represented by a set of triple patterns, where each triple pattern is a tuple $t \in Var \times U \times (U \cup Var \cup L)$ and Var is an infinite set of variables. The state of an edited query is composed of a partial graph pattern and a *cursor position* (cf. pivot). The cursor position is either blank (i.e., empty query) or points to a variable in the query. If the query is empty, the selection of a concept v from W2 results in a new tuple $\langle x, \texttt{rdf:type}, v \rangle \in Var \times U \times U$ in P, where x is a fresh variable. If the cursor points to a variable x, of type v, then each selection of a object property o with target class w from W1 (corresponding to an edge $\langle v, o, w \rangle \in G$) adds the following two triple patterns to P: $\langle x, o, y \rangle \in Var \times U \times Var$ and $\langle y, \texttt{rdf:type}, w \rangle \in Var \times U \times U$, where y is a fresh variable. Every selection and projection operation realised over a data property d in W3, while cursor is on a variable x, adds a new tuple $\langle x, d, y \rangle \in Var \times U \times (Var \cup L)$ to P. Finally, the selection of a subclass v for a typed variable x in W3 results in a new triple in P: $\langle x, \texttt{rdf:type}, v \rangle \in Var \times U \times U$.

3   Adaptive Query Formulation

Currently, the widgets W2 and W3 (see Fig. 1) present all the available concept-object property pairs and data properties to users respectively. However, the lists grow quickly due to *ontology size, number of relationships between concepts, sub-properties, inverse properties, inheritance of restrictions* etc. As the lists grow, the time required for a user to find elements of interest increases; therefore ranking ontology elements with respect to previously executed queries and suggesting highly ranked elements first as possible query continuations have potential to increase the efficiency of the users. The nature of OptiqueVQS requires suggestions to be done for the pivot (i.e., cursor point) rather than for any part of a query.

In what follows, we first present a running example and then describe our ranking method for context-aware suggestions. The running example is built on one of the industrial Optique use cases, namely the *Statoil* use case. Statoil[3] is a large international energy company focused on upstream oil and gas operations. The company reports that value creation processes could be improved considerably, if domain experts are to be able to access data on their own.

3.1   Running Example

The exploration department of Statoil has to find new hydrocarbon reserves in a cost effective way and ultimately the only way to prove the presence of a reserve is to drill an exploration well, which may consist of one or several well paths, i.e., wellbores. But since drilling is very expensive, it is important to maximise the chances of success. To do this, all available data from previous and ongoing exploration and production projects to extrapolate a model of the geology of a field, which then allows to anticipate the presence of hydrocarbon reserves.

A partial simplified ontology for Statoil exploration department is depicted in Fig. 2. The ontology currently contains 344 concepts, 148 object properties, 237 data properties, and 8190 axioms and it is yet to grow. In Fig. 3, an example query log with three queries is assumed for the sake of brevity. The first query, *Q1*, is the one that is depicted in Fig. 1 and asks for the names of wellbores with a drilling facility and a drilling company. The second query, *Q2*, asks for the content of all shallow wellbores that belongs to a well and has a drilling company of type operator. The final query, *Q3*, asks for the content of all exploration wellbores that has a fixed drilling facility and a drilling company.

In Fig. 3, *PQ* refers to an example partial query. The query in its incomplete form asks for all exploration wellbores with a drilling company; the cursor point is the variable of type exploration wellbore. At this point of query formulation session, the widgets W2 and W3 need to suggest the most relevant continuations, by comparing the partial query with the queries in the query log.

3.2   Ranking Method

A query log QL is basically a set of SPARQL queries: $QL = \{Q_1, Q_2, ..., Q_n\}$. We define a function p that takes a query Q as an input and returns its graph pattern P. We define S as a set suggestions $\{T_1, T_2, ..., T_m\}$. Each suggestion in S is a triple set T_i, which either contains two triples for W2 in the form of $\{\langle x, o, y \rangle \in Var \times U \times Var, \langle y, \texttt{rdf:type}, w \rangle \in Var \times U \times U\}$ or one triple for W3 in the form of $\{\langle x, d, y \rangle \in Var \times U \times (Var \cup L)\}$, where x corresponds to

---

[3] http://www.statoil.com/

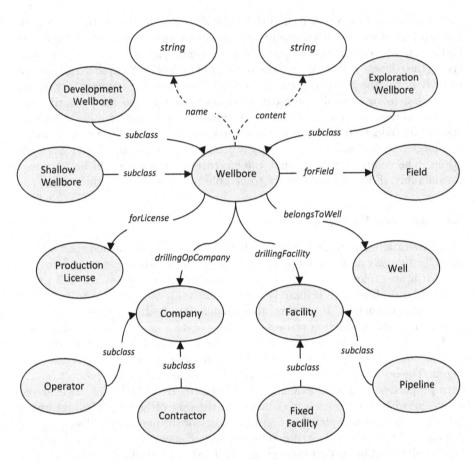

Fig. 2. A partial simplified ontology for the Statoil use case

the cursor variable in a partial user query Q_a. Note that subclass suggestion is not included in the ranking, since it is always suggested by default.

The ranking score, at this point, basically corresponds to the *conditional probability* for each suggestion T_i in S, given a partial query Q_a and a query log QL, that is $Pr(T_i \mid p(Q_a))$. Conditional probability and probability functions are defined in the followings.

Within a query log QL, the probability of a graph pattern P is defined as the fraction of graph patterns in QL that are *supergraphs* [18] of P, as shown in Eq. 1.

$$Pr(P) = \frac{|\{Q_i \in QL | P \subseteq p(Q_i)\}|}{|QL|} \tag{1}$$

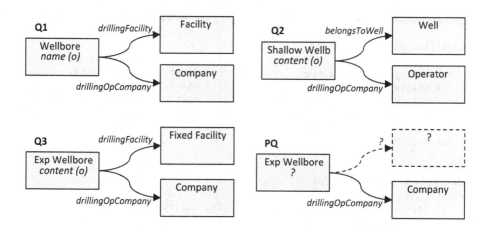

Fig. 3. A query log with three queries and an example partial user query

The conditional probability of a triple set T given a graph pattern P is defined as the quotient of the probability of the union of T and P, and the probability of P as shown in Eq. 2.

$$Pr(T \mid P) = \frac{Pr(T \cap P)}{Pr(P)} \tag{2}$$

Now two important questions come into play. First, how do we find super-graphs in the query log, given a partial user query? Second, how do we extract possible extensions, i.e., suggestions, for the partial query from found super-graphs? As far as the first problem is concerned, it boils down to a *graph match-ing* problem. We consider a graph pattern P_1 to be subgraph of another graph pattern P_2, if all the triple patterns of P_1 are covered by P_2, independent of variable names, ordering of triple patterns, and the values of constraints. Dividino and Groner [19] review different approaches for checking graph similarity, where our interest falls into *content-based* approaches. We propose a method that relies on SPARQL itself and provides us with an exhaustive solution, as it allows us to exploit semantic knowledge while matching queries.

The method starts with the instantiation of graph patterns of queries in the query log by replacing variable names and constraints on data type properties with blank nodes; blank node names are marked with a query identifier for preventing any overlap and identification purposes. Then, the resulted RDF graphs are stored in a common dedicated triple store; the instantiation of the query log depicted in Fig. 3 is given in Fig. 4. By applying the partial query over this triple store, one can retrieve all the queries that are the supergraphs of the partial query.

As far as the second question is concerned, i.e., finding possible extensions, the partial query is extended with a triple pattern from the cursor point to retrieve all extensions occurred in the matching supergraphs. The output of partial query

Query log: SPARQL form	Query log: triple form

Q1 SELECT DISTINCT ?c1 ?a1 ?c2 ?c3
WHERE {
  ?c1 ns1:type ns2:Wellbore.
  ?c2 ns1:type ns2:Facility.
  ?c3 ns1:type ns2:Company.
  ?c1 ns2:drillingFacility ?c2.
  ?c1 ns2:drillingOpCompany ?c3.
  ?c1 ns2:name ?a1.
}
	_:q1c1 ns1:type ns2:Wellbore.
	_:q1c2 ns1:type ns2:Facility.
	_:q1c3 ns1:type ns2:Company.
	_:q1c1 ns2:drillingFacility _:q1c2.
	_:q1c1 ns2:drillingOpCompany _:q1c3.
	_:q1c1 ns2:name _:q1a1.

Q2 SELECT DISTINCT ?c1 ?a1 ?c2 ?c3
WHERE {
  ?c1 ns1:type ns2:ShallowWellbore.
  ?c2 ns1:type ns2:Operator.
  ?c3 ns1:type ns2:Well.
  ?c1 ns2:drillingOpCompany ?c2.
  ?c1 ns2:belongsToWell ?c3.
  ?c1 ns2:wellboreContent ?a2.
}
	_:q2c1 ns1:type ns2:ShallowWellbore.
	_:q2c2 ns1:type ns2:Operator.
	_:q2c3 ns1:type ns2:Well.
	_:q2c1 ns2:drillingOpCompany _:q2c2.
	_:q2c1 ns2:belongsToWell _:q2c3 .
	_:q2c1 ns2:wellboreContent _:q2a1.

Q3 SELECT DISTINCT ?c1 ?a1 ?c2 ?c3
WHERE {
  ?c1 ns1:type ns2:ExpWellbore.
  ?c2 ns1:type ns2:Company.
  ?c3 ns1:type ns2:FixedFacility.
  ?c1 ns2:drillingOpCompany ?c2.
  ?c1 ns2:drillingFacility ?c3.
  ?c1 ns2:wellboreContent ?a1.
}
	_:q3c1 ns1:type ns2:ExpWellbore.
	_:q3c2 ns1:type ns2:Company.
	_:q3c3 ns1:type ns2:FixedFacility.
	_:q3c1 ns2:drillingOpCompany _:q3c2.
	_:q3c1 ns2:drillingFacility _:q3c3.
	_:q3c1 ns2:wellboreContent _:q3a1.

Fig. 4. The instantiation of query graph patterns

is modified to retrieve the identifiers of matching queries, properties, and the types of variables for the returned extension. An example is given in Fig. 5 for the partial query depicted in Fig. 3 and the triple store depicted in Fig. 4. The rest of the method involves calculation of conditional probabilities for the suggestions, as exemplified in Fig. 5.

If one inspects the results in Fig. 5 closely, she will realise that reasoning is involved. This is because in the query log, only Q3 is an exact match for the partial query. However, thanks to reasoning support, Q1 is also matched, since exploration wellbore is a subclass of wellbore. Likewise, this guarantees a match for any query that has a *semantic similarity* [20] to the partial query, involving subclasses, subproperties, inverses etc. Later in the paper, this is to be discussed further, as there is a *semantic distance* involved between the partial query and the matched query. Yet, it is possible to query the triple store without any reasoning, if one wants to eliminate such matches, hence avoiding any semantic distance.

Partial user query	Modified partial user query

`SELECT DISTINCT ?c1 ?c2`
`WHERE {`
`  ?c1 ns1:type ns2:ExpWellbore.`
`  ?c2 ns1:type ns2:Company.`
`  ?c1 ns2:drillingOpCompany ?c2.`
`}`
	`SELECT DISTINCT ?c3 ?prop ?type`
	`WHERE {`
	`  ?c1 ns1:type ns2:ExpWellbore.`
	`  ?c2 ns1:type ns2:Company.`
	`  ?c1 ns2:drillingOpCompany ?c2.`
	`  ?c1 ?prop ?c3.`
	`  OPTIONAL { ?c3 rdf:type ?type }`
	`}`

Matches

?c3		?prop	?type	Pr(T|P)	Widget
`_:q1c2`	T_1	`ns2:drillingFacility`	`ns2:Facility`	0.16	W2
`_:q1c3`	T_2	`ns2:drillingOpCompany`	`ns2:Company`	0.33	W2
`_:q1a1`	T_3	`ns2:name`		0.16	W3
`_:q3c2`	T_2	`ns2:drillingOpCompany`	`ns2:Company`		
`_:q3c3`	T_4	`ns2:drillingFacility`	`ns2:FixedFacility`	0.16	W2
`_:q3a1`	T_5	`ns2:wellboreContent`		0.16	W3

Fig. 5. Modified partial user query and possible query extensions

The final stage involves ordering and dividing S into two sets, S_1 for W2 and S_2 for W3, with respect to ranking score and type of each suggestion (i.e., concept-relationship pair vs. data type property). Then, suggestions in each set are paginated into $\frac{|S_i|}{j}$ pages, where i is the set identifier and j is the *window size* for a page (i.e., the required number of suggestions for a page).

4   Related Work

There are a number of visual query formulation tools available in the literature (e.g., [2,21,22,23]); however, to the best of authors knowledge none of them supports adaptive visual query formulation. Existing approaches for adaptive query formulation are largely developed for *context-sensitive* textual query formulation.

Khoussainova et al. [24] provide a system, named *SnipSuggest*, for context-aware composition of textual SQL queries with respect to a given query log. The authors translate each SQL query in the query log into a set of features (e.g., a table name appearing in the *FROM clause*). Similarly, the partial query of the user is also translated into a set of features. Possible features for extension are identified by matching the feature sets of the partial query and the feature sets of queries in the query log and are ranked by calculating conditional probabilities. The approach generates suggestions for extending any part of the partial query rather than a single cursor point. Authors also propose a set of supportive algorithms and techniques for, such as feature set matching (i.e., what if the partial query does not appear in the query log), the selection of suggestions (i.e., accuracy vs. diversity), and query log elimination (i.e., to reduce the size). The elaborate approach provided by SnipSuggest system is relevant to our contribution in many aspects. However, a fundamental difference is in feature comparison; while the features of SnipSuggest system are a set of syntactic elements and the feature comparison is string based, for OptiqueVQS feature sets (i.e., correspond to the triple sets of graph patterns) have a semantic nature and compared semantically. The semantic aspects not only concern how the matching is done, but also the calculation of rankings, which we discuss in the following section.

As far as approaches for SPARQL are concerned, Campinas et al. [25] propose an approach for assisting textual SPARQL query formulation, however in a different context. The approach assumes that an ontology describing the data set is unknown. Therefore, the authors propose a model that summarises the underlying data graph and extracts ontology elements to suggest. The approach extends a given partial user query from the cursor point, similar to our approach, and then evaluates it over the data graph summary to retrieve possible extensions. However, the approach does not realise any ranking of suggestions based on the previously executed queries and does not take semantic similarities between queries into account, possibly due to lack of rich domain knowledge (e.g., lack of subclass, inverse property axioms).

Kramer et al. [26] present a tool, named *SPACE*, to support autocompletion of textual SPARQL queries. For this purpose, it takes a SPARQL query log as an input and then builds an *index structure* for the computation of query suggestions. The index structure has a root node at level 0, representing a set of queries, while each vertex at level 1 represents a SPARQL query. The vertices from level $n - 2$ to index level 1 represent graph patterns recursively. Finally the vertices at the highest level ($n - 1$) represent IRIs, blank nodes, literals, variables, and binary operators such as *AND*, *UNION*, and *FILTER*. The suggestion process is done by subgraph matching for the partial user query in the index graph in a bottom up manner. However, the authors describe neither the subgraph matching process nor the details of ranking calculation. Finally, the index structure could grow quickly as it is built on recursive decomposition of graph patterns.

5   Discussion

The fact that there exist SPARQL engines capable of handling large triple sets effectively [27,28] is a positive evidence for the execution performance of our approach, since our proposal relies on SPARQL querying for matching partial user queries against a query log. One should also note that the size of a triple store for a query log is only expected to be in the order of thousands triples, if maintained – e.g., pruned, clustered etc.

As far as the *precision* of suggestions is concerned, approaches that take the partial query into account are reported to be better than *popularity-based* approaches purely built on the number of occurrences of terms in the query log [24].

Note that, initially, when no kernel concept is selected, our approach behaves like a popularity-based approach, as it extends an empty query. Below, we discuss a set of issues that need to be addressed:

Semantic distance: In Fig. 3, the match between the first query and partial query is due to their semantic similarity and is not exact (e.g., exploration wellbore is a subclass of wellbore); and in Fig. 5, the drillingFacility - Facility and drillingFacility - FixedFacility suggestions are semantically similar. Therefore one could incorporate the semantic distance involved as a cofactor into the ranking function, so that semantically distant queries contribute less to the ranking. Huang et al. [20] suggest a similarity measure, which can readily incorporated to our proposal. It uses the depth of compared concepts and properties and their least common ancestors from the root of hierarchy to compute similarity between concepts and properties and combine them to compute similarity between triple patterns, hence queries.

No match: A problematic situation arises when no match is found for the partial query in the query log (cf. [24]). A possible solution could be pruning the partial query until a match is found. At each step of a pruning process, a leaf node, which is not the cursor point, could be randomly selected and deleted (or with respect to some heuristics), so that partial query graph pattern does not get disconnected and the cursor point is preserved.

Cold start: The proposal cannot draw any suggestions, when the query log contains no or insufficient number of queries. Mostly likely sources to use for addressing this problem are the ontology and data set. A statistical inspection of ontology, e.g., concept centrality with respect to the number of incoming and outgoing relationships, and the data set, e.g., the number of times each concept and property appears in the dataset, could reveal useful information to overcome the cold start problem.

Collective, group, or individual: The ranking and suggestions could be applied on an individual basis for each user, i.e., only over the portion of query log that belongs to the subject user, on group basis, i.e., only over the portion of query log that belongs to the users of same type, and on a collective basis, i.e., over the whole query log for every user (cf. [11]). The decision possibly should consider whether users are homogeneous or there exist different user groups, each using a part of the ontology heavily – e.g., geologist and chemists. In the former case, a group or even user specific approach is more feasible, as each user group/user focuses on a specific part of the ontology.

6   Conclusion and Future Work

Ontology-based end-user visual query formulation is promising for enhancing value creation processes; yet existing approaches are not scalable against large ontologies. Although there are some attempts for assisted textual query formulation in the literature; they are either not elaborate enough to be readily used in our case or do not take previously executed queries into account. In this paper, we proposed a method for ranking and suggesting SPARQL query extensions, which relies on the partial user query, the queries in the query history, and their semantic similarity. We also identified notable issues to be addressed in order to reach an elaborate solution.

The future work involves comparative evaluation of the proposed method and its variants (e.g., with/without semantic similarity) in terms of precision. End-user studies are also planned to measure the *perceived usefulness*, i.e., whether in practice users find ranking approach useful or not.

Acknowledgements. This research is funded by the FP7 of the European Commission under Grant Agreement 318338, "Optique".

References

1. Giese, M., Calvanese, D., Horrocks, I., Ioannidis, Y., Klappi, H., Koubarakis, M., Lenzerini, M., Moller, R., Ozcep, O., Rodriguez Muro, M., Rosati, R., Schlatte, R., Soylu, A., Waaler, A.: Scalable End-user Access to Big Data. In: Rajendra, A. (ed.) Big Data Computing. Chapman and Hall/CRC (2013)
2. Catarci, T., Costabile, M.F., Levialdi, S., Batini, C.: Visual query systems for databases: A survey. Journal of Visual Languages and Computing 8(2), 215–260 (1997)
3. Lieberman, H., Paternó, F., Klann, M., Wulf, V.: End-User Development: An Emerging Paradigm. In: Lieberman, H., Paternó, F., Wulf, V. (eds.) End-User Development. Human-Computer Interaction Series, vol. 9, pp. 1–8. Springer, Netherlands (2006)
4. Soylu, A., Giese, M., Jimenez-Ruiz, E., Kharlamov, E., Zheleznyakov, D., Horrocks, I.: OptiqueVQS – Towards an Ontology-based Visual Query System for Big Data. In: Proceedings of the International Conference on Management of Emergent Digital EcoSystems (MEDES 2013), pp. 119–126. ACM (2013)
5. Soylu, A., Skjæveland, M., Giese, M., Horrocks, I., Jimenez-Ruiz, E., Kharlamov, E., Zheleznyakov, D.: A Preliminary Approach on Ontology-based Visual Query Formulation for Big Data. In: Garoufallou, E., Greenberg, J. (eds.) MTSR 2013. CCIS, vol. 390, pp. 201–212. Springer, Heidelberg (2013)
6. Siau, K.L., Chan, H.C., Wei, K.K.: Effects of query complexity and learning on novice user query performance with conceptual and logical database interfaces. IEEE Transactions on Systems, Man and Cybernetics - Part A: Systems and Humans 34(2), 276–281 (2004)
7. Spanos, D.E., Stavrou, P., Mitrou, N.: Bringing relational databases into the Semantic Web: A survey. Semantic Web 3(2), 169–209 (2012)
8. Kogalovsky, M.R.: Ontology-Based Data Access Systems. Programming and Computer Software 38(4), 167–182 (2012)
9. Katifori, A., Halatsis, C., Lepouras, G., Vassilakis, C., Giannopoulou, E.: Ontology visualization methods - A survey. ACM Computing Surveys 39(4), 10:1–10:43 (2007)
10. Grau, B.C., Giese, M., Horrocks, I., Hubauer, T., Jimenez-Ruiz, E., Kharlamov, E., Schmidt, M., Soylu, A., Zheleznyakov, D.: Towards Query Formulation and Query-Driven Ontology Extensions in OBDA Systems. In: Proceedings of the 10th OWL: Experiences and Directions Workshop (OWLED 2013). CEUR Workshop Proceedings, vol. 1080. CEUR-WS.org (2013)

11. Brusilovsky, P., Kobsa, A., Nejdl, W. (eds.): Adaptive Web 2007. LNCS, vol. 4321. Springer, Heidelberg (2007)
12. Harris, S., Seaborne, A.: SPARQL 1.1 Query Language. W3C Recommendation, W3C (March 2013)
13. Ter Hofstede, A.H.M., Proper, H.A., Van Der Weide, T.P.: Query formulation as an information retrieval problem. Computer Journal 39(4), 255–274 (1996)
14. Tunkelang, D., Marchionini, G.: Faceted Search. Synthesis Lectures on Information Concepts, Retrieval, and Services. Morgan and Claypool Publishers (2009)
15. Motik, B., Shearer, R., Horrocks, I.: Hypertableau Reasoning for Description Logics. Journal of Artificial Intelligence Research 36(1), 165–228 (2009)
16. Motik, B., Grau, B.C., Horrocks, I., Wu, Z., Fokoue, A., Lutz, C.: OWL 2 Web Ontology Language Profiles. W3C Recommendation, W3C (October 2009)
17. Grau, B.C., Horrocks, I., Motik, B., Parsia, B., Patel-Schneider, P., Sattler, U.: OWL 2: The Next Step for OWL. Web Semantics: Science, Services and Agents on the World Wide Web 6(4), 309–322 (2008)
18. Ray, S.S.: Subgraphs, Paths, and Connected Graphs. In: Graph Theory with Algorithms and its Applications. Springer India (2013)
19. Dividino, R., Groner, G.: Which of the following SPARQL Queries are Similar? Why? In: Proceedings of the 1st International Workshop on Linked Data for Information Extraction (LD4IE 2013). CEUR Workshop Proceedings, vol. 1057. CEUR-WS.org (2013)
20. Huang, H., Liu, C., Zhou, X.: Computing Relaxed Answers on RDF Databases. In: Bailey, J., Maier, D., Schewe, K.-D., Thalheim, B., Wang, X.S. (eds.) WISE 2008. LNCS, vol. 5175, pp. 163–175. Springer, Heidelberg (2008)
21. Catarci, T., Dongilli, P., Di Mascio, T., Franconi, E., Santucci, G., Tessaris, S.: An ontology based visual tool for query formulation support. In: Proceedings of the 16th Eureopean Conference on Artificial Intelligence (ECAI 2004). Frontiers in Artificial Intelligence and Applications, vol. 110, pp. 308–312. IOS Press (2004)
22. Kapetanios, E., Baer, D., Groenewoud, P.: Simplifying syntactic and semantic parsing of NL-based queries in advanced application domains. Data & Knowledge Engineering 55(1), 38–58 (2005)
23. Barzdins, G., Liepins, E., Veilande, M., Zviedris, M.: Ontology Enabled Graphical Database Query Tool for End-Users. In: Proceedings of the 8th International Baltic Conference on Databases and Information Systems (DB&IS 2008). Frontiers in Artificial Intelligence and Applications, vol. 187, pp. 105–116. IOS Press (2009)
24. Khoussainova, N., Kwon, Y., Balazinska, M., Suciu, D.: SnipSuggest: Context-aware Autocompletion for SQL. Proceedings of the VLDB Endowment 4(1), 22–33 (2010)
25. Campinas, S., Perry, T.E., Ceccarelli, D., Delbru, R., Tummarello, G.: Introducing RDF Graph Summary with Application to Assisted SPARQL Formulation. In: Proceedings of the 23rd International Workshop on Database and Expert Systems Applications (DEXA 2012), pp. 261–266. IEEE (2012)
26. Kramer, K., Dividino, R., Groner, G.: SPACE: SPARQL Index for Efficient Autocompletion. In: Proceedings of the ISWC 2013 Posters & Demonstrations Track (ISWC-PD 2013). CEUR Workshop Proceedings, vol. 1035. CEUR-WS.org (2013)
27. Schmidt, M., Hornung, T., Lausen, G., Pinkel, C.: SP^{2}Bench: A SPARQL Performance Benchmark. In: Proceedings of the IEEE International Conference on Data Engineering (ICDE 2009), pp. 222–233. IEEE Computer Society (2009)
28. Bizer, C., Schultz, A.: The Berlin SPARQL Benchmark. International Journal on Semantic Web and Information Systems 5(2), 1–24 (2009)

Approach for Instance-Based Ontology Alignment: Using Argument and Event Structures of Generative Lexicon

Abderrahmane Khiat and Moussa Benaissa

LITIO Lab, University of Oran, B.P 1524 El M'Naouar 31000, Oran, Algeria
abderrahmane_khiat@yahoo.com,
moussabenaissa@yahoo.fr

Abstract. Ontology alignment became a very important problem to ensure semantic interoperability for different sources of information heterogeneous and distributed. Instance-based ontology alignment represents a very promising technique to find semantic correspondences between entities of different ontologies when they contain a lot of instances. In this paper, we describe a new approach to manage ontologies that do not share common instances. This approach extracts the argument and event structures from a set of instances of the concept of the source ontology and compared them with other semantic features extracted from a set of instances of the concept of the target ontology using Generative Lexicon Theory. We show that it is theoretically powerful because it is based on *linguistic semantics* and useful in practice. We present the experimental results obtained by running our approach on Biblio test of Benchmark[1] series of OAEI[2] 2011. The results show the good performance of our approach.

Keywords: Instance-Based Ontology Alignment, Generative Lexicon Theory, Ontology Matching, Semantic Interoperability, Semantic Web.

1   Introduction

Ontology alignment, is defined as the process of identification of semantic correspondences between entities of different ontologies to be aligned [1], is prerequisite and necessary for a better understanding and interactions between not only people but also software agents [2]. It likewise represents the solution to the problem of semantic interoperability between different sources of distributed information.

The work proposed in this article is in the context of extensional alignment i.e. instance-based ontology alignment. In fact, when ontologies contain a lot of instances there is a very good opportunity to use the extensions of concepts in order to align them using instance-based techniques. In practice, two situations may arise in terms of sharing instances between ontologies to align [4]. When they have common instances, it is recommended to use metrics, such as JACCARD metric [1], which evaluates the overlap of

---

[1] http://oaei.ontologymatching.org/2011/benchmarks.

[2] OAEI (Ontology Alignment Evaluation Initiative) organizes evaluation campaigns aiming at evaluating ontology matching technologies. http://oaei.ontologymatching.org/

S. Closs et al. (Eds.): MTSR 2014, CCIS 478, pp. 120–127, 2014.

instances between concepts, and these concepts are considered similar when their overlap is important [7]. In contrast, when ontologies do not share or share few instances, one generally proceeds to aggregate the information of instances between concepts to align.

Contrary to our approach, the approaches that use the technique of similarity based on WordNet to calculate the similarities between the instances, has a disadvantage that is you can lose the similarity because of *distinct meanings of a word i.e. distinct meanings of a lexical token correspond to distinct lexical tokens*, if we based only on WordNet, especially to calculate the similarities between the instances *that are complex i.e.* the instances which are composed of several propositions.

The approach that we propose in this paper fits into the category of instance-based ontology-alignment methods when the ontologies to align do not have many common instances (these instances can be words or labels sentences), which makes the task of identifying the semantic relation between concepts very difficult. Our approach consists to extract the *argument structure* and *event structure* (*semantic features*) described in Generative Lexicon Theory of Pustejovsky 1995, from a set of asserted instances which are definitely share a set of argument and event structures (semantic features) of a concept of the source ontology.

Our approach aims to *strengthen the similarity*; and can also resolve the problem of *ambiguity*. This set of common semantic features (argument and event structures) presented in a document will be compared with semantic features of a concept of the target ontology. Finally we combine these similarities with similarities calculated by WordNet.

The rest of the paper is organized as follows. First, we present a background in Section 2, and related work is presented in Section 3 on existing approaches. Section 4 describes our contribution, and Section 5 presents the experimental results of our system. Section 6 contains concluding remarks and sets directions for future work.

2   The Generative Lexicon Theory

The Generative Lexicon [16] is a promising approach, it consists to explain the semantics of all the lexical units in context. Pustejovsky proposes to associate with each lexical unit four distinct levels of representation to capture the semantics of the words:

- *Lexical Typing Structure*: giving an explicit type for a word positioned within in a type system for the language i.e. organizes lexical concepts in network.
- *Argument Structure*: indicating the predicative structure of the word i.e. specifying the number and nature of the arguments to a predicate.
- *Event Structure*: indicating the type of event: state, transition.
- *Qualia Structure*: a structural differentiation of the predicative force for a lexical item, which decomposes itself into four roles:
  - *Formal*: the basic category of which distinguishes the meaning of a word within a larger domain.
  - *Constitutive*: the relation between an object and its constituent parts.
  - *Telic*: the purpose or function of the object, if there is one.
  - *Agentive*: the factors involved in the object's origins or "coming into being".

This approach seeks to analyze the meaning of a word by decomposing it into different facets that constrain the way it combines with others in a sentence [16].

3 Related Work

Recently, instance-based alignment has become a promising family of solutions to find semantic relations among concepts of ontologies. There are two main categories [4] for instance-based ontology alignment: approaches in the presence of common instances [7] and approaches in the absence of common instances such as RiMOM [5, 6], GLUE [9], CSA [15] and others (such as MAFRA, LSD, COMA++). We present below the principle of CSA system which has been the object of a comparison with our system.

CSA [15]: is an acronym of **C**luster-based **S**imilarity **A**ggregation for Ontology Matching. The principle of CSA is to calculate the similarity between the content of instances using WordNet-based similarity metric with other similarity measures.

This approach uses WordNet-based similarity to calculate similarities between instances. It does not work well when instances are complex and do not use the same vocabulary to describe entities.

When ontologies contain disjoint instances, most of the ontology alignment approaches proceed generally, to aggregate the information of the instances by building a document containing these information; using machine learning techniques; methods of calculating similarities or using external resources such as documents.

Contrary to CSA approach and many other approaches which use the WordNet similarity metric, the values of similarities become small between concepts that contain complex instances (the instances which are composed of several propositions) because of the *distinct meanings of a word i.e. distinct meanings of a lexical token correspond to distinct lexical tokens*, which is the case in *the instances descriptions of the real word*, i.e. the textual content of WebPages.

4 Our Ontology Alignment Approach

The approach that we propose in this paper, is situated in *linguistic-knowledge-based methods to resolve the problem of ontology alignment when the ontologies to align do not share the same instances*. Our approach consists first to extract the argument and

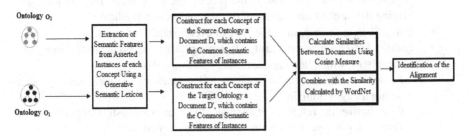

Fig. 1. Process of our Ontology Alignment Approach

event structures using the generative lexicon, from each instance of a concept of the source ontology, and the common semantic features will be grouped in a document. Then this document will be compared with another document that contains the semantic features of instances of a target concept combined with Wordnet in order to *strengthen the similarity*; these semantic features can also resolve the problem of *ambiguity*.

The main contribution of our approach is that the comparison of instances is done at a higher level of abstraction i.e. the semantic features have a single annotation which are truly reflects what those concepts of the ontologies to align really refer to in practice. We summarize the process of our approach in Fig.1. It consists in the following successive steps:

4.1   Step 1: Extraction of Semantic Features

In this step, it consists to extract the argument structure and event structure for each instance of a concept of the source ontology based on Pustejovsky model "the generative lexicon" that uses two aspects: the relational model (WordNet) and compositional semantics. We rely on this model for extracting the semantic features in order to identify a better selection of the semantic correspondences in both cases, i.e. in order to *strengthen the similarity* or resolving the *ambiguity*.

We justify the use of this linguistic-knowledge information by the following two points:

1- Difficulty to explicit the link between the lexical entries, while the link is often easily noticeable.
2- Knowledge (without "the generative lexicon") generates ambiguity in the lexicon.

We use our approach by extracting the argument and event structures using the generative lexicon on the one hand, from asserted instances which are necessarily shared common semantic features on the other hand, we can strengthen *the similarity* or resolving the *ambiguity*.

To resolve the problem of *strengthen the similarity* or *ambiguity* depends also on the number of asserted instances i.e. get more semantic features.

Argument structure and Event structure

1. Argument Structure
Example1: John eats an apple   **Example2**: I butter my tartine

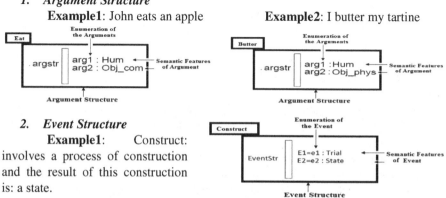

2. Event Structure
Example1:   Construct: involves a process of construction and the result of this construction is: a state.

Our approach extracts semantic features: the argument structure (jean: human, apple: comestible object, I: human, tartine: physic object) and event structure (trial and state) like presented in the examples above and be regrouped in a documents.

4.2   Step 2: Construction of the Document

In this step, it consists to construct for each concept of the source and target ontology, a document contain all common semantic features extracted in the previous step.

4.3   Step 3: Calculation of Similarities

In this step, we apply the document-based metric such as the COSINE measure (1) to calculate the similarities between the documents that represent the concepts.

$$cos(d_j, d_k) = \frac{\vec{d_j} \cdot \vec{d_k}}{|\vec{d_j}|.|\vec{d_k}|} = \frac{\sum_{i=1}^n w_{i,j}.w_{i,k}}{\sqrt{\sum_{i=1}^m w_{i,j}^2}\sqrt{\sum_{i=1}^n w_{i,k}^2}} \tag{1}$$

Where $w_{i,j}$ is the weight of term i in document j, such as calculated by the method tf.idf, m and n are the numbers of the respective terms of the two documents.

4.4   Step 4: Identification of Alignment

In this step, we identify the semantic correspondences by exploiting similarities calculated in the previous step with similarities calculated by WordNet. Our method was combined with other alignment methods with the average aggregation strategy (Fig. 2 (b)). We selected a threshold s to operate the filter and realize the selection of correspondences.

5   Evaluation

5.1   Illustrative Example

To test our approach we need to obtain the information to identify the set of semantic features of each word component instance. However, as there is no lexicon available annotated with this information, we need to get this lexicon from large text corpora.

1)   Resolve the problem of ambiguity
Example:

    1. E1= A fast decision.   2. E2= A fast car.
    3. E3= A fast track.   4. E4= A fast secretary.

If we compare each instance with WordNet Table .1 we find the similarities between these instances is very close, which mean we can resolve the ambiguity problem with WordNet but with our approach we find that the similarities are reduced (which means that these sentences are not the same) because these instances do not have the same argument and event structure of generative lexicon (the column of Argument and Event structure in Table. 1). The mean of each instance: E1= that quickly takes, E2=rolling quickly, E3=that can go faster drive, E4= that works quickly.

Table 1. Ambiguity Problem

Matching each instance	WordNet Similarity	Our Approach Similarity	Argument and Event structure
E1, E2	0,5	0,25	E1 (action), E2 (physic object)
E1, E3	0,65	0,40	E1 (action), E3 (way)
E1, E4	0,5	0,18	E1 (action), E4 (Human, animated)
E2, E3	0,65	0,40	E2 (physic object), E3 (way)
E2, E4	0,7	0,40	E2 (physic object), E4 (Human, animated)
E3, E4	0,6	0,35	E3 (way), E4 (Human, animated)

2) Resolve the problem of strengthen the similarity
Example:
1. E1= Ali began to read a book.   2. E2= The professor began to write an item.
3. E3= I began to reread the newspaper. 4. E4= The students began to write an article.

If we compare each instance with WordNet Table .2 we find the similarities between these instances is small, but with our approach we can **strengthen the similarity** because these instances do have the same argument and event structures ((the column of Argument and Event structure in Table. 2) of generative lexicon.

Table 2. Problem of Strengthen the Similarity

Matching each instances	WordNet Similarity	Our Approach Similarity	Argument and Event structure
E1, E2	0,32	0,55	E1=E2 (human ,animated, physic object)
E1, E3	0,40	0,68	E1=E3 (human ,animated, physic object)
E1, E4	0,45	0,70	E1=E4 (human ,animated, physic object)
E2, E3	0,26	0,46	E2=E3 (human ,animated, physic object)
E2, E4	0,48	0,71	E2=E4 (human ,animated, physic object)
E3, E4	0,41	0,64	E3=E4 (human ,animated, physic object)

5.2   Evaluation Metrics

To evaluate the performance of our system we have used the standard metrics that are the precision, recall and F-measure. These measures of are defined as follows:

$$\text{Precision} = P(A, R) = \frac{|R \cap A|}{|A|} \quad \text{Recall} = R(A, R) = \frac{|R \cap A|}{|R|} \quad \text{F-measure} = \frac{2 * \text{Recall} * \text{Precision}}{\text{Recall} + \text{Precision}}$$

Where |R| is the number of correspondences of the reference alignment and |A| is the number of correspondences found by our approach. The results obtained are shown below.

5.3   Experimental Results

We tested our approach using the ontologies of biblio test of benchmark track obtained from OAEI 2011 Campaign. We compared our approach with the similarities calculated by WordNet.

The figure (Fig. 2) summarizes the results obtained in the comparison of our approach successively with similarities calculated by WordNet (Fig. 2 (a)); and CSA system[3] (Fig. 2 (b)) participated in OAEI 2011, which use WordNet matcher on biblio test.

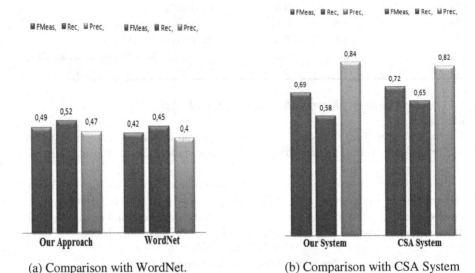

(a) Comparison with WordNet.   (b) Comparison with CSA System

Fig. 2. Comparison of Our Approach

The experimental results show that:

1) The results of our approach are better than the similarities calculated using WordNet (Fig. 2 (a)) in terms of precision, recall and F-measure.
2) The results of our system are better than CSA system (Fig. 2 (b)) in term of precision but less good in term of recall.

Our approach seems promising using the argument and event structures, and the results show the reliability and efficiency of the proposed method.

6   Conclusion

In this article, we introduce a new linguistic-knowledge-based approach for instance-based ontology alignment. Our solution is very useful to identifying semantic correspon-

---

[3] http://oaei.ontologymatching.org/2011/results/benchmarks/
biblio-benchmarks-r1.html.

dences between concepts of different ontologies when they do not share common instances.

Our approach consists to extract the argument structure and event structure (semantic features) from asserted instances that describe a concept, then a document is constructed which contain the common semantic features of all instances of this concept. The document of this concept of the source ontology will be compared with another document of a concept of the target ontology using the cosine measure then we combined with similarities calculated by WordNet similarity measure.In addition, we have implemented a platform in order to test our approach.

As future perspectives of our work, we envision to intensify the evaluation of our approach, and a better exploitation of the semantic features, in future we envision to use the *Qualia Structure of the lexicon generative* in our approach.

References

1. Euzenat, J., Shvaiko, P.: Ontology Alignment. Springer, Heidelberg (2013)
2. Ehrig, M.: Ontology Alignment: Bridging the Semantic Gap. Springer (2007)
3. Schopman, B., Wang, S., Isaac, A., Schlobach, S.: Instance-Based Ontology Alignment by Instance Enrichment. Springer, Vrije Universiteit Amsterdam, Netherlands (2012)
4. Rahm, E.: Towards large-scale schema and ontology Alignment. ReCALL (2011)
5. Wang, Z., Zhang, X., Hou, L., Zhao, Y., Li, J., Qi, Y., Tang, J.: Rimom: a dynamic multistrategy ontology alignment framework. OAEI (2010)
6. Li, J., Tang, J., Li, Y., Luo, Q.: Rimom: a dynamic multistrategy ontology alignment framework. IEEE Trans. Knowl. (2009)
7. Bouquet, P., Euzenat, J., Franconi, E., Serafini, L., Stamou, G., Tessaris, S.: Specification of a common framework for characterizing alignment (2004)
8. Maedche, A., Motik, B., Silva, N., Volz, R.: Mafra – A mapping framework for distributed ontologies. In: Gómez-Pérez, A., Benjamins, V.R. (eds.) EKAW 2002. LNCS (LNAI), vol. 2473, pp. 235–250. Springer, Heidelberg (2002)
9. Doan, A., Madhavan, J., Domingos, P., Halevy, A.: Ontology Alignment: a machine learning approach. Springer, Berlin (2004)
10. Stumme, G., Maedche, A.: Fca-merge: bottom-up merging of ontologies. In: Proceedings of the 17th International Conference on Artificial Intelligence (IJCAI 2001), Seattle (2001)
11. Zaiss, K.S.: Instance-based ontology Alignment and the evaluation of Alignment systems. Ph.D. thesis, Heinrich Heine Universität Düsseldorf (2010)
12. Todorov, K., Geibel, P., Kühnberger, K.-U.: Mining concept similarities for heterogeneous ontologies. In: Perner, P. (ed.) ICDM 2010. LNCS (LNAI), vol. 6171, pp. 86–100. Springer, Heidelberg (2010)
13. Tellier, I.: Introduction au TALN et à l'ingénierie linguistique (2012)
14. Pustejovsky, J., Boguraev, B.: Lexical Knowledge Representation and Natural Language Processing. In: Artificial Intelligence (1993)
15. Tran, Q., Ichise, R., Ho, B.: Cluster-based Similarity Aggregation for Ontology Matching (2011)
16. Pustejovsky, J.: The Generative Lexicon. MIT Press, Cambridge (1996)

Facets and Typed Relations as Tools for Reasoning Processes in Information Retrieval

Winfried Gödert

Cologne University of Applied Sciences, Institute of Information Science, Cologne, Germany
`winfried.goedert@fh-koeln.de`

Abstract. Faceted arrangement of entities and typed relations for representing different associations between the entities are established tools in knowledge representation. In this paper, a proposal is being discussed combining both tools to draw inferences along relational paths. This approach may yield new benefit for information retrieval processes, especially when modeled for heterogeneous environments in the Semantic Web. Faceted arrangement can be used as a selection tool for the semantic knowledge modeled within the knowledge representation. Typed relations between the entities of different facets can be used as restrictions for selecting them across the facets.

Keywords: Knowledge representation, Facets, Typed relations, Inferences, Information retrieval.

1   Introduction

Knowledge representation regarded as information retrieval tool has to find solutions for representing knowledge elements beneficial for human use. Traditional indexing languages are strongly oriented towards a cognitive interpretation of their content representatives, the entities. This interpretation is primarily based on the user's knowledge and formally supported only by providing some different types of relationships between the entities. Normally, no formal definition of an entity is given, e.g. by assembling the set of content characterizing attributes. Assigned relationships between terms have to be verified mainly by plausibility. Likewise, no criteria are provided for the attributes that have been chosen for the decision to establish just these and no other relationships.

Due to these circumstances, the represented knowledge usually can only be retrieved based on the entities. Inference processes along the relational paths cannot be performed. Only forms of drill down searches supported by the hierarchical structure of the knowledge representation can sometimes be processed. The quality of the result sets strongly depends on the transitivity of the established hierarchies, a formal property that cannot always be taken for granted [3], [5], [18]. In this respect, indexing languages differ from knowledge structures built upon the principles of formal knowledge representations and that are seen as basis for semantic statements in Semantic Web environments.

S. Closs et al. (Eds.): MTSR 2014, CCIS 478, pp. 128–140, 2014.
© Springer International Publishing Switzerland 2014

We make a proposal for combining the two approaches in order to build retrieval systems with enhanced power. The aim is to discriminate a specific documents' *aboutness*[1] as far as its *a posteriori* content is regarded. Part of this proposal is the compatibility between a human understanding of the knowledge represented and to ensure the formal correctness of reasoning along the relational paths by machine inferences. The main methodological tools are faceted representation of entities, typed relations between the entities, and inferences along the relational paths.

We start the discussion by presenting a short summary of essentials necessarily to be observed for the task of indexing understood as a statement about a documents' content, its aboutness.

2   Aboutness and Indexing

Providing index terms can only be justified if the corresponding concepts are covered issues within the context of the document. Generally, this cannot be seen only with respect to isolated terms. Every concept is part of a semantic context and may be treated in syntactic connections to other concepts. The sum of all covered concepts and their embedding into semantic or syntactic relationships may be seen as the documents' aboutness. Indexing should represent this aboutness by means of a knowledge representation containing conceptual entities and semantic relationships between them. We will discuss the requirements to be observed when solving some nontrivial indexing and retrieval tasks.

The semantic context gives rise for the establishment of *a priori* relationships between the elements of an indexing language. Usually there are three types of relationships, *synonymy*, *hierarchy*, and *association*. The decision, which type of relationship should be established between two concepts is based on an intellectual content analysis of the concepts. Formal characteristics are usually not given, neither for the content definition of the elements nor for the relationships. Consequently, the decision whether an element should be used to represent a part of the documents' aboutness as an index term is also based on the elements' content by intellectual interpretation.

A posteriori relationships specify the context of the content elements on a second level. An identical sum of concepts may constitute a different aboutness if they are connected by different syntactical relationships. For example, one may represent the role 'to be an agent of an action' or 'to be the object of an action'. Up-to-now, there is a controversial discussion about the extent to which one should deal with this type of relationships. Their total amount is too large for including them all into indexing and retrieval environments. Furthermore, as precision tools they require additional effort.

Our concern is to discuss some characteristic features of the aboutness and its representation by the semantic features of an indexing language. We give some simple examples. Let us assume we are interested in *all* documents on *songbirds*. One may think that processing such a search only requires a single index term, e.g. *singing*

---

[1] We prefer to use the term aboutness instead of content, subject, or topic; cf. http://www.iva.dk/bh/core concepts in lis/articles a-z/aboutness.htm

birds to retrieve a complete result set. But there are documents about songbird species that have been indexed by a more specific index term, e.g. *titmice*. Ideally, the knowledge structure for the index terms represents such connections by hierarchical relationships. Automatically collecting the set of all entries along the hierarchical trail could help to generate the complete result set for *songbirds*. The success of such an approach depends on the inheritance of characteristics, in other words, the hierarchical relationship must fulfill the property of transitivity.

Our second example is described by topics that require more than one term as result of a form of coordinate indexing and as search terms for post-coordinate retrieval, e.g. combining the terms by Boolean operators or other syntactical devices. To give an impression, our aforementioned example could be enhanced to the topic *migratory behavior of songbirds*. This case would require that *migration behavior* as well as *singing birds* have been indexed and that they can be searched in combination.

Much more crucial is the type of topics represented by the third example, *songbirds with migratory instinct*. In this case, *migratory instinct* shall not be a covered topic, so it may not have been indexed for the documents to be found. *Migratory instinct* is only a constraining property for selecting the appropriate species of songbirds. There exist a lot of songbird species without such a behavior. Therefore, *migratory instinct* has to be modeled as a constraint for selecting the appropriate entities of the knowledge representation for subsequently generating the result set.

We can generalize our example to the key question: how should such constraints be represented in a knowledge representation in order to benefit indexing and to support inference mechanisms in retrieval environments? We will come back to the example and its generalization in Section 5.

3   Indexing and Facets

Basic tool for intellectual indexing is a structured collection of controlled terms. The concepts of such an indexing language are usually arranged according to their characteristics as determined by intellectual analysis. For building proper hierarchies over several stages of the relational paths, inheritance of these characteristics should be observed. This means that each hierarchically subordinated concept has all characteristics of the parent concept and at least one more. This requirement can best be met by avoiding poly-hierarchies or poly-dimensional connections. This especially means that the additional features must originate from a common aspect area or a certain categorical facet. If the generic context for the determination of characteristics is changed, poly-hierarchies become unavoidable and the result most commonly is a pre-combined conceptual ordering with insufficiently expressed criteria.

As an example one can consider the following terms: table, wooden table, glass table, kitchen table, living room table, art nouveau table, desk, changing table, side table. Any attempt to organize these concepts – or even an extension – into a single hierarchy must fail because of the reasons stated. Therefore, a subordination by changing aspects, as it is often found in pre-combined classifications or thesauri with extensive use of conceptual composition (e.g. by using compound nouns), cannot be a suitable condition for drawing conclusions by relational inferences.

To support inferences we need a faceted structure preserving the generic contexts within each hierarchy string. It is commonly agreed that a faceted arrangement of knowledge elements supports best the requirements for indexing and retrieval [2]. Using faceted indexing terms for representing the documents' aboutness allows to specify each content component at the desired level of granularity without ignoring the structural requirements of building transitive relational paths. Figure 1 may serve as a visualization of a faceted structure suitable for the topic: *Illustrated book of European songbirds*, composed by subjects of three aspects.

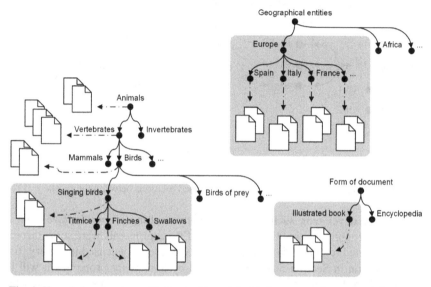

Fig. 1. Knowledge structure with facets, hierarchical inferences and associated documents

Such an arrangement has strong advantages for establishing proper hierarchies that avoid ambiguities. Connections established by common cultural use, scientific tradition, or statistical co-occurrences may be seen as beneficial but cannot be expressed by relationships within the facets. Integrating a topic like *European songbirds with migratory instinct* as a single entity would create a pre-combined knowledge structure with poly-dimensional connections between the entities. It cannot be properly connected to the entities of only one facet without violating the requirements of transitivity and transparency of the resulting structure. We have to find another solution to represent such topics by the entities and the structural features of a knowledge representation.

4   Facets and Typed Relations

The conceptual parts of our example can be differentiated into faceted components. One facet may be characterized as a taxonomical facet (*songbirds*) and a second one as a behavioral facet (*migratory instinct*). The connection between both facets can be represented by a relationship specified as a type of association from an inventory of typed relationships. The general pattern of such connections is given in Figure 2 with an exemplification of three types of associative relationships between the hierarchical organized entities of four facets.

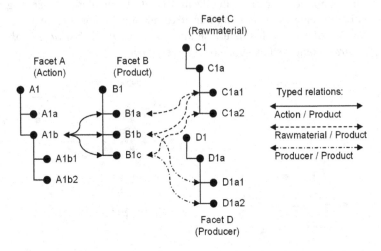

Fig. 2. Faceted systematic structure with typed relations between the facets

Analyses for developing such inventories with resulting proposals have been reported in the literature, e.g. in [12], [19]. Basis of these proposals were some theoretical studies reported for example in [8], [17]. We will use a condensed inventory [6, 7] for our discussion in Section 5. If characterized by transitivity properties it will become possible to draw inferences along the paths of typed associative relationships between entities of different facets and not only for entities connected by hierarchical relationships. In this way we want to demonstrate the potential of combining faceted structures with inferences along the paths of combinations of different typed relations.

5   Typed Relations and Inferences

Rule-based (formal) reasoning is supported by inferences about the underlying knowledge. For indexing and retrieval, this knowledge is given by the entities and the structure between them. Both elements, the indexed entities and also the relationships between them should therefore be used to form result sets.

Within our approach we distinguish two types of filter processes. One type allows drawing inferences on the *a priori* statements modeled in the knowledge representation. The second type is applied to the results of an indexing process representing the *a posteriori* statements of a document. This second type is the more common one, typically realized by the use of Boolean operators or other syntactical devices.

Figure 3 gives a visualization of the requirements for the first process by using abstract labels. This illustration stresses the importance of structural properties of such knowledge representations instead of only interpreting the content of the semantic entities intellectually. The labels should be read as follows:

- E_jF^i – Entity j in Facet i
- E_jxF^i – Entity in Facet i that is in a *is a* relationship to E_jF^i, $x \in \{a\text{-}z\}$
- E_jxyF^i – Entity in Facet i that is in a *is a* relationship to E_jxF^i, $x \in \{a\text{-}z\}$, $y \in \{a\text{-}z\}$
- Rel_i - Relationship of type i

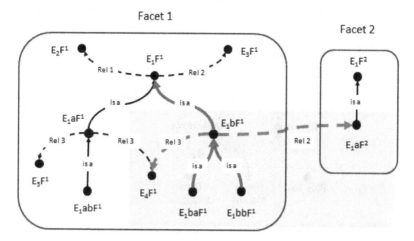

Fig. 3. Knowledge representation with typed property assignments and inferences

This visualization stands for a search interest that may require the selection of *all* entities that can be characterized as 'all entities of facet 1 that can be described as entities related to E_1F^1 by a *is a* relation under the restriction given by an entity E_1aF^2 of facet 2', in short $E_1b\$F^1 {}_*Rel2{}_* E_1aF^2$. Neither the entity E_1F^1 nor the entity E_1aF^2 should be used as a search term, the search should only be processed by the entities $E_1b\$F^1$.

Considering *songbirds with migratory instinct* as an example of this abstract setting, neither *songbirds* nor *migratory instinct* must have been assigned as index terms to the relevant documents. We are looking for documents that make statements *about* certain concepts (*songbirds*) with specified properties (*have migratory instinct*) without these properties themselves being covered in the documents.

Facet 1 of our knowledge representation contains the knowledge about the entity E_1F^1 *(Singing birds)*, e.g. that E_1bF^1 is a songbird species. A typed relation (Rel2) to entity E_1aF^2 of facet 2 provides the constraint *(has migratory instinct)* for all entities $E_1b\$F^1$ of facet 1 that is not valid for E_1F^1. An inference about the hierarchical relation paths allows to generate the set of all applicable songbirds and thus to carry out the respective search. The dashed line connecting E_1bF^1 to E_1aF^2 gives an illustration for this inference.

The example provides a proper illustration of the aforementioned abstract rule to choose the appropriate hierarchical node for linking it to another node of a second facet by a typed relation in order to avoid the necessity for exception clauses. For better comprehension we will illustrate this statement by discussing three figures that present different small knowledge structures. It is not difficult to generalize the examples' structural content to the general situation.

Figure 4 shows first an assignment of typed relations to an entity *Singing birds* that must be qualified as incorrect. One of these relationships is given by '*Singing birds* has *Migration pattern*'.

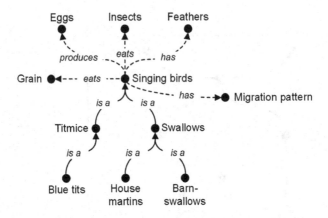

Fig. 4. Knowledge structure with incorrect connection of typed relations

Of course there are songbirds having a migratory instinct, but this is not true for *all* species. A solution for modeling this fact might be to connect only those subordinated species to *Migration pattern* that really do have a migratory instinct. Despite a lot of effort this solution causes a lack of transparency within the knowledge structure. This fact is indicated in Figure 5 for connecting only very few instances. It should be imagined as a simulation of the general situation with possibly hundreds of connections.

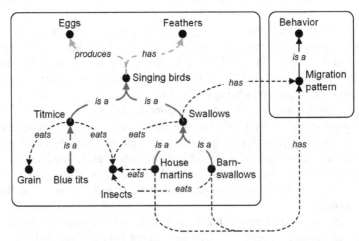

Fig. 5. Knowledge structure with typed property assignments but without inferences

Another solution of this problem may be the application of exception clauses following the approach of expert systems.

Our proposal given by Figure 3 combines mainly two elements,

— choosing the appropriate hierarchical node for linking it to another node by a typed relation,
— inferences along the relational paths.

Figure 6 gives an exemplification of the general setting for our example. Not all species of songbirds are connected to *Migration pattern* but only those with migratory instinct. To avoid the danger of building structures with less transparency and to ensure the content-oriented consistency of the formal properties, only the species of respective highest hierarchical level have been chosen for the connections.

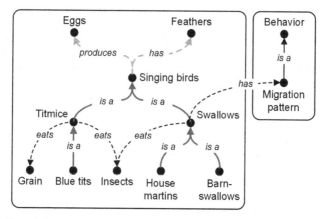

Fig. 6. Knowledge representation with typed property assignments and inferences

A further enhancement for using inferences in the domain of information retrieval is given by building result sets along relational paths of combinations of different relationships. As has been mentioned, such a mechanism is not well supported by traditional indexing languages. Therefore, it may be beneficial to analyze different combinations of semantic *a priori* relations in order to make some propositions about transitive inferences along the relational paths. Because of the content-based decisions about the type of relationships in indexing languages it is not possibly to give exact proofs for such transitivity statements. Especially for associative relationships one is restricted to plausibility arguments. We present a summary of our findings in three tables, where we make use of the following enhanced inventory of the usual relationships [6, 7].

Equivalence
   Synonym
Hierarchy
   Abstraction, generic context
   Whole / Part
   Abstraction, generic context
   Whole / Part

Chronological context
   Earlier / Later
   Later / Earlier
   Earlier / Later
   Later / Earlier
Association
   Unspecific association
   Raw material / product
   Causality (cause – effect)
   Person as actor / action
   Institution as actor / action
   Person as actor / product
   Institution as actor / product
   Action / product

The guiding principle for our transitivity statements is always the inheritance of characteristics. As has been discussed, for the hierarchical relationships this is supported by a faceted approach in order to avoid ambiguities. A more detailed analysis and presentation of the arguments has been given in [7].

The transitivity statements are always indicated in the last column by the symbols:

+: Transitivity is given
-: Transitivity cannot be expected
O: Not allowed for indexing languages

Table 1 shows the transitivity statements for combining relationships of same type.

Table 1. Transitivity in case of same type of relationships

Type of relation	Relation 1	Relation 2	Transitivity
Equivalence	Synonym	Synonym	O
Hierarchy	Abstraction, generic context	Abstraction, generic context	+
	Whole / Part	Whole / Part	+
	Abstraction, generic context	Whole / Part	-
	Whole / Part	Abstraction, generic context	-
Chronological context	Earlier / Later	Earlier / Later	+
	Later / Earlier	Later / Earlier	+
	Earlier / Later	Later / Earlier	-
	Later / Earlier	Earlier / Later	-
Association	Unspecific association	Unspecific association	-
	Raw material / product	Raw material / product	+
	Causality (cause – effect)	Causality (cause – effect)	+
	Person as actor / action	Person as actor / action	-
	Institution as actor / action	Institution as actor / action	-
	Person as actor / product	Person as actor / product	-
	Institution as actor / product	Institution as actor / product	-
	Action / product	Action / product	-

Table 2 shows the transitivity statements for combining different types of hierarchical relationships.

Table 2. Transitivity in case of different types of hierarchical relationships

Type of relation	Relation 1	Relation 2	Transitivity
Hierarchy	Synonym	Abstraction, generic context	+
	Synonym	Whole / Part	+
	Abstraction, generic context	Synonym	O
	Abstraction, generic context	Synonym	O
	Whole / Part	Synonym	O
	Whole / Part	Synonym	O
Chronological context	Synonym	Earlier / Later	+
	Synonym	Later / Earlier	+
	Earlier / Later	Synonym	O
	Later / Earlier	Synonym	O
	Abstraction, generic context	Earlier / Later	+
	Abstraction, generic context	Later / Earlier	+
	Earlier / Later	Abstraction, generic context	+
	Later / Earlier	Abstraction, generic context	+
	Whole / Part	Earlier / Later	+
	Whole / Part	Later / Earlier	+
	Earlier / Later	Whole / Part	+
	Later / Earlier	Whole / Part	+

Finally, Table 3 shows the transitivity statements for combining different types of hierarchical relationships with typed associative relationships. Only combinations with a positive statement have been included.

Table 3. Transitivity for combinations of typed associative with hierarchical relationships

Type of relation	Relation 1	Relation 2	Transitivity
Association	Unspecific association	Abstraction, generic context	+
	Unspecific association	Whole / Part	+
	Unspecific association	Earlier / Later*	+
	Raw material / product	Abstraction, generic context	+
	Raw material / product	Whole / Part	+
	Raw material / product	Earlier / Later*	+
	Action/ product	Abstraction, generic context	+
	Action/ product	Whole / Part	+
	Action/ product	Earlier / Later*	+
	Person as actor / action	Abstraction, generic context	+
	Person as actor / action	Whole / Part	+
	Person as actor / action	Earlier / Later*	+
	Institution as actor / action	Abstraction, generic context	+

Table 3. (*continued*)

Type of relation	Relation 1	Relation 2	Transitivity
	Institution as actor / action	Whole / Part	+
	Institution as actor / action	Earlier / Later*	+
	Causality (cause – effect)	Abstraction, generic context	+
	Causality (cause – effect)	Whole / Part	+
	Causality (cause – effect)	Earlier / Later*	+
	Person as actor / product	Abstraction, generic context	+
	Person as actor / product	Whole / Part	+
	Person as actor / product	Earlier / Later*	+
	Institution as actor / product	Abstraction, generic context	+
	Institution as actor / product	Whole / Part	+
	Institution as actor / product	Earlier / Later*	+

* Also: Later / Earlier

Such a list of transitivity statements may be used for a formal mark-up in knowledge representations when characterizing the properties of combinations of typed relationships for the design of semantically enhanced search environments.

6   Web Retrieval and Semantic Interoperability: An Outlook

The ideas presented in this paper can be used in any indexing and retrieval environment. But they may be especially useful when applied in heterogeneous information environments, e.g. in the context of Semantic Web applications and its standards for semantic representation. To demonstrate this usefulness in principle, a prototype with a search form was built at the *Institute of Information Science* at the *Cologne University of Applied Sciences* and can be accessed via a Web interface[2]. This prototype was based on existing data originating from the database *Literatur zur Informationserschließung (Information science literature)*[3]. The scope of the documents corresponds to an extract from the *ASIS&T Thesaurus* [1], which was transformed into a *topic map* ([4], [10], [15, 16]) by using the software *Ontopia*[4]. This environment was chosen for its special potential to represent entities and the relationships between them by typed relations as topic maps. The features of *Ontopia* comprise a visualization of the topic map and an ability to support a Web retrieval system. We refrain from giving more details or examples in this paper, more material has been presented in [6, 7].

Web retrieval and heterogeneous information environments include issues of semantic interoperability. Compared with the already given suggestions in the *SKOS* recommendations [9], [13, 14] or in *ISO 25964* [11], using typed relations may provide an advanced support for implementing inference processes and methods of faceted retrieval across heterogeneous indexing languages. The semantic representation stan-

---

[2] http://ixtrieve.fh-koeln.de/ghn/
[3] http://ixtrieve.fh-koeln.de/LitIE/
[4] http://www.ontopia.net

dards *RDF* or *OWL* support an enhancement of existing relationships without a need for complete reorganization of the indexing language.

Further research and practical implementation projects will be necessary to get benefit for real information environments constituting of data records indexed by one or more of the well-known knowledge organization systems. This paper could only present a sketch of the approach. Any realization in a real world setting requires the combination of already elaborated linked data techniques with a labor intensive restructuring of knowledge organization systems used in heterogeneous indexing and retrieval environments.

References

1. Redmond-Neal, A., Hlava, M.M.K. (eds.): ASIS&T Thesaurus of Information Science, Technology and Librarianship, 3rd edn. Information Today, Medford (2005)
2. Broughton, V.: Faceted classification as a basis for knowledge organization in a digital environment: the Bliss Bibliographic Classification as a model for vocabulary management and the creation of multi-dimensional knowledge structures. New Review of Hypermedia and Multimedia 7(1), 67–102 (2001)
3. Buxton, A.B.: Computer searching of UDC numbers. Journal of Documentation 46(3), 193–217 (1990)
4. Garshol, L.M.: Metadata? Thesauri? Taxonomies? Topic maps!: making sense of it all. Journal of Information Science 30(4), 378–391 (2005)
5. Gödert, W.: Die Dezimalklassifikation im Online-Retrieval. Nachrichten für Dokumentation 41(3), 155–158 (1990)
6. Gödert, W.: Ein Ontologie basiertes Modell für Indexierung und Retrieval. Information - Wissenschaft und Praxis 65(2), S.83–S.98 (2014); an English version has been accepted for publication in the Journal ofthe Association for Information Science and Technology. A preliminary version can be found under: http://arxiv.org/abs/1312.4425
7. Gödert, W., Hubrich, J., Nagelschmidt, M.: Semantic knowledge representation for information retrieval. DeGruyterSaur, Berlin (2014)
8. Green, R., Bean, C.A.: Aligning systems of relationships. In: Raghavan, K.S., Prasad, K.N. (eds.) Knowledge Organization, Information Systems and Other Essays: Professor A. Neelameghan Festschrift, pp. 111–128. EssEss Publ., New Delhi (2006)
9. Isaac, A., Summers, E.: SKOS simple knowledge organization system primer. W3C working group note (2009), http://www.w3.org/TR/skos-primer (retrieved)
10. ISO 13250. Topic maps. Information technology. ISO, Geneva (1999)
11. ISO 25964. Thesauri and interoperability with other vocabularies: Part 1: Thesauri for information retrieval. Part 2: Interoperability with other vocabularies. ISO, Geneva (2011-2013)
12. Michel, D.: Taxonomy of subject relationships (1997), Under: http://web2.ala.org/ala/alctscontent/CCS/committees/subjecta nalysis/subjectrelations/msrscu2.pdf, Part of: Final Report to the ALCTS/CCS Subject Analysis Committee (June 1997), Under: http://web2.ala.org/ala/alctscontent/CCS/committees/subjecta nalysis/subjectrelations/finalreport.cfm

13. Miles, A., Bechhofer, S.: SKOS Simple Knowledge Organization System. W3C recommendation (2009), `http://www.w3.org/TR/skos-reference` (retrieved)
14. Miles, A., Brickley, D.: SKOS mapping vocabulary specification (2004), `http://www.w3.org/2004/02/skos/mapping/spec/2004-11-11.html` (retrieved)
15. Park, J., Hunting, S. (eds.): XML topic maps: creating and using topic maps for the Web. Addison-Wesley, Boston (2003)
16. Pepper, S.: The TAO of topic maps: finding the way in the age of infoglut, Under: `http://www.ontopia.net/topicmaps/materials/tao.html`
17. Bean, C.A., Green, R. (eds.): Relationships in the organization of knowledge. Kluwer Academic, Boston (2001)
18. Shiri, A.: Powering search: the role of thesauri in new information environments. ASIST, Medford (2012)
19. Tudhope, D., Alani, H., Jones, C.: Augmenting thesaurus relationships: possibilities for retrieval. Journal of Digital Information 1(8) (2001), under: `https://journals.tdl.org/jodi/index.php/jodi/article/view/181`

The Effectiveness of Big Data in Health Care: A Systematic Review

Panorea Gaitanou[1,2], Emmanouel Garoufallou[3], and Panos Balatsoukas[4]

[1] Database & Information Systems Group (DBIS),
Laboratory on Digital Libraries and Electronic Publishing,
Department of Archives, Library Science and Museum Studies, Ionian University,
Ioannou Theotoki 72, 49100 Corfu, Greece
rgaitanou@ionio.gr
[2] Benaki Museum Library,
Koumbari 1, 10674, Athens, Greece
gaitanou@benaki.gr
[3] Department of Library Science and Information Systems,
Alexander Technological Educational Institute (ATEI) of Thessaloniki,
57400, Thessaloniki, Greece
mgarou@libd.teithe.gr
[4] HeRC, University of Manchester, UK
panagiotis.balatsoukas@manchester.ac.uk

Abstract. There is a consensus among scientists that the analysis of Big Data in health care (such as electronic health records, patient reported outcomes or in-motion data) can improve clinical research and the quality of care provided to patients. Yet there is little knowledge about the actual effectiveness of Big Data in the health care sector. The aim of this study was to perform a systematic review of the literature in order to determine the extent to which Big Data applications in health care systems have managed to improve patient experiences and clinicians' behavior as well as the quality of care provided to patients. All searches for relevant articles were performed in the PubMed database. From the 108 potentially relevant articles 12 satisfied the inclusion criteria for this study. The findings showed that in the case of nine articles the researchers reported positive effect of Big Data. However, some negative results were recorded in the case of three articles. The main benefits of Big Data application involved positive behavior change, improved usability and efficient decision support. However, problems were identified for technology acceptance. Most problems occurred in the case of systems processing heterogeneous datasets, patient reported outcomes and in motion data, as opposed to electronic health record systems. The paper concludes by highlighting some areas of investigation where further research is needed to understand the use of Big Data in health care and improve its effectiveness.

Keywords: Health Informatics, Big Data, Electronic Health Records, Effectiveness.

S. Closs et al. (Eds.): MTSR 2014, CCIS 478, pp. 141–153, 2014.

1   Introduction

The collection and analysis of big volumes of heterogeneous data sets is an important predicate of modern science and one of the key drivers of innovation and economic growth in developed countries. From a practical point of view, the harvesting and analysis of social and scientific data can generate new knowledge and intelligence needed to inform better decision making, improve the understanding of social and natural phenomena, explore new hypothesis, identify hidden patterns, and finally increase the relevance and timeliness of public policy making. Despite the fact that data has been used for a long time in the sciences   to understand natural phenomena (especially through simulations and computational algorithms), the modern term Big Data refers to data whose scale, diversity, and complexity require new architectures, techniques, algorithms, and analytics to manage it and extract value and hidden meaning from it [9]. In particular, Big Data is a combination of four very important characteristics: volume, velocity, variety, and veracity [1]. Volume refers to the amount of data. Velocity refers to data in motion and more specifically to the speed at which data is created, processed and analyzed. Variety is about managing the complexity and heterogeneity of multiple data sets, including structured, semi-structured and unstructured data. Finally, veracity refers to data uncertainty and to the level of reliability/quality associated with certain types of data [1].

Over the last decade a Big Data revolution is under way in the health care sector. In this context, scientists have been focused on the improvement of public health policies, clinical research and the care provided to patients through the analysis of health-related big datasets [10]. Traditionally, this type of data included electronic health records (EHRs), genomics and imaging data. However, the advent of modern ubiquitous and social networking technologies have given rise to new forms of patient generated data, such as electronic patient reported outcomes (ePROs); physiological and psychometric data (especially real-time data collected directly through sensor devices); and data generated online (for example, patients' comments and posts in online social networking tools). There are several examples of technological interventions developed for public health benefit in this respect. For example, EHRs have been processed to improve the application and analysis of clinical guidelines and online integrated care pathways in health care [11, 12]. ePROs have been used extensively as a means of enhancing already existing electronic patient health record systems and improve the design of clinical decision support tools in primary and secondary care [13]. Also, mobile technologies and sensor devices have facilitated the development of novel online interventions for health monitoring that record and analyze big volumes of physiological and psychometric data collected directly from patients [14, 15]. Moreover, the extraction and analysis of patients' posts in online health forums and social networking tools has given rise to novel infodemiology tools used to track and monitor disease outbreaks and patients' concerns [16].

Nevertheless, despite the fact that several technologies in healthcare have been focused on the analysis of Big Data, we know little about the effectiveness of these new technologies in the daily clinical work. Previous work has shown positive evidence about the effectiveness of Big Data in clinical research, especially in the case of data-driven hypothesis generation [30]; collaborative biomedical research [31]; and the identification of relationships between heterogeneous data-sets of genomic data, environmental variables and patient health records [32]. However, evidence about the effectiveness of Big Data becomes more blurred as we shift from clinical research to daily clinical work. In the later case, patients, doctors and public health policy makers are the immediate beneficiaries of data-driven systems and tools (as opposed to clinical research where the application of Big Data technologies targets primarily academics and researchers. Reviewing the literature on Big Data applications in daily routine health care systems (such as clinical decision support, diagnostic tools and other types of health information systems) is therefore critical to understand whether these technologies have managed to improve patient experiences and clinicians' behavior as well as the quality of care provided to patients.

The aim of this paper was to review the literature on Big Data and identify empirical studies focused on how Big Data actually help to improve or hinder the effectiveness of tools and systems used for the promotion of health in primary and secondary care. The review of the existing evidence on the effectiveness of Big Data in this context will inform the design of more user-centered tools and highlight some of the main challenges and problems related to the application of Big Data.

The rest of the paper is structured as follows: In Section 2 we review the literature on the effectiveness of Big Data implementation in health care. The next two sections include the methodology and the results of this study respectively. Finally, Section 5 presents some discussion and conclusions.

2   Background

Only a few similar reviews have been published in the health care domain. In [7], authors present a review that includes 11 studies from the US that illustrate the range of what has been done in diverse health care settings for clinical care, quality improvement and research. This review was focused on PRO data collection systems that were linked to an EHR system. The results of this review highlighted several barriers associated to the uptake and use of PROs, as well as factors impending their integration with electronic health records. Despite the fact that the authors provided a comprehensive view of the different types of PROs in use across the US health care sector, they did not report findings about the effectiveness of systems collecting and analyzing data about patient outcomes. In [27] the authors systematically reviewed the literature around the effectiveness of the EHRs in primary care. Despite the fact that the authors did not focus specifically on EHRs with a Big Data, or, a data analytics component, the results showed some mixed evidence. In particular, the application of EHRs had structural and process-related benefits for primary care, but showed no positive effect on clinical outcome.

A more business-oriented and operational review of Big Data implementation in healthcare was conducted by [28]. The authors examined whether the use of Big Data could effectively reduce healthcare concerns of governments and healthcare providers regarding the quality of care provided to patients, the integration of heterogeneous data-sets and the analysis of real-time data. The study highlighted the need for insightful analysis of current Big Data applications, led by champions in this area, as a means of providing guidelines and facilitate informed decision making for governments and stakeholders who are interested in using this type of applications but lack the means necessary to evaluate/analyze them.

Finally, in [8] the authors performed a literature review on the application of Big Data in medicine. The paper, which was focused on providing a general overview of the field of Big Data in medicine, showed several factors that can influence the storage and analysis of clinical data in health care and identified some of the mainstream technologies and methods used for Big Data management and processing.

3   Methodology

Our study aimed to review the literature on Big Data for health care promotion and identify empirical papers that report on the effectiveness of Big Data applications in this context. We conducted the literature review using the following strategy: <effectiveness-related keywords> AND <big data-related keywords> AND ["healthcare" OR "clinical decision support" OR "clinical trial registry" or "registries" OR analytics OR "clinical work" OR "primary care" OR "secondary care" OR Physicians OR "General Practitioners" OR Patients].

Effectiveness-related keywords and Big Data related keywords were combinations of the following: [effectiveness OR usability OR "behavior change" OR satisfaction OR validation OR evaluation OR "decision making" OR "policy making"] AND ["big data" OR "electronic health records" OR "patient health records" OR "patient reported outcomes" OR Genomics OR Imaging]. Queries were submitted to the Pub-Med database, which comprises more than 23 million citations for biomedical literature from MEDLINE, life science journals, and online books. Research was conducted between January and April 2014. Only articles written in English were included.

3.1   Inclusion and Exclusion Criteria

We included only studies focused on the evaluation of the effectiveness of Big Data in the context of clinical work (primary and secondary care). This decision was made because there is a lack of clear evidence on the effectiveness of Big Data in this context (as opposed to the context of clinical research where positive evidence exists).

Selected studies should document the use of technologies where Big Data was the key component of the effectiveness evaluation process. In this manner, traditional knowledge-based systems and tools that rely on relatively simple rules for the processing of data were not included in this review. For such as system or tool to qualify for inclusion in this study should have employed analytics and data mining techniques for automatically mining and analyzing distributed and heterogeneous collections of Big Data. There was no restriction as to the type of Big Data qualified for inclusion in this study. However, an emphasis was placed on the following types of data:

- Electronic Health Records: These large-scale datasets contain data regarding the results of clinical and administrative encounters between a provider (physician, nurse and others) and a patient that occur during episodes of patient care as well as demographic details of each individual patient, history records etc.
- Patient Reported Outcomes: PROs are defined as any report coming directly from patients about their health condition and treatment and include a range of outcomes such as symptoms, functional status, and health-related quality-of-life [29].
- Genomics and Imaging data: These types of data sets are more common in the case of clinical research. For example, Big Data analytics techniques have been used to identify associations between genomic data and environmental variables or patient health records [32]. In the same manner data mining and analytics methods have been used to improve the design of diagnostic tools in the case of imaging data and the data-driven generation of relationships and patterns [17]. The review explored whether instances of these data were used in the case of tools used by professionals in the context of primary and secondary care.
- Data collected from wearable sensors: The majority of wearable devices enable the collection of biochemical, physiological and motion sensing data [18]. The analysis of this type of data, when integrated with electronic health records, can support health monitoring and diagnosis for different chronic conditions (e.g. [19]).
- Data mining from social networking tools: Patients' posts in online social networking tools can be mined to extract knowledge about disease trends, patients' satisfaction and concerns. Twitter is a typical example where data analytics methods have been used for disease monitoring and health related trends (e.g. [16]).

Studies may have described a new technology or model to be used in the health related domain and reported an evaluation of the effectiveness of an actual intervention using the technology. In the context of this study we defined effectiveness as: a) system usability; b) system effectiveness c) user satisfaction; d) technology acceptance e) behavior change; and finally e) effectiveness in health policy making and decision making.

We excluded the following kinds of studies: a) research surveys that referred to cost or benefit effectiveness of Big Data technologies in the health care domain, b) studies reporting on the effectiveness of Big Data in the context of academic or clinical research, as opposed to studies focused on everyday clinical work; c) opinion, position, or concept papers on the use of Big data in health care, as well as review papers and papers reporting on planned, but not actually implemented, effectiveness evaluation studies; and finally d) papers describing the analysis of data-sets using traditional knowledge-based systems that rely on simple rule-based methods, as opposed to the use of data analytics methods. This latter criterion was also the reason why many studies were excluded from this review. This decision was made in order to keep the focus of the study on Big Data, thus differentiating it from previous work in the area of knowledge-based health information systems.

3.2   Data Extraction

Following a review of title and abstracts, the search identified around 108 potentially relevant articles. Of these, 12 satisfied the inclusion criteria after a full-text review. As it is shown in Table 1, for each paper included in the study a record was kept with the following information:

- The specific type of health technology used (e.g. clinical decision support, diagnostic tool);
- The type of Big Data that was analyzed (e.g. Electronic Health Records (EHRs), Electronic Patient-reported Outcomes (ePROs), genomic data; data from clinical trials, or drug testing);
- The aim of the effectiveness evaluation (e.g. Usability evaluation; Technology acceptance; System effectiveness; Behavior change (behavior change can be either objective or subjective – objective change is normally measured through the use of quantitative measures, while subjective change is based on qualitative data reporting users' experiences); Satisfaction; Engagement; Effectiveness of public health policy and decision making);
- The methodology followed, by presenting the method, sample and measures used (e.g. Randomized Control Trial / 60 adult patients / Blood pressure);
- The findings of the effectiveness evaluation: the findings refer to the main findings of the effectiveness evaluation.

4   Results

The results showed the presence of four main types of health information systems that supported processing of Big Data. These were: Pharmacosurveillance systems [2]; Clinical Decision Support [3, 4, 6, 22, 23]; Diagnostic tools [5, 20, 25]; and Health monitoring systems [21, 24, 26].

In terms of the type of Big Data processed by the aforementioned systems, the findings showed that EHRs were the most commonly used datasets. In particular, EHRs were processed in the case of eight out of the twelve studies. Despite the fact that EHRs were implemented across all different types of health information systems, the four studies that did not include the use of EHRs were diagnostic tools [5, 20] and Health monitoring systems [21, 24]. PROs were used in the case of two studies, both implementing a clinical decision support tool [4, 6]. Finally, in motion physiological data (collected through the use of wearable sensors) and psychometric data were used in the case of three health monitoring tools [24, 26], while electroencephalography data was analyzed in the case of two diagnostic tools [5, 20].

Table 1. Effectiveness of Big Data in health care

Reference	Health topic System	Source of Big Data	Aim of Effectiveness Evaluation	Methodology/ Sample/ measures	Findings of the effectiveness Evaluation
Holbrook et al. [2]	Pharmaco-Surveillance	Large Administrative Data (LAD) / Electronic Health Records (EHRs) / Electronic Patient Registries (EPRs)	System Effectiveness	Expert Evaluation / Data from three different sources (LAD, EHRs, EPRs) were analyzed by experts against a set of criteria / data type availability, data type importance, data quality and privacy.	There is a lack of integration between different databases / Bias and incomplete privacy legislation can reduce the effectiveness of linked datasets for analysis and decision making.
Hrovat et al. [3]	Clinical Decision Support	Electronic Health Records (EHRs)	Effectiveness of decision Making / System effectiveness	Reduction in hemoglobin levels for the intervention Group (clinical change) – Change in medication prescription by physicians (behavior change) - Positive levels of satisfaction for both patients and physicians.	The application of Big Data and Visual Analytics on the analysis of EHRs facilitated the discovery of trends that would be Impossible to identify using traditional techniques, thus improving the effectiveness of decision making.
Valuck et al. [4]	Clinical Decision Support (Depression)	Electronic Health Records (EHRs) / Patient Health Questionnaires (PHQ-9)	Public health policy/ Decision making effectiveness	Feasibility study (aims at showing the potential for integrating electronic patient health records with the PHQ-9 questionnaire) / 61.464 patient health records + data from 4900 PHQ-9 questionnaires.	The findings showed that the integration of EHRs with data from the PHQ-9 Questionnaire could improve the management of depression and the effectiveness of the public health policy making process.
Shen et al. [5]	Diagnostic tool (depression)	Electro-Encephalography (EEG) data	System effectiveness	Experiment / 2 sets of EEG data (1st set from 13 patients, 2nd set from 5 patients) / Classification accuracy, prediction time.	The application of big data analysis on both sets of EEG data improved the diagnostic accuracy of the tool and prediction times.
Holzner et al. [6]	Clinical Decision Support	Patient Reported Outcomes (PROs) /Electronic Health Records (EHRs)	Technology Acceptance/ User Engagement	Case study / Two hospitals (inpatient and Outpatient unit) / quantitative data – usage Statistics.	Although the tool was used effectively to collect and analyze PROs for clinical studies, in the case of both hospital case studies the findings showed that the tool could not be integrated into daily clinical routine, thus the data collection and analysis process of PROs could not be used by clinicians for individual patient treatment.
Jayapandian et al. [20]	Diagnostic tool (epilepsy)	Electro-encephalography (EEG) data	System Effectiveness / Usability (response time)	Experiment / five patient EEG recordings / Time (to process data); Time (to execute Data)	The proposed method (based on Hadoop) performed significantly faster than the baseline system (both in terms of data processing and execution time).

Table 1. (*continued*)

Graf et al. [23]	Clinical Decision Support (Coronary Artery Disease)	Electronic Health Records (EHRs)	Behavior change	Observational study / Data from 200 practices (providing care to a total of 17,000 patients) / Objectively measured physiological measures (e.g. Body Mass Index; Blood pressure) and administrative clinical data (e.g. % of vaccination; visits to the doctors).	The health of patients with CAD improved across Several measures including "Body Mass Index"; "Blood Pressure"; "Vaccination";"LDL"; "adherence to therapy".
Tseng et al. [21]	Health Monitoring System	Physiological data	Technology Acceptance	Survey / elderly residents in a nursing home / Acceptability was measured in terms of: performance expectation - endeavor expectation - social influence - user Intention - Facilitating condition	Positive effect of performance expectation, endeavor expectation, social influence, and facilitating condition on user intention to use the system. However, there was no effect of user intention on actual behavior.
Shams et al. [22]	Clinical Decision Support (re-admissions predictor)	Administrative data / Electronic Health Records (EHRs)	System effectiveness	Retrospective cohort study / Dataset (7200 records that correspond to 2985 patients)	The proposed solution could identify more accurately avoidable or unnecessary readmissions than baseline approaches (that do not analyze administrative data, along with patient health records).
Suh et al. [24]	Health Monitoring System (diabetes)	Physiological / Psychometric data	Usability (ease of use)	RCT / Adults with Type 2 Diabetes / Confidence, Efficiency	Compared with a baseline system, the proposed method showed higher levels of confidence and efficiency in terms of rule-based data associations, which resulted in improved ease of use.
Perer and Sun [25]	Clinical Diagnosis Tool (Heart Failure)	Electronic Health Records (EHRs)	Usability	Expert evaluation / 4 medical experts	Comments made by the experts during the evaluation included: doctors can easily track the progress of the disease – earlier diagnosis can be made – use of visualization can help doctors select the best strategy to avoid onset of heart failure – ability to compare cohorts.
Quinn et al. [26]	Health Monitoring System (Diabetes)	Physiological data /Electronic Health Records (EHRs)	Behavior change / Clinical change / User Satisfaction	RCT / Adults with Type 2 Diabetes	Reduction in hemoglobin levels for the intervention group (clinical change) - Change in medication Prescription by physicians (behavior change) - Positive levels of satisfaction for both patients and physicians.

Despite the fact that only 12 studies satisfied the inclusion criteria for this review, the findings showed that in the case of nine studies the researchers reported positive effect of Big Data implementation. However, some negative results were recorded in the case of three studies [2, 6, 21]. Two out of the 12 studies reported results about the effect of Big Data application on actual behavior change (i.e. effect on patients' health; change of health behaviors and/or change in clinical practice). Both studies reported a positive effect in the context of diabetes and coronary heart disease respectively [23, 26]. In the study by Graf et al. [23] the findings showed that the analysis of EHRs improved clinical decision support and the care provided to patients with coronary heart disease. The health of patients with CAD improved in terms of Body mass index, blood pressure and therapy adherence. The integration of EHRs with real time physiological data collected through wearable sensors improved also the effectiveness of a health monitoring system for patients with type 2 diabetes [26]. The system enabled both patients and doctors to track the progress of the disease. The collection of real time physiological data updated the data held in patients' electronic health record database and supported integrated analysis and visualization of both types of data. The results of the RCT showed that patients' health was improved, as well as the flexibility of clinicians' prescription behavior.

In addition to behavior change, two studies studied the role of the analysis of EHRs in improving the effectiveness of decision and public health policy making [3, 4]. Despite the fact that the results communicated in both studies were preliminary, it becomes clear that the application of visual analytics methods to the processing of EHRs can support the disclose of hidden patterns and trends that would be impossible to identify using traditional techniques, such as the identification of temporal trends and missed opportunities, critical for the management of the disease.

The effect of Big Data on the usability and technology acceptance was the most common form of effectiveness evaluation. Specifically, this issue was reported in five out of the 12 papers. However, the results of these studies were mixed. For example, although Big Data improved the usability of health information systems, the findings of technology acceptance evaluation showed some negative effects that impeded the use and integration of this type of systems in clinical care. In terms of usability evaluation the authors found that Big Data improved the data processing time [20]; led to higher levels of confidence and efficiency in terms of rule-based data associations [24]; and enabled detailed visualizations of the processed data, as well as the comparison of different patient cohorts across several variables (including genomic, environmental and administrative) [25]. However, studies focused on the investigation of technology acceptance issues showed that the integration of PROs into a clinical decision support tool could not be incorporated successfully by doctors into daily clinical routine [6]; while in the case of a health monitoring system for the elderly, which collected and processed in motion physiological data, the authors concluded that there was no effect of intention to use the system on actual behavior [21].

Finally, a panel of expert reviewers evaluating a pharrmaco-surveillance system, in the study by Holbrook et al. [2], found several factors where Big Data implementation reduced system effectiveness. These factors included: lack of integration between heterogeneous datasets (e.g. EHRs, LAD and EPRs); incomplete linked data technologies for structured and unstructured data sets; data quality problems; and finally, bias and incomplete privacy legislation.

5   Conclusions

In this paper we aimed to present a systematic overview of the literature in order to determine the extent to which Big Data applications in health care systems have managed to improve patient experiences and clinicians' behavior, as well as the quality of care provided to patients. The results show that significant research has been focused on EHRs implementation, while we also found that relatively few studies are explicitly focusing on other types of Big Data, such as PROs, genomic data, etc. Therefore, despite the benefits of the PROs, described analytically in [6, 7, 13], as their importance is evidenced by their increased use in clinical trials, in this review we observed that the systematic use of PROs assessment in clinical care is too rare. Nevertheless, we should highlight the fact that our survey misses journal articles and conference papers, which are not indexed in PubMed and that we also did not include gray literature, such as white papers and unpublished reports.

Furthermore, we observed that in the majority of papers, Big Data implementation in the health care domain presents several positive effects, regarding actual behavior change and decision and public health policy making. This happens because the application of novel analytics technique to big datasets of clinical data can show hidden patterns and associations between data variables; and enable decision makers to visualize and make sense of big volumes of data. This was common in the case of clinical decision support and diagnostic tools that processed electronic health records. On the other hand, in a few papers some negative effects of Big Data implementation were stated. In particular, there is a need for research to explore how data-driven systems can be incorporated effectively into daily clinical work. Also, it is important to investigate what health behaviors are needed for patients to effectively engage with in-motion data, and in particular, technologies that collect and analyze physiological and psychometric data in real time. For this type of data-driven health technologies to succeed there is a need to understand how patients engage with health data and translate their requirements into usable interfaces. Despite the positive effect of Big Data on behavior change, there is a need for more long-term randomized controlled trials to examine the effectiveness of data-driven clinical decision support on patients' health and clinicians' diagnostic accuracy. While the harnessing of big volumes of Big Data can improve the depth of traditional analysis and systems performance, we need to make sure that patients and clinicians can make sense of Big Data and benefit themselves by the new knowledge produced. The results of the preliminary review reported in this paper were a step towards this objective. Finally, we need to highlight the fact that this survey is limited to a small subset of studies found in PubMed, and that we have to repeat the study in the near future in a larger sample. Therefore, the findings should be interpreted with caution.

References

1. Schroeck, M., Shockley, R., Smart, J., Romero-Morales, D., Tufano, P.: Analytics: The real-world use of Big Data: How innovative enterprises extract value from uncertain data. IBM Global Business Services, Business Analytics and Optimization, Executive Report (2012), http://public.dhe.ibm.com/common/ssi/ecm/en/gbe03519usen/GBE03519USEN.PDF

2. Holbrook, A., Grootendorst, P., Willison, D., Goldsmith, G., Sebaldt, R., Keshavjee, K.: Can current electronic systems meet drug safety and effectiveness requirements? In. In: AMIA Annual Symposium Proceedings 2005, pp. 335–339 (2005), http://www.ncbi.nlm.nih.gov/pubmed/16779057

3. Hrovat, G., Stiglic, G., Kokol, P., Ojsteršek, M.: Contrasting temporal trend discovery for large healthcare databases. Computer Methods and Programs in Biomedicine 113(1), 251–257 (2014)

4. Valuck, R.J., Anderson, H.O., Libby, A.M., Brandt, E., Bryan, C., Allen, R.R., Staton, E.W., West, D.R., Pace, W.D.: Enhancing electronic health record measurement of depression severity and suicide ideation: a Distributed Ambulatory Research in Therapeutics Network (DARTNet) study. Journal of the American Board of Family Medicine 25(5), 582–593 (2012), http://www.jabfm.org/content/25/5/582.long

5. Shen, C.P., Zhou, W., Lin, F.S., Sung, H.Y., Lam, Y.Y., Chen, W., Lin, J.W., Pan, M.K., Chiu, M.J., Lai, F.: Epilepsy analytic system with cloud computing. In: 35th Annual International Conference of the IEEE Engineering in Medicine and Biology Society (EMBC), pp. 1644–1647 (2013)

6. Holzner, B., Giesinger, J.M., Pinggera, J., Zugal, S., Schöpf, F., Obergguggenberger, A.S., Gamper, E.M., Zabernigg, A., Weber, B., Rumpold, G.: The Computer-based Health Evaluation Software (CHES): a software for electronic patient-reported outcome monitoring. BMC Medical Informatics and Decision Making 12(126) (November 9, 2012), http://www.biomedcentral.com/1472-6947/12/126

7. Wu, A.W., Jensen, R.E., Salzberg, C., Snyder, C.: Advances in the use of Patient Reported Outcome measures in Electronic Health Records: including case studies. Technical report (2013), http://www.pcori.org/assets/2013/11/PCORI-PRO-Workshop-EHR-Landscape-Review-111913.pdf

8. Wang, W., Krishnan, E.: Big Data and Clinicians: a review of the state of the science. JMIR Medical Informatics 2(1) (2014)

9. Slonim, N., Carmeli, B., Goldsteen, A., Keller, O., Kent, C., Rinott, R.: Knowledge-Analytics synergy in clinical decision support. Studies in Health Technology and Informatics 180, 703–707 (2012)

10. Simpao, A.F., Ahumada, L.M., Galnez, J.A., Rehman, M.A.: A review of analytics anaclinical informatics in health care. Journal of Medical Systems 38(4), 45 (2014)

11. Ainsworth, J., Buchan, I.: COCPIT: a tool for integrated care pathway variance analysis. Studies in Health Technology and Informatics 180, 995–999 (2012)

12. Olive, M., Laswood, A., Solomonides, T.: Care pathway records with ontologies: potential uses in medical research and healthcare. International Journal of Care Pathways 15(1), 15–17 (2011)

13. Jensen, R.E., Snyder, C.F., Abernethy, A.P., Basch, E., Potosky, A.L., Roberts, A.C., Loeffler, D.R., Reeve, B.B.: Review of electronic patient-reported outcomes systems used in cancer clinical care. Journal of Oncology Practice (December 2013)

14. Ainsworth, J., Palmier-Claus, J.E., Machin, M., Barrowclough, C., Dunn, G., Rogers, A., Buchan, I., Barkus, E., Kapur, S., Wykes, T., Hopkins, R.S., Lewis, S.: A comparison of two delivery modalities of a mobile phone-based assessment for serious mental illness: native smartphone application vs text-messaging only implementations. Journal of Medical Internet Research 15(4) (2013)

15. Kelty, T.L., Morgan, P.J., Lubans, D.R.: Efficacy and feasibility of the "girls' recreational activity support program using information technology": a pilot randomized controlled trial. Advances in Physical Education 2(1), 10–16 (2012)

16. Chew, C., Eysenbach, G.: Pandemics in the age of twitter: content analysis of Tweets during the 2009 H1N1 outbreak. PLOS One 5(11) (2010), http://www.plosone.org/article/info%3Adoi%2F10.1371%2Fjournal.pone.0014118

17. Kohli, M.D., Warrnock, M., Daly, M., Toland, C., Meenan, C., Nagy, P.G.: Building blocks for a clinical imaging informatics environment. Journal of Digital Imaging 27(2), 174–181 (2014)

18. Patel, S., Park, H., Bonato, P., Chan, L., Rodgers, M.: A review of wearable sensors and systems with application in rehabilitation. Journal of Neuroengineering and Rehabilitation 9(21) (2012),
http://www.ncbi.nlm.nih.gov/pmc/articles/PMC3354997/

19. Clifton, L., Clifton, D.A., Pimentel, M.A.F., Watkinson, P.J., Tarassenko, L.: Predictive monitoring of mobile patients by combining clinical observations with data from wearable sensors. IEEE Journal of Biomedical and Health Informatics 18(3), 722–730 (2014)

20. Jayapandian, C.P., Chen, C.H., Bozorgi, A., Lhatoo, S.D., Zhang, G.Q., Sahoo, S.S.: Electrophysiological signal analysis and visualization using Cloudwave for epilepsy clinical research. Studies in Health Technology and Informatics 192, 817–821 (2013)

21. Tseng, K.C., Hsu, C.L., Chuang, Y.H.: Designing an intelligent health monitoring system and exploring user acceptance for the elderly. Journal of Medical Systems 37(6), 9967 (2013)

22. Shams, I., Ajorlou, S., Yang, K.: A predictive analytics approach to reducing 30-day avoidable readmissions among patients with heart failure, acute myocardial infarction, pneumonia, or COPD. Health Care Management Science (May 2014)

23. Graf, T., Erskine, A., Steele Jr., G.D.: Leveraging data to systematically improve care: coronary artery disease management at Geisinger. Journal of Ambulatory Care Management 37(3), 199–205 (2014)

24. Suh, M.K., Moin, T., Woodbridge, J., Lan, M., Ghasemzadeh, H., Bui, A., Ahmadi, S., Sarrafzadeh, M.: Dynamic self-adaptive remote health monitoring system for diabetics. In: 2010 Annual International Conference of the IEEE Proceedings of Engineering in Medicine and Biology Society (EMBC), pp. 2223–2226 (2012)

25. Perer, A., Sun, J.: MatrixFlow: temporal network visual analytics to track symptom evolution during disease progression. In: AMIA Annual Symposium Proceedings, pp. 716–725 (2012), http://www.ncbi.nlm.nih.gov/pmc/articles/PMC3540494/

26. Quinn, C.C., Clough, S.S., Minor, J.M., Lender, D., Okafor, M.C., Gruber-Baldini, A.: WellDoc mobile diabetes management randomized controlled trial: change in clinical and behavioral outcomes and patient and physician satisfaction. Diabetes Technology & Therapeutics 10(3), 160–168 (2008)

27. Holroyd-Leduc, J.M., Lorenzetti, D., Straus, S.E., Sykes, L., Quan, H.: The impact of the electronic medical record on structure, process, and outcomes within primary care: a systematic review of the evidence. Journal of the American Medical Informatics Association 18, 732–737 (2011),
http://jamia.bmj.com/content/18/6/732.full.pdf+html

28. Kyoungyoung, J., Gang-Hoon, K.: Potentiality of Big Data in the Medical Sector: Focus on How to Reshape the Healthcare System. Health Informatics Resources 19(2), 79–85 (2013), http://synapse.koreamed.org/search.php?where=aview&id= 10.4258/hir.2013.19.2.79&code=1088HIR&vmode=FULL
29. Acquadro, C., Berzon, R., Dubois, D., Leidy, N.K., Marquis, P., Revicki, D., Rothman, M.: Incorporating the patient's perspective into drug development and communication: an ad hoc task force report of the patient-reported outcomes (PRO) harmonization group meeting at the Food and Drug Administration, February 16, 2001. Value Health 6(5), 522– 531 (2003)
30. Wu, X., Zhu, X., Wu, G.-Q., Ding, W.: Data mining with big data. IEEE Transactions on Knowledge and Data Engineering 26(1), 97–107 (2014)
31. Shaikh, A.R., Butte, A.J., Schully, S.D., Dalton, W.S., Khoury, K.J., Hesse, B.W.: Collaborative biomedicine in the age of big data: the case of cancer. Journal of Medical Internet Research 16(4), 101 (2014)
32. Yoo, C., Ramirez, L., Liuzzi, J.: Big Data Analysis Using Modern Statistical and Machine Learning Methods in Medicine. International Neurourology Journal 18(2), 50–57 (2014)

Using FOAF for Interoperable and Privacy Protected Healthcare Information Systems

Okan Bursa, Emine Sezer, Ozgu Can, and Murat Osman Unalir

Ege University, Department of Computer Engineering,
35100 Bornova-Izmir, Turkey
{okan.bursa,emine.sezer,ozgu.can,murat.osman.unalir}@ege.edu.tr

Abstract. Healthcare information systems needs to share and to reuse the patient's information not only in a department where the information is being formed, but also between the departments of an organization and also among the different organizations. The requirements of health services like providing efficient services and ensuring continuity causes privatization of information. As patient health information is dispersed and specialized, sharing personal health information became more prevalent. A blood test ontology in a clinical information system could help physicians to learn more about the patient's health status. Hence, patients medical history is widely recognized as a good indicator for the patient's treatment plan. In this work, a methodology is proposed to infer the opportunities of using blood test with the help of semantic web knowledge representation. In order to provide a personalized, manageable and privacy protected system, user profiles are fully integrated with blood test ontology and consent management model.

Keywords: Medical Knowledge Management, Personalization, Semantic Web, Blood Test Ontology, Consent Management.

1 Introduction

Blood as the life fluid, has a major role in the immune system to defense the body against diseases. When a patient consults a physician for any complaint, the physician listens the patient's medical history and requests some medical tests. Among various medical tests, blood test is the first and most important test to analyze the human body. Abnormal results in a blood test might be a sign of a disorder or disease. Many diseases and medical problems couldn't be diagnosed with blood tests alone. However, blood tests help the physician to learn more about the patient's health status and to find potential problems early. In health domain, besides its importance, blood test contains information that might be useful to any clinic. Unfortunately, the same tests are being performed repeatedly when the patient goes to different clinics. This repeat process causes the loss of time for the diagnosis and a rise in the healthcare costs.

Until recently, it was not reasonable to share a patient's data between the departments of the healthcare organizations. In fact, the information obtained from records of a health information system is only the administrative data, such as patient's name, age, insurance information and other personal data. However,

S. Closs et al. (Eds.): MTSR 2014, CCIS 478, pp. 154–161, 2014.
© Springer International Publishing Switzerland 2014

in recent years, information technologies are focused on using and sharing the clinical data in a higher-level structured form of semantic rich information. Thus, sharing personal health information became more prevalent in distributed healthcare environments.

As patients are the center of medical treatment, user profiles are the center of personalization. Profile gives the demographic properties and history of the patient. Thus, doctors get to know their patients better. Friend of a Friend project (FOAF, http://www.foaf-project.org/) is the basic representation of profile in Resource Description Framework (RDF) language (http://www.w3.org/RDF/) and most common document to represent the demographical properties of a person. FOAF is widely used inside many different domains to describe personal information. In this work, FOAF is used to describe a patient with demographic and dynamic properties. Moreover, we extend the FOAF description with profile and blood test ontology connections to describe a complete patient profile with full support of different ontological structures. Using FOAF for personal information and integrating FOAF with blood test ontology, provides an interoperable, personalized and more manageable personal data. A personal health care system needs a detailed personal definition. Besides, personal records must be saved accurately. FOAF is the most interoperable data format to describe the patient's personal data. Moreover, it supports extendable, open and sharable data and can be used as the basic description to create a personalized patient system. By using FOAF, the patient can have fully control over her data and the system can give a personalized experience to her during her treatment. However, patient data needs privacy and security. As we extend the FOAF descriptions with blood test ontology, we also connected consent policy to patient's FOAF file to protect patient privacy. Consent management is a policy that allows a patient to determine rights for access control requests to her personal health information. Therefore, FOAF is fully integrated with blood test ontology and consent management to create a personalized, manageable and interoperable system. As a result, the stored personalized blood test result information could be queried and reused. The paper is organized as follows: Section 2 presents the relevant related work. Section 3 explains the proposed model primarily. Later, knowledge representation and development of the blood test ontology is clarified. Also, consent management model for the patient privacy is expressed in this section. The overall architecture of the proposed model is given in Section 4. Finally, Section 5 contributes and outlines the direction of the future work.

2   Related Work

Healthcare domain is one of the rare areas that has a huge amount of domain knowledge. Infectious Disease Ontology (IDO) [1,2], Saliva Ontology (SALO) [3] and Blood Ontology (BLO) [4] are ontologies that are described by formal ontology languages. IDO provides a consistent terminology, taxonomy, and logical representation for the domain of infectious diseases [1]. IDO has 185 concepts, but has not any object properties between these concepts and data properties. IDO covers the terms common for all infectious diseases, but diseases themselves are not defined in the ontology. SALO is defined as a consensus-based controlled vocabulary of terms and relations dedicated to the salivaomics domain and to saliva-related diagnostics. SALO is an ongoing exploratory initiative. BLO is designed to serve as a comprehensive infrastructure to allow the exploration of information relevant to scientific research and to human blood manipulation [4]. It is an ongoing project and the ontology is still continued to be developed. BLO describes the structure, diseases and abnormalities of the blood. However, BloodTest_Ontology is focused on substances of the blood that are measured to analyze a patient's general state of health.

There are many profile adaptations of patient properties within ontological structures. There are two kinds of patient knowledge: demographic properties of a patient which are not changing over time and dynamic properties such as patient blood test results or treatment plan. In [5] and [6], patient knowledge is dynamic and changing over time. Thus, the patient profile must be updated and managed by administrators over time. Case Profile Ontology [6] is changing and merging with other ontologies that are based on the treatment plan. However, this profile isn't connected to any social status or relationship knowledge bases and there is no description of a manageable user profile or roles, no connection with policies which gives privileges to a patient to control privacy rights over her patient file. A concept profile modeling of general person is presented in [7]. The profile model lacks of the structural development of a user model. Therefore, there will be a problem when the system needs to integrate the patient data with other information systems. Also, the user model ontology neither has any connection to FOAF nor has a meta-modeling structure that gives a manageable and extendable ontological environment. In [8], a multi-layered framework is defined to represent personal profiles. As all of these existing user models don't have an active working online ontology, we couldn't compare any ontological structure with our work at the moment.

The protection of patient information in healthcare system is one of the essential need to provide patient privacy. Consentir [9], Clinical Management of Behavioral Health Services (http://www.dshs.state.tx.us/cmbhs), HIPAAT (http://www.hipaat.com) and Cassandra [10] are systems for patient consent management and personal health information privacy. Also, [11] focuses on creating and managing of patient consent with the integration of the Composite Privacy Consent Directive Domain Analysis Model of the HL7 and the IHE Basic Patient Privacy Consents profile. The proposed consent management model differs from the relevant works in that we combine access control techniques with personalization based on semantic web technologies and FOAF profiles.

3 Combining FOAF with Blood Test Ontology and Consent Policy

In our model, ontologies are centered on patient's FOAF profile. As FOAF is a static description of personal properties, we connected the profile with the blood test ontology to save the blood test data of the profile. Therefore, this blood test result could be used to diagnose and to treat the possible diseases of a patient. In order to add blood test result; blood type and blood test result should be both described inside the ontology and connected to FOAF. Blood type is already represented inside FOAF (http://kota.s12.xrea.com/vocab/uranai/). However, the blood test result that we defined gives more detailed and temporal information about the condition of a patient. In order to represent a blood test inside a FOAF profile, p, we are using blood ontology elements to represent results. As a person could have more than one blood test, we described a time stamp for the personal blood test result. hasBloodTest property connects the Person, p, description of FOAF to BloodTest description, a, of BloodTest_Ontology:

$$\exists p.hasBloodTest(a)|a \in BloodTest \land hasBloodTest \in ObjectProperty$$

Our model uses the Meta Object Facility (MOF, http://www.omg.org/spec/MOF/2.4.1/PDF/) description of Ontology Management Group (OMG). MOF is the metadata representation and layering of knowledge representation based on semantic capabilities of elements. It is a Domain Specific Metamodel used to define metamodels. Figure 1 shows the overall structure of our model. At M1 (Model) Level, BloodTest_Ontology and FOAF definitions are connected together. M1 Level stores definitions about blood test result, personal preferences and profiles about these results. Policy and profile ontologies are derived from M2 (Meta Model) Level's Policy and Profile Meta Ontologies. At M0 (Instance) Level, these definitions are used to create personal FOAF profiles of patients.

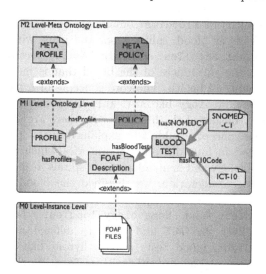

Fig. 1. Structure of the proposed model

In our model, ontologies are connected together with object properties. BloodTest_Ontology is being connected to FOAF description with hasBloodTest property. Profile and consent policy descriptions are being connected together with `hasProfile` property. Overall ontological descriptions are being connected together inside the patient's FOAF file. As FOAF files are being derived from FOAF descriptions, a patient file has the following properties:

$$\exists Person.hasProfile(p) \land Profile(p)$$
$$\exists Profile.hasBloodTest(b) \land BloodTest(b)$$

$$\exists Policy.hasProfile(p) \land \exists Policy.isOwnerOf(p,b) \land Policy.hasConsentPolicy(p)$$

These connections are the central point of our profile management. The knowledge behind the profile, consent policy and blood test ontology are being connected together inside the patient information. This centrality gives an efficiency in twofold: to the doctor to describe a treatment plan for the patient and to the patient to handle with her consent policy description.

3.1   Blood Test Ontology

The blood test ontology (`BloodTest_Ontology`) provides information about the blood test results to physicians, health workers and patients. In this work, we aim to represent the recent blood test result status with the `BloodTest_Ontology` and to use it as a part of an information base for the clinical information system. Thus, it could be used to give services to patients and health workers to organize blood information, to support the clinical decision system and to improve the clinical trials. The primary objectives of the `BloodTest_Ontology` are to perform interoperability, information sharing and reusability in the healthcare domain.

A medical test can be any test that is applied to a patient to assess patient's general state of health. In `BloodTest_Ontology`, these tests corresponds to the human body fluids as blood, saliva, stool and urine with the concepts of `BloodTest`, `SalivaTest`, `StoolTest` and `UrineTest`, respectively. In this work, we have focused on the substances of the blood that is measured to analyze a patient's general state of health. The core concepts of a blood test that are defined in `BloodTest_Ontology` like AST, ALT, Albumin, etc. do not exist in the current blood ontologies of the literature. As there are so many blood test concepts, all of these concepts couldn't be explained in this paper. In hospitals, the blood is analyzed in four different laboratories which are endocrinology, biochemistry, microbiology and hematology, in hospitals, respectively. By taking these situations into consideration, we classified the blood test concept into four sub-concepts: `EndocrinologyBloodTest`, `BiochemistryBloodTest`, `MicrobiologyBloodTest` and `HematologyBloodTest`. For example, the blood tests about liver like AST and ALT are defined as sub-concepts of `BiochemistryBloodTest`, blood tests about thyroid like FT3 and FT4 are defined as sub-concepts of `EndocrinologyBloodTest`. As the reference values may vary according to the test laboratory, patients's age or gender, the reference values of the substances, which are test concepts, are not defined as an object or a data property. `BloodTest_Ontology` has $\mathcal{ALCRIF(D)}$ DL (Description Logic) expressivity. The main goal of developing this ontology is using it as an information base for clinical information system. The `BloodTest_Ontology` is still being developed and extended with new concepts, object and data properties.

3.2   Patient-Oriented Consent Management

Information sharing has a significant importance in health domain. Patients personal information and medical history provides an essential indicator for the patient's treatment plan. However, patients have the right to know who collects, stores and accesses their data. As different people have different privacy needs, each patient should determine her own privacy level. Therefore, a patient-oriented consent management is used to guarantee patient privacy. European Standards on Confidentiality and Privacy in Healthcare (http://www.cpme.eu/european_standards_on_confidentiality_and_privacy_in_healthcare/) states that *patient information is confidential and should not be disclosed without adequate justification. The justification for disclosure should normally be consent.* Patient consent policy allows the patient to permit or deny the disclosure of her medical information to particular people.

The proposed model is based on a personal consent management model [12]. The consent management model has the following concepts: Subject, User, Role, Organization, Action, Object, Quasi-Identifier, Constraint, Purpose, Policy Objects and Consent Data Policy. Details of the related concepts could be found in [12]. In this work, roles of the consent management model is being represented with Friend-Of-A Friend profiles. The following example defines a permission and a prohibition:

Mary who has a pregnant profile permits her doctor (Bob) to see her blood test results for treatment purpose and prohibits her doctor to publish her blood test results for research purpose.

$hasProfile(Mary) \equiv Pregnant, \; hasProfile(Bob) \equiv Doctor$

$hasDoctor(Mary, Bob), \; isOwnerOf(Mary, BloodTest)$

$hasQuasiIdentifier(Mary, (Name, Gender, DateOfBirth, SocialSecurityNumber))$

$hasRequest1(Bob) = (Bob, Mary, Read, BloodTest, Treatment)$

$hasRequest2(Bob) = (Bob, Mary, Publish, BloodTest, Research)$

$CD(Mary) = hasConsentData(Mary, BloodTest)$

$hasConsentPolicy1(Mary) - (Mary, Bob, PermissionDoctor, CD(Mary))$

$hasConsentPolicy2(Mary) = (Mary, Bob, ProhibitionDoctor, CD(Mary))$

The consent policy example has the consent data concept named CD(Mary). Therefore, patients can categorize their records as consent data, control who can access to their health records and for what purposes these data can be used.

4   Architecture

A patient treatment system is a complex system. It has to cover medical knowledge fully and should be supported by doctors. A single missing data in a patient information may lead doctors to make wrong suggestions or assumptions while deciding a treatment plan. An efficient system must provide a semantically rich representation for patient's personal, diagnosis, disease and treatment information. Thus, in our work, ontologies are being used to represent fully structured patient information. Patient treatment system have a multi-layered

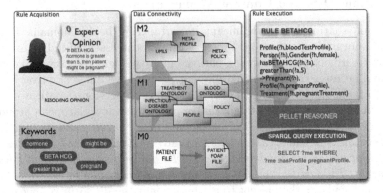

Fig. 2. Architecture of the proposed model

ontological structure at the core of our proposed system. In addition to ontological representations, the patient information and doctor's domain knowledge have to be represented in the system. The proposed patient treatment system seen in Figure 2 consists of three parts: a domain knowledge decomposition (rule acquisition pillar), a knowledge representation (data connectivity pillar) and a knowledge reasoning (rule execution pillar). Inside rule acquisition pillar, we take the expert opinions to construct basic rules about the blood test. For example; *If BETA HCG hormone is greater than five, the patient might be pregnant* sentence represents the domain knowledge of a doctor. First, we resolve this opinion into keywords such as `hormone`, `might be`, `BETA HCG`, `greater than` and `pregnant`. In the data connectivity pillar, these keywords need to be matched with the right ontological elements to create a rule about this opinion. Thus, we created a three layered knowledge representation of semantic structures to create blood test result and connected diseases with the user profile and personalized consent policies. In the rule execution pillar, rules are being created, stored and executed. In order to execute a complex rule and to infer new knowledge, we are using DL-based PELLET reasoner (`http://clarkparsia.com/pellet/`). These new discovered pieces of knowledge could cover the missing part of the doctor's opinions and could support the doctor sufficiently in her treatment plan decision.

5   Conclusion and Future Work

In this work, we have created the base of a personalized treatment system. In order to support the interoperability and information exchange, we will insert the ICD-10 codes and SNOMED-CT ConceptID inside the `BloodTest_Ontology`. Thus, when there will be an another information system using SNOMED-CT vocabulary, that system could exchange health information with a clinic information system which is using `BloodTest_Ontology` as the information base. Although blood tests are not sufficient to diagnose diseases, some blood tests named markers can show certain diagnose results. For example, if a patient's

HIV blood test result is positive, then the patient could certainly be diagnosed as AIDS. In order to make such decisions, infectious disease ontology is needed. As a future work, we will add a disease ontology to our model. Thus, we will integrate IDO to work with `BloodTest_Ontology`. However, if IDO's descriptions for the diseases do not meet our semantical requirements (our primary researches show that IDO has no concepts like `AIDS`, `Hepatitis`, `Mumps`, etc.), our work would expand to describe the infectious disease to overcome the shortcomings. Also, we will integrate the infectious disease ontology with FOAF to create personal treatment plans for patients. Therefore, we will integrate the treatment ontology [6] within our model. This integration will provide to define interfaces for experts to collect expert opinions, interfaces for doctors to select a possible treatment plan or to create new treatment plan using the diagnoses and interfaces to patients to inspect how their treatment plan is going and how they can manage their personal data.

References

1. Goldfain, A., Smith, B., Cowell, L.G.: Dispositions and the Infectious Disease Ontology. In: Proc. of FOIS 2010, pp. 400–413 (2010)
2. Cowell, L.G., Smith, B.: Infectious Disease Ontology. In: Infectious Disease Informatics, pp. 373–395 (2010)
3. Ai, J., Smith, B., Wong, D.T.: Saliva Ontology: An ontology-based framework for a Salivaomics Knowledge Base. BMC Bioinformatics 11, 302 (2010)
4. Almeida, M.B., Freitas, A.B., Proietti, C., Ai, C., Smith, B.: The Blood Ontology: An Ontology in the Domain of Hematology. In: Int. Conf. on Biomedical Ontologies, Working with Multiple Biomedical Ontologies Workshop (2011)
5. Bouamrane, M.M., Rector, A.L., Hurrell, M.: Using OWL ontologies for adaptive patient information modelling and preoperative clinical decision support. Knowl. Inf. Syst. 29(2), 405–418 (2011)
6. Riano, D., Real, F., et al.: An ontology-based personalization of health-care knowledge to support clinical decisions for chronically ill patients. Journal of Biomedical Informatics 45(3), 429–446 (2012)
7. Skillen, K.-L., Chen, L., Nugent, C.D., Donnelly, M.P., Burns, W., Solheim, I.: Ontological user profile modeling for context-aware application personalization. In: Bravo, J., López-de-Ipiña, D., Moya, F. (eds.) UCAmI 2012. LNCS, vol. 7656, pp. 261–268. Springer, Heidelberg (2012)
8. Can, O., Sezer, E., Bursa, O., Unalir, M.O.: Personalized Vaccination Using Ontology Based Profiling. In: Garoufallou, E., Greenberg, J. (eds.) MTSR 2013. CCIS, vol. 390, pp. 213–224. Springer, Heidelberg (2013)
9. Khan, A., Nadi, S.: Consentir: An Electronic Patient Consent Management System. In: 4th Annual Symposium of Health Technology (2010)
10. Becker, M.Y., Sewell, P.: Cassandra:Flexible Trust Management,Applied to Electronic Health Records. In: Proc. of the 17th IEEE Computer Security Foundations Workshop (CSFW 2004), pp. 139–154 (2004)
11. Ko, Y.-Y., Liou, D.-M.: The Study of Managing the Personal Consent in the Electronic Healthcare Environment. World Academy of Science, Engineering and Technology 65, 314 (2010)
12. Can, O.: A Semantic Model for Personal Consent Management. In: Garoufallou, E., Greenberg, J. (eds.) MTSR 2013. CCIS, vol. 390, pp. 146–151. Springer, Heidelberg (2013)

A Privacy-Aware Semantic Model
for Provenance Management

Ozgu Can and Dilek Yilmazer

Ege University, Department of Computer Engineering,
35100 Bornova-Izmir, Turkey
ozgu.can@ege.edu.tr, dilekyilmazer@gmail.com

Abstract. The history of data has a crucial importance almost in every scientific application. In order to trust the correctness of data, the ability to determine the origin of data becomes an important issue. Provenance information summarizes the origin of items, the history of the ownership of items and the actions performed on them. Ensuring that data is kept safe from corruption or illegal accesses and detecting privacy breaches on data should be achieved by integrating provenance concepts with security concepts. Information such as an individuals infectious disease history is highly sensitive and should not be revealed to an unauthorized user. This historical data needs privacy. We propose a privacy-aware provenance management model by creating policies and querying provenance data to detect policy violations. We illustrate our proposed model by integrating it with infectious disease and vaccination domains.

Keywords: Provenance Management, Process Tracking, Semantic Web, Healthcare Information Systems.

1 Introduction

In data management, data is continuously being created, updated, copied and deleted. Due to this dynamic nature, the background knowledge of data needs to be trusted in order to determine the quality on query results. Hence, the knowledge of provenance is essential for the integrity of data. As provenance is widely used in art, archeology and archives, it has also an importance in forensics and legal proceedings of data [1]. Provenance information (also called *lineage*) describes the origins and the history of data in its life cycle [2]. Thereby, provenance is metadata, not data [3]. Data provenance concerns how the data was processed and by whom. Thus, providing data provenance helps users to value and trust the data.

Data provenance has been studied in several fields and researchers have used provenance data to trace data from different sources, such as by whom the file is created, updated or copied. Researchers need to trust that the provenance information associated with the data is accurate. In order to make provenance records trustworthy; *completeness, integrity, availability, confidentiality* and *efficiency* should be guaranteed [4]. Therefore, the provenance model should be integrated with a security model.

S. Closs et al. (Eds.): MTSR 2014, CCIS 478, pp. 162–169, 2014.

We propose an ontology-based privacy-aware provenance management model to provide semantically correct results to imposed queries with a privacy-preserving architecture. For this purpose, the proposed model aims to prevent privacy breaches by using policies and querying provenance data, to track data in a privacy-aware manner in order to infer new relationships between resources and to improve the quality of data integration. In order to achieve these goals, we apply the model over the infectious disease and vaccination domains. In this manner; retrospective patient data held in the infectious diseases domain can be provided, confidentiality of patient data will be granted by determining access control privileges, the progress of infectious diseases can be monitored, the history of infectious diseases of the closest relatives of the patients can be examined, the progress of infectious diseases of other patients in similar circumstances can be examined to manage the patient's infectious disease in the future, the support for critical decisions about applicable treatments and tests can be provided, the vaccination history of a patient can be monitored and necessary vaccines can be determined on time.

The paper is organized as follows: Section 2 discusses the related work. Section 3 defines prerequisites of the privacy-aware provenance management model. The model components and the case study examples are presented in Section 4. Finally, Section 5 concludes and suggests the future work.

2 Related Work

Provenance has been the part of research in many areas, such as databases [5], workflow management systems [6], e-science [7] and Semantic Web [8]. Provenance is considered to be one of the primary issue in security. A provenance access control model and a comprehensive access control language is proposed in [9]. In [10], a provenance-aware policy definition and execution language (PAPEL) is described. PAPEL models provenance information by integrating OPM and extensible access control markup language (XACML). Differently from these works, our model is based on OPM and Dublin Core terms. An OPM based provenance model for web is performed to assess information quality in [11]. However, this study contains a provenance model and an ontology to meet core requirements for web. In [12], a study has been performed on the execution of structural queries over workflow repositories to analyze privacy. [13] proposes a provenance based access control (PBAC) that handles dynamic separation of duties, workflow control, origin-based control and object versioning. In our work, we do not focus on workflows.

As privacy is a critical issue in healthcare domain, provenance is also studied in healthcare applications. [14] presents the privacy aspects of provenance into healthcare information systems. One of the most challenging study is based on the organ transplant management domain [15]. The records of the performed donations and the original data of each donation are held within Organ Transplant Management Application (OTMA). The OTMA ensures the management and accessibility of patient records and donation records in the distributed healthcare systems. The OTMA supports pre-transplant donor identification and assessment, realization of transplantation, post-transplant monitoring of the health status of the recipient. Application can analyze reasons why transplant was rejected by the body, issues whether a transplant is conducted in accordance with rules and if a patient is a suitable donor or a recipient.

Privacy-aware provenance management model aims to detect access control violations and to reduce privacy risks by using policies and querying provenance data. Hence, we integrate OPM and Dublin Core terms within our model. We use infectious disease domain in order to improve medical processes and integrate infectious disease and vaccination domain to track the vaccination history.

3   Prerequisites

The proposed model is built on Open Provenance Model (OPM) and OPM Profile for Dublin Core Terms. OPM (http://openprovenance.org/) is a model for provenance. The model supports the digital representation of provenance and allows provenance information to be exchanged between systems [16]. OPM represents the provenance data as a directed acyclic graph (DAC). The OPM model is based on three primary entities: *artifact, process* and *agent*. Artifact defines the immutable piece of state which is a data object. Process is an action and resulting in new artifacts. A process takes an artifact as an input and outputs an artifact. Agent is a cause of a process taking place [16]. In order to capture casual dependencies between these entities, OPM defines three types of direct dependencies and two types of indirect dependencies. Direct dependencies consist of used, wasGeneratedBy and wasControlledBy. Indirect dependencies are wasDerivedFrom and wasTriggeredBy. Simply; a process used an artifact, an artifact wasGeneratedBy a process, a process wasControlledBy an agent, a process P1 wasTriggeredBy a process P2, and an agent A2 wasDerivedFrom an agent A1.

Provenance related Dublin Core metadata terms map to OPM graphs [17]. Dublin Core terms integrate with OPM data and allow Dublin Core provenance-related metadata to be expressed as an OPM graph. Therefore, Dublin Core terms provide a common vocabulary of provenance resource metadata. A resource could'nt be linked directly to the model in OPM. Hence, there is a mapping process to define resources and functionalities that manipulate them. Records or physical resources in different states are represented as an artifact in OPM. Therefore, representations of the same resource in different states are needed. Dublin Core provides terms to define which resources are derived from another and to represent the relationship between resources. In this manner, an artifact based on version could be held in the model.

4   Privacy-Aware Provenance Management Model Components

The common purpose of security is to ensure privacy. In order to provide privacy, the disclosure of personal information must be controlled and unwanted disclosures must be prevented. As provenance allows to determine the origin of data and to track the authentication of information, it could be used to detect unwanted disclosures and to strengthen privacy. The aim of the privacy-aware provenance management model is to use provenance as a security control to achieve privacy needs. The model is based on Open Provenance Model (OPM) and Dublin Core Profile for OPM.

In privacy-aware provenance management model, a *subject* is a responsible for creating records, making contributions to the recorded data and making the recorded data available. An *artifact* represents data or physical resources same as an OPM artifact. The artifact can be generated by a subject. An *operation* is a manipulation performed by a subject. It modifies an artifact and creates new version of this artifact. In our model, we used Dublin Core terms. For example, a `subject` in our model matches with Dublin Core terms of `dct:creator`, `dct:contributor` and `dct:publisher`, `operation` matches with `dct:instructionalMethod`. Therefore, we need the version history of artifacts, dependencies between these versions and detailed information of creation and modification. The Dublin Core terms of `dct:available`, `dct:created`, `dct:creator`, `dct:dateCopyrighted`, `dct:hasFormat`, `dct:hasPart`, `dct:hasVersion`, `dct:isFormat`, `dct:isPartOf`, `dct: isRequiredBy`, `dct:isVersionOf`, `dct:modified`, `dct:priorVersion`, `dct:versionInfo`, `dct:rights` and `dct:modified` are directly used in our model. In addition to these terms, we also defined new terms in order to create permissions and roles to control access to artifacts and to trace the access history of each artifact. The terms defined in privacy-aware provenance model consist of `Permission`, `Role`, `AccessHistory`, `name`, `hasRole`, `isOwnerOf`, `hasRequest`, `value`, `hasPermission`, `hasOwner`, `isInputOf`, `isOutputOf`, `hasInput`, `hasOutput`, `isPerformedBy`, `isPerformedFor`, `isRequestedBy`, `performed`, `started`, `expired`, `artifactIsAccessedBy`, `isAccessHistoryOf`, `hasAccessHistory`, `accessed`, `wasAccessedBy` and `accessDetail`.

`Permission` determines the accessibility of an artifact and includes access rights. The artifact can be accessed according to a `Role` or `Subject`, `started` and `expired` date of the authorization. After an artifact is created, it is related with a `Permission` object. `Role` represents the position of each subject in an organization. The `Role` is used to identify authorization in a permission object. The `Permission` object provides a limited access to an artifact. However, unauthorized access may occur maliciously. Therefore, detailed records of access are required to detect unauthorized access to records. Hence, we used an `AccessHistory` object that consists of date, accessed artifact and access details. `accessDetail` is an information about access details like by whom the artifact is accessed. `AccessHistory` is used to trace all authenticated/unauthenticated accesses that are performed on an artifact.

The privacy-aware provenance model has $\mathcal{ALCQ}$ DL (Description Logic) expressivity and has the following atomic concepts and roles:

- atomic concepts are Subject, Artifact, Operation, Permission, Role, AccessHistory.

- the atomic roles hasRole links a subject to a role, hasPermission links an artifact to a permission, artifactIsAccessedBy links a permission to a subject, wasAccessedBy links an access history object to a subject.
- the atomic roles isOwnerOf and hasOwner are inverse roles and create a link between a subject and an artifact.
- the atomic role hasRequest and isRequestedBy are inverse roles and create a link between a subject and an operation.
- the atomic role hasAccessHistory and isAccessHistoryOf are inverse roles and create a link between an artifact and an access history object.
- the atomic role isInputOf and hasInput are inverse roles and create a link between an artifact and an operation.
- the atomic role isOutputOf and hasOutput are inverse roles and create a link between an artifact and an operation.
- the atomic role isPerformedBy and performs are inverse roles and create a link between an operation to a subject.
- the atomic role isPerformedFor and hasOperation are inverse roles and create a link between an operation and an artifact.
- the atomic role isVersionOf and hasVersion are inverse roles and create a link between two artifacts.

The privacy-aware provenance management model rules are in the following forms:

$\forall Subject\ hasRole(Subject, Role),\ \ Role \sqsubseteq hasRole.Subject$
$\forall Artifact(hasOwner(Artifact, Subject)) \leftrightarrow$
$\quad\quad \exists Subject(isOwnerOf(Subject, Artifact))$
$\forall Operation(isRequestedBy(Object, Subject)) \leftrightarrow$
$\quad\quad \exists Subject(requests(Subject, Operation))$
$\forall AccessHistory(isAccessHistoryOf(AccessHistory, Artifact)) \leftrightarrow$
$\quad\quad \exists Artifact(hasAccessHistory(Artifact, AccessHistory))$
$\forall Operation(hasInput(Operation, Artifact)) \leftrightarrow$
$\quad\quad \exists Artifact(isInputOf(Artifact, Operation))$
$\forall Operation(hasOutput(Operation, Artifact)) \leftrightarrow$
$\quad\quad \exists Artifact(isOutputOf(Artifact, Operation))$
$\exists Artifact(hasVersion(Artifact1, Artifact2)) \leftrightarrow$
$\quad\quad \exists Artifact(isVersionOf(Artifact2, Artifact1))$
$\forall Operation(isPerformedBy(Operation, Subject)),$
$\quad\quad Subject \sqsubseteq isPerformedBy.Operation$
$\exists Operation(isPerformedFor(Operation, Artifact))$
$\forall Permission(artifactIsAccessedBy(Permission, Subject)),$
$\quad\quad Subject \sqsubseteq artifactIsAccessedBy.Subject$
$\exists AccessHistory(wasAccessedBy(AccessHistory, Subject)),$
$\quad\quad Subject \sqsubseteq wasAccessedBy.Subject$
$Subject \times Permission \times Artifact \rightarrow hasPermission.Subject$
$Subject \times Artifact \times AccessHistory \rightarrow hasAccessHistory.Artifact$

4.1   Case Study

Provenance of data is known as the documented history of the data and being used in various domains. Domain experts use this provenance data to perform analysis and reasoning. When the importance of its consequences are taken into consideration, the medical domain is an important research field for provenance management. We integrate infectious disease domain and vaccination domain with privacy-aware provenance model for twofold: (i) to detect privacy violations in provenance data (ii) to track vaccine information and to remind the people related with the relevant vaccine information.

The Infectious Disease Ontology (IDO) is a core ontology providing a consistent terminology, taxonomy and logical representation for all infectious disease domain [18]. IDO is constructed according to the Open Biomedical Ontology Foundry and uses Basic Formal Ontology (www.ifomis.org/bfo) as an upper ontology. Vaccination prevents humans from infectious diseases that may result in mortality or morbidity. Vaccine domain is specifically handled with regards to the usage of stakeholders who are persons and organizations that participate in vaccination process. Vaccine_Ontology is used in vaccine information system in order to provide all services that occur in the vaccination process [19]. We illustrated our model for infectious disease and vaccine ontologies:

Detecting Privacy Violations: An instance of the privacy-aware provenance management model over the infectious disease domain is illustrated for the case study. Subject represents patients and healthcare workers such as *doctor, nurse, practitioner, laboratory assistant*, etc. Operations are *clinical tests* and *treatment processes*. Artifact contains the *personal information, clinical test results, diagnoses* and *applied treatments of patients*. The case study is designed towards the diagnosis of *Hepatitis C* and presented according to the model rules given in Section 3.

In the case study, the doctor (John) listens complaints of his patient (Mary) and suspects that she is a carrier of the Hepatitis C virus. A number of diagnostic tests, including *HCV antibody enzyme immunoassay (ELISA), recombinant immunoblot assay* and *quantitative HCV RNA polymerase chain reaction (PCR)* can be applied to diagnose Hepatitis C. While John requests an ELISA test for Mary, Mary wants to protect her medical records from unauthorized accesses.

$hasRole(John) \equiv Doctor, \ hasRole(Mary) \equiv Patient$

$hasRole(Lucy) \equiv Nurse, \ hasRole(Mark) \equiv LaboratoryAssistant$

$isPerformedFor(ELISA, DOID\_1883) \equiv hasOperation(DOID\_1883, ELISA)$

$hasRequest(John, ELISA) \equiv isRequestedBy(ELISA, John)$

$creator(Artifact1) = Lucy, \ Artifact1 = Mary's ELISATestRequest$

$isOwnerOf(Mary, Artifact1) \equiv hasOwnerOf(Artifact1, Mary)$

$hasPermission1(Artifact1) = (Permit, Nurse, OnlyWriteForClinicalTests,$
$$2014 - 07 - 01, 2014 - 07 - 10)$$

$isInputOf(Artifact1, ELISA) \equiv hasInput(ELISA, Artifact1)$

$Artifact2 = ELISA - TestResult$

$isOutputOf(Artifact2, ELISA) \equiv hasOutput(ELISA, Artifact2)$

$isOwnerOf(Mary, Artifact2) \equiv hasOwnerOf(Artifact2, Mary)$

$hasPermission2(Artifact2) = (Permit, Doctor, ReadAndWriteForTreatment,$
$$2014 - 07 - 01, 2014 - 08 - 01)$$

$hasPermission3(Artifact2) = (Permit, LaboratoryAssistant,$
$$ModifyTestResultForTreatment, 2014 - 07 - 01, 2014 - 08 - 01)$$

$hasAccessHistory1(Artifact2) = (Artifact2, 2014 - 07 - 04, John, Read)$

$isInputOf(Artifact2, UpdateArtifact2) \equiv hasInput(UpdateArtifact2, Artifact2)$

$isPerformedBy(UpdateArtifact2, Mark) \equiv performs(Mark, UpdateArtifact2)$

$hasAccessHistory2(Artifact2) = (Artifact2, 2014 - 07 - 07, Mark,$
$$ModifiedAndCreatedAnewVersion)$$

$isOutputOf(Artifact3, UpdateArtifact2) \equiv hasOutput(UpdateArtifact2, Artifact3)$

$hasPerrmission2(Artifact3) = (Permit, Doctor, ReadAndWriteForTreatment,$
$$2014 - 07 - 01, 2014 - 08 - 01)$$

$priorVersion(Artifact3) = Artifact2$

$isVersionOf(Artifact3, Artifact2) \equiv hasVersion(Artifact2, Artifact3)$

$hasAccessHistory3(Artifact3) = (Artifact3, 2014 - 07 - 30, John, Read)$

In this manner, access history can be queried to detect privacy violations. Thus, Mary can control who can access her infectious disease record and for what purposes this record can be used. As a result, the infectious disease record of Mary will be protected from unauthorized accesses.

Tracking Vaccine History: The vaccine history is an essential information that can be learned by using provenance data over the privacy-aware provenance management model. Therefore, the vaccine history could be accessed in critical times in order to apply necessary vaccines to the patient on time and to prevent unwanted vaccination processes. For example; when an unconscious patient is brought to the hospital with a large incision on his arm, the doctor would like to learn patient's tetanus vaccine history. As he can't learn it from the patient (we accept that the doctor knows patient's social security number), by executing a query on the provenance data of patient's personal vaccine information the latest tetanus vaccination date will be controlled from the query result. Therefore, if the tetanus vaccine is applied to the patient in last ten years, it should not be applied again. Otherwise, the patient can die or the re-applied tetanus vaccine can cause permanent damage to the patient.

5   Conclusion and Future Work

The proposed privacy-aware provenance management model provides privacy and traceability of data. Users can trace the records of events and dependencies between events and also manage the access control. Thus, data can be protected from unauthorized accesses, all versions of data can be tracked and analyzes can be performed by using provenance data. As a future work, policy ontologies will be created and queries will be written, infectious disease and vaccination ontologies will be extended with new concepts and instances, and the privacy-aware provenance access control engine will be developed.

References

1. Hasan, R., Sion, R., Winslett, M.: Introducing Secure Provenance: Problems and Challenges. In: Proc. of ACM Workshop on Storage Security and Survivability, pp. 13–18 (2007)
2. Cheney, J., Chiticariu, L., Tan, W.-C.: Provenance in Databases: Why, How, and Where. Foundations and Trends in Databases 1(4), 379–474 (2007)
3. Braun, U., Shinnar, A.: A Security Model for Provenance. Technical Report, TR-04-06, Harvard University (2006)
4. Hasan, R., Sion, R., Winslett, M.: The Case of the Fake Picasso: Preventing History Forgery with Secure Provenance. In: Proc. of the 7th USENIX Conf. on File and Storage Technologies, pp. 1–14 (2009)
5. Tan, W.-C.: Provenance in Databases: Past, Current, and Future. IEEE Data Eng. Bull. 30(4), 3–12 (2007)
6. Davidson, S.B., Freire, J.: Provenance and scientific workflows: challenges and opportunities. In: Proc. of the ACM SIGMOD Int. Conf. on Management of Data, pp. 1345–1350 (2008)
7. Sahoo, S.S., Sheth, A., Henson, C.: Semantic Provenance for eScience:Managing the Deluge of Scientific Data. IEEE Internet Computing 12(4), 46–54 (2008)
8. Halpin, H.: Provenance: The Missing Component of the Semantic Web for Privacy and Trust. In: Workshop on Trust & Privacy on the Social and Semantic Web (2009)
9. Ni, Q., Xu, S., Bertino, E., Sandhu, R., Han, W.: An Access Control Language for a General Provenance Model. In: Jonker, W., Petković, M. (eds.) SDM 2009. LNCS, vol. 5776, pp. 68–88. Springer, Heidelberg (2009)
10. Ringelstein, C., Staab, S.: Papel: Provenance-Aware Policy Definition and Execution. IEEE Internet Computing 15(1), 49–58 (2011)
11. Freitas, A., Knap, T., O'Riain, S., Curry, E.: W3P: Building an OPM based provenance model for the Web. Journal Future Generation Computer System 27(6), 766–774 (2011)
12. Davidson, S.B.: On provenance and privacy. In: McGuinness, D.L., Michaelis, J.R., Moreau, L. (eds.) IPAW 2010. LNCS, vol. 6378, pp. 1–1. Springer, Heidelberg (2010)
13. Park, J., Nguyen, D., Sandhu, R.: A Provenance-based Access Control Model. In: 10th Annual Int. Conf. on Privacy, Security and Trust, pp. 137–144 (2012)
14. Kifor, T., Varga, L.Z., et al.: Privacy Issues of Provenance in Electronic Healthcare Record System. Journal of Autonomic and Trusted Computing (2007)
15. Álvarez, S., Vázquez-Salceda, J., Kifor, T., Varga, L.Z., Willmott, S.: Applying Provenance in Distributed Organ Transplant Management. In: Moreau, L., Foster, I. (eds.) IPAW 2006. LNCS, vol. 4145, pp. 28–36. Springer, Heidelberg (2006)
16. Moreau, L., Clifford, B., et al.: The Open Provenance Model Core Specification (v1.1). Future Generation Computer Systems 27(6), 743–756 (2011)
17. Miles, S., Moreau, L., Futrelle, J.: OPM Profile for Dublin Core Terms, v0.3 (2009), http://twiki.ipaw.info/pub/OPM/ChangeProposalDublinCoreMapping/dcprofile.pdf
18. Goldfain, A., Smith, B., Cowell, L.G.: Dispositions and the Infectious Disease Ontology. In: Proc. of the FOIS 2010, pp. 400–413 (2010)
19. Can, O., Sezer, E., Bursa, O., Unalir, M.O.: Personalized Vaccination Using Ontology Based Profiling. In: Garoufallou, E., Greenberg, J. (eds.) MTSR 2013. CCIS, vol. 390, pp. 213–224. Springer, Heidelberg (2013)

EPOS: Using Metadata in Geoscience

Keith G. Jeffery[1] and Daniele Bailo[2]

[1] Keith G Jeffery Consultant, Faringdon, United Kingdom
keith.jeffery@keithgjefferyconsultants.co.uk
[2] INGV- Istituto Nazionale Geofisica e Vulcanologia, 00143, Rome, Italy
daniele.bailo@ingv.it

Abstract. One of the key aspects of the approaching data-intensive science era is integration of data through interoperability of systems providing data products or visualisation and processing services. Far from being simple, interoperability requires robust and scalable e-infrastructures capable of supporting it. In this work we present the case of EPOS, a project for data integration in the field of Earth Sciences. We describe the design of its e-infrastructure and show its main characteristics. One of the main elements enabling the system to integrate data, data products and services is the metadata catalog based on the CERIF metadata model. Such a model, modified to fit into the general e-infrastructure design, is part of a three-layer metadata architecture. CERIF guarantees a robust handling of metadata, which is in this case the key to the interoperability and to one of the feature of the EPOS system: the possibility of carrying on data intensive science orchestrating the distributed resources made available by EPOS data providers and stakeholders.

Keywords: Research Infrastructure, e-infrastructure, data integration, data intensive, metadata, cerif, epos.

1   Introduction

We describe the use of metadata in EPOS: European Plate Observing System (www.epos-eu.org), an ESFRI (European Strategic Framework for Research Infrastructures) project. In EPOS, metadata is used not only to describe datasets but also users, software and ICT resources thus providing a virtualized e-infrastructure environment for geoscientists. We describe a 3-layer model of metadata to provide the required functionality including interoperability. We approach the end of EPOS-PP (Preparatory Phase) with a developed architecture and prototype e-Infrastructure environment and expect to develop the full production system starting in 2015.

EPOS is the result of changing expectations and requirements in science, and the use of ICT for science. According to Tony Hey [HeTaTo09] research passed through different eras, and we are leaving the computational science era and moving to the data-intensive science era, where the amount of produced data outstrips our capacity for collecting and analysing it. The vision is that "the goal is to have a world in which all of the science literature is online, all of the science data is online, and they

S. Closs et al. (Eds.): MTSR 2014, CCIS 478, pp. 170–184, 2014.

interoperate with each other". Data interoperability is therefore fundamental. Extending the Tony Hey et al vision, another complementary view, promoted by [HaRaOr06] states that integration of data, which is one of the main reason for system interoperability, is another core concept: "Data integration is crucial [...] for progress in large-scale scientific projects, where data sets are being produced independently by multiple researchers [and] for better cooperation among government agencies". The key to achieving the vision is virtualization (hiding from the end-user the complexity of the underlying system) and virtualization is achieved by the use of metadata. Metadata provides the raw material for the middleware necessary to allow interoperation across datasets, across software, across users (using electronic means) and across computing resources.

2   Related Work

Interoperability of data has long been recognized as important. In the 1970s attempts to integrate data from heterogeneous sources in geoscience were already underway [SuJeGi77] and in that work metadata (so-called structural information records) were the key to matching syntactically heterogeneous datasets. However this work only touched on the semantic aspects.   Much research has been done since including the seminal paper [ShLa90]; an approach using in combination data, software and knowledge engineering [JeHuKaWiBeMa94] and the use of graph theory in hypermedia databases [KoJe95] although no fully satisfactory automated technique has yet been developed.   In fact a semi-automated method involving much human interaction named Dataspaces has been proposed [FrHaMa05] and subsequent work has focused largely on semi-automated mechanisms.

Software interoperability is even more problematic.   Attempts have been made with catalogs or directories of software components.   However, the binding of software to data in the Object-Oriented environment precludes general use of software across heterogeneous data structures. The answer lies in atomic software services that are agnostic to data structures (or semantics) which implies that the software reads first the metadata describing the data of interest and then self-modifies to meet the data structure encountered.   In the relational database world this is more easily achieved because the data structures are normalized and – at least for data management – a set of atomic software services are already defined, namely the relational algebra.   Many software packages (e.g. in statistics or visualization) build on this concept and access relational tables because they provide a generic data interface using the relational schema.   The key is execute-time binding of software to data which precludes compile-time typing and thus requires typing checks to be carried out at execute time (at least for data ingest and update) to ensure integrity.

Interoperability across computing resources has been – so some extent - achieved. With homogeneous systems (same hardware, operating system and same organizational management) there have been solutions available for some time to make a distributed system appear homogeneous although even in this environment maintenance of catalogs or directories of the systems characteristics is non-trivial. With heterogeneous systems it is more complex. Not only are we dealing with different hardware with different characteristics (e.g. specialized processors in supercomputers) but also differences in accuracy and precision especially for double-precision floating point numerics commonly used in scientific research. Worse, we also have different organisations and their management policies to deal with. Great advances were made in the period 2000-2008 based on GRIDs technology; perhaps summarized best in the work of the CoreGRID project http://coregrid.ercim.eu/mambo/ although much has been carried forward through the European Grid Infrastructure http://www.egi.eu/ and on into CLOUD Computing.

The importance of interoperability means that design papers for system interoperability and for data integration are plentiful in scientific literature: these papers range from theoretical models developed by huge companies and academic researchers [HaRaOr06], [Le02] to database models and implementation of seismogenic sources [BaVaVaBuFrMaBo08], to reviews and summaries on the topic of integration [DoHaIv12] and many others. These (and other) papers provide a range of visions with part-solved approaches to each of the kinds of interoperability outlined above although the maximum amount of work has been done on data interoperability. Matching the wide range of papers are many local e-Infrastructure implementations, with local data formats, specialised metadata standards and data delivery systems which only in a few cases are in regular production use and able to share data with common standards. One example of a production system in Geoscience comes from seismology [SuEcGi08].

Because of the distribution and heterogeneity of many scientific research resources the fundamental task of integration is usually carried on by European-wide organizations or European projects, with long term vision and consequent investment both in human and financial resources. Examples come from astronomy, astrophysics and remote sensing, where huge organizations such as European Space Agency (ESA), National Aeronautics and Space Administration (NASA), Japan Aerospace Exploration Agency (JAXA) and many others can manage and coordinate in a consistent way all the resources required to carry on research: satellites, telescopes, other sensors or machinery and also the e-Infrastructures which enable researchers to retrieve, store, exchange and elaborate data, thus reducing the amount of different data and metadata formats, software and procedures. When all the resources required to carry on research in a certain science field are managed centrally, then an e-infrastructure with a high interoperability factor is likely designed and implemented. The key factor is that the sensors / detectors and associate systems are expensive and shared among researchers and thus there is a need for standardization of data formats, software and procedures.

With the exception of earth observation, such an approach is not found in Geoscience. The relatively low cost of sensors and hardware required to create a research infrastructure (RI) allow any institution to create its own RI and of the underlying e-infrastructure. Thus there is a lack of integration even within each sub-discipline of geoscience let alone between those sub-disciplines – except in seismology where there is some coordination. This is because of the economic and social consequences of seismic activity and the better science that can be achieved by utilising many seismic observatories with their sensor arrays providing higher precision in the data.

Attempts to provide cross-discipline integration have started. At low level (storage and preservation) the EC-funded project EUDAT http://www.eudat.eu/ is providing an e-layer to store, securely preserve and curate the data and encourage discovery of datasets across all disciplines. Interestingly, their initial trials of DC (Dublin Core) and subsequent use of CKAN (Comprehensive Knowledge Archive Network, www.ckan.org) metadata proved inadequate and they are now pursuing other possibilities including the metadata standard used by EPOS (of which more below).

Similar integration is being attempted in the Global Earth Observation System of Systems (GEOSS www.earthobservations.org/geoss.shtml), devoted to "proactively link together existing and planned observing systems around the world and support the development of new systems where gaps currently exist". In both cases the common goal is to provide a certain degree of integration of data and datasets coming from different science fields, so that a user may discover information with one discovery action (query). Although such global initiatves are important and fundamental, dealing with such diverse data poses problems because of the heterogeneity intrinsic to multilingual semantics.

3   EPOS

This paper takes a particular example case from geoscience, the European Plate Observing System (EPOS) which deals with data coming from solid Earth Sciences. A major problem is the varied group of communities and their different approaches, their distributed locations and groupings. There is a tension between the local institutional organization covering one or several fields and the international cooperation in any one field – in some cases with one or more European centres. Thus the EPOS e-infrastructure team interacted with ten major community groupings to discover their assets (datasets, software, computing and other equipment, services offered). This inventory – together with contact information – was stored in a database named RIDE (Research Infrastructures Database for EPOS) and made widely available. This encouraged communities to 'open up' more assets. It also allowed EPOS-PP to demonstrate the scale of research infrastructures already funded and available and therefore the benefits of integrating across them all in the EPOS project.

Thus, EPOS aims to have a real integration of science data and common access to services (including software services but also, e.g., access to rock mechanics equipment or supercomputers) from one single integrated online environment, namely EPOS Integrated Services. These services utilise metadata namely a specialised, extended implementation of the Common European Research Information Format (CERIF) model. CERIF was designed initially for research information interoperation and has been an EU Recommendation to Member States since 1991. Information on CERIF is available at the website of the not-for-profit organization tasked to maintain, develop and promote CERIF, euroCRIS www.euroCRIS.org and specifically at http://eurocris.org/Index.php?page=CERIFreleases&t=1. In this paper we outline the main features of the EPOS system, and in particular the metadata catalog and its implementation.

The EPOS mission is to integrate existing and new, distributed research infrastructures (RIs) for solid Earth Sciences warranting increased accessibility and usability of multidisciplinary data from monitoring networks, laboratory experiments and computational simulations. This is intended and expected to enhance worldwide interoperability in the Earth Sciences and establish a leading, integrated European infrastructure offering services to researchers and other stakeholders. In fact EPOS is designed to interoperate with equivalent RIs in other continents and work is ongoing with them.

EPOS represents the solution and expresses a scientific vision and an IT approach in which innovative multidisciplinary research is made possible. However, EPOS also requires a sustainability plan and business model and has to organize and leverage other funding sources. Additionally the legal aspects of providing such integrated services and the associated rights over data, software, equipment and even scholarly publications require managing. In an online integrated research environment all these aspects require metadata.

Hence, EPOS is not only a portal to domain-specific (thematic) datasets for download. The ambition of EPOS is to overcome the general complexity faced by a researcher when using a wide diversity of data and data products to perform her/his research, by providing a simple "one-stop shop" environment and interface. The technical goal is to provide an integrated environment where the user can browse, preview and/or select, download data. However, in addition, the novel aspect of EPOS compared with other portals – is to allow the user to perform analytics, data mining, visualisation and modelling directly online.

4   e-Infrastructure Design

The EPOS architecture is structured as follows (Fig.1):

- *Integrated Core Services (ICS)* provide access to multidisciplinary data, data products, and synthetic data from simulations, processing and visualization tools. However, because EPOS means to integrate, analyse, compare, interpret, and present data and information, ICS does not simply mean data access, they are the place where integration occurs;
- *Thematic Core Services (TCS)* are infrastructures that provide data services to specific communities (they can also be international organizations, such as ORFEUS for seismology www.orfeus-eu.org);
- *National Research Infrastructures and facilities* provide services at national level and send data to the European thematic data infrastructures.

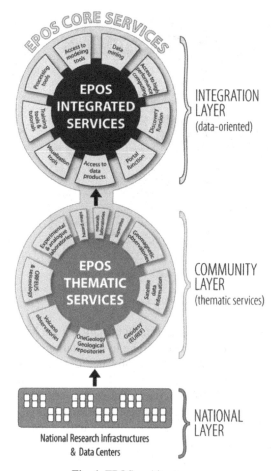

Fig. 1. EPOS architecture

The main concept is that the EPOS TCS data and services are provided at the layer where the integration occurs, that is to say by and into the ICS. It is achieved by means of a communication layer called the compatibility layer, as shown in the functional architecture (Fig. 2). This layer contains all the technology to integrate data, data products and services (including software services and access to resources) from many communities into a single integrated environment: the Integrated Core Services (ICS).

Therefore, the ICS, being devoted to the real integration of data, data products and services, represent the "core" of the whole e-infrastructure. The ICS is conceptually a single, centralized facility but in practice is likely to be replicated (for resilience and performance) and localized for particular natural language groupings or legal jurisdictions. In the actual design, ICS are made up of several, modular, interoperable building blocks (as shown in the top part of Fig. 2):

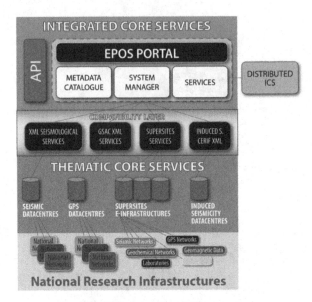

Fig. 2. Functional Architecture

Metadata catalog is the key component. It contains all the information that the system might be willing to deal with describing in a digital representation the objects of the EPOS e-Infrastructure including data, software, users and resources such as computers, detectors or laboratory equipment. It uses CERIF as a tool to harmonize information on research. CERIF describes datasets but also software, services, users and resources such as computers, datastores, laboratory equipment and instruments. This catalog requires dynamic maintenance. This can be done either by human or by automated means (the latter is recommended and we are working on such services). Automation naturally is depending on the technologies implemented at the TCS layer, to which the metadata catalog will connect through the compatibility layer. This is a typical task accomplished by the System Manager.

System Manager can be considered as the "intelligence" of the system and is basically middleware which manages the whole metadata system. The System Manager takes advantage of the information contained in the catalog (which is the "knowledge base" of the system) and makes proper decisions according to: (i) user requests, (ii) metadata contained in the EPOS metadata catalogue covering users, resources, software services and data. Therefore, in an EPOS context, this is the place where the brokering techniques – but driven by the metadata made explicit in the catalog rather than by program code hidden in the software – will be effective.

EPOS Portal and API are functional blocks dedicated to the interaction between users (both human and machine) and the system. The portal deals with the interaction between a human user and the system. A generic user will be enabled to perform actions like: (i) data/data products/sensors/facilities discovery; (ii) data/data products download; (iii) data /data products analytics; (iv) data/data products visualization; (v) data/data products modeling and simulation. However, this portal functionality is not sufficient because EPOS wants to (i) be interoperable with other systems, (ii) be compliant with major European standards, (iii) deliver a high quality service that enables a user to perform programmatically some actions. A locus dedicated to machine-machine interaction is therefore needed. This is exactly the Application Programming Interface (API), which includes a set of native functions enabling a machine use of the EPOS system, as for instance RESTful queries of the type: GET /entity?data_types=[seismwav,GPS,satdata]&lat=45.5345&lon=16.334&startime="datetime". For this latter purpose, the reliable and fully CERIF compliant CERIF-XML standard is used at the present stage in the form of a RESTful service that can be queried to obtain XML-formatted metadata.

Services interface module includes all the software and interfaces required to connect outsourced resources as, for instance, linkage to HPC centres or workflow management infrastructure (e.g. VERCE www.verce.eu).

5   Data Model

The metadata catalog is the key to the implementation and is dependent on the metadata model. Metadata can be viewed or considered in two dimensions:

- Metadata to describe the objects of the "EPOS ecosystem" in such a way that the descriptions (including restrictions of usage) can be used by the middleware and by application software;
- Metadata for to provide the appropriate level or depth of metadata for the required task or processing;

5.1   Metadata to Describe EPOS Ecosystem Objects

This dimension of the metadata concerns the objects of the EPOS "ecosystem": these are classified into users, services (including software), data and resources (computing, data storage, instruments and scientific equipment) as shown in Fig. 3.

The *User Model* describes how a subject (human user, but also a program, or a process) can interact with the EPOS e-infrastructure and determines the design of the EPOS web-portal. This is important to ensure all kinds of people, regardless their location, language, expertise, permissions, responsibilities, authorities and disabilities (or differently-abled abilities e.g. when driving), can easily access and use the system. Therefore, it will provide the technical information to ensure users' security, privacy and trust through its identification, authentication, authorization and accounting (IAAA). IAAA are based on the data policy and access rules describing the degree of openness of the information, data usability, data ownership, and the stakeholders' metric aimed at analysing the impact, influence, engagement, exchanges and ethical risks associated to each user category and the possible utilization of EPOS data and services.

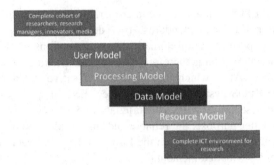

Fig. 3. The four models to describe the EPOS ecosystem objects

The *Processing Model* is by far the most difficult to create because it has to include sufficient information on how the system performs the calculations and visualization on the different data available within EPOS to allow composition of appropriate software services to accomplish the application requirement. It provides the core information of ICS, in particular the know-how on integrating data and data products beyond the simple data mining and data archiving currently distributed but still available (with very different services, access and policies) at a community and national level. The model also has to describe the rights and responsibilities of users of the software services including (if appropriate) costs.

The Data Model serves to describe the data and availability and their associated detailed, domain-specific metadata in order to allow the user to find them, work with them (integrate) and download them or utilize them in a composition of software services. Again the rights asserted over the data are recorded with access to licence information. EPOS is working with others on ways to encode licence information such that it can be processed automatically by middleware to ensure the end-user does not violate any rights inadvertently [BuJe13].

The Resource Model is a technical description of the physical resources owned by the data providers (i.e. national RIs and Thematic Core Services) that are available for EPOS integration and of those owned outside the EPOS delivery framework that will provide specific IT services (see the processing model). This model is needed to provide the description of the organization of the facilities in both their hardware and software components that will guarantee: (i) data repository facilities (including long-term preservation and provenance as well as discoverability), (ii) data processing (calculations), (iii) simulation and modelling and (iv) visualization (rendering). For each category the model provides a detailed technical IT description with specifics on how to ensure a sustainable and efficient connectivity and therefore to allow the user to reach their content (the data) or to use them (processing and visualization).

5.2   Metadata Depth for the Required Task

The other dimension of metadata provides the appropriate level or detail of metadata information which enables a user to perform actions and functions over data and data products. This model, the so-called three-layer model [JeAsHoJö13] is structured as follows (see also Fig. 4):

1. The discovery layer, which utilises not only (a subset of) the underlying CERIF directly for discovery but also has the capability to generate from the underlying contextual CERIF layer DC, DCAT, INSPIRE (to integrate with other existing datacentres utilizing these standards) and both CKAN and eGMS (the latter two to encourage particularly integration with government open data (data.gov) sources);
2. The contextual layer, using CERIF to assist in assessing the relevance of data (or other artefact) for the purpose of the application request, to assist in assessing the quality and validity of the data (or other artefact) and to disambiguate conflicting identities. Also this is the layer from which the other discovery level metadata standards can be generated and which also points to individual datasets or services characterized by metadata in the detailed layer;
3. The detailed layer, which includes detailed metadata standards usually domain or sub-domain specific for each kind of data (or software, computer resources or detectors/instruments) to be (co)-processed. For example, detailed metadata for a dataset may include the database schema (giving attributes, types etc.) but also - for each attribute – precision and accuracy.

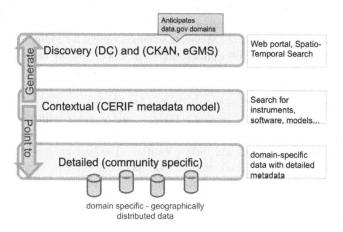

Fig. 4. Three layer Metadata Architecture

5.3   CERIF Model in the Context of EPOS

The core of the proposed structure is the contextual layer, which is built following the concepts and guidelines of the euroCRIS organization www.eurocris.org. CERIF was originally designed for research information interoperability and the version from 2000 onwards – based on extended entity-relations modelling – replaces the earlier CERIF1991 version. The 1991 version was very like Dublin Core with single records having Project as the key and having elements such as title, abstract, contact person etc. as attributes. The problems predicted with such a structure – including violation of referential and functional integrity - were experienced 1991-2000 which led to the reconvening of the expert group and the development of the replacement CERIF2000.

CERIF2000 covers - as base entities - persons, organisations, projects, products (including datasets and software), publications, patents, facilities, equipment, funding and more. The novelty of CERIF is in the linking entities; these describe the relationships between instances of base entities. Each linking entity consists of the keys (unique identifiers) of the two base entities being related, a role (the relationship) and both start and end date/time; thus providing temporal information for the period of validity of the assertion implicit in the instance of the linking entity. A role might be 'author' in the linking entity between person and publication; it could equally well be 'editor' or 'reviewer'. Similarly a role between organisation and person might be 'employs'; multiple instances with diffreent values of start date/time and end date/time (and possibly with different organisations) form a list of employments (career history) of a person. In the case of datasets related to datasets appropriate roles describe replication or partitioning and (with appropriate dates/times) provenance. Clearly it is possible to relate daatasets to software, licences, organisations, equipment (sensors) etc.

The design of CERIF respects both referential and functional integrity which is an advantage over simpler metadata schemes and the reason why CERIF was chosen for EPOS (and other projects). For example, in CERIF a person exists independently of whether they are employed, an author, a copyright holder or a software developer – all of which might be coincident. Metadata schemes which, for example, have person as an attribute in an instance of a publication (where the attribute name might be author or creator) violate functional integrity and may – depending on cardinality – violate referential integrity. CERIF provides for multilinguality; each text string can have multilingual variants.

Additionally, CERIF has a semantic layer – interoperable with the well-known W3C standards OWL and SKOS – which has the same design philosophy as the rest of CERIF. It has base entities and linking entities. The base entities of the semantic layer are classification schemes (rather like namespaces) and classification (i.e. terms). The linking entities allow terms from different classification schemes to be related by roles such as is equivalent to, is broader than, is narrower than and so on – like a thesaurus or ontology. This flexibility is important and having the semantic layer integrated within the model – and using conventional data processsing technology - makes for efficient processing especially when crosswalking to interoperate across semantc domains is reuqired. In implementation, the terms representing role from linking relations in the rest of CERIF are unique identifiers which – in the semantic later – are translated to terms. This allows for multilingual terms for the same role. Similarly, the semantic layer holds valid terms for values of a particular attribute in the rest of CERIF – for example the values for country code from the ISO standard. Holding all term values in the semantic layer and referencing them through unique identifiers from the rest of CERIF allows terminological /semantic contol and improves the accuracy and interoperability of the data.

However the original CERIF design was aiming to describe all aspects of research process which ended up with the publication, product or patent as a final output.

Within the context of EPOS, the output (product) of research is a more complex object, a product which can potentially include very diverse kind of data and data products. Some developments in this area to extend CERIF were already started. In 2013 a data extension proposal for CERIF for the purposes of EPOS was initiated by investigating CKAN, DCAT and eGMS and was guided by a draft proposal of the Jisc-funded CERIF for Datasets (C4D) project (cerif4datasets.wordpress.com). In EPOS, as a comprehensive list of all the possible data products would have been very difficult, if not impossible, to draft, a categorization has been carried out taking into account previous work done on levels of data products from NASA (science.nasa.gov/earth-science/earth-science-data/data-processing-levels-for-eosdis-data-products), Interface Region Imaging Spectrography (IRIS) (www.lmsal.com/iris_science/doc?cmd=dcur&proj_num=IS0076 &file_type=pdf), UNAVCO (pbo.unavco.org/data/gps) and others including the particle physics community and datacentres in the natural environment communities.

This work yielded the EPOS data levels categorisation:

- **Level 0:** raw data, or basic data (example: seismograms, accelerograms, time series, etc.)
- **Level 1:** data products coming from nearly automated procedures (earthquake locations, magnitudes, focal mechanism, shakemaps, etc.)
- **Level 2:** data products resulting by scientists' investigations (crustal models, strain maps, earthquake source models, etc.)
- **Level 3:** integrated data products coming from complex analyses or community shared products (hazards maps, catalogue of active faults, etc.)

The extension to CERIF proposed by C4D – and now adopted in the current version of the CERIF model as published - is able to handle all the data encompassed by this categorisation. Furthemore, the relationships between datasets at the different levels - and the processing or operations that caused the generation of a new derived dataset – can be recorded together with software, persons, organisations involved and the temporal duration of the transition.

5.4   Data Discovery with EPOS ICS

The three-layer metadata structure can effectively represent and manage the levels of commonality among all the metadata describing datasets provided by the data providers (or similarly for users, software services and resources). Discovery level is somewhat abstract but provides a target list of potentially relevant data (or software, resources) while contextual level provides the lowest common metadata across all domains and allows an end-user or software to assess the relevance and quality of the data for the purpose at hand. The community specific metadata (lowest level) is hence not ingested by the system as a whole: only a subset of it is mapped into the Metadata Catalogue – sufficient for (a) providing the end-user or software with information to characterise the object(s) being accessed and assess their quality related to the purpose at hand; (b) to provide the acces route (usually an API). However in order to have a reliable access to the local data, the Integrated Core Services had to set up efficient communication mechanisms into the so called compatibility layer. This layer makes possible the linkage between ICS and TCS (and when required institutional RIs) thus enabling discovery and integration capabilities. The thematic core services (TCS) are developed independently by their respective communities and in order to provide data and metadata to the ICS (but more in general to be interoperable at international level) they provide software interfaces to access their systems, usually just end-user services to discover appropriate datasets or software and –in some cases – limited processing.

To fetch and discover the desired data and metadata, ICS can then: (i) access to TCS web-services, (ii) access TCS generic APIs, (iii) link directly to datasets and ingest the metadata by means of some automated process or – if it is an infrequent access channel - manually. The automated process is a conversion driven by an earlier metadata matching and mapping exercise which can be manual (once and thereafter automated using the convertor driven by the mapping parameters) or part-automated using one of the techniques mentioned in the Previous Work section (Section 2).

To enable such a communication (compatibility layer) a new entity was introduced in the CERIF scheme – the cfServiceInterfaceDescription – and the cfService was used with a special meaning: the entity is supposed to store information about the webservice or API providing data. The purpose of these two new proposed entities is to store all the information necessary to enable the system to connect to the desired service and map the metadata of interest into the cfResulProduct entity.

6   Using EPOS for Science

The aim of EPOS is to provide for the solid Earth community a research infrastructure for data intensive science making use of integrated data and community-constructed software services by users utilizing resources (computing, laboratory equipment, sensors/detectors). To achieve this, two clearly differentiated steps are needed: (i) integration, (ii) intensive data processing. The latter goes beyond the determined capability of the EPOS Preparatory Phase Project and the e-Infrastructure just depicted, whose role is to orchestrate the use of distributed processing facilities (and for instance determine whether it is convenient to move data to HPC centers or code to local datacenters / repositories with some processing capabilities). However, the EPOS e-Infrastructure architecture has been designed to accommodate data-intensive processing with analytics, data mining, simulation and visualization. Nonetheless, the data integration (and to some extent user, software service and resource integration) is covered by the EPOS ICS.

It is here that the requirement for rich metadata becomes apparent. Some general purpose discovery tools, protocols and mechanisms, as for instance OAISTER for query with Open Archives Initiative Protocol for Metadata Harvesting (OAI-PMH) for data transfer, can be effective for discovery of data repositories or of datasets. However, given the variety and complexity of objects in the EPOS e-Infrastructure a robust handling of metadata is needed. The relevance (precision) and recall (completeness) of retrieval has to be better than that achieved with the commonly available technologies. The complexity of data structures (which usually imply some meaning in terms of methods of data collection or initial processing) and the detail of the semantics require rich metadata in order to achieve quality results.

When heterogeneous data are confined within the field of Earth Sciences, a general discovery can be carried on using the contextual layer of the three-layers structure described above, which contains the maximal level of commonality among all the data products (i.e. it is the lowest level (between abstract and detail) that is applicable across all the digitally represented objects in the e-Infrastructure). Using the information contained in the metadata catalog, the system can hence retrieve community specific metadata, thus enabling the user to perform a fine tuning of the discovery parameters (i.e. using specific metadata elements rather than generic ones) and the system itself to orchestrate higher level functions (visualization and processing) over distributed resources. With such a robust management of metadata through a CERIF-based catalog, the path to data-intensive science gets closer and easier, thus creating new perspectives for science data processing.

7   Conclusion

In this work we outline the main concepts of EPOS, and describe its e-infrastructure devoted also to data intensive science. Such an e-infrastructure makes use of the CERIF data model not for its usual domain of   managing research information but to run a complex metadata catalog system which will – with middleware - enable EPOS services to perform advanced functions. These functions, in turn, will improve the capabilities of scientists dealing with Earth Sciences. EPOS – or more precisely EPOS-PP - has therefore demonstrated with a prototype for the full EPOS system the power and utilization of the CERIF data model for building a data-intensive e-infrastructure for geoscience.

Acknowledgements. The authors acknowledge the work of their colleagues in EPOS WG7 e-Infrastructure team, in particular the work of Luca Trani, Frieder Euteneuer, Damian Ulbricht and also the work of Alessandro Bartoloni, Carmela Freda and others from the EPOS Management Office. The continual encouragement of the EPOS-PP project leader, Massimo Cocco, is acknowledged gratefully. EPOS-PP e-Infrastructure design has been influenced heavily by the requirements and planned requirements of community groups within EPOS covering a wide range of aspects of earth sciences: intensive discussions with those groups are acknowledged. The team has received much support from euroCRIS and particularly Nikos Houssos. Finally, Keith Jeffery is pleased to acknowledge the financial support of NERC/BGS part-provided by EC funding to lead the e-Infrastructure team and thus after many years working in many aspects of ICT to return to the domain of his initial degree and PhD.

References

[BaVaVaBuFrMaBo08] Basili, R., Valensise, G., Vannoli, P., Burrato, P., Fracassi, U., Mariano, S., Boschi, E.: The Database of Individual Seismogenic Sources (DISS), version 3: Summarizing 20 years of research on Italy's earthquake geology. Tectonophysics 453(1-4), 20–43 (2008)

[BuJe13] Bunakov, V., Jeffery, K.: Licence Management for Public Sector Information. In: Proceedings Conference for E-Demoracy and Open Government (CeDEM), pp. 292–302. Donau University Krems (2013) ISBN 978-3-902505-30-9

[DoHaIv12] Doan, A.H., Halevy, A., Ives, Z.: Principles of Data Integration. Elsevier Science (2012)

[FrHaMa05] Franklin, M.J., Halevy, A.Y., Maier, D.: Halevy, David Maier: From databases to dataspaces: a new abstraction for information management. SIGMOD Record 34(4), 27–33 (2005)

[HaRaOr06] Halevy, A., Rajaraman, A., Ordille, J.: Data integration: the teenage years. In: Conference on Very Large Data Bases (2006)

[HeTaTo09] Hey, T., Tansley, S., Tolle, K.: The fourth paradigm. Data-Intensive Scientific Discovery. Microsoft Research (2009)

[JeAsHoJö13] Jeffery, K., Asserson, A., Houssos, N., Jörg, B.: A 3-Layer Model for Metadata. In: Proc. Int'l Conf. on Dublin Core and Metadata Applications, pp. 3–5 (2013)

[JeHuKaWiBeMa94] Jeffery, K.G., Hutchinson, E.K., Kalmus, J.R., Wilson, M.D., Behrendt, W., Macnee, C.A.: A Model for Heterogeneous Distributed Databases. In: Bowers, D.S. (ed.) BNCOD 1994. LNCS, vol. 826, pp. 221–234. Springer, Heidelberg (1994)

[KoJe95] Kohoutkova, J., Jeffery, K.G.: Hypermedata: Interoperability for Health-care Systems. In: Proceedings MBB 1995, Slovakia (September 1995)

[Le02] Lenzerini, M.: Data Integration: A Theoretical Perspective. In: Proc. of the ACM Symp.on Principles of Database Systems (PODS), pp. 233–246 (2002)

[SuEcGi08] Suarez, G., Van Eck, T., Giardini, D.: The International Federation of Digital Seismograph Networks (FDSN): An Integrated System of Seismological Observatories. Systems Journal (3), 431–438 (2008)

[SuJeGi77] Sutterlin, P.G., Jeffery, K.G., Gill, E.M.: Filematch: A Format for the Interchange of Computer Based Files of Structured Data. Computers and Geosciences 3, 429–468 (1977)

Finding Agriculture among Biodiversity: Metadata in Practice

Jane Bromley, David King, and David R. Morse

Department of Computing and Communications,
The Open University,
Milton Keynes,
MK7 6AA, UK
{j.m.bromley,david.king,david.morse}@open.ac.uk

Abstract. The breadth of biodiversity literature available through the Biodiversity Heritage Library (BHL) is potentially of great use to agricultural research. It provides access to literature drawn from across the world, and its archives document the Earth as it was one hundred years ago and more. However, this strength of BHL is also its weakness: the breadth of coverage of BHL can complicate finding relevant literature. In this short paper, we will explore the practical issues arising from attempting to filter out relevant legacy literature to support agricultural research.

Keywords: agriculture, biodiversity, metadata, AGRIS, AGROVOC, agrotags, KEA, BHL, LCSH, search, keywords, subjects, classification, information retrieval.

1 Introduction

The work described in this paper comes from the EU FP7 funded agINFRA project [1], which aims to promote data sharing in agricultural sciences. We are seeking to enhance an existing specialist agricultural resource, AGRIS [2], with content from a more comprehensive – but general – resource, the Biodiversity Heritage Library (BHL) [3], without introducing too many items that are irrelevant to agriculture. In doing this we are not attempting to develop new filtering algorithms. Rather our core task is to create a simple workflow to harvest and filter relevant content from BHL to make it accessible through AGRIS.

We describe how we use AGROVOC [4], a specialist agricultural controlled vocabulary, to assist in accurate filtering of BHL content, and how these vocabulary terms both help and hinder that process. The issues that we are addressing throughout this paper are "what is a suitable list of terms to use to filter?" and "what should we filter on – provided metadata such as the title, classification and subject, or the whole text?"

A brief overview of the relevant repositories and workflows follows.

S. Closs et al. (Eds.): MTSR 2014, CCIS 478, pp. 185–192, 2014.

AGRIS. The UN Food and Agriculture Organization's AGRIS (International Information System for Agricultural science and technology) is a mainstay of agriculture research. AGRIS began in 1976 as a bibliographic reference library to which all interested researchers could contribute, promoting access to agricultural information. It now has more than seven million references, and links to relevant data resources on the web.

AGROVOC. To complement AGRIS, FAO developed AGROVOC, a controlled vocabulary to be "used by researchers, librarians and information managers for indexing, retrieving and organizing data in agricultural information systems and web pages". The consistency provided by using a specific set of defined terms to access agricultural information, including AGRIS, assists productive use of that information. Applying AGROVOC terms to filtered BHL content exposed through AGRIS brings the benefits of discoverability through linked open data to that content.[1]

Biodiversity Heritage Library. The BHL is a large digital archive of legacy biodiversity literature, comprising (in July 2014) over 44 million pages scanned from books, monographs, and journals. The BHL project began in 2005 when ten natural history museum libraries, botanical libraries, and research institutions in the UK and the USA agreed to collaborate in digitizing their legacy literature [5], with texts dating back as far as the c16th. It now draws on libraries "that cooperate to digitize and make accessible the legacy literature of biodiversity" from all of the inhabited continents [6].

Complementing the public domain literature in their collections, the BHL partners have obtained permission from publishers to digitize and publish significant copyrighted content. In conjunction with the partners' geographical scope, this makes the BHL a valuable resource of accessible biodiversity literature. This long-term view can prove invaluable in locating wild relatives of crops and understanding their relationship to local habitats and ecosystems.

Workflow – Filtering BHL. BHL's metadata is available as a download [7], updated monthly. Our workflow processes the downloaded metadata to identify agriculturally relevant content, for which we then request the full bibliographic record directly from BHL using its public API [8]. We then pass those records to FAO who imports them into AGRIS. The workflow uses Python scripts that will be freely available on completion of our work.

Related Work. Previous writings about BHL's metadata [9] do not discuss its utility. Instead, they consider only the practical problems of assigning metadata to BHL content, given the need to maintain a high throughput in the digitization process, and handling the vagaries of historic biodiversity literature such as separate foldout pages. The current paper does not address these digitization workflow issues.

---

[1] We acknowledge there are related filtering options we could use, eg CAB thesaurus and NALT. However, AGROVOC has the advantage of being an enhancement to AGRIS. In the future, GACS should supersede AGROVOC but is still in development.

Previous writings about BHL's content have focused on specific tasks such as named entity recognition [10] within its content in order to improve information retrieval. The current paper does not investigate such methods to enhance retrieval, but to filter BHL content using existing content and search capabilities.

2   Filtering Options

This section discusses using four sources of data available to filter out agriculturally relevant resources from BHL, beginning with the item's title, then considering the metadata attributes in subject and classification, and finally using the whole text itself.

2.1   Filtering on Full Title

Our initial approach to filtering was to look for AGROVOC terms in titles because this is the one data source we knew would always be available. Using the October 2012 BHL data export of 56,568 titles, we found that 85% (37,793 titles) of English-language titles contained at least one AGROVOC term, and 73% (41,455 titles) of all titles contained at least one AGROVOC term. This initially promising result masked three problems.

First, 85% (or even 73%) seems a high estimate for the proportion of titles in BHL that are agriculturally relevant. Reviewing the first 20 titles identified suggested they could be appropriate. However, reviewing the top 5 terms that matched[2] to something in a title (birds, plants, history, animals, species) struck us as not particularly *agricultural*, and indeed led to inappropriate titles being selected for inclusion in AGRIS, as identified when we manually reviewed the complete list of filtered titles.

Second, we were not the first researchers to find that AGROVOC can be very broad, and consider that a smaller, focused set of terms could be more discerning. ICRISAT (The International Crops Research Institute for the Semi-Arid Tropics) led the work [11] that produced AGROTAGS [12], a subset of AGROVOC. With some minor edits to aid matching of AGROTAGS terms in item titles, such as removing brackets from the terms, we applied an edited AGROTAGS list as a filter to BHL and retrieved a list 17,670 English-language titles. While the AGROTAGS results list is about half the size of the AGROVOC results list, similar issues in the filtered titles relevance to agriculture emerged when we reviewed the output.

Third, the underlying issue affecting our use of both AGROVOC and AGROTAGS to filter BHL titles is that terms in both lists are not unique to agriculture. An example of the many rather general terms is dry season. In reviewing the accuracy of the results lists we found that a human, reading just the title, cannot tell if the material is relevant: hidden away in the text can be relevant and useful information that is not explicitly explained in the title. Unfortunately, from our perspective, we were not dealing solely with tightly descriptive scientific publications having meaningful titles:

---

[2] The matching algorithm applies the list of AGROVOC terms alphabetically and stops when a match is found somewhere in the title. Hence, this is not a proper frequency analysis.

BHL's content is broader than that. However, this is a well-known phenomenon, for which the solution is to assign keyword metadata to each item. Therefore, we next investigated the use of keywords to filter BHL content.

2.2   Filtering on Subject

Keywords, or subjects as BHL names them, aid searching for relevant material. Works can have multiple subjects assigned to them and are intended to indicate the content of a work. Hence, they could be used for filtering, as well as searching, BHL.

The subjects applied to BHL's content come from several sources. Most subjects are already associated with the material in the donating institution and are added to the content's BHL metadata as part of the digitization process. These subjects typically include the Library of Congress Subject Heading (LCSH) [13], because many consortium members are libraries and curate their collections using this system. Additional ad hoc metadata can be supplied manually during the digitization process and after. Text mining is used to identify taxonomic names automatically in the content, providing another means to search the literature [14]. Other potential search criteria, such as people and places, are not currently automatically identified using text mining, though BHL would like to enhance its workflow to include this process. The net result is that currently, the metadata subjects might not provide a comprehensive insight into the content of a document.

The July 2014 BHL export data shows that 72,034 out of 77,552 (or 92.88%) titles have subject words associated with them.. That this value is slightly down on typical metadata completeness, as reported for example by Tsiflidou and Manouselis when assessing metadata tools [15], is a product of the BHL data import process. However, we felt there is sufficient coverage of the content to make selection on subjects a valid filtering technique.

Our filtering is based on looking for appropriate LCSH terms in the BHL Subjects field. This is effective not only because the majority of BHL's contributing libraries manage their collections using the Library of Congress cataloging scheme, but where other schemes are used, the subject terms are broadly similar. An added benefit of using LCSH to filter the titles is that the Subjects associated with each title can be translated to AGROVOC using the mapping developed as part of the AGROVOC Linked Open Data project [16, 17]. This mapping simplifies the integration of BHL metadata into AGRIS.

Using monocot as our topic of interest identified seven BHL titles. Interestingly, four titles used the LCSH preferred term 'Monocotyledons', while three used the older and still recognized though no longer to be used 'Monocotyledones'. This offers the possibility of automating record curation before import into AGRIS, bringing all seven items in line with current usage, though at the expense of maintaining detailed matching lists of variant terms. Therefore, we considered exploiting the hierarchical nature of LCSH, and to select titles based on higher-level subjects only. In this example, the broader term for Monocotyledons is Angiosperms.

We experimented by just using the high-level LCSH term "Agriculture" to filter the Subject field, which returned 2,123 titles (2.74%) as relevant. Filtering the Subject field using the wider criteria of any term that includes the word "agriculture" returned 2,314 items (2.98%), while using "agricultural" returned 881 items (1.14%).

Repeating the experiment starting with a narrow filter using just the LCSH term "Horticulture" returned 3,047 titles (3.93%) as relevant. Filtering on the wider criteria of terms that include the word "horticulture" returned 3,834 items (4.94%), while using "horticultural" returned 83 items (0.11%).

There was some overlap in these results, hence the total titles filtered as agriculturally relevant using LCSH "Agriculture" and "Horticulture" was only just over 4,000 titles. This represents less than 10% of the content of BHL, which was surprisingly small given the large number of titles previously identified as potentially agriculturally relevant.

Many titles have very restricted Subjects, e.g. Banana is used as the Subject for five items and none of them would have been retrieved if "Agriculture" or "Horticulture" had been used as the filter term because they did not have these higher-level terms in their Subject fields. The issue can lead to relevant titles being hard to select. While using a few common LCSH terms, such as "Agriculture", seems a good way to filter it means that many useful items are missed. Therefore, we next considered returning to a larger list of LCSH terms, but only agriculturally relevant ones.

To achieve this goal we exploited the set of LCSH terms that map directly to an AGROVOC term. Reviewing the list of mapped terms did not induce confidence because it contains generic terms such as "Bread", "Density" and "Mouth". Therefore, we began to contemplate repeating the manual curation adopted by ICRISAT when producing AGROTAGS, and to produce our own list of terms to filter BHL Subjects.

We began to prepare a hand-crafted list by reading LCSH and selecting all related terms in suitable hierarchies, but soon realized this would not be sustainable beyond the end of the agINFRA project to accommodate updates to LCSH. In addition, our discovery work with BHL content quickly exposed items whose Subjects do not reveal the true content of the item. For example, David Livingstone's *Missionary travels and researches in South Africa* [18], has the following subjects: 1813-1873; Description and travel; Livingstone, David; Missions; South Africa; Travel. Neither the title nor the Subject list suggest that this is relevant to agriculture, but the table of contents shows: domestic animals, The Boers as Farmers, Discovery of grape-bearing vines, The sugar-cane, Coffee Estate, Coffee Plantations amongst others.

Therefore, we turned to another means of identifying books used by librarians, and which should also benefit from their curation of the titles before submission to BHL.

2.3   Filtering on Classification

Libraries assign a unique Classification to the items in their collection using a Classification Authority, such as Library of Congress Classification LCC and Dewey Decimal Classification DCC. For example, LCC classifications starting with S mean the item is Agricultural, as does DCC 630. This Classification also informs the item's shelf-mark or Call Number, which is the physical location of the item. Being unique for each item, we investigated the utility of the Classification for filtering material.

In the July 2014 BHL data export, around 13,000 items have LCC Agriculture. Hence, selecting items with LCC Classification "Agriculture" would net just over 15% of the content of BHL. Unfortunately, the classification is not always present. In the July 2014 data export, only 43,848 of the titles in BHL (56.54%) have a Classification associated with them. Therefore, this could be good enough to filter BHL material as a rough and ready method with a high proportion of the retrieved titles being relevant, but would fail to retrieve many relevant titles. In technical terms, filtering on Classification would easily deliver high precision but with low recall [19].

Further, we have found we would be at the whim of each library's local practice. It is up to each library to assign a Call Number, which may include looking at the title, introduction and content, while using a classification manual for guidance. The final choice is up to the particular library; and depends on things like its particular size and remit. So, for instance, what one library places on the Agriculture shelf, another may place under Horticulture, or Economics. Hence, L'Illustration horticole [20] is listed under Botany (LCC QK), though it contains useful information about Floriculture, Gardening, Greenhouses and Horticulture. Should we filter on QK, however, we would identify many items that are not agriculturally relevant because the Classification 'Botany' is too broad a term.

Returning to our Subject example in the previous section, of the five texts with the Subject Banana, four are classified as S, Agriculture, and one as QH, Natural history - Biology. Hence, filtering purely with the Classification S can produce relevant results, but it is not sufficient to identify all relevant literature. Yet filtering including the more general QH will prompt the retrieval of a wide range of natural history material not relevant to agriculture.

Therefore, it appears that filtering on terms in titles and subjects, and by classifications lead to the same problem: with a narrow set of terms we can achieve high precision but poor recall, and as we widen the set of terms used so precision falls off to such a degree as to invalidate our filtering. Hence, we turned to another source of information, the full content itself.

2.4   Filtering on the Whole Text

Given the accuracy and completeness issues with using metadata to filter relevant literature, we have begun to explore the option of filtering based on analyzing the whole text. This approach has two disadvantages. Firstly, we need access to the whole text not just the metadata export. Following an earlier collaboration with BHL, we have a 5Gb local copy of sample articles for our research. This avoids the issue of downloading and analyzing the text of BHL content during our research, though the issue of access remains for any possible later harvesting of the full BHL content. Secondly, there is the issue of the processing power required by the filtering process when compared with the previous metadata-based approaches.

We analyzed the whole text of a sample of articles using KEA [21], a keyword extraction tool trained to apply the AGROVOC vocabulary to the analyzed text. Applying this approach to analyzing the agriculturally relevant book, The arthropod fauna of potato fields [22], KEA identifies the key subjects as Arthropoda; Agriculture;

Canada; Control methods; New Brunswick; Research; Species; Fields; North America; Yields. This indicates it is a relevant item. In contrast, the BHL supplied key subjects Arthropoda; New Brunswick; Nomenclature, do not indicate the book's agricultural relevance. This suggests that whole text processing can be useful so we are continuing to develop this promising approach to filtering.

A probable refinement to our workflow will be to continue with a first level analysis of the metadata using a narrow set of manually curated AGROVOC terms to identify immediately relevant literature, and only incur the overhead of accessing and processing the whole text for the remaining texts whose relevance we cannot confidently determine solely from metadata.

3   Conclusion

This paper has documented briefly our experience with filtering the known content of one resource to make a relevant subset available to a new audience, enhanced with its discoverability through linked open data. We faced two key issues in our work.

The first issue was to identify "what is a suitable list of terms to use to filter?" While we are fortunate that our target domain of agricultural research has an established vocabulary, AGROVOC, in practice AGROVOC is too generic to be usefully applied unmodified to BHL. The degree of modification necessary to achieve high precision with acceptable recall is still under test.

The second issue was to ask "what should we filter on – provided metadata such as title, classification and subject, or the whole text?" The answer seems to be a combination of these data sources for we can relatively quickly assess the relevance of much material solely from its supplied Subject and Classification metadata, leaving a candidate body of material suggested by the presence of AGROVOC terms in the title to be further refined through whole text analysis.

There is an interplay between these two issues, for it is possible that we can accept poor recall when addressing issue one because it can be overcome by our whole text work to address issue two. Our work to develop this complete workflow, and provide metrics on its efficacy, continues.

Acknowledgements. The work is supported by agINFRA, a project funded by the EU Seventh Framework Programme (FP7) under objective Infra 2011 1.2.2, Data infrastructures for e-Science. Grant agreement no 283770. We are grateful to Valeria Pesce and Fabrizio Celli for their help in defining subsets of AGROVOC terms and importing references into AGRIS, and Guntram Geser for discussions.

References

1. agINFRA, http://aginfra.eu/ (accessed July 18, 2014)
2. AGRIS, http://agris.fao.org/es/content/about (accessed July 18, 2014)
3. BHL–Portal, http://www.biodiversitylibrary.org/ (accessed July 18, 2014)

4. AGROVOC, http://aims.fao.org/website/AGROVOC-Thesaurus/sub (accessed July 18, 2014)
5. Gwinn, N.E., Rinaldo, C.: The Biodiversity Heritage Library: sharing biodiversity literature with the world. IFLA Journal 35(1), 25–34 (2009)
6. BHL–Africa, http://blog.biodiversitylibrary.org/2013/04/making-bhl-africa-reality-bhl-africa.html (accessed July 18, 2014)
7. BHL–Export, http://biodivlib.wikispaces.com/Data+Exports (accessed July 18, 2014)
8. BHL–API, http://biodivlib.wikispaces.com/Developer+Tools+and+API (accessed July 18, 2014)
9. Pilsk, S.C., Person, M.A., Deveer, J.M., Furfey, J.F., Kalfatovic, M.R.: The Biodiversity Heritage Library: Advancing Metadata Practices in a Collaborative Digital Library. Journal of Library Metadata 10(2-3), 136–155 (2010)
10. Wei, Q., Heidorn, P.B., Freeland, C.: Name Matters: Taxonomic Name Recognition (TNR) in Biodiversity Heritage Library (BHL). Paper, iConference 2010 (2010), http://hdl.handle.net/2142/14919
11. Balaji, V., Bhatia, M.B., Kumar, R., Neelam, L.K., Panja, S., Prabhakar, T.V., Samaddar, R., Soogareddy, B., Sylvester, A.G., Yadav, V.: Agrotags – A Tagging Scheme for Agricultural Digital Objects. In: Sánchez-Alonso, S., Athanasiadis, I.N. (eds.) MTSR 2010. CCIS, vol. 108, pp. 36–45. Springer, Heidelberg (2010), http://dx.doi.org/10.1007/978-3-642-16552-8_4
12. AGROTAGS, http://agropedia.iitk.ac.in/content/agrotags (accessed July 18, 2014)
13. Library of Congress Subject Heading files, http://www.loc.gov/aba/publications/FreeLCSH/freelcsh.html (accessed July 18, 2014)
14. BHL–scientific names, http://biodivlib.wikispaces.com/Developer+Tools+and+API#Developer%20Tools-Scientific%20Names (accessed July 18, 2014)
15. Tsiflidou, E., Manouselis, N.: Tools and Techniques for Assessing Metadata Quality. In: Garoufallou, E., Greenberg, J. (eds.) MTSR 2013. CCIS, vol. 390, pp. 99–110. Springer, Heidelberg (2013), http://dx.doi.org/10.1007/978-3-319-03437-9_11
16. AGROVOC Linked Open Data project, http://datahub.io/dataset/agrovoc-skos (accessed July 18, 2014)
17. Caracciolo, C., Stellato, A., Morshed, A., Johannsen, G., Rajbahndari, S., Jacques, Y., Keizer, J.: The AGROVOC Linked Dataset. Semantic Web 4(3), 341–348 (2013), http://eprints.rclis.org/20648/ (accessed July 18, 2014)
18. Download from, http://www.biodiversitylibrary.org/bibliography/60038#/summary
19. Van Rijsbergen, C.J.: Information retrieval. Butterworths, London (1979)
20. Download from, http://www.biodiversitylibrary.org/bibliography/131#/details
21. KEA, http://www.nzdl.org/Kea/ (accessed July 18, 2014)
22. Download from, http://www.biodiversitylibrary.org/bibliography/63088#/summary

LabTablet: Semantic Metadata Collection on a Multi-domain Laboratory Notebook

Ricardo Carvalho Amorim[1], João Aguiar Castro[1],
João Rocha da Silva[1], and Cristina Ribeiro[2]

[1] Faculdade de Engenharia da Universidade do Porto/INESC TEC, Porto, Portugal
{ricardo.amorim3,joaoaguiarcastro,joaorosilva}@gmail.com
[2] DEI—Faculdade de Engenharia da Universidade do Porto/INESC TEC,
Porto, Portugal
mcr@fe.up.pt

Abstract. The value of research data is recognized, and so is the importance of the associated metadata to contextualize, describe and ultimately render them understandable in the long term. Laboratory notebooks are an excellent source of domain-specific metadata, but this paper-based approach can pose risks of data loss, while limiting the possibilities of collaborative metadata production. The paper discusses the advantages of tools to complement paper-based laboratory notebooks in capturing metadata, regardless of the research domain. We propose LabTablet, an electronic laboratory book aimed at the collection of metadata from the early stages of the research workflow. To evaluate the use of LabTablet and the proposed workflow, researchers in two domains were asked to perform a set of tasks and provided insights about their experience. By rethinking the workflow and helping researchers to actively contribute to data description, the research outputs can be described with generic and domain-dependent metadata, thus improving their chances of being deposited, reused and preserved.

1 Introduction

The laboratory notebook is a well-established device to document the laboratory activity and may be organized according to the recommendations of an institution or a research group. Researchers involved in laboratory experiments are comfortable with paper notebooks and there is a long tradition of their acceptance as authoritative information sources and as legal documents [1]. It is however recognized that their major drawback is the difficulty in searching, sharing, and generically re-purposing the information in the notebook.

When data are created in a research environment, recording the context of their creation is essential to allow others to understand their meaning or to replicate the results of any derived analysis. Proper documentation of data also increases the likelihood of data being reused. This calls for the association of metadata to the collected data, a process which is recognized as hard due to the overhead it creates on the researchers and to the lack of specific tools [2].

S. Closs et al. (Eds.): MTSR 2014, CCIS 478, pp. 193–205, 2014.

As laboratory research is typically recorded in laboratory notebooks, they are a valuable source of domain-level metadata. Paper notebooks offer simplicity and flexibility, but besides the risk of loss and deterioration, the use of the information therein as metadata for the recorded experiments requires its transcription and the choice of an appropriate format for the metadata. Even when the transcription of the notebook's contents to a digital support is performed, this task is often left to later stages in the research process.

Both funding [3] and research institutions are already concerned with the preservation of their data, thus acknowledging that laboratory notebooks should also be included in the earlier stages of the research [4,5,6]. This has resulted in the emergence of several applications—electronic laboratory notebooks (ELNs)—intended to help researchers manage their observations and record personal notes.

The recent popularity and affordability of mobile devices such as smartphones and tablets has contributed to an increase in the number of ELN solutions[7]. These applications provide ways of recording written notes, pictures, and other information that can be sourced from portable devices. However, there is room for improvement when it comes to sharing those notes and integrating them with the remainder of research activities. We argue that ELNs should place a stronger emphasis on semantically-enabled and customizable representations of the metadata records they produce and export.

This work proposes an electronic laboratory notebook as part of a research data management workflow. It innovates by closely integrating with researchers' daily data management workflow and placing a stronger emphasis on metadata record production. It allows users to gather experimental context metadata (images, audio, notes, sensor information, etc.) but goes a step further than existing solutions by guiding researchers through the process of giving exact semantics to them. In our approach, every descriptor used in the application is drawn from an ontology; for example, `foaf:depiction` can be used to specify the semantics of a picture taken in the field that aims to provide a visual representation of an observed specimen. Since describing datasets from different domains calls for distinct sets of descriptors, the application can be customized according to the domain in which it is being used.

The complete workflow includes the synchronization of the metadata in the electronic notebook with an intermediate research data management platform—Dendro—developed to support the daily research activities, and a third stage where researchers can decide to deposit their data on a repository aimed at publication and long-term preservation, making them available to the scientific community and citable. The main goal is to bring researchers closer to the data management activities by allowing them to easily describe their data as soon as they are produced.

The paper is organized as follows. Section 2 is an overview of the current data management workflows, identifying the key concerns related to the creation and preservation of metadata records. Section 3 describes the LabTablet application, to be used by researchers to streamline metadata recording. Section 4 presents some preliminary evaluation results based on the feedback obtained from researchers in two domains who tested the application through a set of pre-defined tasks. Some ongoing extensions to the LabTablet platform are presented in the conclusions.

2 Improving the Data Management Workflow

Current research data management workflows follow similar stages in different research groups. Figure 1 shows three phases that data and metadata usually go through: gathering, improving and sharing. In the first phase, laboratory notebooks play an important role, whereas in the second a collaborative environment can be used to help researchers to save and manage the collected data. Finally, when a dataset is ready to be published (associated to a publication, for example), a data repository designed for long-term preservation comes into play.

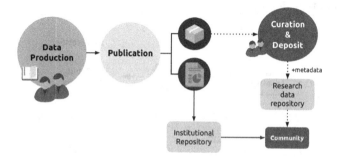

Fig. 1. Common data management workflow

To support the collaborative data creation phase, researchers often resort to tools designed to manage the data in the research group, before they can be disclosed. Email messages are the prevalent collaboration tool, but other popular solutions are collaborative file management platforms such as *Dropbox* or *Google Drive* that give researchers the ability to specify access control rules, while keeping record of changes. Other platforms specifically tailored to the research domain, such as LabFolder[1] and *labarchives*[2] also enable researchers to upload their data while providing them with tools to describe them through personal annotations. While these may be enough for creators to understand their own data in the short term, the reuse of the datasets may become impossible due to the lack of appropriate metadata and compliance with domain standards.

The final stage of the workflow includes the deposit of the dataset in a data repository. In some areas, namely in the life sciences and the social sciences, there are well-established repositories (NCBI[3] and ICPSR[4] are respective examples)

---

[1] https://www.labfolder.com/
[2] https://www.labarchives.com/
[3] http://www.ncbi.nlm.nih.gov/
[4] http://www.icpsr.umich.edu/

where researchers are used to deposit. In these cases the metadata models are also stable and the data curation routine has become part of the research process. We are dealing here with the so-called long-tail of research data, i.e. groups with insufficient resources to create their own data management tools [8] and where data description and publishing has yet to be established.

Figshare and Zenodo are examples of popular cross-domain repositories that, due to their ease of use and low usage costs, are more suited to the needs of these small research groups. These platforms allow dataset creators to include metadata such as the creator and a description of the new dataset, its associated license and, if applicable, an embargo period. In some cases, this information is limited to a small set of metadata elements and does not comply with any established metadata schema. In others, where there is this kind of compliance, the available elements are limited to generic, high-level descriptors. To help cope with these limitations, some platforms such as CKAN allow researchers to include domain-specific metadata at the time of deposit, complementing the generic mandatory descriptors.

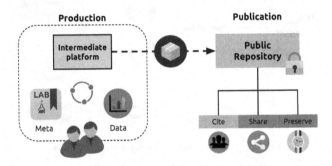

Fig. 2. Improved research data management workflow

Since research results may have already been published at this final stage, it is risky to assume that the creators of the original datasets will be available to participate in the description of their data. Also, as data creators, researchers hold the best knowledge about their data and therefore are key stakeholders when describing them [9]. Actively involving researchers in data description early in the process is therefore essential for the timely description of research datasets, which is necessary to ensure data publishing [10,11]. Laboratory notebooks were therefore selected for improvement and integration in a systematic research data management workflow, as they are a valuable source of contextual information regarding the production of many datasets [1].

While paper notebooks are inexpensive and portable, they are also a vulnerable storage media, as they can sometimes be misplaced or lost. Moreover, their contents are often structured according to the practices of an individual researcher or a research group, which can make them hard to interpret by others. As research is often a collaborative effort, it is common for the metadata recorded in the notebooks to be shared in the research group. For a paper-based notebook, however, sharing metadata for newly produced datasets among group members requires either physical contact with the notebook or the transcription of its information into a digital format (commonly a text document or a spreadsheet).

A representation of an improved workflow is shown in Figure 2. Instead of following an *a posteriori* approach to data description, we aim to integrate data description throughout the entire research workflow, an approach already followed in the past [8,12,13]. We identify a group of tools (Production) that researchers use to describe and manage their data, along with valuable domain-level metadata. In this scenario, a different collaborative platform, supporting both general-purpose and domain-level descriptors can help prepare data for the deposit in a repository. After the deposit process, data creators can reference the dataset in their publications and make it available to the research community while complying with their research data management plans. This seamless integration of rich metadata has to be supported by the entire ecosystem, meaning that the ELN solution, the collaborative environment and the selected repositories must be flexible enough to record domain-specific metadata records that take advantage of established semantics.

Popular note-taking solutions such as Evernote already allow researchers to manage simple metadata records [14,5]. Evernote is a general-purpose solution that helps users to produce not only text-based notes but also images and voice recordings. However, these general purpose environments can show their limitations when the number of managed notes increases. Researchers may find it difficult to look for a specific record in the ad-hoc, non-standard structure. At the same time, the absence of a structured metadata model means that the notes have to be organized at a later time, when they need to be associated with data records.

When analyzing ELN solutions, there are three types of application environments: purely web-based, mobile-only application and an integrated environment where the two work together. A web-based notebook is cross-platform since it works on any web browser, as a consequence it is compatible with a greater number of devices [4], but is not as portable nor capable of gathering sensor-based data. A purely mobile approach can take advantage of its portability to mimic some of the interaction with a traditional laboratory notebook [5], while the presence of many onboard sensors inside the device allows a native application to automatically gather richer metadata such as GPS positioning, temperature or altitude. The hybrid alternative combines the advantages of the two approaches. It provides both a web-based interface for collaborative data management and a native application for data production, enabling the gathering of sensor-based metadata but allowing subsequent manipulation using a computer terminal, which is more comfortable for researchers to use when handling large numbers of metadata records—*LabFolder*, *labarchives* and our own data management ecosystem are examples of these hybrid platforms.

3   The LabTablet Application

LabTablet is designed for ease of use and seamless integration with the research workflow, helping researchers produce better data descriptions by harnessing a mobile device's capabilities. These can then be used to produce standardized metadata records that can be shared within the group through a collaborative web-based data management platform. Provenance and descriptive metadata can be included, much like in a traditional notebook [1], making activities like metadata validation and exchange faster and easier. Designed for the long tail of research, the LabTablet application can be customized to better suit common data description needs of researchers from different domains by including different sets of ontology-based descriptors in its application profile.

3.1   Demonstration and Walkthrough

To support different research domains, LabTablet uses previously prepared descriptors that are loaded into the application through an application profile. As a mobile application, it takes advantage of the operative system features such as the set of available sensors—position, magnetic field, ambient light and temperature—as well as the built-in microphone and camera to help in the description process. According to our revised workflow, metadata collected during research activities can be exported to describe a folder in the collaborative platform. This folder can then be used by researchers to deposit the actual data gathered in their activities. After the data is processed and the results are published, datasets can be exported from the collaborative platform to a long-term repository so that both data creators and other researchers can cite the datasets. Since some researchers may not be interested in disclosing their data [15], this final step is optional as they can keep their data within the intermediate repository where they can have full control over data access.

The selected collaborative data management environment is Dendro [16]. Dendro consists of an ontology based repository focused on allowing researchers to describe their data with domain specific metadata, regardless of their research domain. To maintain the interoperability with other data management platforms, Dendro complements the generic purpose metadata schemas with specific descriptors extracted from ontologies designed for the description of resources from different domains. Furthermore, it is also possible to create and manage projects as sets of folders and files, in a similar way as it is done by popular cloud based storage services such as *Dropbox*.

Since Dendro does not implement important features for long-term data management such as detailed deposit workflows, embargoes or licensing, we have assessed the capabilities of three major data repositories that already do—CKAN, Figshare and Zenodo. After our evaluation, we opted for CKAN as the long-term repository platform for finished research datasets. This repository features a fully functional API, and while not explicitly encouraging the use of structured metadata, it enables its users to complement any metadata record with domain-specific descriptors through sets of key-value pairs.

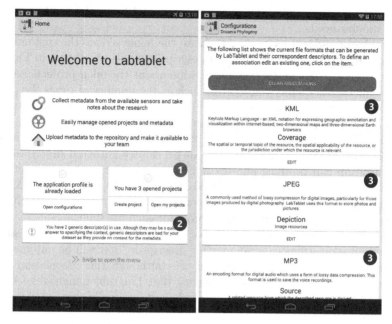

Fig. 3. Initial screen and customization features

Metadata records produced by LabTablet follow a standard representation as soon as they are added to the Dendro platform, but a translation process is necessary when exporting them to CKAN, due to the different capabilities of the platforms. Dendro stores a domain-specific metadata value, for example the `achem:sampleCount`[5] of a dataset as an edge in its underlying graph. When exporting the dataset to CKAN, one will be limited to key-value pairs when specifying dataset metadata, so that particular pair would have to be exported as a human-readable textual representation of the edge, for example: `Field Name: Sample Count`[6]`, Value: 142`. This way, each descriptor can be uniquely identified, even if they have the same `rdf:label` property within Dendro. The only foreseeable consequence is that the ontology has to be available for reference when interpreting the dataset in the future; some domain-specific ontologies may not be widely used and become unavailable in the long term, but those that are well established will ensure the durability of metadata records.

As an open-source project, CKAN has the support of many entities, including government agencies that use it to disclose institutional data[7]. CKAN can, unlike subscription-based competitors, be installed and managed entirely within a research institution. This approach can be beneficial for institutions that intend

---

[5] A property defined in a purpose-built ontology for describing chemistry datasets, representing the number of samples used in an experiment

[6] http://dendro.fe.up.pt/ontology/achem/sampleCount

[7] http://ckan.org/instances/

to keep data in a repository under their control and tailor the solution itself to their particular needs.

LabTablet provides three main interfaces: the home screen, the customization area and the project management and description tools. As shown in Figure 3, the home screen shows statistical information about the open projects (Area 1) as well as metadata quality related tips such as the number of times the generic descriptor is used across all the projects (Area 2). From this page, the user can either navigate to the list of open favorites or start a new one.

The second module allows users to customize their application by loading an application profile, containing a set of previously gathered descriptors. As this application can produce non-textual metadata—for instance, a picture to be included as the object of a `foaf:depiction` property, or a Keyhole Markup Language (KML) file as the `dcterms:coverage` of the dataset being produced—it makes sense to specify default descriptors for each file type.

With this in mind, the user can associate frequent file extensions—such as images or voice recordings—to an existing descriptor, that will be automatically suggested whenever the extension is in use (although this association is not permanent). For each of the file extensions that LabTablet manages (Area 3) the researcher can choose one descriptor to be automatically associated with the corresponding records.

The last module is responsible for the core functionalities of the application, from viewing and editing the recorded metadata, up to preparing and uploading it to the repository. Within the application, we also defined the concept of favorite as a folder in Dendro that the researcher chooses to describe. For instance, an ecology research team would create a favorite for each field trip and then proceed to describe the data collected in that activity. At this time, though, it is not required that the folder exists in the destination.

3.2 Metadata Collection

To describe a dataset, a previously created application profile puts together the descriptors that will be available as soon as the researcher starts using the application. LabTablet can also import descriptors from an existing Dendro project, thus complementing the pre-loaded application profile. Recording metadata can be done either by adding values to each descriptor, or by starting a session and collecting several records from the onboard sensors of the mobile device, as well as manual researcher inputs.

To add a metadata value, the researcher needs to select a descriptor and then proceed to assign its value (a textual value, for example). In the second case, presented in Figure 4, researchers can add values provided by the device's onboard sensors (1), including freehand drawing on the touch screen, recorded audio notes, or photos (2). Another implemented feature is the continuous GPS monitoring (3) that generates a KML file—an XML-based (and thus preservation-friendly) format used by *Google Earth*—containing all the recorded coordinates in a standard representation. By turning on this feature, researchers can gather a geographic boundary or represent a specific route, recording the geographical

Fig. 4. Field mode and metadata validation, together with the result of uploading the records

locations visited during their field experiments. Upon ending the session, the researcher is prompted to validate the collected records. At this stage, it is possible to assign a descriptor to each of the gathered values or discard the unwanted ones. After this validation, all the accepted metadata records will be added to the session and thus be available to be uploaded to the repository.

After each session, the researcher can edit (4) and upload the metadata to the group's shared working area in a data management repository. This upload ensures that the records are backed up to the data management platform (5) and allows the researcher to continue editing the metadata record after it has been uploaded. If mistakes are found in the uploaded record, they can simply be corrected in the LabTablet application and uploaded again. Dendro will replace the metadata records, keeping track of all versions.

3.3 Data Management Improvements

The proposed data management workflow starts with the researcher creating data and, at the same time, describing it using the application. The key difference when comparing to a regular workflow is that metadata records will already be recorded in Dendro and associated with standard descriptors when the actual data is ready to be shared in the research group, thus keeping data and metadata together.

LabTablet does not require an active Internet connection to the repository up to the time when data is sent to the research group's working area in Dendro. During the entire data production process, the application is available to collect records and locally store them, just as with regular laboratory notebooks. In the event of the presence of a network connection, metadata records can of course be available from the moment they are recorded.

The resulting workflow can be less dependent on both the research team and the curator, specially as some validation of the collected metadata is already done as it is recorded. As the device can be synchronized frequently, researchers are able to backup their metadata records at the end of each activity. Seamless integration with a long-term data repository such as CKAN allows data creators to quickly deposit datasets that can be cited, either by them in their publications or by others.

4   Preliminary Evaluation

The development of the LabTablet application has followed the strategy already adopted for Dendro: working in close partnership with the users. A panel of researchers have been engaged in the identification of requirements for research data management and in the validation of the tools. Their involvement is in itself a proof of the growing interest of researchers in data management actions. For the preliminary evaluation of LabTablet, researchers from two domains accepted our invitation and provided feedback. The first domain is the chemical engineering and our subject is well acquainted with the data management practices followed at his laboratory. The second domain is biodiversity and our subject is an expert on the fields of biodiversity and evolutionary biology.

For each of the research groups, both Dendro and LabTablet had to be parameterized in order to provide researchers with adequate sets of descriptors for their specific domains. Dendro's parameterization is performed by loading available ontologies on the web, such as *Dublin Core* or *FOAF*, to obtain generic descriptors. For the domain-specific descriptors not available in a public ontology, a lightweight ontology was modeled and loaded [17]. The parameterization of LabTablet, on the other hand, is performed by building an application profile which, while not currently being specified in RDF format, uses descriptors sourced from the ontologies that are loaded into Dendro.

4.1   Chemical Engineering

In the chemical engineering laboratory, metadata from each research activity is mostly recorded in laboratory notebooks and translated to a digital media at the end of the research work. Regarding data storage, research data is kept on local storage devices such as USB thumb drives or personal computers. The researchers sometimes use cloud-based solutions such as *Dropbox* and *Google Drive* to share their datasets locally, but data from external institutions or companies is not shared at all due to legal restrictions. We had access to one of these datasets in order to evaluate their requirements in terms of metadata descriptors. The data, as described by the data creators, concerns measurements of the concentration of a specific sediment in the sea water. As they routinely perform studies of this kind, we were told that they can make particularly good use of a pre-defined application profile. An application profile has been designed for this purpose, including the basic Dublin Core descriptors, as well as domain specific ones—for example, the *sample* (a word or phrase describing the collected sample), and the *compound_group* (a description of the analyzed elements). To understand the concepts related with metadata, our subject suggested that a preliminary introduction to the concepts of *descriptor* and *descriptor value* would be useful. After this explanation, they quickly understood the similarity between LabTablet and their familiar laboratory notebooks.

After performing a series of tasks using the application, the researcher went over some of the aspects considered interesting to improve the daily work in the laboratory. He considered it useful to have the metadata records promptly available as soon as the activity ended, and also recognized that using a traditional laboratory notebook would require the transcription of the records to a digital support, which was not guaranteed. In this particular case, the researcher was not interested in uploading data to a public repository, due to contractual constraints. Nevertheless he acknowledged the usefulness of the electronic laboratory notebook. As for the negative aspects, he pointed out that it was harder to input text in the tablet, since the touch keyboard can be cumbersome. We recorded this and observed that, to input longer texts for certain descriptors, the task could be performed directly in Dendro, in a computer with a full keyboard.

4.2 Biodiversity

After the contact with the researcher from the chemical engineering domain, we gathered feedback that was used to refine important aspects of the interface of LabTablet, therefore improving the application's overall usability. After performing these improvements, the second researcher was asked to perform the same set of tasks. In contrast with the chemical engineering laboratory, the biodiversity laboratory follows a data management plan and has an established set of rules for data description. Due to existing ties with other European research facilities, their metadata records must comply with the INSPIRE[8] directive, which outlines a set of guidelines to describe and manage data. As for the context of the produced data, they are frequent users of both geographic coordinates and boundaries to specify, for example, the locations of field studies and specimen occurrences. Additionally, they also use photos and sketches as part of the metadata associated to their datasets. For the purpose of creating the application profile, some of the most frequently used descriptors were extracted from the INSPIRE directive—including, for instance, the *geographicBoundBox*,

---

[8] http://inspire.ec.europa.eu/

to represent the geographic area covered by an experiment. Another advantage of using ontologies became apparent in this context: relationships between different descriptors can be easily established (for example, an equivalence between the *geographicBoundBox* data property and the *coverage* of Dublin Core).

This group organizes several field trips to monitor specific species, so the portable nature of the tablet device and the usefulness of its sensor package was highlighted by the researcher. He found it very useful to have a tool to collect all the related metadata such as the location, and to be able to take photos of the specimen. Additionally, as a more advanced user, this researcher suggested that the device might be useful to gather data, and not just metadata. An example of this would be to quickly capture geographic coordinates and photos of specimens as "opportunity observations". These would not be included as metadata records, but rather constitute new data to be include in the same dataset or in a new one.

5   Conclusions

In this paper, we have presented LabTablet, an electronic laboratory notebook designed to generate standard-compliant metadata records to describe research datasets. LabTablet integrates with a staging repository (Dendro) to manage research data on a daily basis within a research group. It is integrated with a research data repository (CKAN) to preserve research datasets in the long-term. To capture metadata in a semi-automated way, the application also makes use of the device's sensors to record and represent contextual information such as location and temperature.

By collecting metadata as soon as it is available and recording it in a research data repository, the initial curation stages become be less demanding for researchers and curators. As the process becomes faster, it becomes possible for data creators to make their datasets ready for deposit even before the corresponding paper is published, making it possible for them to cite the dataset associated to a paper. Although this doesn't currently happen very often, interviewed researchers stated that it would be a valuable possibility to be able to do so. They also showed that, after an initial briefing, LabTablet can be integrated in their daily activities to gradually complement the currently used laboratory notebooks to record metadata.

In the future, we will continue to develop LabTablet alongside Dendro. Additional testing will be carried out with our panel of researchers in order to further improve its interface, while fine tuning some interoperability improvements to make the application increasingly standards-compliant. At the current state of development, LabTablet's application profiles are loaded from JSON files, but in the future we will be updating the application to directly load lightweight ontology serialized in RDF or OWL, much like Dendro already does.

Acknowledgements. This work is supported by project NORTE-07-0124-FEDER000059, financed by the North Portugal Regional Operational Programme (ON.2–O Novo Norte), under the National Strategic Reference Framework (NSRF), through the European Regional Development Fund (ERDF), and by national funds, through the Portuguese funding agency, Fundação para a Ciência e a Tecnologia (FCT). João Rocha da Silva is also supported by research grant SFRH/BD/77092/2011, provided by the Portuguese funding agency, Fundação para a Ciência e a Tecnologia (FCT).

References

1. Talbott, T., Peterson, M., Schwidder, J., Myers, J.: Adapting the electronic laboratory notebook for the semantic era. In: Proceedings of the 2005 International Symposium on Collaborative Technologies and Systems, pp. 136–143 (2005)
2. Rocha da Silva, J., Ribeiro, C., Lopes, J.C.: UPData: A Data Curation Experiment at U. Porto using DSpace. In: iPres 2011 Conference Proceedings (2011)
3. Foundation, N.S.: Grants.gov Application Guide A Guide for Preparation and Submission of NSF Applications via Grants.gov. (2011)
4. Myers, J., Mendoza, E., Hoopes, B.: A Collaborative Electronic Laboratory Notebook. IMSA (2001)
5. Walsh, E., Cho, I.: Using Evernote as an electronic lab notebook in a translational science laboratory. Journal of Laboratory Automation 18(3), 229–234 (2013)
6. Kumar, M.: Electronic Lab Notebooks-Collaborative Tool for Managing Knowledge in Pharmaceutical Research and Development. Journal of Engineering Computers & Applied Sciences 2(11), 14–19 (2013)
7. Rubacha, M., Rattan, A.K., Hosselet, S.C.: A review of electronic laboratory notebooks available in the market today. Journal of Laboratory Automation 16(1), 90–98 (2011)
8. Hodson, S.: ADMIRAL: A Data Management Infrastructure for Research Activities in the Life sciences. Technical report, University of Oxford (2011)
9. Lyon, L.: Dealing with Data: Roles, Rights, Responsibilities and Relationships. Technical report, UKOLN, University of Bath (2007)
10. Martinez-Uribe, L., Macdonald, S.: User engagement in research data curation. In: Agosti, M., Borbinha, J., Kapidakis, S., Papatheodorou, C., Tsakonas, G. (eds.) ECDL 2009. LNCS, vol. 5714, pp. 309–314. Springer, Heidelberg (2009)
11. Castro, J.A., Ribeiro, C., Rocha da Silva, J.: Designing an Application Profile Using Qualified Dublin Core: A Case Study with Fracture Mechanics Datasets. In: Dublin Core 2013 Conference Proceedings, pp. 47–52 (2013)
12. Shotton, D.: The JISC UMF DataFlow Project: Introduction to DataStage. Technical Report (2012)
13. Rocha da Silva, J., Barbosa, J.P., Gouveia, M., Lopes, J., Ribeiro, C.: UPBox and DataNotes: a collaborative data management environment for the long tail of research data. In: iPres 2013 Conference Proceedings (2013)
14. Geyer, F., Reiterer, H.: Experiences from Employing Evernote as a Tool for Documenting Collaborative Design Processes. In: Proceedings of the DIS12 Workshop on Supporting Reflexion in and on Design Processes (2012)
15. Borgman, C.L.: Advances in Information Science. Journal of the American Society for Information Science and Technology 63(6), 1059–1078 (2011)
16. Rocha da Silva, J., Castro, J.A., Ribeiro, C., Lopes, J.C.: Dendro: collaborative research data management built on linked open data. In: Presutti, V., Blomqvist, E., Troncy, R., Sack, H., Papadakis, I., Tordai, A. (eds.) ESWC Satellite Events 2014. LNCS, vol. 8798, pp. 483–487. Springer, Heidelberg (2014)
17. Castro, J.A., da Silva, J.R., Ribeiro, C.: Creating lightweight ontologies for dataset description: Practical applications in a cross-domain research data management workflow. In: Proceedings of JCDL, the ACM/IEEE Joint Conference on Digital Libraries (2014)

Semantic Enrichment of Research Outputs Metadata: New CRIS Facilities for Authors

Sergey Parinov

Central Economics and Mathematics Institute of RAS, Moscow, Russia
sparinov@gmail.com

Abstract. A CRIS system with implemented semantic linkage technique opens new opportunities for authors of research outputs. Using facilities of such a CRIS authors can essentially enrich metadata of their research outputs after the papers have been published and have become available at the CRIS. The proposed approach allows for authors providing some data for enrichment purposes. These data include their personal roles and contributions into the collective research, comments and notes for updating publication abstracts, data about motivations for citing the papers in the reference lists, research association with newer relevant publications, etc. Technically authors make such enrichment as a semantic linking of related publications' metadata. They don't overwrite the initial publishers' metadata. In the paper we present this approach and its pilot implementation at the Socionet CRIS with focus on servicing the big international community of RePEc users. We expect that results of such enrichment will improve a professional recognition of "who did what" and "how research outputs were used". Also we expect interest from research management and evaluation organizations.

Keywords: semantic enrichment, semantic annotation, semantic linkage technique, scientific relationship taxonomy, CRIS, tools for authors, Socionet, RePEc.

1 Introduction

This paper continues a discussion started in [9,10] of possible applications of a semantic linkage technique within a research information system environment. In these papers we showed that by establishing semantic linkages between information objects in a research Data and Information Space (DIS) the scientists can express their knowledge or hypotheses about research relationships between linked objects [10]. In particular, using a semantic linkage technique, authors can curate and enrich metadata of their research outputs even if the metadata is created by a publisher and after it became available for users within contents of research information systems.

Authors have at least two reasons to enrich ordinary information about their papers typically provided by publishers: (a) there is something that is not supported by the traditional publication metadata model (e.g. roles/impacts of co-authors in making a paper, motivations why authors used publications listed at their papers references section, etc.); (b) something important is happened after the paper was published

S. Closs et al. (Eds.): MTSR 2014, CCIS 478, pp. 206–217, 2014.

(e.g. authors found some important methodological associations and theoretical hier-archical relations, etc. with research outputs published after their papers).

Authors also have an increasing motivation to provide such enrichment since: (a) funders and research assessment organizations would like to have more detailed data about authors' contributions (who did what) to collaborative research output [1]; (b) citation indexes and other usage indicators are widely used to evaluate research performance so many authors seek any opportunity to popularize and promote their publications to maximize their professional recognition and research impact as demonstrated by more citations.

Among possible technical solutions that allows authors to enrich metadata of their publications the semantic linkage technique looks the most preferable. A semantic linkage consists of ID of linked objects, a relationship type value taken from taxono-my of scientific relationships, a comment, a provenance data, creation/revision dates, etc.[1] These data elements are usually enough to express the additional information.

A semantic linkage technique allows creating linkages as separate information ob-jects [11]. Additional enrichment data is stored at the CRIS as separate information objects and displayed at the publication metadata web page together with initial metada-ta created by a publisher. The publication metadata as some information entity provided by a publisher is not changed after the enrichment. Such virtual form of enrichment can be important for many research information systems because the information systems typically just federate publishers' metadata and have no rights to change it.

Since the semantic linkage that virtually enrich a publication metadata exists as a separate information object it can be easily exported from originating information systems to be aggregated in and connected with contents of other systems. It opens an opportunity to make such data completely portable and re-usable within research DIS based on common identification systems for information objects.

A research information system designed according (or compatible with) recom-mendations of a Current Research Information System (CRIS) approach [4,5] and based on a CERIF data model [6] provides a proper and convenient environment for implementing enrichment facilities for authors. The growing popularity of the CRIS-CERIF approach improves basic standardization and interoperability among numer-ous research information systems that are necessary for integrating its contents in a form of common research DIS. Adoption of CRIS-CERIF guarantees that enrichment data created at one CRIS can be easily moved, visualized and re-used outside the originating information system at other CRIS or at an Institutional Repository (IR).

Another aspect of enrichment data portability is the use of common taxonomy. Us-ers of different CRIS use the same taxonomy to assign some semantic meanings to linkages. Our approach assumes that scientific relationships taxonomy which also covered a publications metadata enrichment is centrally maintained as a set of con-trolled semantic vocabularies [7].

We used the Socionet CRIS, which is one of RePEc units, as a platform to imple-ment the proposed approach of virtual enrichment of publication metadata by its

---

[1] A discussion on a semantic linkage approaches and its specification details are provided in [12].

authors. The design within the Socionet environment facilities is based on the Semantic Linkage Technique [12] and the Open Annotation approach[2]. A set of controlled semantic vocabularies embedding taxonomy of scientific relationships into enrichment facilities was created in collaboration with Mikhail Kogalovsky [7]. We also used some part of the Annotator open source Java-script library (http://annotatorjs.org/). Roman Puzyrev worked with the Annotator code; Victor Lyapunov developed all other software.

In the paper we discuss opportunities and tools for authors to semantically enrich metadata of their research outputs available in CRIS content. We consider two situations: 1) an author browses a CRIS web page that displays metadata of their publication, i.e. a publication is linked with their personal profile); and 2) an author opens in a browser a CRIS web page with other's publication metadata which have relationship with some author's research output linked with their personal profile.

In the next section we provide details about semantic enrichment, including taxonomy which can be applicable for thus actions in different situations. The third section is about an implementation of this approach in the form of author tools designed within Socionet CRIS environment (http://socionet.ru/). Section four concludes the paper.

2   Semantic Enrichment of Research Outputs Metadata

Traditionally a semantic enrichment or a semantic annotation of a research output metadata is understood as a result of some computer processing of the research output full text to extract some additional useful information. For example Bertin and Atanassova [3] write: "The semantic annotations are used to enrich the document metadata and to provide new types of visualizations in an information retrieval context".

In our approach an enrichment act is made by a person who establishes a scientific relationship between a pair of research DIS objects. The person classifies the scientific relationship by some taxonomy and can also provide a text comment [12].

Technically an enrichment of certain publication metadata can be made by any person who has been given access rights to perform such action at a certain CRIS. However, the focus of this paper is the specific case where an author creates scientific relationships with own publications.

A relationship has a direction from a source information object to a target one. In our context, the directed relationship can be created: a) from an author personal profile to an author's publication metadata; or b) from some author's publication metadata to other publication metadata, which may describe a work by the same author, or describe a work authored by other people.

The taxonomy of relationships depends on the types of the source and the target information objects. For the relationship "author personal profile" -> "author publication metadata" it can carry data such as the author's role in collective preparing of the publication (who did what, if there are co-authors, see more in [1], or such as the author updating notes for the publication, etc.

---

[2] http://www.w3.org/community/openannotation/

In the second case "author publication metadata" -> "author another publication metadata" the taxonomy can classify dependences between different research outputs of the same author, e.g. relationships between components of a research composition (some research output can be used as a part of another, see a semantic vocabulary in [13], or provide links to supplementary materials, etc.

In the third case "author publication metadata" -> "another author publication metadata" the author can use taxonomy to specify why and how the materials listed in reference section of their publications were used in a research and for preparing the publications. It includes usage/impact relationships, scientific inference relationships (see associated semantic vocabularies in [13]), etc. Another situation occurs when an author would like to establish relationships with newer publications of other authors. Here the taxonomy can classify e.g. hierarchical and associative scientific relationships (see a semantic vocabulary in [13]), etc.

In Table 1 we list possible cases of enrichment in connection with suggestions where appropriate enrichment has to be anchoring within publication metadata. Examples of visualization of enrichment data over a publication metadata web page are in the next section.

Table 1. Anchoring and taxonomy for cases of publication metadata semantic enrichment

Part of metadata for anchoring	Semantic vocabulary name / *Types of related objects*	Type of enrichment *)
Data about authors	1. Researcher contributions to collaborative publication / *Author personal profile -> Author publication metadata*	Authors can specify the roles of co-authors like "study conception", "methodology", "computation", etc.
Abstract	2. Professional evaluations / *Author personal profile -> Publication metadata*	Users can express their opinion about a publication like: "innovative result", "very interesting result", "potentially dangerous effect", "result based on confusion", etc.
	3. Hierarchical and associative relationships between research outputs / *Author publication metadata -> Publication metadata*	Authors can indicate relations between own publication and newer one like: "extends or broader", "related or relevant to", "narrower", etc.
	4. Usage proposals / *Author personal profile -> Publication metadata*	Authors can make a relationship between own and newer publication to propose own one for purposes like: "can improve", "can illustrate", "can replace", etc.

Table 2. (*continued*)

Full text link	5. Relationships between components of a research composition and supplementary materials / *Author publication metadata -> Author publication metadata*	Authors can make a relationship between a pair of own materials like: "revised or new version", "abstract", "part of", "duplicated copy", etc.
References	6. Usage/impact relationships between research outputs / *Author publication metadata -> Publication metadata*	Authors can add usage types to publications from a reference section like: "uses method from", "corrects", "refutes", etc.
	7. Scientific inference relationships between research outputs / *Author publication metadata -> Publication metadata*	Authors can also add usage types to publications from a reference section like: "obtain background from", "confirms", "qualifies", etc.

*) Current content of all semantic vocabularies used for enrichment of publication metadata see at http://socionet.ru/section.xml?h=metrics_interdisciplinary&l=en

3   Implementation

The proposed enrichment of publication metadata has been partly implemented as a set of tools and services within the Socionet CRIS (http://socionet.ru/) environment. Some general information about Socionet CRIS can be found in [14]. For options 1, 2 and 6, 7 from Table 1, the implementation is complete. We provide some descriptions and screenshots. All other options from Table 1 are currently under development. For these we only give general descriptions.

CRIS facilities for authors to do enrichment according cases from the Table 1 have to include:

a) an identification service, which using data from a user personal profile can recognize if a user is an author of a currently opened web page with a publication metadata from CRIS content. If that is the case, the system provides for a user some additional menu;

b) user tools to create semantic linkages with enrichment data;

c) user tools to manage created semantic linkages (editing, deleting, etc.);

d) administrator tools to control an input flow of created semantic linkages;

e) a visualization service for the enrichment at a CRIS publication metadata web page.

For a complete description of necessary information objects, tools and services see [12].

3.1   Identification of Authors

A proper authors identification at CRIS to provide them ability for semantic enrichment of their publication metadata has two basic requirements: 1) users who are going to make semantic enrichment have to be represented at CRIS by some information objects, e.g. they should have some personal profile at the CRIS; and 2) users should have ability to identify themselves as authors by claiming to have publications at CRIS content.

There is an approach when users identify themselves as authors of some publications by linking their personal profiles with appropriate research output. An approach pioneered by the RePEc Author Service, see [8].

A real scale of such activity can illustrate, e.g. the IDEAS Author Information web page (http://ideas.repec.org/i/eall.html), which currently visualizes about 40K (thousands) personal profiles created at RePEc Author Service and linked with publications. This activity is based on metadata aggregated by RePEc services from about 4.5K sources worldwide with in total about 1500K publications. Owners of these profiles registered with the service RePEc Author Service (http://authors.repec.org/) and identified themselves as authors by claiming to have written papers in RePEc content during the registration process. They can add papers to their profiles when new publications appear at RePEc.

Another example is Socionet CRIS (http://socionet.ru/), which also satisfied to the requirements and provides additionally to RePEc Author Service about 180K personal profiles of Russian scientists linked with their research outputs. Most of personal profiles in Socionet CRIS are generated by software and only few of them connected with identification data of real Socionet users. This is the main difference with RePEc, where all personal profiles are created by real people.

A scale of potential enrichment activity can be also illustrated some numbers from CitEc data. Currently about 40K personal profiles in RePEc have in total about 1000K linkages to 675K[3] publications from RePEc content. It means that for about 50% of publications from RePEc content the identification service can recognize at least one of its authors. All these people get ability to enrich their publications.

3.2   Author Tools to Make Enrichment of a Publication Metadata

In this section we consider the case where an author looks at their own publication metadata web page within a CRIS. The author has at the CRIS a personal profile with linked own publications and she/he would like to add to the initial publication metadata generated by a publisher some updates or useful information for readers of the publication and/or demanded by research management/assessment organizations.

---

[3] Number of linkages is bigger than number of linked publications, since co-authors have linkages with the same publication.

Enrichment of Author(s) Data

Usually a publication metadata represents authors like this[4]

Fields name	1st author	2nd author
author-name	Sergey Parinov	Mikhail Kogalovsky
author-workplace	CEMI RAS	MEI RAS
author-email	sparinov@gmail.com	kogalov@gmail.com

At the first stage of enrichment, just because the author's personal profile is linked with their publication, the CRIS service inserts a link to the profile on the fly. This if displays at the publication metadata page a hyperlink to the author's personal profile, with the total number of their claimed publications linked to the publications list. Figure 1 for an example.

If a user is recognized as an author the system provides at the publication metadata web page a hyperlink to specify roles/impacts of authors in preparing the publication. For an example see the anchor at the Figure 1 at the right starting with "You are the author…". This menu item is visible only if the publication has more than one author.

The online form to create a semantic linkage, which will enrich traditional data about authors by information "who did what" includes:

a) taxonomy selector of roles/impacts of authors in collective work to prepare the publication, see option 1 from the Table 1;

b) optional comment which can provide some additional information;

c) a selector of a "container" where this linkage will be stored at user's personal data storage at CRIS.

You can see the form at the Figure 1 in the right bottom corner.

By default the system also includes into the linkage attributes: user's personal profile ID (as source object of the linkage); current publication ID (as target object of the linkage), a provenance data (who create the linkage) and creation date. See more about semantic linkage data format in [12].

At the Figure 1 you can see a fragment of publication metadata web page at Socionet CRIS with enriched authorship data and a form to add more enrichment data.

---

[4] All examples and illustrations below use the same publication metadata –
http://socionet.ru/publication.xml?h=repec:rus:mqijxk:31&l=en

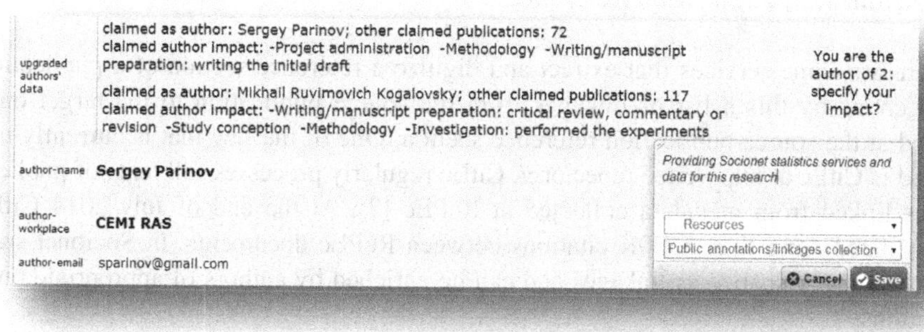

claimed as author: Sergey Parinov; other claimed publications: 72
claimed author impact: -Project administration -Methodology -Writing/manuscript
preparation: writing the initial draft

upgraded authors' data

claimed as author: Mikhail Ruvimovich Kogalovsky; other claimed publications: 117
claimed author impact: -Writing/manuscript preparation: critical review, commentary or
revision -Study conception -Methodology -Investigation: performed the experiments

You are the
author of 2:
specify your
impact?

author-name   Sergey Parinov

*Providing Socionet statistics services and
data for this research*

author-workplace   CEMI RAS

Resources   ▾

author-email   sparinov@gmail.com

Public annotations/linkages collection ▾

⊗ Cancel   ✓ Save

Fig. 1. A fragment of a publication metadata web page with enriched data about authors and a form to add new data about author role

Enrichment of the Abstract

Authors can annotate their publication's abstract to provide readers with new relevant information appeared after the paper was published. It can be used to add author's comments to some text fragment of the abstract and an optional taxonomy value. This allows authors to make some kind of continuous actualization of the publication data. Figure 2 shows an example.

An online form to annotate the abstract is almost the same as in previous cases, but here an author first has to select a text fragment within an abstract of the publication and only after that the form will open. Another specific aspect of this linkage is the semantic vocabulary number 2 from the Table 1. It is optional for this type of semantic linkages.

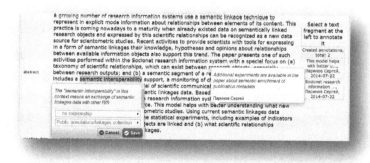

Fig. 2. A fragment of a publication metadata web page with annotated abstract and a form to add a new annotation

Enrichment of Publication References

There are some services that extract and digitize a reference section of a publication and create by this a list of linkages from the source publication to the target ones listed at the source publication reference section. One of the few that is currently updated is CitEc at http://citec.repec.org/. CitEc regularly processes full texts of publications linked from metadata collected at RePEc [2]. At the end of July 2014 CitEc recognized more than 6300K citations between RePEc documents. In Socionet such citation data visualize as linkages and can be enriched by authors of appropriate publications.

CitEc data allows making some numeric illustrations of possible enrichment activity.

An average number of citation linkages for one publication is about 10. Among 639K publications processed by CitEc there are a few having in its reference section more 300 recognized citations. E.g. a book "Regional Growth and Regional Decline" has 331 linkages to publications listed in its reference[5].

If we look at authors, currently among 40K RePEc authors with personal profiles there are people claiming about 1K own publications (e.g. Michael McAleer, http://ideas.repec.org/e/pmc90.html), but an average number for one author is about 25 claimed publications.

If we count for each author a total number of linkages from reference sections of their claimed publications some authors have about 10K records. The profile of already mentioned above Michael McAleer has about 9.5K references[6]. On average the total number of references per author is about 250 records. That makes for a lot of records that can be enriched.

A CRIS can merge citation data to publication metadata. Its interface can then display the titles of and hyperlinks to publications that were listed as references. Figure 3 has an.

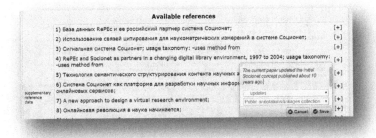

Fig. 3. A fragment of a publication metadata web page with enriched reference list and a form to add a usage characteristic

---

[5] http://socionet.ru/publication.xml?h=
repec:eee:grochp:2-683&l=en

[6] http://socionet.ru/stat-lnk.xml?h=repec:per:pers:pmc90&l=en

For each cited publication displayed at the source publication metadata CRIS system can provide to its users a hyperlink to an enrichment form. On the Figure 3 we have the hyperlinks at the right as a column of [+]. A click on any [+] opens the enrichment form visible here at the right bottom corner.

In general the enrichment form is the same as in previous cases. The taxonomy is the one from Table 1, options 6 and 7.

3.3   Other Enrichment Facilities

This section presents facilities that are not completely implemented at the moment.

Enrichment of the Full Text Link

An author can supplement information about the full text of their publication initially provided by a publisher by making relationships listed in the Table 1, option 5. This opportunity can be used by an author to "enrich" a typical for commercial publishers' payment access to the article full text by linking, for example, to an open access version of this publication.

An online form to make this type of enrichment differs from previously described forms by a semantic vocabulary (Table 1, option 5) and by an additional menu to get a list of author's publications to select one from the list as a target publication for creating a linkage. The source publication of the linkage is the current one which metadata is opened by the author in a browser.

User Tools to Make Enrichment of Publications Metadata

This is the case when a user opens in a browser a web page from CRIS content with a publication metadata to read it. The user is not the publication author. He/she has at CRIS a personal profile linked with own publications. After reading the publication the user intends establishing a relationship (semantic linkage) from some own publication (as a source for the linkage) to this one read currently in a browser (as a target of the linkage). The added information may be useful for authors of the target publication; for readers of both linked publications; and/or for research management/assessment organizations.

If a user opens a publication metadata web page after authorization at a CRIS the system "knows" the user is not its author and displays at the publication web page a menu configured for this current situation. In a menu a user gets a tool to specify a relationship between some own publication selected from the list and the currently reading publication.

This tool is very similar to one described above in the section "Enrichment of the full text link". But the semantic vocabulary is different. It must allow a user to specify research associations and hierarchical relationships (Table 1, option 3) between a pair of linked publications.

Using this tool an author can enrich metadata of their own published research outputs by connecting them with other research be they younger or older. It works as some kind of actualization of older research results by comparing them with the newer ones. Users can also use this approach.

Another side of such actualization is ability of users to make suggestions to authors to enrich metadata of some their publication. In this case a user would use the same form with a semantic vocabulary of Table 1, option 4.

4   Conclusion

Additionally to the enrichment facilities Socionet CRIS provides an e-mail notification service making awareness of users about creating/changing semantic linkages with their publications and also specific scientometrics based on processing of accumulated data about semantic linkages [13]. Altogether these facilities can create a more efficient professional communications for the research community and a better information source for research management and assessment organizations.

We expect that presented enrichment facilities will be adopted by the community and it will improve professional recognition of "who did what" and "how research outputs were used".

Acknowledgments. This research is partly funded by Russian Foundation for Basic Research, grant 12-07-00518-A. Thanks to Mikhail Kogalovsky and Thomas Krichel provided comments on an earlier version of this paper.

References

1. Allen, L., Brand, A., Scott, J., Altman, M., Hlava, M.: Credit where credit is due. Nature 508, 312–313 (2014), doi:10.1038/508312a
2. Barrueco, J.M., Krichel, T.: Building an autonomous citation index for GL: RePEc, the Economics working papers case. The Grey Journal 1(2), 91–97 (2005)
3. Bertin, M., Atanassova, I.: Semantic Enrichment of Scientific Publications and Metadata. D-Lib Magazine 18(7/8) (2012)
4. Jeffery, K., Asserson, A.: CERIF-CRIS for the European e-Infrastructure. Data Science Journal 9 (2010), http://www.codata.org/dsj/special-cris.html
5. Jeffery, K., Asserson, A.: The CERIF Model as the Core of a Research Organisation. Data Science Journal 9 (2010), http://www.codata.org/dsj/special-cris.html
6. Jörg, B., Jeffery, K.G., Dvorak, J., Houssos, N., Asserson, A., van Grootel, G., Gartner, R., Cox, M., Rasmussen, H., Vestdam, T., Strijbosch, L., Clements, A., Brasse, V., Zendulkova, D., Höllrigl, T., Valkovic, L., Engfer, A., Jägerhorn, M., Mahey, M., Brennan, N., Sicilia, M.-A., Ruiz-Rube, I., Baker, D., Evans, K., Price, A., Zielinski, M.: CERIF 1.3 Full Data Model (FDM): Introduction and Specification. euroCRIS (2012), http://www.eurocris.org/Uploads/Web%20pages/CERIF-1.3/Specifications/CERIF1.3_FDM.pdf
7. Kogalovsky, M., Parinov, S.: Metrics of online information spaces. Economics and Mathematical Methods 44(2) (2008), http://socionet.ru/publication.xml?h=repec:rus:mqijxk:17 (in Russian)

8. Krichel, T., Zimmermann, C.: Author identification in economics,... and beyond. Working Paper Series des Rates fürSozial-und Wirtschaftsdaten No. 222 (2013)
9. Parinov, S.: CRIS driven by research community: benefits and perspectives. In: Proceedings of the 10th International Conference on Current Research Information Systems, June 2-5, pp. 119–130. Aalborg University, Denmark (2010), http://socionet.ru/publication.xml?h=repec:rus:mqijxk:23
10. Parinov, S., Kogalovsky, M.: A technology for semantic structuring of scientific digital library content. In: Proc. of the XIIIth All-Russian Scientific Conference, RCDL 2011. Digital Libraries: Advanced Methods and Technologies, Digital Collections, October 19-22, pp. 94–103. Voronezh State University (2011), http://socionet.ru/publication.xml?h=repec:rus:mqijxk:28 (in Russian)
11. Parinov, S.: Open Repository of Semantic Linkages. In: Proceedings of 11th International Conference on Current Research Information Systems e-Infrastructure for Research and Innovations (CRIS 2012), Prague (2012), http://socionet.ru/publication.xml?h=repec:rus:mqijxk:29
12. Parinov, S.: Towards a Semantic Segment of a Research e-Infrastructure: necessary information objects, tools and services. Journal: Int. J. of Metadata, Semantics and Ontologies 8(4), 322–331 (2012), http://socionet.ru/pub.xml?h=RePEc:rus:mqijxk:30, doi:10.1504/IJMSO.2013.058415.
13. Parinov, S., Kogalovsky, M.: Semantic Linkages in Research Information Systems as a New Data Source for Scientometric Studies. Scientometrics 98(2), 927–943 (2013), http://socionet.ru/pub.xml?h=RePEc:rus:mqijxk:31
14. Parinov, S., Kogalovsky, M., Lyapunov, V.: A Challenge of Research Outputs in GL Circuit: From Open Access to Open Use. In: Proceedings of the Fifteenth International Conference on Grey Literature: The Grey Audit, A Field Assessment in Grey Literature (December 23, 2013), compiled by D. Farace and J. Frantzen; GreyNet International, Grey Literature Network Service. TextRelease, Amsterdam (2014), http://socionet.ru/pub.xml?h=RePEc:rus:mqijxk:33

Best Practices for Current Learning Repositories: The Case of Agrega

Isabel Alcaraz-García[1] and Gema Bueno-de-la-Fuente[2]

[1] University Carlos III of Madrid, Madrid-Puerta de Toledo Library, Spain
isabel.alcaraz@alumnos.uc3m.es
[2] University Carlos III of Madrid, Library and Information Science Department, Spain
gbueno@bib.uc3m.es

Abstract. In recent years the presence and importance of learning objects repositories like Agrega has increased in the educational community. Meanwhile, several trends have gained momentum, notably open education, cloud computing or the web of linked data as a realization of the Semantic Web. Educational repositories should encompass all these trends to maintain high levels of service. This paper proposes a set of best practices to the Spanish Learning Object repository Agrega, aiming to improve on its current retrieval, interoperability and reuse capabilities. As a guiding principle, the user's perspective and needs are given priority. The most recent learning technologies and semantic web standards are considered in this approach, including ISO/IEC MLR, LRMI and RAMLET metadata specifications. This set of recommendations aims to serve as a basis for other learning resources repositories, as well to any other kind of repository, currently planning to adopt the new generation of standards and technologies, like the linked data web.

Keywords: learning object repositories, educational resources, metadata, linked data, Agrega.

1 Introduction

Agrega, the Spanish federation of educational digital object repositories, is a platform with nodes in all regional government education departments. Agrega holds a collection of more than 90,000 educational resources organized around the curriculum covering pre-university education. To describe these resources, the LOM-ES application profile is used. LOM-ES was developed adapting the IEEE Learning Object Metadata to the Spanish curriculum particularities, and was published as an official national standard (UNE 71361-2010 AENOR) [1]. Agrega educational resources can be downloaded in IMS Content Packaging, SCORM 1.2 and SCORM 2004 standardized packaging models. Moreover, to improve interoperability with other repository ecosystems through metadata exchange, Agrega is compliant with the OAI-PMH (Open Archives Initiative-Protocol for Metadata Harvesting) [2, 3, 4].

S. Closs et al. (Eds.): MTSR 2014, CCIS 478, pp. 218–225, 2014.

Despite the efforts made, and the good set of standards applied, Agrega has experienced some shortcomings in its retrieval, reusability and interoperability capabilities. Among them, we can highlight the cataloguing issues due to the use of the standard LOM and its profile application LOM-ES, which have proved some inconsistencies of their metadata definitions [5]. As a result, a high proportion of metadata records are not correctly completed lowering the performance of the retrieval system. Also, the interoperability which provides the OAI-PMH must be based on simple Dublin Core due to the fundamental   incompatibly among LOM application profiles.

These technologies were chosen in Agrega's design as the most innovative at the time (2007). However the Semantic Web and learning technology standards areas have developed further over the last few years, offering better and more powerful technologies to adopt. Agrega along with many contemporary repositories, have both the challenge and the opportunity to adapt themselves and transform their resources into Linked Data.

In 2013, INTEF [6] started a process of adopting semantic web technologies. The pilot project, called Procomun [7] published a dataset of Agrega educational resources described with a wide range of open vocabularies as well as newly developed OWL ontologies (e.g. odeAgrega [8]), linked with some open datasets such as Dbpedia. Procomun provides a faceted search engine both for Agrega's resources and external resources by teachers and other educational agents, alongside many other new social media features. This promising project is still in progress, and many of the linked data assumptions and requirements are not yet met: the new Agrega ontologies are not publicly available; their URIs are not dereferenceable; and there is no SPARQL endpoint. The current implementation just offers one-way links, from Procomun to other datasets, and it is impossible to make links from other datasets to the Agrega collection.

This paper proposes alternative strategies to adapt Agrega —or other repositories in a similar situation— to current learning and linked data technologies. The approach taken is based on the consideration of Agrega expected users' perspective, under the principle that a repository should be designed to serve its users, and not just depend on economic and political trends. Several groups of stakeholders have been considered according to their main objectives and necessities: students and general public; teachers and other content authors; and cataloguers together with other repository' administrators. Following their different user intentions and interactions with the platform, a set of priorities have been identified that would guide Agrega's developments:

- facilitate the creation, description and reuse of new educational resources,
- improve Agrega's cataloguing system easiness and usability,
- enhance Agrega's interoperability model,
- facilitate users' discovery and retrieval of educational resources .

We analyze these objectives in the context of three different function areas of a repository: resource management, search and retrieval, and interoperability.

2   Management Area

The Management Area covers the operation of the repository, its main functions being the classification and organization of digital object collections and their metadata.

2.1   Objective 1: Improve Agrega's cataloguing

Agrega uses the Spanish application profile of the metadata standard IEEE LOM, LOM-ES. IEEE LOM is a metadata schema specially designed to be used in educational contexts and to be compatible with other learning standards such as SCORM.

However, both IEEE LOM and its application profile LOM-ES have proved to have many inconsistencies that hinder Agrega's cataloguing: incompatibility between different application profiles, a lack of precision in metadata definitions, insufficient metadata and a lack of well-defined data formats.

Proposal 1.1: Metadata records migration to a new standard: from LOM-ES to ISO/IEC MLR

The standard ISO/IEC Metadata for Learning Resources [9] aims to be internationally inclusive, as well as solve LOM's deficiencies, and focus on cataloguing issues. Also, MLR extensions are compatible between each other and with the standard.

The migration could be based on ISO/IEC MLR part 11, whose main purpose is being a guide for LOM to MLR migration [10]. Also, there are digital tools in development which will allow automatic transformation of LOM records into MLR ones [11].

These mapping techniques and tools should be carefully reviewed and customized to meet Agrega's requirements. The LOM-ES application profile includes new elements beside IEEE LOM ones, as well as vocabularies developed specifically for LOM-ES. The conversion method should not present significant difficulties, as the MLR schema proposes also more metadata elements than IEEE LOM.

2.2   Objective 2: Facilitate the Creation and Description of New Educational Resources

At present, teachers can create and integrate new resources into the Agrega collection thanks to the cataloguing tool —*catalogador*— available both on-line and as a desktop application. This tool allows teachers to perform an initial metadata assignment process. To prevent them having to struggle with LOM-ES cataloguing complexity, teachers should just provide some basic information for compulsory metadata elements. Agrega cataloguers review and complete these metadata records before their final publication. This implies redundant work that is not always done properly, as it is common that cataloguers do not complete the records because of time restrictions or knowledge limitations related to educational or subject-specific content.

Proposal 2.1: Automated metadata extraction cataloguing aids

We propose the adoption of automatic metadata extraction features, integrated in or offered together with the existing cataloguing tool. These would reduce the time required for cataloguing technical and basic descriptive information of digital objects, thus leaving more time for quality cataloguing of educational and other complex metadata content. Existing automatic generation tools as SAmgI (Simple Automatic Metadata Generation Interface) have shown good results extracting metadata from learning resources [12]. Learning content repositories such as those of the LACLO federation [13] are already using an automatic metadata generation system successfully [14].

3   Search and Retrieval Area

The Search and Retrieval area is fundamental to repositories, both for teachers and final users, being one of the key purposes for which the repositories are created.

3.1   Objective 3: Facilitate Users to Find Educational Resources

Up to now, Agrega resources may be retrieved by general web search engines such as Google or Yandex, although usually their page rank is not high, so they do not reach top positions in the search results list. Search engine optimization of Agrega resources will help users to find educational resources more quickly and easily, and thus increase the repository's popularity. This objective may be achieved by adopting different strategies as we propose below.

Proposal 3.1: Adopt schema.org with LRMI specification

Adopting schema.org, and tagging the educational records according to the Learning Resource Metadata Initiative (LRMI) [15] specification will help to improve visibility and retrievability of Agrega content in web search engines such as Google, Bing, Yahoo! or Yandex. Internationally known learning content repositories such as MERLOT [16] or JORUM [17] have already adopted LRMI, an example that Agrega should follow.

Proposal 3.2: Publication of Agrega metadata collection as a linked open dataset

The publication of Agrega learning resources' collection metadata as a linked dataset will help to create new interfaces with other repositories and a wide range of different information sources. Fulfilling the linked data premises would allow other repositories and datasets to point to Agrega resources too, providing significant benefits in terms of visibility and ease of retrieval for Agrega. For instance, the ARIADNE repository [18] has created a dataset of metadata records linked with DBpedia and WordNet.

3.2   Objective 4: Improve Educational Resources Retrieval in the Agrega Repository

The current Agrega search engine has an advanced search option which allows filtering by format type, license, content properties (identifier, resource type, publishing date, etc.), aggregation level, educational thesaurus terms and taxonomies (there are four: competences, availability, curriculum tree and educational level). This system is quite complete but also complicated. Students and general public have some difficulties using it, as some filters are not easy to understand for non-expert users.

Moreover, some of the default search rules correspond to non-mandatory LOM-ES metadata elements. Since not every record is complete a biased or incomplete retrieval is likely.

Proposal 4.1: Adoption of an ontology based retrieval system.
The introduction of an ontology-based retrieval system will allow Agrega to become a Semantic Learning Object Repository (SLOR). The platform would act as a connection point between users seeking information and software agents, which   search for and retrieve it. A SLOR has flexible information storage, for example, the same resource may have more than one description, with non-normalized information [19].

An ontology-based system will permit retrieval of related resources which do not include any of the specific search terms in their metadata record. Also, it will allow new information to be generated from by making inferences over stored data and established rules.

Proposal 4.2. Implementation of recommendation technologies
The application of recommendation technologies in Agrega will improve the retrieval of learning resources more suitable for user needs [20]. Some of the current proposals in this area include collaborative filtering or web mining, as reviewed in [21]. We recommend the initial adoption of an automatic recommendation strategy, as the Case Based Reasoning system implemented in AIREH (Architecture for Intelligent Recovery of Educational content in Heterogeneous Environments) [20].

4   Interoperability Area

The interoperability area focuses on the availability of resources to be deployed and used in Learning Management Systems and other platforms, as well as connection and interaction with other educational repositories.

4.1   Objective 5: Facilitate Educational Resources Reusability

Currently, Agrega's educational resources can be downloaded in the established aggregation formats SCORM 1.2, SCORM 2004 (with or without sub-manifests) and IMS Content Package.

Agrega repository works only with aggregation packages. Because single components or objects that are part of the packages are not individually described there is no way to retrieve them.

In addition, if someone wants to introduce repurposed resources in Agrega, these have to be re-catalogued, as the system does not allow the inclusion of new versions of the same objects sharing common metadata. This lack of interoperability between aggregation formats and metadata schemas is probably the main technical barrier for resource reusability.

Furthermore, it should be noted that Agrega allows the authors to chose a wide range of licences, including copyright, public domain or different types of Creative Commons licences resulting from the combination of their terms and conditions: attribution, ShareAlike, NonCommercial, and NoDerivatives. Problems arise when new resources are created aggregating multiple assets distributed under different and contradictory licenses.

Proposal 5.1: Implement automatic aggregation capabilities based on RAMLET
RAMLET is a recently published IEEE standard proposing a conceptual model for learning resources aggregation. It aims to facilitate interoperability by providing an ontology that allows mapping from existing aggregation formats. We recommend Agrega adopt RAMLET, as it is already compliant with some of the aggregation formats for which RAMLET is developing crosswalks [22]. This would increase the exchange formats of educational resources available through automatic mapping without the need to re-catalogue them.

Proposal 5.2 Increase the granularity of description and retrieval
The implementation of cataloging and retrieval functionalities at the granularity of objects or assets would result in higher and easier reusability of Agrega learning resources. The cataloging tool should be modified to facilitate the description of these resources, through automatic extraction of technical metadata, and when applicable inheritance of descriptive metadata from the aggregated resources they belong to. The SCORM aggregation model could work as a reference model though it should be adjusted to offer an effective modularity [23].

Proposal 5.3 Limit the licensing choices and recommend CC-BY
A smaller choice of licences would reduce complexity and foster reusability of learning resources. When possible, the use of more open licences such as CC-BY should be prescribed, to lower barriers to repurposing and reusing resources.

4.2   Objective 6: Improve Agrega's Interoperability Model

Agrega interoperability model is based on the OAI-PMH, therefore the Dublin Core metadata format (oai_dc) is the minimum common denominator. While it guarantees interoperability with a wide range of repositories and other information management tools, the use of this general-purpose metadata schema also means a loss of information richness [24]. Also, the Procomun project does not provide the best interoperability due to limitations already mentioned: ontologies are not publicly available, URIs are not dereferenceable and there is no SPARQL end-point.

Proposal 6.1: Adopt a "follow your nose" interoperability model based on linked data

If learning content repositories publish their metadata records collections as real Linked Data, thus following its main concept and technical principles [25]; it would be possible to establish semantic connections between them, regardless of the metadata schema used internally and avoiding the loss of representativeness of these schemas.

A "follow your nose" model would allow the connection of repositories joining the linked data cloud without the need for a bridge, e.g. a metadata mapping tool.

5   Conclusions

The learning content repositories created during the first decade of the Twenty-First century need to be adapted to current semantic web technologies. While significant efforts have been made, the adaptation is still too slow and lacks coordination.

There is no single shared strategy to carry out this adaptation process. As an example we have analyzed the Procomun approach to take Agrega, the Spanish federation of learning content repositories, to the Semantic Web. In this paper, alternative strategies are proposed with this aim. As a guiding principle, the users' perspective and needs are considered paramount.

The specific strategies that collectively form our approach are based in the most recent linked data premises and standards, especially those designed for learning technologies and systems. It includes the adoption of the brand new ISO/IEC MLR standard, which would improve Agrega cataloging in comparison with LOM and its application profile LOM-ES. Adoption of the LRMI specification and schema.org for resource tagging would improve visibility and discoverability of Agrega resources by the best known general web search engines. Additionally, other specifications and methods adopting Semantic Web core technologies, such as RDF and OWL ontologies, would provide a significant improvement to Agrega's current capabilities for retrieval, interoperability and reuse of objects.

To sum up, the strategies proposed could serve as a best practice basis to other learning resources repositories, as well as to any other kind of repository currently planning to adopt the new generation of standards and technologies, like the linked data web. For those already in this enterprise, this would remind them of the need to be alert and anticipate future improvements in the areas of educational and web technologies.

References

1. UNE 71361:2010 AENOR, http://www.en.aenor.es
2. Sarasa, A., Canabal, M., Sacristán, J.C., Jiménez, R.: Agrega: Repositorios de Objetos de Aprendizaje Interoperables. In: V Simposio Pluridisciplinar Sobre Diseño y Evaluación de Contenidos Educativos Reutilizables, p. 10 (2008)
3. Proyecto Agrega, http://www.agrega2.es/web/

4. OAI-PMH (Open Archives Initiative-Protocol forma Metadata Harvesting), http://openarchives.org/pmh
5. Nevile, L.: DC Metadata is Alive and Well (and has Influenced a New Standard for Education). In: Pro. Int'l Conf. on Dublin Core and Metadata Applicationsl Conf. on Dublin Core and Metadata Applications, pp. 162–171 (2013)
6. INTEF (Instituto Nacional de Tecnologías Educativas y Formación del Profesorado), http://www.intef.educacion.es/
7. Procomún, http://procomun.educalab.es/
8. Ode Agrega, http://procomun.gnoss.com/Ontologia/odeAgrega.owl#
9. ISO/IEC 19788-1:2011, http://www.iso.org
10. Gauthier, G., Guay, P.J.: Rationale for an ISO/IEC 19788 Multipart Standard Project Subdivision – Part 11 Migration from LOM to MLR (2013)
11. Gauthier, G.: MLR Bindings. Part 1: OWL, RDFS, RDF & XML. Published by GTN-Québec (2012)
12. Meire, M., Duval, E., Ochoa Chehab, X.: SAmgI: Automatic Metadata Generation v2.0. In: Proceedings of the ED-MEDIA 2007 World Conference on Educational Multimedia, Hypermedia and Telecommunications, pp. 1195–1204 (2007)
13. LACLO (Latin-American Community on Learning Objects), http://laclo.org
14. Ochoa, X., Klerkx, J., Vandeputte, B., Duval, E.: On the use of learning object metadata: The GLOBE experience. In: Kloos, C.D., Gillet, D., Crespo García, R.M., Wild, F., Wolpers, M. (eds.) EC-TEL 2011. LNCS, vol. 6964, pp. 271–284. Springer, Heidelberg (2011)
15. LRMI (Learning Resource Metadata Initiative), http://www.lrmi.net
16. MERLOT (Multimedia Educational Resources for Learning and Online Teaching), http://www.merlot.org/
17. JORUM, http://www.jorum.ac.uk/
18. ARIADNE (Alliance of Remote Instructional Authoring and Distribution Networks in Europe), http://www.ariadne-eu.org/
19. Joshi, S., Thakur, N., Mehrotra, D.: Schemes and Practices of Learning Object Repository: A Literature Review. International Journal of Computer Applications 65(20), 27–32 (2013)
20. Gil, A.B., Rodríguez, S., de la Prieta, F., De Paz, J.F.: Personalization on E-Content Retrieval Based on Semantic Web Services. International Journal of Computer Information Systems and Industrial Management Applications 5, 243–251 (2013)
21. Manouselis, N., Vuorikari, R., Van Assche, F.: Collaborative recommendation of e-learning resources: an experimental investigation. Journal of Computer Assisted Learning 26, 227–242 (2010)
22. IEEE LTSC: 1484.13.1-2012 IEEE Standard for Learning Technology. Conceptual Model for Resource Aggregation For Learning, Education and Training. IEEE Computer Society (2012)
23. Meyer, M., Rensing, C., Steinmetz, R.: Multigranularity Reuse of Learning Resources. ACM Transactions on Multimedia Computing, Communications, and Applications 7(1), 1–23 (2011)
24. Bermès, E.: Convergence and Interoperability: A Linked Data Perspective. In: 77th IFLA World Library and Information Congress, Puerto Rico, pp. 1–12 (2011), http://conference.ifla.org/past-wlic/2011/149-bermes-en.pdf
25. Bernes-Lee, T.: Linked data. In: Design Issues. W3C, The World Wide Web Consortium (2006), http://www.w3.org/DesignIssues/LinkedData.html

Information Continuity: A Temporal Approach to Assessing Metadata and Organizational Quality in an Institutional Repository

Erik Radio

The University of Kansas, Watson Library, Lawrence, KS

Abstract. Repositories provide a vital infrastructure for an institution to aggregate and disseminate creative output, yet this task is only as successful as the effective organization of its content. The University of Kansas is currently undergoing a systematic review to analyze metadata and content organization in its own repository. This paper argues that for a full assessment to be achieved it is necessary to not view the repository as a fixed item, but as an entity with its own continuity. This temporal approach has a significant impact on establishing resource provenance for metadata policy adjustments, disciplinary migration, and resource extensibility. For any repository it is essential for ensuring long-term viability.

Keywords: Institutional Repositories, Information Hierarchy, Author Generated Metadata, Temporality.

1   Introduction

The organization of an institutional repository (IR) has a significant impact on its ability to enable discovery and disseminate resources. Processes to analyze both metadata and information hierarchy are critical to ensure consistency of records and clarity of structure. Repositories can be understood as having both horizontal and vertical dimensions, the former concerning records' conformance to metadata standards across the corpus and the latter to ensure consistency between organizing classes. While examining both dimensions is necessary to any analysis as a step towards identifying needed remediation, they are not entirely sufficient in providing the clearest picture of an IR's structure.

Information continuity is the idea that a resource, be it item, collection, or repository, has an ongoing narrative. This temporal aspect to information systems plays a significant role in providing vital provenance information about resources and their place within an IR. This information also provides an important way to organize content that is consistent with the history of the institution, disciplinary migration, and IR policies. This paper will define this principle and its impact on these critical aspects, and provide examples of how they may be understood by using the University of Kansas' (KU) repository, ScholarWorks as a model. [1] Finally, it will provide possible use cases for implementing information continuity as well as the next steps to be taken in the context of KU ScholarWorks (KUSW).

S. Closs et al. (Eds.): MTSR 2014, CCIS 478, pp. 226–237, 2014.

2   Dimensional Aspects of Institutional Repositories

An IR can be described most fully as having three dimensions: horizontal, vertical, and temporal. Briefly, the horizontal aspect can be thought of as a way of assessing resources at the item level with regards to their metadata. Consistency regarding adherence to policies about required elements, content standards, and other similar qualities can be analyzed from this perspective to ensure maximal discoverability of resources across the repository. Ensuring that appropriate semantic units are being employed for the corresponding element is required before any scalable enhancement can be considered.

The vertical dimension of an IR refers to the organizational structures present within the IR in terms of an information hierarchy. For example, the Dspace framework allows for the creation of both communities and collections. In KUSW, this has actually been a source of inconsistency with communities like 'Office of the Provost' being listed alongside 'Mathematics'. While the aim of this paper is not to assess the repository on this level, this is merely provided to show an instance of when classes may not have equivalency and in turn obfuscate the hierarchy of the IR; an unnecessary challenge for users to navigate.

The horizontal and vertical approaches to repository quality should be familiar as they reflect a common, persistent way of viewing information resources. In this case metadata and the organizing structures that contain it are understood as relatively unchanging objects. However, these dimensions provide a misleading notion of the repository and its resources as fixed items. This view is perhaps owing to the time of the physical card catalog in which the metadata record, as a mostly static object, stood as a surrogate for the information resource. When the most atomic metadata in a system is seen as unchanging, so also will its organizing containers. This persistent view fails to take into account not only the capabilities of current technology to track changes to information over time, but the fact that information is not a static entity. Rather, information's ability to change is a critical component of any system. It is important that records may change over time, and that a repository's structure may adapt to accomplish new organizing objectives.

Concern for temporality is required to gain the fullest context for information resources. Significant work has already been achieved in this area by Isabelle Boydens, who begins from the notion that an unequivocal interpretation of 'observable reality' is impossible. [2] As closed world systems, databases, the ubiquitous system for storing what we will for simplicity's sake call 'facts', are generally in opposition to this fundamental idea. Her thesis, neatly distilled by Bade, is that

"...The world changes for us because we ask and expect different things of it at different times; that being so, both our data and our metadata need to change to reflect that new state of the world." [3]

Information stored in a database represents a particular, fixed view of reality. That picture should change with time and by the functional needs of those using it to remain consistent with the changing world around it. An IR is no exception. Being databases with a culturally significant bent, they are acutely tied to temporal changes. Furthermore, there are many ways in which these temporal elements affect IR administrators' ability to manage and enhance metadata. By incorporating elements that capture continuity, administrators will be able to present a clearer, hopefully more useful, bibliographic system to users.

3   Temporal Perspectives

3.1   Policy Adjustments

Policies for metadata creation are necessary to ensure consistency across records. Before any standardization can occur (e.g. naming conventions), it is necessary to know what guidelines are already in place. However, these policies change by the adoption of new schema, identifiers, content standards, and other similar considerations. Fortunately, the time a record is created can be captured by repository technology, making it a straightforward process to determine which records were created after a specific policy had been put in place. It is then possible to more accurately adjust records to reflect a newer policy.

While this capability is certainly essential to effective record management, it is unfortunately insufficient, especially for an IR. KUSW metadata consists of author generated (AG) records provided at the time of a resource's submission into the repository. While this process has saved cataloging staff from a substantial workload, it has understandably led to creative interpretations of schema elements, causing a wide level of inconsistency across records. This obviously raises concerns for those interested in providing an effective retrieval system. The remediation process will require substantial work, particularly as it pertains to subject terms.

Some examples of author-generated subject terms include 'parent-child talk', 'agency', 'reading with distraction', and 'future selves' to name only a few. These types of terms, in some cases at once both specific and vague, make up the majority of subjects populating the corpus. There is a clear disparity between these terms and what one would expect to see had they been populated from an authority source such as Library of Congress Subject Headings or another more discipline appropriate vocabulary. From a retrieval perspective they are generally not very useful given their frequency of use; most are employed only once. Indeed, collocation is essentially impossible for those browsing by subjects. From a linked data perspective they are useless as there is no URI available for them to reference.

It was initially suggested that these terms be mapped onto terms from an authority source, an idea that will likely be implemented in the future. But should AG terms then be discarded? As Lubas notes, it is recommended to retain terms from AG metadata, however this does come at the cost of increased 'noise' within a repository, an obvious hindrance to any bibliographic system. [4] While the terms may not be useful in the context of a retrieval system, they remain valuable as artifacts. AG metadata provides a unique prism to view how an author understood their work, with subject terms adding a particularly acute distillation of what terms they thought might also be used by other practitioners.

Preserving AG records raises questions of access and audience. Tracking provenance as it conforms to the Dublin Core element set has been built into Dspace. However, there currently is no mechanism to store meta-metadata or what changes were made and why. Even if such a system existed, such changes would probably only be viewable from an administrator perspective, which while still valuable, does not lend itself to openness. Indeed part of the motivation for saving AG records is so that users would be able to observe these changes, in turn informing their own assessment of the resource and its relevance.

A straight normalization of subject terms, or their mapping onto a pre-existing controlled vocabulary eliminates this unique perspective of the author regarding their work. Yet if we continue to think of databases as a snapshot of a particular instance in time, an edited record, while positively adding consistency to the corpus, will come at the cost of provenance or even more precisely, a cultural artifact unique to the institution. Capturing the evolution of metadata allows for the ability to analyze how it changes and understand why it changes, becoming itself an object of critical inquiry.

Transparency, usually referring to openness about the internal workflows and policies a trusted repository follows, should be extended to providing the clearest accounting of a resource's lifespan, including adjustments to its metadata. By retaining an original record and making it accessible to users as an optional view on the same splash page with the new record is an important way of establishing trust through providing additional context for a resource rather than covering it up. For KUSW, since there was little guidance regarding what metadata should look like, this will play an important part for an administrator's ability to understand how and why records changed over time and more effectively monitor the utility of records or lack thereof.

Continuity is important on many different timescales. While the previous example focused on metadata through its entire lifecycle, metadata may also be improved by understanding its current usage. Working from a micro-temporal level, a dynamic prototype interface designed by Boydens and Hooland allows for users to choose which elements to search by in the interface through a drag and drop mechanism, customizing their experience to their specific information seeking behavior. [5] Besides its flexibility for users, it also allows collection managers to prioritize work based on the most frequently used elements and monitor how this changes over time. This demonstrates promising possibility for determining appropriate metadata scope that is informed by temporal considerations. Furthermore it addresses capturing the narrative of the record, in this case, why certain elements are more important at a given time than others. As a basic way of understanding user behavior, dynamic interaction with metadata will provide insight into the effectiveness of interfaces and inform user experiences decisions in a more rigorous way.

3.2   Disciplinary Migration

If policy adjustments over time may be understood as referring to the horizontal dimension of an IR, disciplinary migration represents the vertical. Disciplinary migration is, as its name suggests, when a particular discipline undergoes some sort of rebranding or refocusing to reflect more current appellations consistent with the larger academic community. At KU, what was once the *Human Development and Family Life* department broadened in 2004 to be *Applied Behavioral Science*. Such changes are ubiquitous at academic institutions and their changes can be no small feat to navigate.

These migrations present a difficult challenge for IR with static worldviews. Recently deposited resources stored under the most current appellation of a discipline present no problem, but relevance collisions emerge when one considers aggregating resources under the same collection from when the discipline went by other names. Are the resources consistent enough in subject matter to form a cohesive collection? For more recent changes this is likely true, but for subjects that can trace back several decades, even into other centuries, the similarities grow increasingly thin. Likewise, it may be counterproductive to aggregate resources for disciplines that have undergone disruptive foundational changes, particularly in the physical sciences.

There are a couple of ways in which repositories have sought to mediate this issue. In the University of Illinois at Urbana-Champaign repository, IDEALS, separate top-level collections were created for each iteration of a discipline or department, with dates listed to delineate when the department existed or went by a different name. [6] Within each collection a description was provided indicating the origin of the discipline/department and when it transitioned into something else. From a statically based perspective, this is an acceptable if somewhat less than ideal solution. The tracking of migrations is documented and it avoids the problems of disparity caused by aggregating resources across a century of development under one roof. However, for users navigating the system it creates an even grander domain to traverse. Similarly, relations between iterations of a discipline, while noted, are not built into the infrastructure. There is no attempt to meaningfully connect these relationships on a deeper level.

Another method has been to ignore it as a problem. In KUSW a collection of pre-1923 Theses and Dissertations have been aggregated under the broader collection of Theses and Dissertations that includes those resources from 1923 to the present. While the more recent ETDs are also housed within their respective disciplines, the pre-1923 works can only be found in this one collection. One work, 'Aspects of the Gothic Romance', has a discipline marked unambiguously as 'English' and if desired could easily be mapped into the existing discipline collection of the same name, especially since the content is less likely to be dated.

By contrast, another work, 'Additional Peculiarities in the Spermatogenesis of Phrynotettix Magnus' has for its discipline 'Zoology'. While valuable as representing an important historical perspective on an evolving subject, it has not been joined to its current related discipline 'Biological Sciences'. It is possible that its content has been superseded by new research, but if that is the case, who will go looking for it if it is not stored under what would be its current discipline? For similar examples, separating these resources from their current disciplinary descendent may be a bit of detraction; they appear now as simply relics of a certain time period, perhaps not worthy of consideration alongside more recent research. The solution of aggregating resources in an appropriate collection, even though it may not represent the best, most specific location for it categorically speaking, is fraught with inconsistencies and difficultly resolved content arrangements.

The limits of assessing a repository without a temporal perspective are significant. It may be argued that the methods mentioned above to address disciplinary migration are really more compromises than permanent solutions as some element of the information hierarchy and continuity is lost after implementation. In the context of KUSW, Dspace does not have any built in method of applying these nuanced details within its architecture. Indeed, this is beyond the scope of what a Postgres database can offer on its own. However, linked data provides a possible solution to the challenges of representing information continuity.

As stated above the specter of the physical card catalog continues to influence bibliographic systems. Memory institutions are still strongly tied to the record format, which while useful still suggests a view of the record as an immutable object. Of course current technologies allow for a degree of interoperability that in the light of our discussion can go some way to addressing these temporal concerns, transitioning a record more to data along the spectrum outlined by Glushko and McGrath. [7] In a promising study, Peponakis describes a system for building semantic relationships into an IR, primarily by a combination of RDF informed by FRBR and FRAD principles to create a network of authority files for individuals and departments that can be tied to works. [8] Additionally, a time span was attached to each triple to allow an even more powerful method of coordinated searching, though as Peponakis notes, the implementation of time with RDF has not reached a community consensus despite research into this area. [8, 9] Nevertheless, it remains a unique way of addressing these temporal constraints in an elegant and progressive way. By serializing the history of the departments and disciplines in RDF, one is able to view the relationships between different academic units and their evolution over time through a semantically rich and meaningful way.

As a method of assessing a repository, the continuity of its vertical organization is a critical element with significant implications. To remain with a static view of disciplines, an image of the world at a given time, is to compromise on the meaningful structure of the information hierarchy in addition to creating a system that is at best flawed for navigation and at worst inconsistent and confusing. Initial steps for assessing an IR from this perspective must first to determine what disciplines are represented and if there has been an attempt at documenting the continuity of migrations, then some steps towards integration into a semantic framework may be already in place. If, as in the case of KUSW, the view is of a static present then much of this historical context will need to be discerned before it can be integrated into an authority file and incorporated into a linked environment.

3.3   Resource Extensibility

Format Types
Digital resource types and the software that create them are in a constant state of development. It goes without saying that ensuring resources remain in a currently accessible format is a natural concern for any repository. Fortunately, the push for open formats is a positive step towards ensuring the longevity of repository resources. [10] However, long term utility of resources is not quite so simple a matter of choosing an

initial format. Rather, it is an increasingly nuanced universe, especially as media types continue to change and grow in complexity.

The majority of resources in KUSW are of a text-based nature, consisting of articles, books, project reports, and other similar items. However, there is a slowly growing body of code, data, and videos; formats for which are much more in flux regarding adoption than their text-based counterparts. For example, the resources listed as 'videos' in KUSW often point to embedded videos in web pages. Ignoring the misleading type designation, the resource is subject to a similar problem regarding extensibility. Ensuring that the HTML remains consistent with modern browsers ability to read the page is one concern, but the video in the page, which currently runs on the Adobe Flash, may be replaced by functionalities built into HTML 5. It is inevitable that over time the current format of the video will become obsolete.

The predominance of text resources may diminish over time, requiring the already needed attention given to preservation of more complex resources and consideration for those that are yet to emerge. Resources in KUSW are generally available in the format they were ingested in. Little effort has been made to upgrade resources to their most current, stable format which fortunately has not been a significant problem as most of the resources are in formats that remain widely used (e.g. PDF, CSV). However, if Python code were to be ingested today, how useful will that resource be to the user who finds it a decade from now and by which time a new version of the language will have been released? Similarly, XML metadata for GIS datasets may need conversion to JSON to support future use.

Evolving resource types are an excellent way of demonstrating how the fixed-world view of databases is itself a contradiction. As a repository ages it will grow to contain several iterations of a particular resource type, becoming an inconsistent disseminator of anachronistic resources. Understandably this is in direct conflict with the definition of a trusted repository put forth by RLG-OCLC, particularly that a trusted repository "design its system(s) in accordance with commonly accepted conventions and standards to ensure the ongoing management, access, and security of materials deposited within it." [11] Enabling access is a continuous process, not an event, and ensuring that resources can be not only accessed but also used is a part of that process.

It is evident that resource extensibility is a critical part of any repository's assessment, and particularly that format types, dependencies, and other information needed to enable its use be documented in the preservation metadata. Provided this is accomplished, we may return to the horizontal dimension of the repository and be able to observe that after a certain date, for example, a policy regarding accepted file types was implemented and that previous types were migrated to a more current format. The question of retaining those older versions and how metadata records should reflect their replacements goes beyond the scope of this paper, but it is mentioned now as a possible source of future discussion.

Preservation Narratives
The use of PREMIS for documenting the technical components of a resource at a very granular level is widespread. Given the limitations of other schema to record information of this quality in any sort of all encompassing way, its existence is a needed tool for

managers of repositories. However, the claim that PREMIS data dictionary contains all the information required to ensure preservation has been rightly questioned by Wilson, who notes that the dictionary does not capture anything related to the preservation process, only the resources, events, and related agents. [12] Additional provenance information, he continues, is required to gain the clearest picture of a resource's lifespan beginning from before its ingest and into the future.

Wilson hints at the temporal element by his mention of preservation as a process. Defined by the PREMIS data dictionary, a *representation* is 'a single digital instance of an intellectual entity held in a preservation repository'. [13] This concept seems to exists somewhere between a FRBR manifestation and item. It uses as an example a TIFF image of a statue of a horse as one representation, while a derived JPEG image represents yet another, both being representations of the statue image. The ability to track events and relationships between representations and agents goes some way towards introducing a temporal element, but it is not sufficient. We only know that preservation events happened, but not necessarily why they happened. While the <eventOutcomeDetailNote> element can capture some of this information, it reflects only a small part of the ongoing preservation process.

The contextual element is essential to the notion of information continuity. Without the proper documentation for why certain processes were implemented, we are left with guesswork. But if this information is not to be fully captured in PREMIS, where can it be? While METS does allow for some of this more administrative information to be recorded, it is neither exactly what is needed nor on a scale appropriate to the myriad iterations of digital resources that may populate a system; the structure of a METS record would quickly be overwhelmed. Of course some degree of rational can usually be inferred from a PREMIS event, but leaving these deductions to future stewards when more should be captured at the time of the event is hardly a favor.

It is recognized that to some extent we are reaching the limits of what can be expressed by metadata, at least currently. Again, while events recorded by PREMIS can be given additional details, the ability to form a narrative outlining these changes is really what is required to fully reflect information continuity. How these discrete metadata units can be rebuilt to form a larger picture remains to be seen, but its achievement is required for future administrators to have the most complete picture of the preservation continuum and how it informs their own work. For KUSW, which is only in its initial stages of implementing a preservation system, care will have to be given to these concerns to create an effective and understandable paper trail from the outset to ensure it is achieved.

4   Temporal Modeling and Implementation

4.1   Temporal Parts

Any consideration for modeling how resources exist in time will inevitably require a decision between two trains of thought. The perdurantist view posits that entities have both a spatial and temporal parts, in essence that an institution does not just have its present version, but has in equally important measure its version from yesterday and tomorrow; in essence, a sum of parts. The opposing view, endurantism, says that an entity is wholly present whenever it exists, that parts do not extend beyond the current moment. [14] While not delving into the nuances behind each school of thought, each has significant implications for temporal representation of an IR. Information continuity is most closely aligned with perdurantism as it has been argued that the narrative of a metadata element, document, and institution is important.

Before any implementation of a system can occur it is necessary to model what exactly comprises a perdurant object. Despite the fundamental differences between a resource and an entity in an IR there are similarities in the way they are viewed from temporal perspectives. Figure 1 represents how an admittedly oversimplified perdurant view might represent an object (e.g. article, department):

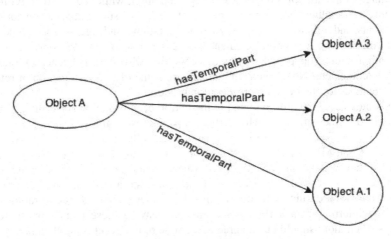

Fig. 1. An object with its perdurant components

The prime object itself is not identical with any one of its iterations, but rather is the sum of the three. While Object A.3 may represent the one currently accessible in a repository, it does not represent the totality of the object. Rather, Object A, an intangible resource, might be considered the prime object, and is not unlike a *Work* in the FRBR sense. This correlation is only meant to illustrate and not to incorporate another model in any systematic way.

It may be judged that temporal parts are just a matter of versioning, and while the similarities are obvious, the primary difference is that continuity is more interested in the matter of the objects as aggregates; one does not supersede another. Indeed, that is the critical element of continuity. That one may succeed another does not change the fact that all are necessary to form the narrative of the object.

4.2   Implementation

It is clear that semantic solutions are required to facilitate the meaningful relationships between resources built around temporal considerations. Otherwise one runs into the same compromises that we have observed in the examples of organizing an IR by discipline. Yet, as noted above, there is no common consensus on how time is to be accounted for within the context of RDF despite research into the area. [9] More recent approaches include the development of a temporal Web Ontology Language (tOWL) though its widespread adoption remains to be seen and it seems likely that its proposed serialization in RDF/XML will pose the same challenges that have encumbered that format so far. [15] Concerns for interoperability are of course critical but beyond the scope of this paper.

This initial exploration seeks to draw on existing models to avoid the proliferation of alternatives among an already competitive ecosystem. RDF is the natural tool for creating these relationships and using JSON-LD will likely provide a more lightweight and flexible method for preliminary investigations into the feasibility of these aggregations. Regarding an appropriate aggregating standard, the most closely related model currently available is that of OAI-ORE [16]; Fig. 1. Is derived from a part of this model. Though the goal of the aggregations are different with OAI-ORE designed to collect resources from various content providers, the specification provides a broadly analogous model for how various perdurant iterations could likewise be collected. [16] To build in a temporal element one may draw on the W3's OWL-Time, which allows for time to be incorporated into an object's metadata as 'instants' and intervals'. [17] There are fundamental differences regarding representations in OAI-ORE that will need to be reconciled with the non-tangible prime object of the perdurant model. This brief discussion has only been meant as a cursory outline of what potential frameworks may be employed towards a serialization of IR resources and structures. It is implied that a more detailed model and analysis of its implementation will be the immediate focus of future research.

5   Conclusions

This paper has outlined that the idea of information continuity is essential to an effective assessment and organization of any information system. By outlining three areas most immediately impacted by temporal concerns, a framework for approaching the needs of a repository can be used and a more thorough analysis achieved. Future work will demonstrate how effectively perceived temporal needs can be implemented in the context of KUSW, with results serving as a model for future development.

While this paper has pointed to potential solutions for each of three areas described, they by no means represent the best or only approaches to consider. As regards preservation metadata there is significant room for research on how to best incorporate the already present sequential aspects into a more meaningful relational context. For archival metadata additional effort is needed to address the final role and perceived utility of author generated records. Finally, the disposition of certain schemas towards capturing important temporal information will provide an important outlet for a wider assessment of schema utility in general.

Finally, the perdurant model outlined above is only an initial step in using existing tools and standards to build a flexible relational model. Since there is yet no standard, allowing for flexibility in proposed models is necessary to ensure responsive adaptability. Further research will involve using the OAI-ORE framework within the context of an IR collection to assess its appropriateness and needed extensions.

Metadata needs to be more flexible. As only one part of the information environment that is a repository, it in some ways can be considered a microcosm of its host structure. If the metadata is considered a static resource, then the organizing structures containing it will follow suit, as there is no temporal element to be considered and built upon. If metadata begins with a concern for capturing temporality and in a way that meaningfully impacts larger structures, a greater symbiosis between resource and repository can be achieved and information continuity more effectively represented.

Information, like the world, is affected by temporality. Monitoring how metadata is used over time and in certain contexts naturally allows for a greater understanding of its effectiveness and how it must change to reflect new information seeking behaviors, social responses, and networked environments. That metadata is an indicator for resources and not just a pointer is a vital way of assessing the narrative of resources themselves. As Boyden notes, this provides a new direction for a type of metadata that is more interactive and responsive to the world around it. [2]

References

1. The University of Kansas, ScholarWorks, `http://kuscholarworks.ku.edu`
2. Boydens, I.: Informatiques, normes et temps. Bruylant, Bruxelles (1999)
3. Bade, D.: It's about Time!: Temporal Aspects of Metadata Management in the Work of Isabelle Boydens. Cataloging & Classification Quarterly 49(4), 328–338 (2011), doi:10.1080/01639374.2011.571096
4. Lubas, R.L.: Defining Best Practices in Electronic Thesis and Dissertation Metadata. Journal of Library Metadata 9(3-4), 252–263 (2009), doi:10.1080/19386380903405165
5. Boydens, I., Van Hooland, S.: Hermeneutics applied to the quality of em-pirical databases. Journal of Documentation 67(2), 279–289 (2011), doi:10.1108/00220411111109476
6. The University of Illinois at Urbana-Champaign, IDEALS, `https://ideals.illinois.edu/`
7. Glushko, R., McGrath, T.: Document Engineering. MIT Press, Cambridge (2005)
8. Peponakis, M.: Libraries' Metadata as Data in the Era of the Semantic Web: Modeling a Repository of Master Theses and PhD Dissertations for the Web of Data. Journal of Library Metadata 13(4), 330–348 (2013), doi:10.1080/19386389.2013.846618
9. Gutierrez, C., Hurtado, C., Vaisman, S.: Introducing time into RDF. IEEE Transactions on Knowledge and Data Engineering 19(2), 207–218 (2007)
10. Rimkus, K., Padilla, T., Popp, T., Martin, G.: Digital Preservation File Format Policies of ARL Member Libraries: An Analysis. D-Lib Magazine 20(3-4) (2014), doi:10.1045/march2014-rimkus
11. RLG-OCLC. Trusted Digital Repositories: Attributes and Responsibilities, Mountain View, CA (2002)
12. Wilson, A.: How Much Is Enough: Metadata for Preserving Digital Data. Journal of Library Metadata 10(2-3), 205–217 (2010), doi:10.1080/19386389.2010.506395
13. PREMIS Editorial Committee. Premis Data Dictionary for Preservation Meta-data, version 2.2. Washington, DC (2012)

14. Hawley, K.: Temporal Parts. In: Zalta, E.N. (ed.) The Stanford Encyclopedia of Philosophy, Winter 2010 edn. (2010), `http://plato.stanford.edu/archives/win2010/entries/temporal-parts/`
15. Milea, V., Frasincar, F., Kaymak, U.: tOWL: A Temporal Web Ontology Language. IEEE. Transactions on Systems, Man, and Cybernetics 42(1), 268–281 (2012)
16. Open Archives Initiative-Object Reuse and Exchange, `http://www.openarchives.org/ore/`
17. OWL-Time, `http://www.w3.org/2006/time`

A Framework for the Evaluation of Automatic Metadata Enrichments

Juliane Stiller, Marlies Olensky, and Vivien Petras

Humboldt-Universität zu Berlin, Berlin School of Library and Information Science,
Berlin, Germany
{juliane.stiller,marlies.olensky,vivien.petras}@ibi.hu-berlin.de

Abstract. Automatic enrichment of collections connects data to vocabularies, which supports the contextualization of content and adds searchable text to metadata. The paper introduces a framework of four dimensions (frequency, coverage, relevance and error rate) that measure both the suitability of the enrichment for the object and the enrichments' contribution to search success. To verify the framework, it is applied to the evaluation of automatic enrichments in the digital library Europeana. The analysis of 100 result sets and their corresponding queries (1,121 documents total) shows the framework is a valuable tool for guiding enrichments and determining the value of enrichment efforts.

Keywords: Evaluation, Europeana, Digital Libraries, Cultural Collections, Framework, Semantic Enrichment.

1 Introduction

Digital libraries see great promise in linking controlled vocabularies and datasets in order to achieve easier access to the material, for example, through the implementation of better browsing functionalities based on category systems [1]. Automatic enrichments of metadata lead to an improved contextualization of the information objects that are enriched and increase the searchable metadata many digital libraries are lacking [2]. The dream of interconnected datasets, which reveal hidden contexts and allow the presentation of semantic relations, seems to be within arm's reach.

In the cultural heritage domain, where structured metadata and, therefore, accessibility is rather scarce, the application of semantic technologies like automatic enrichments seems to be a step in the right direction. Europeana[1], as one of the biggest platforms for retrieving, experiencing and interacting with cultural data from European museums, archives and libraries, is trailblazing the implementation of automatic workflows for linking controlled vocabularies and other datasets to its metadata. As of mid-2014, over half of the metadata-described objects in Europeana had links to

---

[1] http://www.europeana.eu/

S. Closs et al. (Eds.): MTSR 2014, CCIS 478, pp. 238–249, 2014.

external datasets and resources. However, automatic metadata enrichments are not always useful [3]. Ambiguous, vague or even incorrect data could be added to curated and high-quality metadata resulting in reduced effectiveness during the retrieval process or during the relevance decision-making process of a human user.

The impact and quality of the created links could not be studied so far due to a lack of a comprehensive evaluation framework and suitable measures. This paper wants to fill this gap and presents a framework for evaluating automatic enrichments in digital libraries. The framework is applied to evaluate automatic enrichments in Europeana based on a sample of real Europeana queries and (enriched) documents determining their value and impact.

The paper is organized as follows: section 2 provides the state of the art with regard to enrichments and linking datasets in the cultural heritage domain. Section 3 presents the framework for evaluating enrichments including a categorization schema for the impact of enrichments in relation to user queries. To verify the framework, section 4 presents an evaluation of enrichments automatically conducted by Europeana based on the framework. The last section discusses the findings.

2   Background and Literature

The key to unlocking the value of a digital library's content is to provide easy access to its collections [1]. This requires a high quality standard of metadata, which can necessitate an enhancement of metadata to improve the retrieval experience for the user if the provided metadata is scarce or poor. We have defined this process of metadata enhancement as semantic and multilingual enrichment that uses controlled vocabularies to enrich metadata of information objects in a digital library, archive or museum [3]. Schreiber et al. [4] define this process as semantic annotation.

Automatic enrichment efforts in digital libraries have been carried out by Newman et al. [1], who used statistical topic models to generate and add uniform subject headings to information objects from hundreds of different repositories and Jones et al. [5] who experimented with geographical metadata enrichment. The Paths Project[7] implemented several enrichment techniques [6] like mapping items to Wikipedia [7] and developing a web service for the enrichment of cultural heritage data [2].

The basic process for linking datasets is to find a match between the target vocabulary and a source field in the metadata. Metadata quality is crucial to enable a smooth and high quality linking process. Shreeves et al. [8] conclude from their study on implications of local metadata practices on aggregation that variance in the metadata sharply increases. This leads to problems for activities concerning the whole body of the heterogeneous data, especially for automatic metadata enrichment.

In 2012, some of the authors manually analyzed 200 enrichments from Europeana and categorized the different flaws and problems encountered [3]. They concluded that three dimensions influence the quality of enrichment: metadata level, vocabulary

---

[2] http://www.paths-project.eu/

level, workflow level. Domain and language-specific characteristics of metadata need to be considered in the enrichment process. Based on the findings of this study, Europeana created a task force with metadata experts to determine a strategy for multilingual and semantic enrichments in Europeana[3]. While the task force focused on identifying sources for enrichment errors, the framework introduced in the following identifies measures for evaluating the quality of produced enrichments.

3   A Framework for Evaluating Enrichments

Evaluating the effectiveness of automatic metadata enrichments helps to understand their usefulness for information access and reveals potentially harmful enrichment processes. When measuring the effectiveness of enrichments, the focus can be either on the quality of the enrichments themselves (i.e. are the enrichments correct for an object) or their influence on the retrieval performance (i.e. do the enrichments increase success in search). The latter focuses on the outcomes of enrichments from an end-user point of view. Not the enrichment itself is important, but how it influences user satisfaction, i.e. the entire end-to-end process (from the initial query to the result list) is evaluated [9].

For evaluating the quality of the enrichments, one can determine how often objects were enriched and how good these enrichments were with regard to the enriched object. This assumes that logical and appropriate vocabularies and linking rules have already been determined during the enrichment process so that the first quality check of the prerequisite stages of the enrichment process has been assured [10]. Looking at queries, the impact of enrichments on the quality of the search results can determine their usefulness with regard to the retrieval performance. This evaluation can serve to fine-tune the enrichment components but also to improve the integration of enrichment outcomes into the retrieval processes.

To evaluate enrichments and their effectiveness, a framework based on a collection of (metadata) objects and a list of queries is proposed. The queries represent different end-user· information needs retrieving a collection of objects. They are the basis to measure the effectiveness of enrichments from both the quality and retrieval performance perspectives.

Table 1 gives an overview of the framework for evaluating enrichments based on several dimensions. Frequency and coverage provide information about the distribution of enrichments across a collection (of metadata objects). The relevance dimension for the objects measures whether the enrichment is appropriate for the digital object, respectively the field or facet that was enriched. The error rate determines the number of incorrect enrichments per objects and per query. Dimensions can have several measures, that are either dependent on the metadata objects (measures for quality) or on the queries (measures for retrieval performance).

---

[3] http://pro.europeana.eu/web/network/europeana-tech/-
/wiki/Main/Task+force+multilingual+semantic+enrichment

Table 1. Framework for evaluating enrichments

Dimension	Object-dependent	Query-dependent
Frequency	Percentage of enriched objects Enrichments per objects	Percentage of queries that retrieve enriched objects
Coverage	Distribution of enrichments across facets	Proportion of enriched objects per query
		Percentage of queries retrieving enrichment facets
Relevance	Relevance of enrichment to the object	Relevance of enrichments to queries
Error rate	Percentage of incorrect enrichments	Percentage of queries retrieving incorrect enrichments
	Percentage of retrieved objects with incorrect enrichments	

To determine the relevance and error rate of the enrichments with regard to objects and query, the authors developed seven categories (Table 2).

Table 2. Categories and their descriptions for measuring the relevance and error rate dimensions

Category	Description
Retrieved query match	The object was found due to the enrichment, i.e. the query term is only present in the automatically added enrichment terms but not in the original metadata.
Query match	The enrichment is relevant to the query, but the enrichment terms are also part of the original metadata.
Hierarchical term match	The enrichment is a broader or narrower term of the query. It has no influence on the retrieval of the object.
Partly query match	The enrichment is relevant to only a part of the query or only part of the enrichment is relevant to the query.
Query independence	The enrichment is independent from the query, but a correct enrichment for the record.
Incorrect enrichment	The enrichment is incorrect, but does not have influence on the retrieval of the object.
Retrieved incorrect enrichment	The enrichment is incorrect, and has been retrieved because of the incorrect enrichment.

The *retrieved query match* type directly contributes to the retrieval performance for an object, because it adds terms that are in the query – the object would otherwise not have been found. The *partly query match* and *query match* type could also positively contribute to the retrieval performance, because of repeating original metadata terms in the enrichments that are relevant for the query. Europeana, for example, uses a ranking system that uses term frequency (the frequency of a term occurring in a metadata record) as a positive ranking signal, so while repeating terms in the object description might not be useful for the user, it might contribute to the retrieval success. The *hierarchical term match* could be used for increasing the result set by retrieving objects that have a broader or narrower scope of the original query, but are not used in that way so far and, therefore, do not contribute to the retrieval performance. *Query independence* denotes a correct enrichment for the object, which is independent from the query. Hence, it can have potential positive influence on the retrieval for other queries. The *incorrect enrichment* type could actually decrease the retrieval performance because irrelevant objects might be retrieved for a query because of incorrectly added enrichments. *The retrieved incorrect enrichment* type decreases the retrieval performance by ranking irrelevant objects for the query. The error rate is implicitly measured by the categories, since *retrieved query match* up until *query independence* denote a correct enrichment and the remaining two categories *incorrect enrichment* and *retrieved incorrect enrichment* designate an incorrect enrichment.

4   Use Case: Evaluation of Europeana

In order to verify the framework explained in the previous section, it was applied to enrichments in Europeana. The focus was on the enrichments conducted by Europeana after the ingestion of the collections.[4]

Europeana enriches its object metadata automatically with different vocabularies using the AnnoCultor Tagger[5]. It matches certain metadata fields to different vocabularies establishing links between these resources. Additional contextual information is also added to the original objects. These can be multilingual variants of the terms or broader terms. Table 3 shows an overview of the source metadata fields and the target vocabulary for the enrichment facets used in Europeana, namely places (WHERE), agents (WHO), concepts (WHAT) and time periods (WHEN).

Table 3. Enrichment facet, their target vocabulary and source fields

Facet	Target vocabulary	Source metadata fields
WHERE	GeoNames[6]	dcterms:spatial, dc:coverage
WHAT	GEMET[7], DBpedia[8]	dc:subject, dc:type
WHO	DBpedia	dc:creator, dc:contributor
WHEN	Semium Time[9]	dc:date, dc:coverage, dcterms:temporal, edm:year

---

[4] The evaluation was conducted within the EU-funded project Europeana v2.0 (http://pro.europeana.eu/web/europeana-v2.0/home). An earlier version of the framework and parts of the evaluation can be found in the deliverable D7.8 [11].
[5] A thorough explanation of the enrichment process can be found here: http://europeanalabs.eu/wiki/EDMPrototypingTask21Annocultor which is a copy of the following blog post: http://borys.name/blog/semantic_tagging_of_europeana_data.html
[6] http://www.geonames.org/
[7] http://www.eionet.europa.eu/gemet/
[8] http://dbpedia.org/About
[9] http://semium.org/time.html

In the portal display[10], automatic enrichments can be found in certain metadata fields (number 1 in Fig. 1) and in the foldout "Auto-generated tags" (number 2 in Fig 1). The example in Fig 1shows that the dc:type field of the object was delivered with the German term "Denkmal" (monument). Europeana enriched it with the appropriate GEMET entity and its language variants (number 2). Additionally, the broader term of "monument" was added too – "cultural facility".

Fig. 1. Automatic enrichments in the portal display.[11]

4.1   Data Collection and Assessment

In order to build a sample corpus of queries and enriched objects for evaluation, the 1,000 most frequent queries in Europeana were extracted from Google Analytics for the first quarter of 2014. By removing duplicates, advanced queries (e.g.

---

[10] It should be noted that the display does not distinguish between automatic enrichments delivered by providers with their domain-specific vocabularies and the automatic enrichments conducted by Europeana.

[11] http://europeana.eu/portal/record/08501/
5160ED8B5ED7C6D057AAE31C4FAA1FB2A82BAC62.html

what:"Photo"), queries with just one letter, a number, punctuation (except *) or Boolean operators, the corpus was reduced by circa two thirds. A random selection of 100 queries was extracted from the remaining 348 queries.

Each query was searched in Europeana and the first result page (12 objects at most) analyzed. A total number of 1,121 records for 100 queries was assessed, i.e. almost all queries retrieved at least 12 objects (enough for a first result page) that could be analyzed. Based on the relevance categories, each enrichment term was assessed. Table 4 shows the categories with examples from the data sample and their coding.

Table 4. Categories, examples from the sample and codes

Category	Example	Code
Retrieved query match	The query "Bratislava" retrieves a record that only had "Pozsony" in the original metadata, which is a Hungarian translation of Bratislava.	RQM
Query match	The query "Lilien, Ephraim" retrieves objects enriched with the person Ephraim Moses Lilien, yet, Ephraim Moses Lilien was also listed as creator in the original metadata.	QM
Hierarchical term match	For the query "Bratislava" a record was not only enriched with Bratislava, but also with its broader term Slovakia.	HTM
Partly query match	For the German query "sport zeitung", objects were enriched with the concept sports.	PQM
Query independence	The query "Lerski, Helmar" (Swiss photographer) retrieves objects that were enriched with documentation and photograph or industrial process and photography.	QI
Incorrect enrichment	A record with the subject "art" was enriched with "ecological parameter" and "species" (independent from the query).	IE
Retrieved incorrect enrichment	The query "internet" retrieves objects about the Forum Romanum, because Forum was incorrectly enriched with newsgroup and its broader term internet.	RIE

The automatic enrichments added by Europeana were assessed per facet as explained in Table 3. For the relevance dimension of the evaluation only the WHAT-, WHO- and WHERE-facet enrichments were analyzed[12]. Additional enrichments delivered from data providers were considered part of the original metadata and are not subject of this evaluation.

---

[12] Temporal queries (such as year dates or time periods), where enrichments in the WHEN-facet would be helpful, did not occur in our selected corpus and were therefore excluded from this analysis. Consequently, a total number of 507 enrichments were assessed for their relevance to the query and the object.

4.2   Results

Following the results are listed grouped by the dimension from the framework - frequency, coverage, relevance and error rate.

Frequency – Object and Query-Dependent

In total, 1,082 enrichment terms were added to the 1,121 retrieved objects (*Enrichments per objects*). However, only 424 (38%) of these objects were enriched, i.e. when enrichment occurred, more than one enrichment term was added to an object (*Number of enriched objects*). A small percentage of the objects contained only one enrichment (17%), while the rest were enriched with two terms (51%) or more. Almost ¾ of the queries (75%) retrieved at least one object in the first 12 results that contained an enrichment (*Number of queries that retrieve enriched objects*).

Coverage – Object and Query-Dependent

Summarizing the *Distribution of enrichments across facets*, of the 424 enriched records, 72% were enriched with terms in only one facet, 26% in two facets and 2% in three facets. Most enrichment terms were added in the WHEN facet (53%), followed by WHAT enrichments (28%). Personal names (WHO) were rarely enriched. On average, 50% of the objects are enriched per query which retrieved enriched objects (*Proportion of enriched objects per query*).

Relevance – Object and Query-Dependent

The overall results in Fig. 2 show that enrichments from category QI (correct enrichment for the object, but not relevant to the query) are the most frequent ones with 46%, followed by enrichments from category QM (correct enrichment for the object and relevant for the query, but terms also occur in the original metadata) with 21%. Incorrect enrichments (IE and RIE), which can be, and in some cases were, detrimental for the retrieval performance, account for 15% of the assessed cases, whereas enrichments that might contribute to the retrieval success (RQM, PQM and QM) account for 27% of the cases.

Summarized according to the framework, 85% of enrichments are relevant to the object (RQM, QM, HTM, PQM, QI), i.e. *Relevance of enrichment to the object*. For the query relevance, i.e. *Relevance of enrichments to queries*, this means that 39% of the enrichments were relevant to the query. While 27% of enrichments had a potential positive impact on the retrieval performance, 4% of enrichments had a negative impact on the retrieval performance and 2% of enrichments had a positive impact on retrieval.

Error Rate – Object and Query-Dependent

The relevance to the object and query can also be expressed as error rate. Summarizing the categories IE and RIE, 15% of enrichments are incorrect for the object they enriched (*Percentage of incorrect enrichments*). In total, 3.5% of objects had an incorrect enrichment (*Percentage of retrieved objects with incorrect enrichments*). 7% of the queries retrieved incorrect enrichments (*Percentage of queries retrieving incorrect enrichments*).

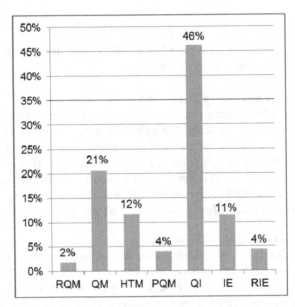

Fig. 2. Relevance and error rate of enrichments

4.3   Summary

While 15% of the analyzed enrichments were incorrect for the object, this affected only 3.5% of the objects. With respect to retrieval performance, only 1% of the queries were affected negatively by the incorrect enrichments. On the other hand, in 7% of the queries, users would find an incorrectly enriched object within the first 12 results of a search, which could lead to mistrust in the system. As a matter of fact, the 7 queries with incorrect enrichments retrieved 6 objects with incorrect enrichments on average. The likelihood of encountering an incorrect enrichment is therefore not to be underestimated.

Of the analyzed enrichments, 85% were factually correct for the object, but only 27% (RQM, QM, PQM) might have contributed to the retrieval performance, i.e. increased the chances of the object being found for the query. Only 2% of the enrichments actually added a term to the original metadata, without which the object would not have been found. The other 25% (QM, PQM) duplicated terms in the original metadata and have probably contributed to the retrieval performance due to the term frequency-based ranking algorithm. Objects which were only retrieved due to the enrichments often tended to be from collections with underrepresented languages. This means that multilingual enrichment can help particularly in multilingual retrieval and contextualization of objects.

Most enrichments are in the temporal facet, most queries are topical, geographic or for person names, meaning that the temporal enrichments will be mostly used for contextualization of information when the user reviews an object. A lot of the topical enrichments did not contribute to the retrieval performance (enrichment terms were not used for searching) and were mostly very broad. A significant number of enrichments were either broader or narrower terms of the query terms. In an expanded search, these could be used to increase precision or recall when used as recommended search terms.

While this analysis has shown that enrichments might not necessarily increase an object's findability or likelihood to be retrieved, they can help in the contextualization of objects, particularly in a multilingual environment. A larger sample and a more rigorous categorization of query categories could even determine viable candidates for enrichments, for example by comparing query terms to enrichment terms. Query-, domain- and language-specific characteristics of the objects play a role in successful enrichment processes. The results from this analysis contribute to identify focus areas for future developments of enrichments.

5   Discussion

The study has shown that the framework can be used to get a holistic view on the quality and impact of enrichments. It allows illuminating the impact of enrichments from different angles. It not only measures the object-enrichment relationship, but also takes into account how visible enriched objects are in the search results.

The Europeana evaluation has shown that query-dependent measures deliver different results dependent on the sample of the query. Enrichments that did not influence the retrieval of the object (categories QM, HTM, PQM, QI and IE) might fall into different categories, even one that does influence retrieval, if the query was different. Hence, the coding of enrichments is determined by the enriched object, the enrichment, the query and their relationships. Results are, therefore, individual for each use.

Additionally, the categories used for determining the relevance of enrichments with regard to the enriched object only determine the states 'correct' or 'incorrect'. For future work, the framework categories should reflect different shades, similar to the relevance with regard to the query. For example, Europeana has millions of objects with very generic enrichments. In the majority of cases, these enrichments are in the subject or type field (e.g. "paper" plus broader term "industrial product" or "photograph" plus broader term "documentation"). They are correct but could also create a lot of noise at the expense of reduced precision. For some users searching for "documentation" in Europeana, it might be useful to get every object of the type document, photograph, CD-ROM, film, video (all narrower terms in the GEMET thesaurus) as a result, but for others those might not be important. It is difficult to decide how useful these enrichments are, especially when considering Europeana as part of the semantic web, where generic terms become very specific just due to the vast amount of datasets. These enrichments are therefore not considered harmful in contrast to incorrect enrichments, which could contribute to objects being retrieved although they are not relevant to the query. For these different views, categories to measure the relevance and error rate dimension could be extended to reflect the diversity of aspects enrichments impact.

Furthermore, the specific data sample used influences the results of the query-dependent measures. In our Europeana evaluation, the most frequent queries in a given time period were used to give an overview on how often users in general encounter either objects, which ranked incorrectly due to enrichments, or an object with incorrect metadata (the enrichments). Another sample with longer, more specific or complex queries representing the long tail might get very different results and should be subject of future research.

Additionally, the framework offers measures that are system-focused and independent of the user's point of view. For example, the user might not even realize that an incorrect enrichment is added to an object. On the other hand, expert user might be very upset to be finding incorrect metadata on objects they want to work with. Evaluations regarding the diversity of stakeholders and their satisfaction with metadata enrichments should be also focus of further research.

The framework is a tool that can be used to evaluate enrichments in a structured manner being able to monitor measures across time spans or systems. It offers a nuanced analysis of enrichments and their impact on findability. Within one system correct automatic enrichments might have no influence on the retrieval of objects whereas incorrect enrichments might be less visible in the search results. The framework helps to thoroughly understand these implications and will result in better, more elaborate discussion about automatic enrichments, i.e. how they can be evaluated and improved.

Acknowledgement. This research was partly financed by the project Europeana v2.0 (grant agreement no: 270902). We would also like to thank Antoine Isaac from the Europeana Foundation for his continuous support and feedback regarding the framework and the evaluation.

References

1. Newman, D., Hagedorn, K., Chemudugunta, C., Smyth, P.: Subject Metadata Enrichment Using Statistical Topic Models. In: Proceedings of the 7th ACM/IEEE-CS Joint Conference on Digital Libraries, pp. 366–375. ACM, New York (2007)
2. Agirre, E., Barrena, A., Fernandez, K., Miranda, E., Otegi, A., Soroa, A.: PATHSenrich: A Web Service Prototype for Automatic Cultural Heritage Item Enrichment. In: Aalberg, T., Papatheodorou, C., Dobreva, M., Tsakonas, G., Farrugia, C.J. (eds.) TPDL 2013. LNCS, vol. 8092, pp. 462–465. Springer, Heidelberg (2013)
3. Olensky, M., Stiller, J., Dröge, E.: Poisonous India or the Importance of a Semantic and Multilingual Enrichment Strategy. In: Dodero, J.M., Palomo-Duarte, M., Karampiperis, P. (eds.) MTSR 2012. CCIS, vol. 343, pp. 252–263. Springer, Heidelberg (2012)
4. Schreiber, G., Amin, A., Aroyo, L., van Assem, M., de Boer, V., Hardman, L., et al.: Semantic annotation and search of cultural-heritage collections: The MultimediaN E-Culture demonstrator. Web Semantics: Science, Services and Agents on the World Wide Web 6(4), 243–249 (2008)

5. Jones, C.B., Purves, R., Ruas, A., Sanderson, M., Sester, M., van Kreveld, M., Weibel, R.: Spatial Information Retrieval and Geographical Ontologies an Overview of the SPIRIT Project. In: SIGIR 2002, Proceedings of the 25th Annual International ACM SIGIR Conference on Research and Development in Information Retrieval, pp. 387–388. ACM, New York (2002)

6. Fernie, K., Griffiths, J., Davies, R.: D 8.1 Final Report. PATHS - Personalised Access to Cultural Heritage Spaces (2014), `http://www.paths-pro-ject.eu/eng/content/download/5274/40160/version/1/file/D+8+1+Final+Report_final.pdf`

7. Agirre, E., Barrena, A., Lopez de Lacalla, O., Soroa, A., Stevenson, M., Fernando, S.: Matching Cultural Heritage items to Wikipedia. In: Proceedings of the 8th International Conference on Language Resources and Evaluation, Istanbul, Turkey, pp. 1729–1735 (2012)

8. Shreeves, S.L., Knutson, E.M., Stvilia, B., Palmer, C.L., Twidale, M.B., Cole, T.W.: Is 'Quality' Metadata 'Shareable' Metadata? The Implications of Local Metadata Practices for Federated Collections. In: Thompson, H.A. (ed.) Proceedings of the Twelfth National Conference of the Association of College and Research Libraries, April 7-10, pp. 223–237. Association of College and Research Libraries, Minneapolis (2005)

9. Van Hage, W.R., Isaac, A., Aleksovski, Z.: Sample Evaluation of Ontology-Matching Systems. In: EON, vol. 2007, pp. 41–50 (November 2007)

10. Stiller, J., Petras, V., Gäde, M., Isaac, A.: Automatic Enrichments with Controlled Vocabularies in Europeana: Challenges and Consequences (to be published)

11. Stiller, J., Olensky, M., Isaac, A., Petras, V.: D7.8. Final Report on Innovative Multilingual Information Access. Europeana Version 2 (2014), `http://pro.europeana.eu:9580/documents/866067/983534/D7.8%2BFinal%2BReport%2BInnovative%2BMultilingual%2BAccess`

Evaluating (Linked) Metadata Transformations Across Cultural Heritage Domains

Kim Tallerås, David Massey, Anne-Stine Ruud Husevåg,
Michael Preminger, and Nils Pharo

Oslo and Akershus University College of Applied Science

Abstract. This paper describes an approach to the evaluation of different aspects in the transformation of existing metadata into Linked data-compliant knowledge bases. At Oslo and Akershus University College of Applied Science, in the TORCH project, we are working on three different experimental case studies on extraction and mapping of broadcasting data and the interlinking of these with transformed library data. The case studies are investigating problems of heterogeneity and ambiguity in and between the domains, as well as problems arising in the interlinking process. The proposed approach makes it possible to collaborate on evaluation across different experiments, and to rationalize and streamline the process.

1 Introduction

Cultural heritage domains have recently experienced substantial efforts in developing new metadata standards intended to increase usability and to enable integration of related resources across established "data silos". In many of the domains, such as in the library community and in broadcasting institutions, these efforts tend to involve Linked data technologies and principles.

The huge amount of existing data produced in compliance with dated standards, requires a significant investigation into transformation processes. In this paper, we describe an approach for the evaluation of different aspects in the transformation of existing metadata into Linked data-compliant knowledge bases. The approach has emerged from work on three partially overlapping and on-going case studies at the Oslo and Akershus University College of Applied Science:

1. The mapping of bibliographic (MARC) records to newly developed ontologies in the library community
2. The (automated) extraction of metadata from semi-structured archive records at the Norwegian Broadcasting Corporation and
3. The interlinking of shared entities across the two domains.

While these case studies have different goals, they share a need for a standardized set of rules for evaluation of performance in a broader context than traditional evaluation of information retrieval and ontologies represent. The presented approach builds upon existing evaluation principles and metrics, but

S. Closs et al. (Eds.): MTSR 2014, CCIS 478, pp. 250–261, 2014.

rationalizes these into a coherent and minimalist system of applicable data sets, representing ground truths for a variety of tasks.

The paper consists of two parts. Firstly, we describe a generic transformation process and provide definitions of the key concepts used in the paper. Secondly, we present the ongoing case studies and the evaluation approach.

2   The Road to Linked Data - Key Concepts and Processes

Linked data is a set of best practice guidelines for the publishing and interlinking of data on the web, recommending the use of standards such as RDF, URI's and OWL ([1,2]). The publishing and interlinking of legacy data (which is the problem context of this paper) must overcome a variety of heterogeneity conflicts between legacy sources. The conflicts can be structural (caused by disparate modelling approaches) or they can concern inconsistencies in the data (caused by typos, local or changing registration practises, ambiguate name forms, schema flexibility etc.) ([3]). Figure 1 illustrates the process of transforming metadata collections into interlinked knowledge bases. In the figure, "Source schema(s)" denotes any metadata standard or rules for content descriptions. The "Target ontology" can be any formal ontology, providing sets of classes, properties and restrictions. The resulting "Knowledge base" denotes a data set of instances transformed in compliance with the target ontology. According to the Linked data guidelines the target ontology should be based on a formal ontology language such as OWL and the knowledge base should be formalized as RDF.

The transformation process primarily consists of three complementary activities:

- Mapping: Structural transformations based on semantic correspondences between the source schema and the target ontology.
- Extraction: Content transformation consisting of entity and relationship recognition and disambiguation (i.e. information extraction) from textual fields within the metadata.
- Interlinking: The linking of identical entities that are members of different data sets. In Figure 1 $A' \bigcap B'$ is the intersection of entities that belongs to both (data) set A' and B'. In this context, entities must be understood as "things-that-exist" in the real world. The representation of entities can differ in the data sets, but as long as a unique identifier is provided for each entity in each set, we can formally relate the entities with proper OWL properties.

3   Case Studies

At Oslo and Akershus University College of Applied Science (in the TORCH project[1]) we are working on three case studies that are focusing on metadata

---

[1] The TORCH project is an activity of the research group Information systems based on metadata: http://tinyurl.com/k8gf7dr

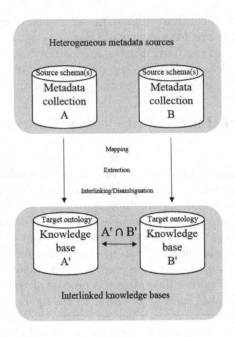

Fig. 1. Overview of a generic transformation process from two sources with related data

transformations in the library and broadcasting domains. The case studies are investigating problems of heterogeneity and ambiguity in and between the domains and problems arising in the interlinking process.

In the library community a huge amount of the metadata are generated in accordance with established international standards. The two most prominent standards are the suite of MARC metadata schemas and the cataloging code AACR2 . MARC has been in use since the late 1960s and was developed as a tool to make the card catalogue machine-readable in order to support metadata exchange between libraries. AACR2 provides rules for the registration of content. Together these standards primarily provide coded fields with string based information intended for human consumption (an inheritance from the card catalogue, see Figure 4 for an example record and [4] for a more detailed discussion of the history and dated features of MARC/AACR2). A "flat" record model (the format was developed prior to both relational database theory and the web) and the string orientation pose severe challenges to the transformation into a data oriented and graph based OWL/RDF environment.

In our case study, we are using a subset of MARC records from the Norwegian National Bibliography. One of the studies is experimenting with mapping based transformations into Knowledge bases compliant with a series of new ontologies provided in the library community such as BIBFRAME[2] , Schema.org[3] and FRBRoo[4].

The archives of the Norwegian Broadcasting Corporation (NRK) have registered metadata describing TV and radio programs since the early 1990s. While the schema and rules that constrain library MARC data are based on (inter)national standards, NRK's archival metadata is created according to schema and rules developed in-house generating so-called SIFT-records (Searching In FreeText, [5]). A major part of the metadata are free text fields that describe the contents of the programs. Valuable entities, such as people, places and events are hidden within the ambiguity of these natural language descriptions, hampering machine processing, and consequently retrieval and interlinking. One of the cases in the project focuses on the evaluation of methods for extracting these entities and the relationships between them.

Ontologies play a pivotal role in the project. We have been studying existing ontologies within the broadcasting domain, such as the BBC Programmes ontology[5] and EBU-Core[6], but felt that they did not fill our needs to decribe entities and relationships between entities that we found in the original NRK metadata collection. This was due to our desire to describe both formal elements related to broadcasting (e.g. the relationships between programs, episodes and series) as well as details from the program content (e.g. different kinds of creative works and their creators mentioned or included in a program). Recently Schema.org ([6]) has been extended with elements for the description of broadcasting resources that brought us closer to our required coverage, but we have still felt the need to develop our own broadcasting ontology (TORCH ontology). The ontology is very much inspired by the aforementioned ontologies, and contains mappings to equivalent classes and properties in these. With 50 classes and 60 properties it is not as big as many of the established cultural heritage ontologies, but the design reflects the SIFT-specific needs regarding coverage and supports its two main goals, firstly to be the target of the automated extraction and thus serve as a model for the resulting knowledge base, and secondly to support the manual annotation described below.

Figure 2 illustrates the different case studies and how they interrelate. Dealing with the relatively structured library data, we are primarily concerned with problems related to structured mapping and the outcome of transformations based on such mappings. In the case of broadcasting data, dealing with semi-structured data closer to natural language, we are concerned with problems related to extraction algorithms. In both cases, we aim at disambiguating and interlink the resulting data that are related, based on established tools and experimental algorithms.

---

[2] http://bibframe.org/

[3] http://schema.org

[4] http://www.cidoc-crm.org/frbr_inro.html

[5] http://www.cidoc-crm.org/frbr_inro.html

[6] http://www.ebu.ch/metadata/ontologies/ebucore/

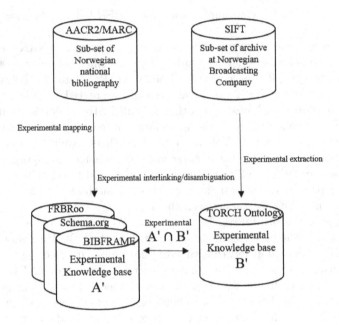

Fig. 2. Overview of the different experimental case studies

4   Automated Extraction and Interlinking - Ongoing Experiments

In the following, we will illustrate and give some examples from the experimental case studies on broadcasting data and the interlinking of these with transformed library data.

A simple prototype for extraction has been developed, that currently consists of a pipeline with three modules: Tokenizing and part-of-speech recognition based on the Oslo-Bergen Tagger[7] ; identification of SIFT-specific formatting patterns; and lookup in local gazetteer files, currently Norwegian first and last person names.

The result of the three modules is an array of features for each token. Candidate entities are identified by rules that combine these features and external Linked Open Data and web services are queried to strengthen the evidence.

The identified entities can be used to populate a knowledge base compliant with the TORCH ontology. In order to automatically generate the proper relationships between the entities (e.g between the author and his novel or between the interviewer and her interviewee) internal and external evidence must be collected and analysed. While library data can be used to support the creator-relationship between Eggen and Hilal (see e.g. MARC record in Figure 4), it does

---

[7] http://www.tekstlab.uio.no/obt-ny/english/index.html

not help to identify the relationship between Eggen and Bratholm that might be dependent on internal (con)textual features.

Figure 3 shows an example of a typical SIFT record and Figure 4 a related MARC record, both with highlighted entities. Figure 5 shows two interlinked RDF graphs based on identified entities and relationships in the SIFT record (the white nodes), and the MARC record (the grey nodes). Corresponding entities in the two graphs are interlinked with the owl:sameAs property. The SIFT records are transformed into a graph compliant with the TORCH ontology and the MARC data is made compliant with the BIBFRAME ontology. Both sets of data were mapped and transformed with the data integration tool Karma [7]. The SIFT data was transformed from the result of the extraction process described above. The MARC data was transformed directly from the record. The project is at a very early stage regarding experimentation on interlinking. The example in Figure 5 is developed manually to illustrate a potential result.

```
Et dypdykk ned i Torgrim Eggens forfatterskap, forfattersjel og
forfatterliv. Inspirert publikum og høy stemning på Rockefeller i Oslo.
(Opptaksdato 960212).

Programleder Eva BRATHOLM (mv) introduserer kveldens forfatter Torgrim EGGEN
(mv).  Intv., innimellom applaus og latter fra salen. Hovedemne er Eggens
siste bok "Hilal", innvandrere, muslimsk kultur, fremmedfrykt, islam .....
Sluttekst.
```

Fig. 3. Excerpts from the content field in a SIFT record. The entities found by the extraction prototype are highlighted. Rockefeller is the venue of the show, located in the city of Oslo. Eva Bratholm is the host interviewing Torgrim Eggen about his novel "Hilal".

```
=100  $aEggen, Torgrim
=24510$aHilal$broman$cTorgrim Eggen
=260  $a[Oslo]$bGyldendal$c2000
```

Fig. 4. Excerpts from a related MARC record from the Norwegian national bibliography. Entities are manually highlighted. "Eggen, Torgrim" is an author, "Hilal" is the title, "Oslo" is the place of publication" and "Gyldendal" the publisher.

5 Evaluation Approach

In order to evaluate the experiments described in the previous section, we generate three sets of ground truth data. Figure 6 illustrates how the ground truth sets, based on selected corpora, are covering the evaluation of each metadata transformation (A and B), respectively, and the eventual interlinking between them. On a conceptual level, these three sets form a coherent approach for the evaluation of metadata transformations and interlinking.

Based on the specific case studies in the TORCH project, we are using this set up for the evaluation of what is described as three complementary activities

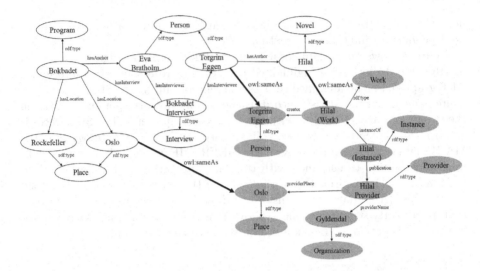

Fig. 5. Two interlinked RDF graphs based on entities in Figur 3 and 4

in Section 2; mapping, extraction and interlinking. The evaluation approach is based on three comparisons between the resulting data from the experimental runs and the ground truth data (our TORCH-specific interests and perspectives are included in parentheses):

- experimental knowledge base A → ground truth A (mapping)
- experimental knowledge base B → ground truth B (extraction)
- experimental $A \cap B$ → ground truth $A \cap B$ (interlinking)

The ground truth data result from (semi-)manual annotations of entities and relationships in the corpus data. In the following, we will briefly describe some of the practical tools we have developed in the TORCH project for the generation of the ground truth data.

5.1 Corpora

To secure a satisfactory level of variety, our corpus of broadcasting data was selected from two different categories of programs; culture and news. 100 SIFT-records from program series in the two categories were chosen. We manually harvested two MARC records related to each of the selected programs from the Norwegian national bibliography, based on entities found in the SIFT records. This procedure also helped to secure an intersection of entities for the evaluation of interlinking.

5.2 Manual Annotation

After reviewing a couple of available annotation tools, we chose to develop our own tool, particularly to gain better control of the different aspects of annotation specific to our project. Annotation productivity was also an important consideration

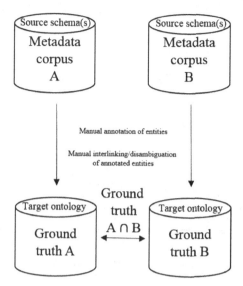

Fig. 6. Illustration of the evaluation approach consisting of three ground truth sets

here. The annotation tool consists of a PHP-based GUI supported by relational database structure for both parameterization and persistence. Figure 7 shows a part of the GUI view. Eventually we use Karma to transform annotation data from the relational database into RDF. The GUI allows annotators

- to highlight and classify mentions with classes from the annotation ontology described below. There is also an automatic suggest-and-select feature for linking[8] entities to Wikipedia articles based on the mediaWiki API[8] search operation.
- to express relations between already classified mentions, using properties from the same ontology(see the table at the bottom of Figure 7). Two special features here are; firstly mentions can relate to the automatically annotated representation of the program (annotated record) itself, and secondly the linking of different mentions of the same entity through a special property, "identicalTo".

The annotation tool uses ontologies to provide classes and properties for classification and expression of relationships. In the case of the broadcasting data, we developed the TORCH ontology described in Section 3 partly for this purpose. The classes and the properties in the ontology are used directly to classify entities and relationships between them. In addition to the afore-mentioned needs concerning coverage, the exposure to test-annotators at an early stage further encouraged the development of a project-specific ontology. The ontology is designed for efficient and consistent annotation by reducing complexity and the intuitive naming of classes and properties [8]. The ontology builds on hierarchies of classes and properties, realized through the RDF

---

[8] http://www.mediawiki.org/wiki/API:Main_page

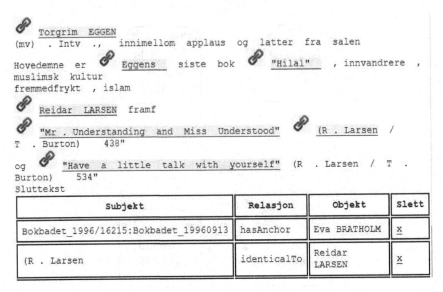

Fig. 7. The annotation tool's main GUI window. Each classified mention in the running text has a special icon to its left, double-clicking on which allows the annotator to establish a relation between it and another, pre-classified mention. The classes, and other information about a mention, are available in a menu window, not shown here, upon selecting a menu or classifying a new mention. The first relation in the table below the running text is between the record (program) representation and the anchor, the second relates two mentions of the same entity to each other.

Schema properties rdfs:subPropertyOf and rdfs:subClassOf (e.g. FictionalCharacter rdfs:subClassOf Person rdfs:subClassOf Agent). This allows for manual annotations on specific levels, which indirectly and at the same time implies general classifications. Such features can be useful e.g. in order to measure the depth obtained by an extraction algorithm.

High quality manual annotation with a high degree of inter-annotator agreement is dependent on guidelines. With some modifications and extensions, we have based our guidelines on work done by Jonsdottir and the Textlab at University of Oslo [9]. The ontology, guidelines and annotation tool have been developed in an iterative process using a group of LIS students as test annotators and domain experts from the NRK archive as a reference group for ontology development.

In order to generate a ground truth set for the MARC data, following the A path in the figures above, we could use the annotation tool with a bibliographic ontology as input. This would have been especially useful (and interesting) for an analysis of the semi-structured description fields (5XX-fields in MARC parlance). Due to our interest in the results of structured mappings, we have nevertheless chosen to experiment with a straightforward RDF serialization of MARC[9] . The

---

[9] The serialization is partly based on the efforts in mapping MARC(21) into RDF found at the metadata registry: http://marc21rdf.info/

chosen approach secures lossless data and semantics for the comparison with the results of transformations based on other ontologies. There are issues with serializing MARC directly as RDF though, for instance related to the handling of string values, but this part of the project is very much work in progress and the issues will need to be discussed in detail elsewhere. This approach can be considered semi-manual. Data are transformed automatically based on mappings, but quality is assessed and corrected manually afterwards.

5.3   Manual Interlinking and Disambiguation

The third ground truth set, $A \cap B$, consists of links between corresponding entities in the two sets described above (A and B). The manually created links can be used for the evaluation of (automated) interlinking between RDF graphs, but also to support algorithmic disambiguation of entities as part of the extraction process. This set could be represented in many ways; in our project, we are using the RDF Alignment format[10].

5.4   Evaluation Metrics

Evaluation in our context is measuring the correspondence between the result of mappings and automatic extractions on one hand, and the manually develop sets of ground truths on the other hand. In the case studies, we are utilizing established metrics originating from traditional information retrieval and ontology evaluations.

The literature of ontology evaluations is pointing in many directions referencing a variety of metrics concerning everything from design complexity and coverage to usability and human reception. In our context, we are mainly concerned with the level of semantic interoperability between two metadata systems [3], measuring loss and gain of information during transformation from one system to another. In the TORCH project, semantic interoperability is investigated from the perspectives of typical heterogeneity conflicts such as inconsistent string data and structural and semantic variations.

Three metrics (originating from evaluations of information retrieval systems) have dominated information extraction campaigns such as Message Understanding Conferences (MUC, see e.g. [10]); recall, precision and F-score. With the introduction of ontology based information extraction, additional metrics exploiting the features of graphs and ontologies have been used and suggested (see e.g. [11] for an overview). Adaptations of the recall and precision oriented metrics are also common in the evaluation of interlinking (see e.g. the Instance matching track in the ongoing Ontology Evaluation Initiative and [12] for definitions of the metrics in this specific context).

---

[10] http://alignapi.gforge.inria.fr/format.html

6 Summary and Concluding Remarks

This paper describes various case studies dependent on systems for evaluation. Such systems exist separately for the evaluation of problems represented by each case study. As our case studies are related through the selection of (corpus) data and the people working with them, we wanted to coordinate such systems in one efficient framework in terms of development and reuse across the studies. We believe that the approach described, consisting of two sets of ground truth data that represent golden standards for the transformations of metadata to RDF, and a third set, consisting of relationships between the previous two, are both efficient and hospitable to (re)use across a variety of problems.

In order to evaluate the experiments, we had to generate three sets of ground truth data. The ground truth data are results of (semi-)manual annotations of entities and relationships in the metadata corpus A and B, and the third ground truth set, $A \cap B$, consists of links between corresponding entities in the two sets A and B. The manually created links can be used for the evaluation of interlinking between RDF graphs, but also to support algorithmic disambiguation of entities as part of the extraction process.

We chose to develop our own annotation tool to annotate entities and relationships in the corpora for the generation of the ground truth data. This allows for manual annotations on specific levels adapted to our projects, which can be useful e.g. in order to evaluate the degree of specificity a certain extraction algorithm is able to achieve. The annotation tool uses ontologies to provide classes and properties for classification and expression of relationships. The ontology and annotation tool have been developed in an iterative process, involving domain experts from the Norwegian Broadcasting (NRK) archive and LIS students as test annotators. The evaluation is based on comparisons between the result of automatic extractions and mappings, and the manually developed sets of ground truth data. This approach can be considered semi-manual. Data are transformed automatically based on mapping, but quality is assessed and corrected manually afterwards. We are mainly concerned about the level of semantic interoperability between two metadata systems, and we are measuring loss and gain of information during transformation from one system to another, using established metrics such as recall, precision and F-score, originating from traditional information retrieval and ontology evaluations.

The case studies described above are still work in progress and will be documented in detail elsewhere. Regarding the further development of the approach, we are looking into the potential provided by the ontology-based features. Using ontologies as the basis of ground truth data gives us the opportunity to evaluate both transformed entities and the relationships between them. In practice, this implies the opportunity to move from entity recognition to information extraction without adding further annotations. We have also mentioned the possibility of exploiting the hierarchical structures in the ontology, for evaluating the specificity-ability of extraction algorithms. As future work we wish to investigate how ontologies can be further exploited as a basis for evaluating metadata transformations.

References

1. Berners-Lee, T.: Linked data: design issues. Technical report, W3C (2006)
2. Heath, T., Bizer, C.: Linked Data: Evolving the Web into a global data space. Morgan & Claypool (2011)
3. Tallerå, S.K.: From many records to one graph: Heterogeneity conflicts in the Linked data restructuring cycle. Information Research 18(3) (2013)
4. Svenonius, E.: The Intellectual Foundation of Information Organization. The MIT Press, Cambridge (2000)
5. Reigem, O.: Sift - searching in free text: A text retrieval system (abstract only). SIGSOC Bull. 12-13(4-1), 59 (1981)
6. Raimond, Y.: Schema.org for TV and Radio markup (2013)
7. Knoblock, C.A., Szekely, P., Ambite, J.L., Goel, A., Gupta, S., Lerman, K., Muslea, M., Taheriyan, M., Mallick, P.: Semi-automatically mapping structured sources into the semantic web. In: Simperl, E., Cimiano, P., Polleres, A., Corcho, O., Presutti, V. (eds.) ESWC 2012. LNCS, vol. 7295, pp. 375–390. Springer, Heidelberg (2012)
8. Hinze, A., Heese, R., Luczak-Rösch, M., Paschke, A.: Semantic Enrichment by Non-experts: Usability of Manual Annotation Tools. In: Cudré-Mauroux, P., et al. (eds.) ISWC 2012, Part I. LNCS, vol. 7649, pp. 165–181. Springer, Heidelberg (2012)
9. Jonsdottir, A.: ARNER, what kind of name is that?: an automatic rule-based named entity recognizer for Norwegian. PhD thesis, University of Oslo (2003)
10. Grishman, R., Sundheim, B.: Design of the MUC-6 evaluation. In: Proceedings of a Workshop on Held at Vienna, Virginia, May 6-8, pp. 413–422. Association for Computational Linguistics (1996)
11. Maynard, D., Peters, W., Li, Y.: Metrics for Evaluation of Ontology-based Information Extraction. In: WWW Conference 2006, Workshop on "Evaluation of Ontologies for the Web", Edinburgh, Scotland (2006)
12. Ferrara, A., Lorusso, D., Montanelli, S., Varese, G.: Towards a benchmark for instance matching. In: Proceedings of the 3rd International Workshop on Ontology Matching, OM 2008 (2008)

Library Data Integration: Towards BIBFRAME Mapping to EDM

Sofia Zapounidou[1], Michalis Sfakakis[1], and Christos Papatheodorou[1,2]

[1] Department of Archives, Library Science and Museology, Ionian University, Corfu, Greece
[2] Digital Curation Unit, IMIS, "Athena" Research Centre, Athens, Greece
{112zapo,sfakakis,papatheodor}@ionio.gr

Abstract. Integration of library data into the Linked Data environment is a key issue in libraries and is approached on the basis of interoperability between library data conceptual models. Achieving interoperability for different representations of the same or related entities between the library and cultural heritage domains shall enhance rich bibliographic data reusability and support the development of new data-driven information services. This paper aims to contribute to the desired interoperability by attempting to map core semantic paths between the BIBFRAME and EDM conceptual models. BIBFRAME is developed by the Library of Congress to support transformation of legacy library data in MARC format into linked data. EDM is the model developed for and used in the Europeana Cultural Heritage aggregation portal.

Keywords: Conceptual models, linked data, interoperability, path-oriented mapping, data integration, BIBFRAME, EDM.

1 Introduction

The advent of the Internet and the World Wide Web emerged powerful tools and possibilities for the development of new, added value information services by museums, libraries and archives. Metadata harvesting and aggregation, as well as linked data technologies enforce a shift towards data and data-driven services that enhance the visibility and impact of memory institutions' collections to research, teaching and learning. Aggregation and harvesting presuppose interoperability and therefore there is the apparent need that metadata (i) are expressed by common vocabularies and (ii) their semantics are harmonized with shared and commonly accepted conceptual models.

This paper focuses on libraries and investigates the integration of their data with third party services and their reuse in new contexts. One of the obstacles for integrating library data into the semantic web and publishing them as Linked Data is the existence of different conceptual models and vocabularies. The most well known conceptual models in the library linked data domain are FRBR [1], FRBRoo [2] and BIBFRAME [3].

Newly-developed aggregation services in the cultural heritage (CH) domain collect metadata regarding cultural heritage objects (CHOs) from libraries and other memory

S. Closs et al. (Eds.): MTSR 2014, CCIS 478, pp. 262–273, 2014.

institutions aspiring to provide a point of access to CH information and advanced research supporting services. Two aggregator efforts are in progress in Europe and North America, that of Europeana (http://www.europeana.eu/) and the Digital Public Library of America – DPLA (http://dp.la/). Europeana focuses on European CHOs, while DPLA is oriented to the United States of America. Both projects have developed data models to enable proper harvesting of metadata from a variety of data providers. Europeana provides the Europeana Data model (EDM) [4] and DPLA provides the DPLA Metadata Application Profile [5], which is also based on EDM.

BIBFRAME is the new library data model that the Library of Congress currently develops within the framework of "modeling the MARC 21 format as a Web of Data" [3, 7]. The Europeana Data Model (EDM) describes the digitized CHOs that the Europeana portal aggregates from European Libraries and other cultural institutions. This paper extends previous work [6] and aims to contribute to interoperability of library data by examining how BIBFRAME core classes and properties could be mapped to EDM according to different paradigms, such as those defined in the library metadata alignment report published in 2012 [8] and the EDM-FRBRoo application profile [18]. For both paradigms contextualized versions of the EDM using the *ore:Proxy* class [9] are considered, as well as non contextualized versions incorporating the BIBFRAME data directly to the *edm:ProvidedCHO* class.

In the next section BIBFRAME and EDM conceptual models are briefly presented, while section 3 describes the methodology followed for the proposed mapping and provides a test case of seven library records. Section 4 presents proposed mappings between the two models following different scenarios and Section 5 discusses and concludes the derived results.

2   Background

Libraries typically describe their holdings using MARC format [7]. MARC records provide information regarding the physical copies held at a library to enable searching and locating on the shelves. On the occasion of the physical copy more information is added to each record, such as the intellectual content of the physical item, bibliographic details regarding the publication process, custodial history, relationships between and among other bibliographic entities, subjects, etc. [2, 8]. The flat record structure in MARC presents many insufficiencies and has been criticized by experts and library-related international organizations [10–14]. Moreover it does not facilitate meaningful representation and interchange of bibliographic data in the semantic web environment.

Library of Congress announced in 2011 [15] its decision to "experiment with Semantic Web and linked data technologies to see what benefits to the bibliographic framework they offer our community and how our current models need to be adjusted to take fuller advantage of these benefits." BIBFRAME is the new model that the Library of Congress develops within the context of the bibliographic framework initiative. Its main classes are: *Creative Work*, *Instance*, *Authority* and *Annotation* [3]. The class *Creative Work* (or simply *Work*) reflects the "conceptual essence of the cataloguing item" [3]. The class *Instance* reflects "an individual, material embodiment of the Work". The class *Authority* is used to identify People, Places, and Organizations involved in the creation or publication of a Work. For the expression of topics, BIBFRAME *Authority* simply works as a linking mechanism to LC Subject Headings published as linked data[1]. The class *Annotation* expresses comments made about a BIBFRAME *Work, Instance,* or *Authority.* Examples of BIBFRAME annotations are: library holdings, cover arts, sample texts, reviews, etc. (see Figure 1).

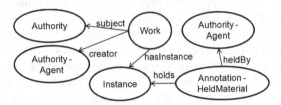

Fig. 1. BIBFRAME model with Annotation for holding

Europeana aggregates metadata about and enables access to digital cultural heritage resources provided by European memory institutions. Descriptions over Europeana are made with Europeana Semantic Elements [16], a basic data model that uses Dublin Core's 15 elements and other 12 additional elements. EDM has been developed for the better semantic expression of the cultural heritage descriptions that Europeana data providers contribute. No community-driven standard was used as a basis for its development and the Semantic Web framework was taken into account [4].

EDM's scope is wider than BIBFRAME's; thus different semantics and abstraction layers are used. For each provider, EDM distinguishes between real provided CHOs and their digital representations, and between provided CHOs and their descriptions. Europeana collects only descriptions for objects having at least one web representation [4]. EDM provides three core classes, namely *edm:ProvidedCHO* (for provided Cultural Heritage Object), *edm:WebResource* (for the *edm:ProvidedCHO* digital representations) and *ore:Aggregation* (for the aggregation of the activities made by the provider of the *edm:ProvidedCHO*).

The alignment of EDM to library metadata is a work in progress. The library metadata alignment report published in 2012 [8] focuses on specific library materials (monographs, multi-volume works and serials), does not adopt current bibliographic records' flat structure and adheres to linked data principles. A key point for the development of the report was the separation of the item in hand (e.g. the book) from its edition which represents the entirety of all identical copies of the item. Despite the fact that the need for compliance with FRBR was recognized by the report, the concept 'edition' was introduced as the union of FRBR Work, Expression and Manifestation entities and thus the desired compliance was postponed.

According to the report the 'edition' level information of the resource is represented by the *edm:ProvidedCHO* class, while the digital representation of the

---

[1] http://id.loc.gov/

real world object is represented by the *edm:WebResource* class. The *ore:Aggregation* class links the description of the provided resource with its digital representations.

EDM in order to contextualize harvested descriptions of the same CHO provided by different institutions utilizes the *ore:Proxy* class [17]. The added value of using proxies is that there will be only one *edm:ProvidedCHO* class instance for each European Heritage object along with multiple instances of the *ore:Proxy* class, provided by different providers. Hence a provider's description (metadata) is assigned as properties at the *ore:Proxy* class (see Figure 2). It is worth mentioning that the *ore:Proxy* class was not considered by [8].

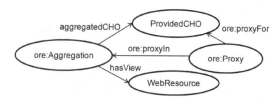

Fig. 2. Europeana data model with use of *ore:Proxy*

The report on alignment of library data to EDM [8] concluded that it should be considered as a milestone and that it needed to be reviewed to "integrate the FRBR entities in EDM using FRBRoo terms". This provision prompted the launch of the EDM-FRBRoo application profile Task Force in July 2012 which completed its activities in April 2013 announcing an application profile [18]. The Task Force in order to translate classes of the FRBR model to EDM, without the introduction of new specialized classes in EDM considered FRBR classes as *skos:Concept* class instances (Figure 3) and then, related *edm:InformationResource* classes with the FRBR vocabulary using the edm:hasType property. In Figure 3 an example of the translation of FRBR Group 1 Work and Expression entities as concepts in EDM is shown.

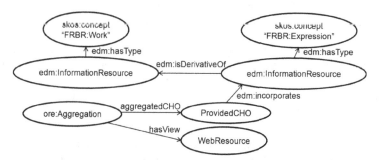

Fig. 3. FRBR Group 1 Work and Expression concepts expressed with EDM classes in the EDM-FRBRoo application profile [18]

Transforming instances from BIBFRAME into EDM, with respect to the above alternative frameworks, will examine key issues in interoperability between the two models, as well as will suggest semantic alignments between the intentions of the two models' communities.

3   Integration Scenarios – Requirements

The methodology adopted in this work is a combination of the ones used in the Europeana Libraries project [8] for the alignment of library metadata with the Europeana Data Model and the EDM – FRBRoo Application Profile Task Force [18]:

1. Selection of specific type(s) of library material
2. Definition of requirements for a BIBFRAME – EDM profile
3. Selection of a real test case and bibliographic records
4. Representation(s) of the test case in BIBFRAME
5. Attempt for a BIBFRAME – EDM mapping following a path-oriented approach
6. Mapping of BIBFRAME representations into EDM using different modeling patterns described in the next paragraph.

The most common library material type is monographs, and therefore this paper focuses on monographs and multivolume works. Different types of monographs include -but are not limited to- simple monographs, multipart monographs, derivations of a monograph such as translations, adaptations, etc, reproductions and aggregates. These categories of monographs are estimated in millions of records in WorldCat according to two studies performed in 2002 [22] and in 2011 [23]. The requirements for our BIBFRAME – EDM mappings are defined as follows:

— BIBFRAME – EDM mappings will be performed using different EDM modeling paradigms; namely the definitions of the Europeana Data Model for Libraries report [8], use of *ore:Proxy* class as described in [17] (see Figure 2), use of *edm:InformationResource* class as used in [18] (see Figure 3) and concurrent use of the *edm:InformationResource* and *ore:Proxy* classes (see Figures 2 and 3).
— BIBFRAME is a linked data model. Therefore the BIBFRAME-EDM profile shall use Resource Description Framework syntax and shall support the use of URIs.
— The BIBFRAME-EDM mappings shall be flexible enough to enable meaningful representations for other types of library material.

Cervantes' "Don Quixote" has been selected as our test case, because it may exemplify different types of monographs, as referred above, enabling complex representations in BIBFRAME and scrutiny of possible BIBFRAME-EDM mappings. Therefore use of the "Don Quixote" case shall enable identification and study of representation issues in BIBFRAME for whole monograph categories, as well as their mapping into EDM.

"Don Quixote" consists of two separate works: the first one entitled "El ingenioso hidalgo don Quixote de la Mancha" was published in 1605 and the second one entitled "Segunda parte del ingenioso cauallero don Quixote de la Mancha" was published in 1615. These two parts have been published, translated and reproduced afterwards as independent volumes, as well as in a single volume. Moreover, there are many adaptations, as well as other works based on variations of the original work. Our test case consists of seven bibliographic records from the National Library of Spain and the Library of Congress that describe (i) the first editions of the two parts (denoted as 'First part' and 'Second part' respectively in Figure 4), (ii) the first edition that incorporated both parts (denoted as 'Two parts'), (iii) a French translation of both parts (denoted as 'French translation'), (iv) an English translation that was based on the former French one (denoted as 'English translation'), (v) an annotated edition of both parts by the Cervantes Institute (denoted as 'Annotated edition') and (vi) a CD-ROM (denoted as 'CD-ROM') that compiled the annotated edition's text with a linguistic database developed on this content. The linguistic database is also represented in BIBFRAME and EDM representations. It must be noted that some of the mentioned records are the same to the ones used by the EDM-FRBRoo Application profile task force [18]. Yet, we selected a few additional records from the National Library of Spain and the Library of Congress to study specific representation cases, such as reproduction and aggregates.

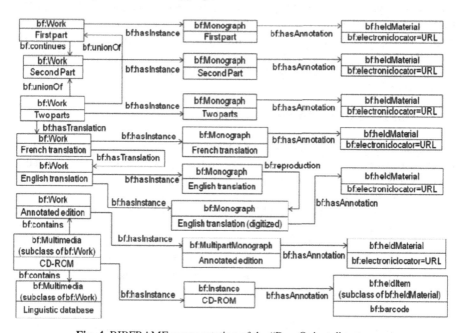

Fig. 4. BIBFRAME representation of the "Don Quixote" test case

In BIBFRAME every record from our sample corresponds to a *bf:Work* class linked with the respective embodiment *Instance* or subclass of Instance (e.g. *bf:Monograph*). Thus, eight individual works are generated to represent the intellectual content of the two independent volumes, the single volume publication for both parts, its translations in English and in French, the Cervantes Institute's annotated edition, the linguistic database derived from the Cervantes Institute's annotated edition and the CD-ROM containing (bf:contains) both the Cervantes Institute's edition with the linguistic database (Figure 4). The relationships between the parts are implemented using the partOf relation of the Work class. All instances, except the CD-ROM, are digitized (*bf:heldMaterial* class with a bf:electronicLocator property) and may be openly accessed online.

Mapping between distinct models that serve different purposes is not a straightforward issue. Therefore we decided to elucidate the semantics of each model and of their mappings following a path-oriented approach [19–21]. Paths are defined as sequences of "domain class – property – range class" statements and enhance comprehensibility of each model's semantics. The paths of the source model (in our case BIBFRAME) are mapped to semantically equivalent paths of the target model (in our case EDM).

Mappings between BIBFRAME and EDM follow different paradigms that may serve distinct library organizations', collections' or end-users' requirements. At first the Don Quixote's test case BIBFRAME representation is mapped to the EDM applying the definitions expressed in the EDM library data alignment report [8]. Then the contextualization of CHOs' ingested descriptions is examined with the use of the *ore:Proxy* class as defined in [17]. Examining the transformation of BIBFRAME to EDM with use of the *edm:InformationResource* class follows. This alternative mapping is based upon the pattern used in the EDM-FRBRoo application profile [18], highlighted in section 2. The final scenario examined is concurrent use of *edm:InformationResource* and *ore:Proxy* classes (Figures 2 and 3).

4   Mapping BIBFRAME to EDM

Europeana aggregates descriptions of CHOs in digital form only. In BIBFRAME the existence of a library object that is in digital form and therefore may be aggregated by Europeana is expressed by the following path "Work –hasInstance – Instance - hasAnnotation - heldMaterial - electronicLocator – URI". In this paper's framework this path is considered the basic BIBFRAME path from which four different mappings to EDM are attempted. It is worth mentioning that in case where EDM is used as the conceptual model for an information integration system and not for aggregating descriptions in the Europeana portal, the basic BIBFRAME path might be slightly different due to the inclusion of non digital materials. This paradigm is out of the scope of this work and is suggested as a further extension to these mappings.

4.1   Mapping According to the EDM Library Data Alignment Report

The EDM library data alignment report was published in 2012 with the aim to "describe how library metadata can be aligned with the EDM" [8]. This report referenced the FRBR WEMI [1] entities (Work, Expression, Manifestation, Item) but did not achieve a one-to-one mapping to EDM classes. Yet it introduced the concept of "edition" to include "all information concerning the Manifestation, Expression and Work entities" and defined that the *edm:ProvidedCHO* class is at this "edition level". The *edm:WebResource* class is defined in this report's framework as the "digital representation of an item".

In BIBFRAME information regarding the intellectual content and its expression (Work and Expression entities in FRBR) is at the *Creative Work* class level. Information regarding the publishing product/object is at the FRBR Manifestation level and is expressed in BIBFRAME through the *Instance* class. Holdings (Items in FRBR) are stated through the following path "Instance - hasAnnotation – heldMaterial - ...". Therefore the basic BIBFRAME path may be mapped to EDM as Figure 5 demonstrates.

The path "Work –hasInstance – Instance" is mapped to a single *ProvidedCHO* instance, and selected properties from the *bf:Work* and *bf:Instance* could be mapped to similar *ProvidedCHO* properties. Existence of the basic BIBFRAME path justifies an instantiation of the *edm:WebResource* class, with id the URI from the BIBFRAME path. For more details describing this paradigm see our previous work in [6].

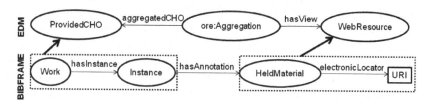

Fig. 5. Mapping of the basic BIBFRAME path to core EDM classes, according to the library metadata alignment report [8]

4.2   Use of ore:Proxy Class

As already mentioned, EDM uses the *ore:Proxy* class to contextualize the CHOs' harvested descriptions. Thus descriptions (metadata) submitted by different organizations will be preserved with use of the *ore:Proxy* class. In this case the BIBFRAME "Work –hasInstance – Instance" path is mapped to a single *ore:Proxy* class instance. It must be noted that any relationships between BIBFRAME *Work* class instances will be most likely mapped to *ore:Proxy* class instances and not to *edm:ProvidedCHO* class instances. Similarly to the previous mapping approach, the BIBFRAME path describing a born-digital or digitized library object justifies an instantiation of the *edm:webResource* class, with id the URI from the BIBFRAME path (Figure 6).

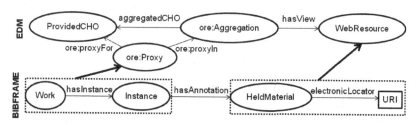

Fig. 6. Mapping of the basic BIBFRAME path to core EDM classes using the *ore:Proxy* class

4.3   Use of edm:InformationResource Class

EDM was developed as a community agnostic model. It serves as the model to aggregate descriptions of digital representations of CHOs mainly for the Europeana portal, while BIBFRAME serves as a model for describing library materials according to the library community objectives. EDM-FRBRoo profile [18] was developed to fulfill the need expressed in [8] for integration of FRBR semantics in EDM using FRBRoo [2] terms.

In this EDM – FRBRoo Application Profile more FRBR semantics may be expressed for an instance of the *edm:ProvidedCHO* class, as described in section 2. FRBR Works -and respectively Expressions- are represented by the path "edm:InformationResource – edm:hasType – frbr:Work". As depicted in figure 7, we propose BIBFRAME *Work* to be mapped to the *edm:InformationResource* class typed as bf:Work, where bf:Work is a *skos:Concept* instance related to *edm:InformationResource* by the edm:hasType property. Therefore a BIBFRAME Work is mapped to the "edm:InformationResource – edm:hasType – bf:Work" EDM path. *Instance* reflects "an individual, material embodiment of the Work" and is mapped to the *edm:ProvidedCHO*. It must be noted that since in this mapping there exists a higher level of abstraction (*edm:InformationResource* class) mapped to the *bf:Work* class, all relationships between Works in BIBFRAME are going to be expressed between the respective *edm:InformationResource* instances.

The transformation of the BIBFRAME representation (see Figure 4) of the "Don Quixote" test case to EDM using typed *edm:InformationResource* class is presented in Figure 8 proving that successful mapping may be achieved for core BIBFRAME classes and properties. This scenario may support translation of different BIBFRAME paths besides the basic one defined earlier. The CD-ROM object along with the linguistic database are not available online and are represented at a more abstract level, as *edm:InformationResource* class instances.

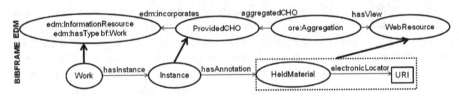

Fig. 7. Mapping of the basic BIBFRAME path to EDM using typed *edm:InformationRecource* class

4.4   Use of edm:InformationResource and ore:Proxy Classes

In order to maintain and preserve information regarding the conceptual content included in provided CHOs along with different providers' views the scenario of using both *edm:InformationResource* and *ore:Proxy* classes was identified. In this case a BIBFRAME *Work* class instance is mapped to the "edm:InformationResource – edm:hasType – skos:Concept – bf:Work" EDM path instance, while a BIBFRAME *Instance* class instance is mapped to an *ore:Proxy* class instance (Figure 9).

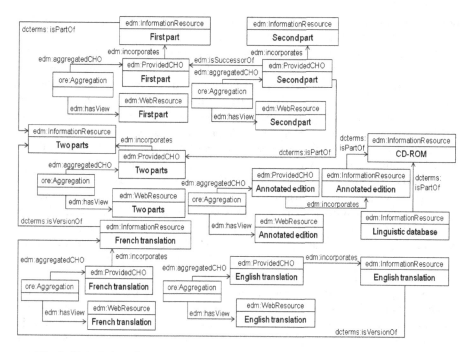

Fig. 8. "Don Quixote" test case in EDM using typed *edm:InformationRecource* class

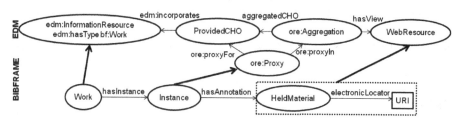

Fig. 9. Mapping of the basic BIBFRAME path to EDM using the *edm:InformationRecource* and *ore:Proxy* classes

5   Discussion and Conclusions

Libraries are expected to engage in interoperability-related activities to enable integration of their bibliographic data into the Semantic Web and their re-use by third-party services. This prospect has motivated our work to attempt translating BIBFRAME conceptualization in the Europeana framework using EDM classes and properties. The mapping of BIBFRAME core classes and properties to EDM has been developed taking into consideration different scenarios expressed as alternative EDM representations; use of the library data alignment report that introduced the "edition" concept [8], use of *ore:Proxy* class that preserves context of CHOs' ingested descriptions, use of *edm:InformationResource* class according to the EDM-FRBRoo application profile and concurrent use of *edm:InformationResource* and *ore:Proxy* classes to better express BIBFRAME semantics and preserve providers' view (descriptive metadata) about the holdings-CHOs they provide to Europeana.

In our mapping a path approach was adopted to avoid possible semantic misinterpretations. Use of source and target paths furnished explicit semantic expressions and mappings between the source BIBFRAME and the target EDM data models, as defined in models' current specifications. Mapping was attempted between a basic BIBFRAME path and the EDM alternative representations. A basic BIBFRAME path was defined in order to satisfy Europeana's focus on born-digital or digitized CHOs available online. BIBFRAME "Work –hasInstance – Instance - hasAnnotation - heldMaterial - electronicLocator – URI" paths of the "Don Quixote" test case were successfully mapped to all possible EDM representation alternatives, proving that various modeling requirements may be satisfied. In case where EDM is used as the conceptual model for an information integration system and not only for aggregating descriptions in the Europeana portal, the above mappings of the BIBFRAME paths require further investigation in order to incorporate descriptions of non digital materials utilizing among others the *edm:PhysicalThing* class.

This is a preliminary work regarding mapping of the core BIBFRAME classes and properties to EDM. More investigations are needed to include more paths and to provide a full application profile. Both models are evolving since BIBFRAME is under development and EDM is regularly updated. Therefore a future application profile should take into account possible changes in each model's semantics. Besides the fact that "Don Quixote" may be considered as a representative example for whole categories of monographs, additional tests need to be performed with a larger set of bibliographic records that will also include more types of aggregates, as well as other types of library materials, such as serials, cartographic material, ephemera, collections, graphic material, etc.

References

1. IFLA Study Group on the Functional Requirements for Bibliographic Records: Functional Requirements for Bibliographic Records. Final Report. IFLA, The Hague (2009), http://www.ifla.org/files/assets/cataloguing/frbr/frbr_2008.pdf
2. Bekiari, C., Doerr, M., LeBoeuf, P., Riva, P.: FRBR object-oriented definition and mapping from FRBRER, FRAD and FRSAD (v.2.0). In: International Working Group on FRBR and CIDOC CRM Harmonisation, Paris (2013), http://www.cidoc-crm.org/frbr_drafts.html
3. Miller, E., Ogbuji, U., Mueller, V., MacDougall, K.: Bibliographic Framework as a Web of Data: Linked Data Model and Supporting Services. Report, Library of Congress, Washington, DC (2012), http://www.loc.gov/bibframe/pdf/marcld-report-11-21-2012.pdf
4. Isaac, A.: Europeana Data Model Primer. Europeana Project, The Hague (2013), http://pro.europeana.eu/edm-documentation

5. Digital Public Library of America: Metadata Application Profile, Version 3. Report, Digital Public Library of America, Boston, MA (2013),
   `http://dp.la/info/developers/map/`
6. Zapounidou, S., Sfakakis, M., Papatheodorou, C.: Integrating library and cultural heritage data models: the BIBFRAME - EDM case. To be appeared in: Panhellenic Conference on Informatics Proceedings, Athens (2014),
   `http://dx.doi.org/10.1145/2645791.2645805`
7. Library of Congress: MARC standards, `http://www.loc.gov/marc/`
8. Angjeli, A., Bayerische, M., Chambers, S., Charles, V., Clayphan, R., Deliot, C., Eriksson, J., Freire, N., Huber, A., Jahnke, A., Pedrosa, G., Phillips, V., Pollecutt, N., Robson, G., Seidler, W., Rühle, S.: D5.1 Report on the alignment of library metadata with the European Data Model (EDM) Version 2.0. Report, Europeana Project (2012),
   `http://www.europeana-libraries.eu/web/guest/outcomes`
9. Lagoze, C., Van De Sompel, H., Johnston, P., Nelson, M., Sanderson, R., Warner, S.: Open Archives Initiative Object Reuse and Exchange ORE Specification - Abstract Data Model (2008), `http://www.openarchives.org/ore/1.0/datamodel`
10. Heaney, M.: Object-oriented cataloging. Information Technology and Libraries 14, 135–153 (1995)
11. Weihs, J. (ed.): International Conference on the Principles and Future Development of AACR, Toronto, Canada, October 23-25. Canadian Library Association (1997); Library Association Publishing; American Library Association, Ottawa; London; Chicago (1998)
12. IFLA Study Group on the Functional Requirements for Bibliographic Records: Functional Requirements for Bibliographic Records Final Report. Saur, München (1998)
13. Tennant, R.: A Bibliographic Metadata Infrastructure for the 21st Century. Library Hi Tech 22, 175–181 (2004)
14. Calhoun, K.: The changing nature of the catalog and its integration with other discovery tools. Report, Library of Congress (2006)
15. Marcum, D.B.: Transforming our Bibliographic Framework: A Statement from the Library of Congress (May 13, 2011),
   `http://www.loc.gov/bibframe/news/index.html`
16. Europeana Semantic Elements Specification and Guidelines. Report, Europeana Project (2013), `http://pro.europeana.eu/ese-documentation/`
17. Definition of the Europeana Data Model v5.2.5. Report, Europeana Project (2014),
   `http://pro.europeana.eu/edm-documentation`
18. Doerr, M., Gradmann, S., Leboeuf, P., Aalberg, T., Bailly, R., Olensky, M.: Final Report on EDM–FRBRoo Application Profile Task Force. Report, Europeana Project (2013),
   `http://pro.europeana.eu/web/network/europeana-tech`
19. Kondylakis, H., Doerr, M., Plexousakis, D.: Mapping Language for Information Integration. Technical report 385, ICS - FORTH, Heraklion, Crete, Greece (2006), `http://www.ics.forth.gr/isl/index_main.php?l=e&pbl=ISL&lab=ISL&author=Doerr`
20. Stasinopoulou, T., Bountouri, L., Kakali, C., Lourdi, I., Papatheodorou, C., Doerr, M., Gergatsoulis, M.: Ontology-based metadata integration in the cultural heritage domain. In: Goh, D.H.-L., Cao, T.H., Sølvberg, I.T., Rasmussen, E. (eds.) ICADL 2007. LNCS, vol. 4822, pp. 165–175. Springer, Heidelberg (2007)
21. Lourdi, I., Papatheodorou, C., Doerr, M.: Semantic integration of collection description. D-Lib Magazine 15 (2009)
22. Bennett, R., Lavoie, B.F., O'Neill, E.T.: The Concept of a Work in WorldCat: An Application of FRBR. Library Collections, Acquisitions and Technical Services 27, 45–59 (2003)
23. Žumer, M., O'Neill, E.T.: Modeling Aggregates in FRBR. Cataloging & Classification Quarterly 50, 456–472 (2012)

Modeling and Managing the Digital Archive of the Pina Bausch Foundation

Kerstin Diwisch and Bernhard Thull

Institute of Communication and Media (ikum),
University of Applied Sciences Darmstadt, Germany
kerstin.diwisch@stud.h-da.de,
bernhard.thull@h-da.de

Abstract. During her lifetime, Pina Bausch had already started to collect material containing her work and in this laid the foundations for an archive. For preserving this cultural heritage in the area of performing arts it was of special interest to integrate ideational resources such as memory fragments or oral storytelling as well as to offer flexible knowledge exploration experiences. Therefore, the digital Pina Bausch archive is realized as a Linked Data archive containing data on various different materials such as manuscripts, choreography notes, programs, photographs, posters, drawings, videos and even oral history related to Pina Bausch's work. In this paper, an insight into the used techniques is presented together with the modeling approach based on FRBR and a machine-readable Dublin Core application profile specifically adapted for managing the archive.

Keywords: Pina Bausch, Performing Arts, Ontology, Linked Data, FRBR, Dublin Core, Application Profile.

1   Introduction

During her lifetime, Pina Bausch had already started to collect material containing her work and to organize the collected objects. In this, she established the foundation for an archive representing her work [1]. After her death, the Pina Bausch Foundation was founded in order to preserve and maintain her lifework. Thereby, preservation and maintenance not only included collecting material, but also preserving memory fragments of people from all over the world [2]. To ensure the archive's accessibility to the public and to allow for the collection of ideational objects (e.g. oral history), a digital archive was decided on.

It is necessary that this archive enables general archiving functions as annotating and linking the archived material. Additionally, it should allow for the collection of ideational objects and the preparation of this material for the development of interpretations, visualizations or interactive experiences [2].

S. Closs et al. (Eds.): MTSR 2014, CCIS 478, pp. 274–285, 2014.
© Springer International Publishing Switzerland 2014

The archive is meant to become publicly available for human users and especially for software interfaces. Accordingly, the use for open standards was envisaged.

For archiving, the ideational objects encountered were in the form of memory fragments, comments and oral history. As there is no written source for these objects, people often have different memories or accentuate different aspects of their shared memories. Thus, one major requirement for the archive was to include contradictory and inconsistent statements and archiving their provenance. Another important requirement was to allow for varying interpretations and interactive experiences with the archived data. However, the details of these actions could not be fully defined at the start of the project, as there was a variety of differing expectations concerning this topic. The data had to be structured to support different representations and purposes in the future.

During the development of the archive it was necessary to provide changing data structures over the course of the project. The needs are provided for through the usage of Semantic Web technologies [3]. Moreover, they enable linking data automatically and create new knowledge through inferencing [4]. Hence, they support exploring and interpreting the archive data according to varying user needs.

To provide the possibility to link the archive with other sources on the web the utilization of Linked Data techniques was foreseen, because they help to structure and connect data on the web [5].

However, even though applying Semantic Web technologies and Linked Data techniques supports all the factors, such requirements also demand for a flexible data model foreseeing a shallow taxonomical hierarchy. In the area of cultural heritage archiving, open standards for different specific areas such as libraries or museums exist. Due to enabling interoperability, the reuse and application of these standards had to be analyzed. Not only is the reuse of existing standards important, but also ensuring the ontology model's flexibility.

Managing data from multiple external sources and providing mappings for a flexible model and ongoing modeling is a major challenge. Varying models and multiple data sources require dynamic configuration of ontology population. Application profiles help maintain modularity and expressivity under these circumstances and provide ways to combine differing metadata schemas [6].

Therefore, the creation of this digital archive incorporated the use of the mentioned technologies and techniques together, which is described in this paper. After this introduction, in Section 2 the related work is presented. In Section 3 the modeling approach is described, followed by a presentation of the specific application profile used to manage data import and export in Section 4. The technical realization in Section 5 shows how these components are combined. Section 6 illustrates the technical process of archiving performance videos and how different types of archive users work with this data. This paper concludes with a short summary and discussion and gives a short outlook onto the further works planned by the Pina Bausch Foundation.

2   Related Work

The archive project brings together topics from differing domains such as cultural heritage and semantic technologies. Data modeling has to be done considering all aspects of these interdisciplinary topics.

There are already several standard ontologies and vocabularies, which can be used for modeling archives in the domain of cultural heritage. According to [7], appropriate models for the library context are FRBR [8], FRBRoo [9], BIBFRAME or EDM[10]. In the domain of museums and (in a broader sense) archives, models such as the ISO21127 release of CIDOC-CRM and FRBRoo are being deployed [11].

Even though the use of these standards is more common for modeling archives, the first version of the Pina Bausch archive ontology is based on an RDF version of core FRBR concepts [12]. Instead of applying and adjusting a rich ontology model, the use of a small core model allowed for easier data integration of several external sources. Furthermore, modeling the ontology and negotiating the model's core schema with the Pina Bausch Foundation could be done simultaneously.

However, these processes demand dynamic configuration of integrating different external data sources and mapping their contents to the model. In addition, the reuse of standard vocabularies was one of the major requirements of the project. Hence, application profiles as a means for configuring and describing the use of standard vocabularies in a compound model [13] qualify for the dynamic configuration of data integration processes in an archive. They were first introduced in UKOLN's work on the DESIRE project [14] and have since been used in several archiving projects, especially in the Linked Data domain, with the most prominent example probably being the application to the Europeana Data Model (EDM) [10].

In particular, machine-readable application profiles allow for interoperability between external data sources and the archives [15] and have been part of many research projects [13, 16]. There are several expressions for machine-readable application profiles. The "RDF Application Profile" Task Group is engaged with RDF [17], as it is one of them. Utilizing RDF or other constitutive vocabularies such as RDF-S and OWL for an application profile expression comes to mind because they are suitable for this application [18, 19] and having the ontology in the same format as its descriptions and restrictions is beneficial for handling purposes. To deploy Dublin Core Application Profiles [20] in RDF, there are two possibilities: Following the "Guidelines for machine-readable representation of Dublin Core Application Profiles" that describe contents and formats with the focus on property usage [19] or formulating an RDF variant of a Description Set Profile (DSP), which is one of the components a Dublin Core Application Profile should consist of [21]. A DSP is meant to describe and constrain resources of an application in accordance with the DCMI Abstract Model [18] and therefore focuses on entities. Hence, their differences lie particularly in the focus of constrained types. In accordance with the decision for

FRBR as a base model and in this focusing on the modeling of entities, a Dublin Core Application Profile with a DSP in RDF was utilized in the digital archive of the Pina Bausch Foundation.

3   Modeling the Ontology

The archive's main purpose is supporting the exploration of Pina Bausch's work for researchers and the interested public. This means that in addition to the collection and annotation of various materials such as posters and videos, the archive also has to provide means for commenting on certain aspects of Pina Bausch's work. At the start of the project, the processes of commenting and discussing Pina Bausch's work in the archive could not be clearly structured and described. Thus, varying and adjusting the model several times was part of the creation process of the archive.

The need for flexible and ongoing modeling led to the decision for a small core model rather than applying a rich ontology such as CIDOC-CRM [22], which could have also been deployed in this context. Since the main use case of the digital archive of the Pina Bausch Foundation derived from a library perspective, FRBR group 1 was merely chosen as a core model. In addition, the first modeling approach focused on digitized objects as the digitization of collected materials paralleled. Thus, the clear structure of FRBR supported this aspect.

In a second step, the archiving focus will slightly shift, including oral history and the creative process, the aforementioned ideational objects. Using FRBR's core concepts as a first step also allows for converting the utilized model to FRBRoo [9] and therefore facilitating further development regarding creation processes [7].

Fig. 1. The first version of the Pina Bausch archive ontology's core model

The application of the FRBR core model in the Pina Bausch archive ontology is briefly shown in Figure 1. Black font is used for FRBR entities and properties, while gray font represents the individual extensions to the model. All 54 plays of Pina Bausch are modeled as individuals of the class Piece, a subclass of *frbr:Work*, representing the intellectual creation. Performances of these plays are individuals of *frbr:Performance*, a subclass of *frbr:Expression*, representing a realization of *frbr:Work*. As the distinction between different types of performances is important for the archive use cases, several subclasses of *frbr:Performance* have been created. Premiere in Figure 1 is representative for these classes. On the manifestation level, there are videos, pictures, programs and posters of a performance, all modeled in subclasses of *pbao:Object*. Divided into physical representations (e.g. a tape of a video) and digital items (e.g. an MPEG-file of a video), all items are modeled as individuals of subclasses of *frbr:Item*.

The example in Section 6 shows that applying FRBR as a core model has proven to withstand the modeling needs of the digital archive of the Pina Bausch Foundation in a previous stage.

4   Managing Archive Data

The need for ongoing and flexible modeling did not only imply the use of a small core model, but it also demanded special treatment of the inclusion of external data sources and data input processes in general. Furthermore, one of the project's requirements was to use standard vocabularies whenever possible in order to conform with Linked Data principles [5].

Application profiles have proven to ensure the modularity and extensibility of an application while allowing for the use of domain-standard vocabularies [6]. Especially in Linked Data software development, where the reuse of existing vocabularies is considered good practice [5], it has become common practice to deploy application profiles. To ensure longevity and interoperability of the application profile, the decision was made to use an open and widely accepted standard and therefore deploy a Dublin Core Application Profile [20, 21]. Utilizing such an application profile in a machine-readable format leads to further advantages:

— Automated data integration and validation
— Database for a form-based editor
— Automated generation of a user manual

As mentioned earlier, Description Set Profiles (DSP) focuses on the constraints of resources. The emphasis on resources led to the decision to utilize a Dublin Core Application Profile with a DSP in RDF-S for managing data import in the digital archive of the Pina Bausch Foundation. In the course of the process, the DSP was not only used for data import and served as a base for an interactive editor, it was also utilized for data representation and selection means which is represented in the DSP model.

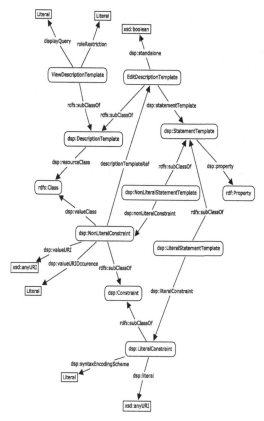

Fig. 2. Description Set Profile extension for the digital Pina Bausch archive

The formalization of the DSP in RDF-S and our extensions for data integration and selection purposes are shown in Figure 2. The general structure comprises of so-called *DescriptionTemplates* for each class. These are linked with several *StatementTemplates*, which represent descriptions of property constraints. The property constraints can be distinguished by their constraint value types: these are either literal or non-literal. The same characteristics apply to the types of Constraint, thus, a distinction is drawn between *LiteralConstraint* and *NonLiteralConstraint*.

The application-specific extensions mainly comprise of templates for editing and data presentation purposes, but there is also an extension for container classes [4]: the property *dsp:descriptionTemplateRef* is used as a link between a *DescriptionTemplate* describing a container and a template describing the constraints of its contained elements.

Defining subclasses of *DescriptionTemplate* leads to the possibility to differentiate between class purposes: *EditDescriptionTemplates* are used for the main purpose of the application profile: defining and constraining the mapping between data sources and the Pina Bausch archive ontology. Whereas *ViewDescriptionTemplates* serve as a means to map classes of this ontology to specific view templates containing SPARQL queries [23] and access rights for frontend applications. Thus, the properties *displayQuery* and *roleRestriction* are defined.

These extensions allow for the use in an interactive editor and as a browser controller for selected frontends.

5   Technical Realization

The Pina Bausch archive ontology and the proposed Dublin Core application profile are both deployed in the digital archive of the Pina Bausch Foundation which implies several components for data import and frontend representation.

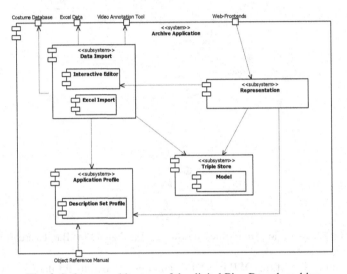

Fig. 3. Software architecture of the digital Pina Bausch archive

Figure 3 shows a brief description of the archive's components. The archive application comprises the Triple Store containing the archive ontology model, the application profile with the machine-readable DSP, a component for data import and one for frontend representation. The Data Import component depends on the Application Profile for mapping external data sources to the archive ontology. Automated imports are available for a costume database, Excel sheets and a video annotation tool which all supply bulk data. In addition, this component provides content for an interactive frontend editor, which is controlled by the Representation component. This component also allocates facilities to browse the archive data, managed through the means of the Application Profile component. In addition, the Application Profile component handles automated generation of a manual which is used for the guidance of archive users.

6   Usage Scenario

To illustrate how the digital archive works, a usage scenario is described in this section: videos of a performance of 'Orpheus and Euridice' are archived and afterwards the related contents can be used through the means of the digital archive in different ways.

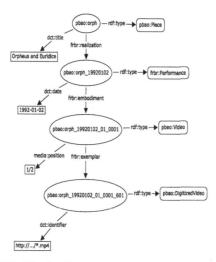

Fig. 4. 'Orpheus and Euridice' and a corresponding video realized in the FRBR model

Figure 4 shows how a video of the aforementioned performance is realized in the Pina Bausch archive ontology with FRBR group 1 entities and the use of several standard vocabularies like Dublin Core. The play itself is modeled as an individual of *pbao:Piece*, a subclass of *frbr:Work*. The performance on Jan 2nd, 1992 is modeled as an individual of *frbr:Performance*. Properties of the Dublin Core vocabularies are used to annotate this performance. The structure of FRBR is kept throughout all tiers. A video of the mentioned performance is linked through the property *frbr:embodiment*, and its digitization is an individual of *pbao:DigitizedVideo*, a subclass of *pbao:DigitizedItem* and therefore a sublass of *frbr:Item*.

In order to annotate those entities in the ontology, an interactive editor uses the DSP to generate input forms. The corresponding part of the DSP in Turtle-Syntax is as follows:

```
:edTemplate_video rdf:type :EditDescriptionTemplate;
  dsp:minOccur "0"^^xsd:nonNegativeInteger;
  dsp:maxOccur "Infinity"^^xsd:string;
  dsp:resourceClass pbao:Video;
  dsp:statementTemplate :litST_title,
    :litST_mediaPosition,
    :nonlitST_depicts,
    :nonlitST_embodimentPerformance.
```

The template is an individual of the class *:EditDescriptionTemplate* and therefore used by the interactive editor to generate forms. The property *dsp:resourceClass* references the type of class the form is generated for, in this case *pbao:Video*. Five attributes are linked with this template by *dsp:statementTemplate*. The interactive editor translates this into a form with five fields (see Figure 5 for the video input form).

pbao:Video

URI

:orph_19920102_01_0001

Titel

|

Teil

1/2

Dargestellte Personen (von links nach rechts)

pbao:aida_vainieri

<<
>>
Clear

pbao:anna_lena_dresia
pbao:anna_martin
pbao:anna_wehsarg
pbao:anna_wloch
pbao:anne_maniglier
pbao:anne_marie_benati
pbao:anne_martin
pbao:anne_rebeschini
pbao:anne_westphal
pbao:annemarie_benati

Aufführung

pbao:orph_19920102

Submit

Fig. 5. An input form for videos generated from DSP contents

The field type (e.g. input field or selection box) depends on the content of the corresponding *StatementTemplate*. In this case, two text fields are generated as the appropriate templates define string values. However, the other two fields are more constrained by the corresponding templates. The selection box for depicted persons allows multiple values while there can only be one performance associated with a video. Multiple values are realized as RDF containers in the archive. Hence, the template for depicted persons uses the container extension of the DSP. Selectable values are taken directly from the archive's triple store, thereby supporting correctness of data input. The editor enables domain experts and users not familiar with knowledge engineering in detail to fill the archive in an unambiguous way.

There are several use cases for the archive's data. Two of them will be illustrated in this example.

Exploring and browsing the archive is one of the main use cases. This is realized through frontend browsers which users can use to navigate through the archive's contents. Figure 6 shows the browser's contents for the performance of 'Orpheus and Euridice' on Jan 2nd, 1992.

Fig. 6. Performance of 'Orpheus and Euridice' on Jan 2nd, 1992 displayed in one of the archive's browsing tools[1]

Which aspects of a performance are displayed in the browser is also managed by the DSP. As shown in the following code listing, *ViewDescriptionTemplates* link entity types to query templates which are used to select the displayed contents.

```
#frbr:Performance
:vdTemplate_perform rdf:type :ViewDescriptionTemplate;
  :displayQuery "performance_sparql.ftl";
  dsp:resourceClass frbr:Performance.
```

Another use case is restaging of a play. There is a mobile app which allows browsing through the individual video scenes of a certain play (see Figure 7). Thus, a dance company would select the individual scenes of the videos taken from the performance of 'Orpheus and Euridice' on Jan 2nd, 1992 in order to restage the play.

Fig. 7. The archive's mobile app for restaging plays

The usage scenario shows how the digital archive of the Pina Bausch Foundation works for different types of use cases.

---

[1] Placeholders for video screens are shown due to confidentiality and copyright reasons.

7   Conclusion

This paper reports on the creation of the digital archive of the Pina Bausch Foundation with a focus on domain-specific obstacles which could have been overcome by the use of Semantic Web technologies, Linked Data techniques, elaborate modeling based on a small core model and the use of a machine-readable Dublin Core Application Profile.

Semantic Web technologies provided means for constantly changing data structures and supported the exploration of new knowledge within the archive's data. The adherence of Linked Data principles helped to provide interoperability and longevity.

To date, FRBR as a base for the ontology model has proven to allow for the archiving of all incurred types of resources. The use of standard vocabularies complemented the ontology and supported Linked Data concepts. Even though, modeling was a constant process throughout the project, data import was possible at all times. This was realized through the use of a small model and the utilization of an extended Dublin Core Application Profile, which has helped to dynamically configure the data integration. Furthermore, it has also been explored as a base for data frontend representation, which can be recommended.

However, frontend representation is still an issue with the digital archive of the Pina Bausch Foundation and Linked Data applications, in general [24]. Especially, the required possibilities for exploring the archive's data in unusual ways leave space for further research regarding visualizations and interactive experiences. Future work will put a strong focus on that feature of the digital archive.

In addition, mapping from the FRBR-based core model to FRBRoo will be further investigated as the main integration analyzing processes are completed and migrating to a more extensive model is possible. This change has to be considered since the project's modeling focus will shift from archiving objects to documenting creation processes.

References

1. Wagenbach, M.: Tanz erben. Ein Archiv als Zukunftswerkstatt. In: Wagenbach, M. (ed.) Tanz Erben. Pina Lädt Ein, pp. 15–20. Transcript, Bielefeld (2014)
2. Thull, B.: Das digitale Pina Bausch Archiv. In: Wagenbach, M. (ed.) Tanz Erben. Pina Lädt Ein, pp. 59–74. Transcript, Bielefeld (2014)
3. Allemang, D., Hendler, J.A.: Semantic Web for the working ontologist. Effective modeling in RDFS and OWL. Morgan Kaufmann, Elsevier Science (distributor), San Francisco, Calif. (2008)
4. Hebeler, J.: Semantic Web programming. Wiley, Indianapolis (2009)
5. Bizer, C., Heath, T., Berners-Lee, T.: Linked Data - The Story So Far. International Journal on Semantic Web and Information Systems 5, 1–22 (2009)
6. Duval, E., Hodgins, W., Sutton, S., Weibel, S.: Metadata Principles and Practicalities. D-Lib Magazine 8 (2002)

7. Zapounidou, S., Sfakakis, M., Papatheodorou, C.: Highlights of Library Data Models in the Era of Linked Open Data. In: Garoufallou, E., Greenberg, J. (eds.) MTSR 2013. CCIS, vol. 390, pp. 396–407. Springer, Heidelberg (2013)

8. IFLA: FunktionaleAnforderungen an bibliografischeDatensätze. Abschlussbericht der IFLA Study Group on the Functional Requirements for Bibliographic Records. Dt. Nationalbibliothek, Leipzig, Frankfurt, M, Berlin (2009)

9. Bekiari, C., Doerr, M., Le Boeuf, P.: FRBR object-oriented definition and mapping to FRBR, http://www.ifla.org/files/assets/cataloguing/frbrrg/frbr-oo-v9.1_pr.pdf

10. Doerr, M., Gradmann, S., Hennicke, S., Isaac, A., Meghini, C., van de Sompel, H.: The Europeana Data Model (EDM). In: IFLA (ed.) Proceedings of the World Library and Information Congress: 76th IFLA General Conference and Assembly. Open Access to Knowledge - Promoting Sustainable Progress (2010)

11. Doerr, M.: Ontologies for Cultural Heritage. In: Staab, S., Studer, R. (eds.) Handbook on Ontologies, pp. 463–486. Springer, Berlin (2009)

12. Davis, I., Newman, R.: Expression of Core FRBR Concepts in RDF, http://vocab.org/frbr/core.html

13. Baker, T., Dekkers, M., Heery, R., Patel, M., Salokhe, G.: What term does your metadata use? Application profiles as machine-understandable narratives. Journal of Digital Information 2 (2001)

14. Heery, R., Patel, M.: Application Profiles: Mixing and Matching Metadata Schemas. Ariadne (2000)

15. Hunter, J., Lagoze, C.: Combining RDF and XML schemas to enhance interoperability between metadata application profiles. In: Proceedings of the 10th International Conference on World Wide Web, pp. 457–466 (2001)

16. Heery, R., Johnston, P., Fülöp, C., Micsik, A.: Metadata schema registries in the partially Semantic Web: the CORES experience. In: Dublin Core Metadata Initiative (ed.) DC-2003, Proceedings of the International DCMI Metadata Conference and Workshop. DCMI (2003)

17. RDF Application Profile Task Group: RDF Application Profiles, http://wiki.dublincore.org/index.php/RDF_Application_Profiles

18. Nilsson, M.: Description Set Profiles: A constraint language for Dublin Core Application Profiles, http://dublincore.org/documents/dc-dsp/

19. European Committee for Standardization: Guidelines for machine-processable representation of Dublin Core Application Profiles, Brussels (2005)

20. Coyle, K., Baker, T.: Guidelines for Dublin Core Application Profiles, http://dublincore.org/documents/profile-guidelines/

21. Nilsson, M., Baker, T., Johnston, P.: The Singapore Framework for Dublin Core Application Profiles, http://dublincore.org/documents/singapore-framework/

22. Le Boeuf, P., Doerr, M., Ore, C.E., Stead, S.: Definition of the CIDOC Conceptual Reference Model, http://www.cidoc-crm.org/docs/cidoc_crm_version_5.1.2.pdf

23. Prud'hommeaux, E., Seaborne, A.: SPARQL Query Language for RDF, http://www.w3.org/TR/rdf-sparql-query/

24. Dadzie, A.-S., Rowe, M.: Approaches to visualising Linked Data: A survey. Semantic Web, 89–124 (2011)

The Europeana Network of Ancient Greek and Latin Epigraphy Data Infrastructure

Andrea Mannocci, Vittore Casarosa, Paolo Manghi, and Franco Zoppi

Consiglio Nazionale delle Ricerche
Istituto di Scienza e Tecnologia dell'Informazione "A. Faedo"
Via Moruzzi 1, 56124 Pisa, Italy
name.surname@isti.cnr.it

Abstract. Epigraphic archives, containing collections of editions about ancient Greek and Latin inscriptions, have been created in several European countries during the last couple of centuries. Today, the project EAGLE (Europeana network of Ancient Greek and Latin Epigraphy, a Best Practice Network partially funded by the European Commission) aims at providing a single access point for the content of about 15 epigraphic archives, totaling about 1,5M digital objects. This paper illustrates some of the challenges encountered and their solution for the realization of the EAGLE data infrastructure. The challenges mainly concern the harmonization, interoperability and service integration issues caused by the aggregation of metadata from heterogeneous archives (different data models and metadata schemas, and exchange formats). EAGLE has defined a common data model for epigraphic information, into which data models from different archives can be optimally mapped. The data infrastructure is based on the D-NET software toolkit, capable of dealing with data collection, mapping, cleaning, indexing, and access provisioning through web portals or standard access protocols.

Keywords: Data Infrastructure, Aggregation System, Metadata Formats, Data Interoperability, Data Harmonization, Cleaning, Epigraphy, D-NET.

1   Introduction

Born approximately in the 16th century, Epigraphy is a modestly ancient field of study with its well-established legacy of best practices. During its early centuries, different communities started their studies independently and developed their local *modus operandi* possibly clashing with other practices from other communities. One of the most important initiatives striving to reduce such fragmentation took place in 1932, with the Leiden conventions [1] which established a set of rules, symbols, and bracketing system to indicate the content and the conditions of an epigraphic or papyrological text when transcribed in a modern edition.

During the nineties, when large portions of epigraphic corpora started being digitized, to make them available online, it became apparent that the Leiden notation, with its symbols and bracketing conventions, had been defined having in mind essentially a

S. Closs et al. (Eds.): MTSR 2014, CCIS 478, pp. 286–300, 2014.

printed representation of the inscription, and was not convenient for searching and browsing digital information online.

The next step forward to facilitate the exchange of epigraphic information was therefore the definition of a new standard, in the early 2010s, for annotating inscriptions and for providing additional information about the epigraphic object itself, such as the physical carrier, the finding place, the present conservation place, and so on. The new standard, called EpiDoc [2], was based on TEI (Text Encoding Initiative), which was a standard already widely used in the Digital Humanities community for XML annotation of manuscripts and old documents [3].

Despite EpiDoc, however, most of the epigraphic archives made available online to support searching, browsing and visualization of inscriptions were developed independently across communities and without any shared guideline, resulting in an a highly fragmented scenario in which information of the same nature is represented according to different conceptual models, making use of heterogeneous back-ends and being offered to the users by different protocols and means. The increased use of Internet and the Web, with its ubiquitous services for searching and browsing information online, has raised the level of expectations of the users of epigraphic material, whether scholars or general public, bringing the need for new paradigms of interoperability and collaboration between different communities and integration of services.

The project EAGLE (Europeana network of Ancient Greek and Latin Epigraphy [4], a Best Practice Network partially funded by the European Commission) intends to provide Europeana [5] with a comprehensive collection of unique historical sources (about 1,5 million digital objects), representing approximately 80% of the total amount of inscriptions in the Mediterranean area. At the same time EAGLE will provide a user-friendly portal to access that same collection, built with material coming from about 15 different epigraphic archives.

More precisely, EAGLE is developing an infrastructure whose aim is to: (*i*) aggregate content from the most prominent European institutions and archives in the field of Classical Latin and Greek epigraphy; (*ii*) harmonize that content according to a single data model; (*iii*) make that content available for ingestion to Europeana and for searching and browsing on the part of end-users (be they epigraphy practitioners or general public). In addition, EAGLE intends to set up a multilingual wiki for the enrichment and curation of epigraphic images and texts, with special emphasis on translations, providing a basis for future translations of inscriptions in modern European languages.

In the present work, we describe the challenges and the solutions adopted in the EAGLE project in order to enable data interoperability and deliver a unified, homogeneous, high-quality information space of cohesive epigraphic material.

The EAGLE data aggregation infrastructure is powered by the D-NET [6] software toolkit, which provides a rich and customizable set of data management services capable of coping with issues such as metadata collection, storage, transformation, cleaning and indexing of the collected data. D-NET also offers services for tailoring search/browse capabilities to the requirements of a target community, and supports the export of the collected (now harmonised) data through standard protocols, such as OAI-PMH [7], SRW/CQL [8], and other exchange formats.

The paper is organized as follows. After the Introduction, in Section 2 we provide some more details about the solutions adopted in the EAGLE project to ensure data interoperability; in Section 3 we provide a detailed description of the different data sources providing input to EAGLE and the common data model harmonizing all of them; in Section 4 we describe how the D-NET toolkit has been customized to satisfy the EAGLE requirements, and describe the different workflows defined to harmonize the collected data; finally, in Section 5, we provide some concluding remarks about the present implementation and future development.

2   Overview of the Problem and Adopted Solution

The EAGLE data infrastructure satisfies two main requirements as identified by the user community: (*i*) single access point to the most prominent European epigraphic archives, and (*ii*) rich and high-quality metadata descriptions.

As mentioned in the introduction, these requisites are hindered by the highly heterogeneous nature of the epigraphic archives. In fact, content of different archives generally conforms to different metadata models and XML schemas, whose structure may vary from complex tree-structured elements to simple flat lists of elements. Other problems arise from the use of different controlled vocabularies to indicate the same concepts, different standards for names, dates and time periods, etc.

In addition, the epigraphic archives also differ in the typology of the objects exported as we will further describe in the next Section. Part of the content describes real-world objects (the physical carrier of an inscription), while other content describes the inscription itself, considered as a string of symbols in some alphabet, and yet other content describes the relationships binding together the different pieces of information, possibly coming from other archives.

EAGLE has tackled such heterogeneity by developing first a common data model (see Section 3.5) onto which incoming metadata records are mapped and then by implementing the EAGLE data infrastructure, whose services provide functionality for: (*i*) collecting records from the different archives and transforming them into records matching the common XML metadata schema; (*ii*) curating the resulting records to identify possible errors and (possibly) to enrich them with additional content.

The data ingestion process, based on the D-NET Software Toolkit, consists of four phases:

1. *Metadata mapping definition.* In cooperation with domain experts from the archives providing records, the structural and semantic rules to map the incoming records into the EAGLE common metadata schema are encoded in the form of D-NET scripts.
2. *Metadata transformation and cleaning.* Metadata records are collected (via FTP, OAI-PMH or other protocols) and processed (using the scripts defined in phase 1) to generate the "EAGLE objects", thus creating the Pre-production Information Space.
3. *Metadata quality control.* The EAGLE records are inspected and validated to identify mapping errors and possible mistakes (e.g., typos). This quality control process

may lead to the redefinition of the mapping rules (in Phase 1) and the repetition of Phase 2.

4. *Metadata provisioning*. The EAGLE records that pass Phase 3 are moved to the Production Information Space, where they are indexed and become available for ingestion to Europeana or for querying and browsing through the EAGLE portal.

3   EAGLE Data Sources and Common Metadata Model

As briefly mentioned in the preceding Sections, EAGLE aggregates content provided by about 15 different archives from all over Europe. While the majority of them is providing records based on the EpiDoc standard, for various reasons a few archives are supplying records in different formats. In addition to epigraphic archives, EAGLE aggregates data from two other different sources: Mediawiki pages, containing translations of inscriptions, and "Trismegistos records", containing information about disambiguated records. Here below we briefly describe those different data sources.

3.1   EpiDoc-Based Epigraphic Archives

The majority of EAGLE data sources provide "editions", i.e. epigraphic documents marked up following the TEI/EpiDoc standard. EpiDoc is today the de facto standard in digital epigraphy and enables a holistic text-centric digital description of an inscription and all its related aspects. EpiDoc documents processed by the EAGLE infrastructure comprise a broad range of information describing the stone (or monument) and its properties, the inscription (as epigraphic field) and its text, contextual information, images, bibliography and so on. Thanks to XML, all this information is provided in a flexible, machine-readable and exchangeable format.

At the same time, an EpiDoc record consists in a monolithic, self-descriptive and self-standing information unit that does not lend itself to an easy search and navigation through big epigraphic databases, with hundreds of thousands of inscriptions. For example, given an EpiDoc document that includes pointers to two images of the described inscription, it is not easy to find another EpiDoc document describing the same inscription, but providing pointers to different images, or to retrieve detailed information about those images, that usually are not included in the EpiDoc documents. For these reasons, as we will see in Section 3.5, the information provided in a single EpiDoc record is (possibly) transformed into more than one "EAGLE object".

3.2   Non-EpiDoc-Based Epigraphic Archives

In a few cases, for historical or technical reasons, some of the institutions providing data to EAGLE will export their data as XML records, but not following the EpiDoc standard. A brief description of those cases follows.

Arachne The Arachne archive [9] is hosted by the Deutsche Archäologisches Institut (DAI) and comprehends a vast collection of photographs, drawings, sketches and scans of ancient volumes. For historical reasons, and because it is more suitable for the type of its information, Arachne exports records expressed in XML, but following the CIDOC Conceptual Reference Model (CRM) [10]. The CIDOC CRM is another standard very popular in the Humanities, especially museums, which is particularly suitable for describing information about physical objects and events (agents, time) related to them, but is less suitable for textual information.

UbiEratLupa The UbiEratLupa archive [11] is hosted by the University of Salzburg (PLUS) and its main focus of interest is on monuments. The archive exports XML records based on its own schema, describing the physical properties of monuments, dating information, plenty of pictorial material, other relevant places related to the monument, and (optionally) describing also information about the text of possible inscriptions on their surface. This type of information does not fit well in the text-centric representation provided by EpiDoc.

The Cyprus Institute The Cyprus Institute [12] is dealing mainly with ancient Cypriote literature and archeology, focusing on 3D modeling of monuments and archeological sites. It exports XML records based on its own metadata schema (STARC), which is very rich in terms of properties related to 3D models. Here also the text-centric representation provided by EpiDoc is not the best mean for representing this type of information.

3.3   Trismegistos

Trismegistos [13], an initiative hosted by the University of Leuven, is a vast archive of information about "texts" spanning approximately from 800 BC to 800 AD. It started focusing especially on texts coming from Graeco-Roman Egypt, but in recent years its domain of interest has expanded to include the entire ancient world.

Trismegistos receives records describing inscriptions (mainly papyrological and epigraphic texts) from many different archives, and by using sophisticated disambiguation technologies (and some heuristics) it determines whether a different edition of the newly arrived inscription is already present in its database or not. As a result of this analysis, if the incoming inscription is considered a "new" one, then a new unique stable Trismegistos identifier (TM-id) is created and associated with that inscription. Otherwise, if the incoming inscription is recognized as being another instance (edition) of an inscription already present in the Trismegistos database, then the TM-id already assigned to the existing inscription is assigned also to the incoming one. In both cases the assigned TM-id is sent to the sending archive for (possible) inclusion in the metadata describing that inscription.

EAGLE too receives records from many different archives and it can happen that the same inscription is held by more than one archive, possibly with different editions and critical apparatus. In order to avoid that as a result of a query EAGLE provides the same inscription more than once, it would be necessary to make duplicate record detection within the aggregator, which could be very onerous. Instead, the use of the TM-ids provided to EAGLE by Trismegistos is particularly useful, as it allows at query time to group together in a single result item all those inscriptions that have the same TM-id.

In conclusion, the information provided to EAGLE by Trismegistos are not records describing inscriptions or inscription related objects, but are records associating a TM-id with all the instances of that inscription that are known to Trismegistos. Those instances are identified with the local identifier assigned to them by the archive providing that instance, and therefore it is easy for the EAGLE aggregator to integrate the TM-id into the records provided by the archives, if not already present.

3.4   Mediawiki

For a project like EAGLE, which aims to be of interest also to the general public, and not just to epigraphy scholars, is a key success factor the availability of good quality translations of the inscriptions (most of them are in Greek or Latin) into modern languages. For that purpose EAGLE has established a Mediawiki platform [14] to be used by the EAGLE partners in order to build a dedicated knowledge base for the translation of the EAGLE inscriptions. Hopefully the use of Mediawiki will stimulate the participation of other interested parties and general public, so that the huge translation task will be accomplished in a collaborative way, like a sort of crowdsourcing. Based on translations already existing in the archives, at the time of writing the EAGLE Mediawiki contains translations (mostly in English and German) for more than 7000 inscriptions, with many inscriptions having more than one translation, in the same or in different languages.

Each Mediawiki page contains all the translations available for a given inscription, identified by its TM-id number (if existing) and by the local identifier assigned to it by the owning archive. If the TM-id is associated with more than one instance of the inscription, all the instances (and their translations, if existing) are on that same page. The Mediawiki page contains also links to the "original objects" contained in the archives that provided those inscriptions. The EAGLE aggregator collects all those information for integration with the information received directly by the archives.

3.5   Epigraphy Aggregation Conceptual Model (EACM)

The need for expressing queries against such heterogeneous material has led to the definition of a data model being able of relating separate concepts and objects in a seamless way, thus allowing both the scholars and the general public to achieve results which could hardly be obtained with the existing EpiDoc archives.

The Epigraphy Aggregation Conceptual Model (EACM) is based on a small number of entities on which the EAGLE Common Metadata Model and Schema is then defined and implemented. The EACM allows expressing all the different facets of epigraphy-related content such as physical supports, texts, translations, images and other context information and enables the user to make sophisticated queries to accurately retrieve the material of interest.

The EACM consists of a root entity (the Main Object) from which four sub-entities can be instantiated: (*i*) Artefact, (*ii*) Inscription, (*iii*) Visual representation, and (*iv*) Documental manifestation. All the information to be aggregated in EAGLE will find its place into one or multiple instances of such sub-entities. In the following we briefly describe each of those. Figure1 shows a high-level view of the model, where solid lines represent a hierarchical relation between two entities (class, sub-class), whilst dashed lines represent a relationship between two entities.

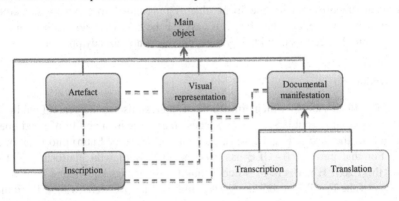

Fig. 1. High-level view of the model

Main object - is an abstract entity that will be materialized into one or more instances of some or all of the sub-entities underlying it. It serves as a placeholder for the information common to all the sub-entities, the main information being the ID of the providing archive and the local ID (in that archive) of the provided object.

Artefact - captures the information about the physical nature of an object in the Epigraphic domain.

Inscription - describes the textual and semantic nature of a text region possibly present on an artefact.

Documental manifestation - contains all information related to the "textual nature" of an inscription. It has two sub-entities: the Transcription, which gathers the information related to the text of the inscription itself, and the Translation, which gathers the relevant properties of possible translations in modern languages of the (interpreted) text of the inscription.

Transcription - describes the inscription text in its original (ancient) language. A Transcription is related to one and only one Inscription instance. At the same time, a Transcription may be related to more than one Translation.

Translation - captures all the aspects relevant to the translation of an ancient text into a modern language. A Translation instance can be put in relation with one or more Inscription instances, of which it is a translation.

Visual representation - collects all the information related to the "visual nature" of a generic artefact, be it a stone, a monument, or an epigraphy-related object providing context to others epigraphic objects of interest. A Visual Representation (always materialized as a digital image) can be put in relation with at most one Artefact (of which it is a picture) and zero or more Inscription instances. There may be cases where a Visual Representation is not in relation with any Artefact, in which case the image represent "context objects".

A more detailed description of the model can be found in [15]. The conceptual model has been implemented as a set of XML objects and a complete schema can be seen at [16].

4   EAGLE Data Infrastructure and Workflows

The EAGLE Data Infrastructure is built on top of the D-NET software toolkit [6], resulting from the experience of CNR-ISTI through its participation in a number of European projects. D-NET is an open source solution specifically devised for the construction and operation of customized infrastructures for data aggregation, which provides a service-oriented framework where data infrastructures can be built in a LEGO-like approach, by selecting and properly combining the required services [6, 17].

The infrastructures implemented by means of D-NET are customizable (e.g., transformation into common metadata formats can be configured to match community preferences), extensible (e.g. new services can be integrated, to offer functionality not yet supported by the toolkit), and scalable (e.g., storage and index replicas can be maintained and deployed on remote nodes to tackle multiple concurrent accesses or very-large data size). D-NET offers a rich set of services targeting aspects such as data collection (mediation area), data mappings from formats to formats (mapping area), and data access (provision area). Services can be customized and combined to meet the data workflow requirements of a target user community. As proven by the several installations and adoption in a number of European projects (DRIVER and DRIVER II [18], OpenAIRE [19], HOPE [20], EFG [21]), D-NET represents an optimal and sustainable solution [17, 22] for the realization of the EAGLE infrastructure.

The customization of the D-NET services implemented for the EAGLE infrastructure is shown in Figure 2. Services are appropriately combined to support the data ingestion workflow defined for the epigraphists' community. In particular the Collecting, Transforming and Cleaning services result from the project design activities. They were devised in order to meet the requirements of the epigraphic archives providing content to EAGLE, but engineered to support their functionalities when operating over arbitrary XML schemas. In addition D-NET has been extended with image processing services to support the Flagship Mobile Application (see Section 4.3), an important application that will be offered by EAGLE to mobile users.

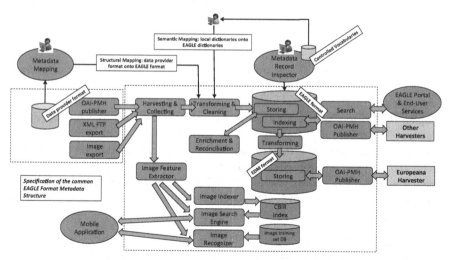

Fig. 2. D-NET customization for EAGLE

4.1   Metadata Mapping Definition, Transformation, and Cleaning

The mapping from the native metadata schema used by an archive to the EAGLE common metadata schema is defined jointly by the experts of the archive (knowledgeable about the structure and the meaning of the objects in the archive) and the infrastructure administrators. The definition has two aspects: (*i*) a *structural mapping* from the archives' local schema to the EAGLE common schema and (*ii*) a *semantic mapping* from the local vocabularies to the ones defined in the infrastructure. A mapping defines a set of rules according to which the infrastructure administrators customize the services that transform the source records into EAGLE records by means of XSLT scripts.

The structural mapping is implemented by the Transformator Service, which implements the rules defining the correspondence among elements and attributes of the local schema and elements and attributes of the EAGLE schema. This is a non trivial task, since input XML records are mapped onto several interrelated EAGLE records, representing different EAGLE data model entities. More precisely, a structural mapping rule for each source element consists of the following information:

1. *Source element*: xpath identifying the schema element relative to the input value;
2. *Target element*: xpath(s) identifying the schema element(s) (and the sub-entity of the conceptual model) onto which the source value has to be mapped;
3. *Mandatory element*: states if the source element is mandatory (if not present, the record is rejected);
4. *Element multiplicity*: states if the source element is repeatable;
5. *Comment*: description of the mapping rule.

The semantic mapping is implemented by the Cleaner Service. Each semantic rule identifies an element of the schema used by the archive and the corresponding element of the EAGLE schema (i.e., source element and target element of the structural rules), and defines the correspondence between the terms of the respective vocabularies.

4.2   EAGLE Workflows

In D-NET, data processing is specified by defining *workflows* (i.e. a tree of elementary steps, with optional fork and join nodes) and *meta-workflows* (i.e. a sequence of *workflows*). A (meta)workflow can be easily configured, scheduled and started through a D-NET tool with a graphical user interface (see Figure 3), while the implementation of the elementary steps is done by writing programs actually executing the needed processing. Each workflow targets one specific and well defined task, such as collection of records, transformation, indexing, etc. [23].

Figure 3 shows a screenshot of the D-NET tool with the definition of the meta-workflow for the processing of EpiDoc documents. It consists of the sequence of the following workflows:

- collect (records from an archive);
- transform (the collected records into the EAGLE metadata format);

- clean (metadata quality control);
- index (build the index of the final records for querying and browsing);
- OAI (put the final records in the format required by an OAI-PMH harvester).

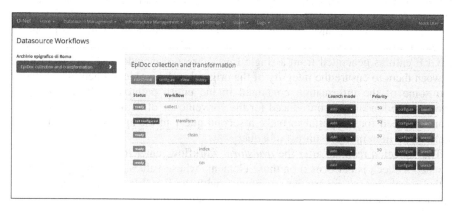

Fig. 3. EpiDoc processing meta-workflow

From a conceptual point of view the meta-workflow of Figure 3 can be shown as in Figure 4, where also the elementary steps of the workflow *transform* are shown.

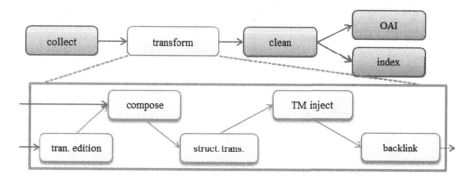

Fig. 4. Collection workflow of EpiDoc content

The original EpiDoc records are collected from the source archive and stored in a local staging area before entering the *transform* workflow. The first transformation (*tran. edition*) processes EpiDoc documents in order to ensure that all transcriptions are uniformly marked-up according to the Leiden conventions. This processing is performed by applying scripts (XSLT transformations) provided by the EpiDoc community [24]. The properly marked-up transcription is then merged back into the original record in the *compose* step.

The next step (*struct. tran.*) is the structural mapping described before, accomplished with XSLT transformations. Following the conceptual model, each EpiDoc record is mapped into a set of interrelated EAGLE entities, since each incoming record will contain data to be included in at least one (possibly more) of the EAGLE

"Artefact", "Inscription", "Transcription" entities and in zero or more EAGLE "Visual representation" entities.

In the next step (*TM inject*) the TM-ids, collected in advance with another workflow and stored in a staging area, are inserted in the Inscription entities generated in the previous step. At query time, this will allow a search engine to perform a *group-by* operation on the result of a query, clustering together all the different instances of an inscription.

The *transform* workflow concludes with a *backlink* step that ensure that all the EAGLE entities generated from a single EpiDoc record include back and forth links between them to ensure the integrity of the original archive object. Each link includes also some of the information contained in the entity pointed to. This (minimal) amount of redundancy is introduced for the convenience of the EAGLE end users, to avoid the need for the portal to make a second query to the aggregator when a user clicks on an item in the result list of a query.

The collected records, after the *transform* workflow, enter the *clean* workflow. In this step a check is performed on those elements whose values are coming from controlled vocabulary to ensure the compliance with the EAGLE common vocabularies highlighting the non-compliant items for human intervention.

The last step before provisioning, non depicted in Figure 4 since it is a manual intervention, is the possible use of a D-NET validation tool (the Metadata Record Inspector, see top of Figure 2) that enables data source curators to search and browse at a low-level the pre-production Information Space (a staging area containing the output of the *transform* workflow) in order to check if the metadata records have been correctly harvested and mapped. Once that the records reach the desired quality, they enter the final provisioning workflows. Figure 5 shows a screenshot of the Metadata Record Inspector user interface.

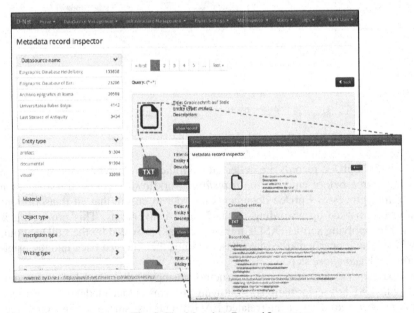

Fig. 5. The Metadata Record Inspector

The two final steps of the data collection meta-workflow are the *indexing* and *OAI* workflows, which can be performed in parallel. EAGLE's metadata can be provided to external consumers via different channels and modes. In the *index* workflow the cleaned final records are given to a SOLR search engine [27] for indexing and for searching and browsing on the part of the EAGLE end users. The EAGLE portal will interact therefore with the SOLR search engine API, and not directly with the aggregator. For the Mobile Application, a specific light-weight API has been developed in order to interact directly with the Image Recognizer.

In the *OAI* workflow the final records undergo a further transformation, to extract from them exactly the information to be provided to Europeana and put them in the format required by the Europeana OAI-PMH harvester (see [25]).

The other types of archive records dealing with epigraphic objects are processed by meta-workflows quite similar to the one described. The meta-workflow to process the non-EpiDoc records (Arachne, UbiEratLupa, Cyprus) is exactly the same, except for the *transform* workflow, which of course will be different for each type of record, to perform the correct mapping from the source format to the EAGLE common format.

The processing of Mediawiki pages, containing translations of inscriptions, is done with a very simple meta-workflow, since in this case there is no need to "clean" the collected data. The *transform* workflow is also very simple, since it only creates the EAGLE entity "Translation" and fills its elements with the appropriate values taken from the Mediawiki page. After that, there is the *backlink* step, as before, to create links between the newly created "Translation" entity and the other (existing) EAGLE objects related to the IDs contained in the Mediawiki page. The meta-workflow for Mediawiki pages will conclude with the provisioning steps as all the other workflows described until now.

The processing of Trismegistos record is different, since its meta-workflow basically consists only in the collection workflow, as the collected records are stored in a staging area waiting to be used by the other workflows, and there is no need for cleaning and provisioning.

4.3   The Mobile Application

For completeness we briefly describe the customization of D-NET to support an important feature of the EAGLE project, namely the Flagship Mobile Application as shown in the bottom part of Figure 2. To increase the visibility of EAGLE and to better exploit the wealth of data aggregated in the central repository, EAGLE is implementing an application targeted at "common end user", i.e. end users who are not scholars in Greek and Roman epigraphy.

A picture of an inscription found somewhere in Europe can be taken with a smartphone and sent to the EAGLE infrastructure. There the software will recognize the picture from within a database of inscriptions, and will provide all the information associated with that picture. For that purpose, during harvesting, the Image Feature Extractor will identify images (or links to images) in the incoming records, will fetch those images and will send them to the Image Recognizer for visual features extraction and indexing.

The application supports two modes of recognition. In the first mode, called "best match", the mobile device will receive back a list of inscriptions (each with a short description) in order of similarity with the image sent, and by selecting one of them the user will receive all the associated information; it may happen that none of the inscriptions in the result list is the image sent to the EAGLE infrastructure. In the second mode, called "exact identification", the mobile device will receive either a "not identified" answer, or all the information associated with the recognized image. To support this mode, in collaboration with the partners providing content to EAGLE, a subset of the material with visual representations will be selected to enrich it with additional historical and touristic material. The main criteria to select this subset will be the historical or touristic relevance of the inscription and the quality and quantity of images associated with it, as this will increase the probabilities of an exact recognition.

A more detailed description of the application can be found in [26].

5   Conclusions and Future Work

We have described the solutions adopted in the EAGLE project to achieve a complete integration of different ancient Greek and Latin epigraphic archives. The solution is based on the definition of a conceptual model and a common metadata schema that have, at the same time, the power to preserve the input metadata quality and the simplicity to enable simple mappings from all different archives. Metadata aggregation is based on the use of D-NET, a software toolkit to support the implementation of Aggregative Infrastructures. D-NET offers services for metadata collection, transformation, and provisioning and offers also a service-oriented framework for the seamless addition of new services and domain specific functionalities. This capability has proven very useful in EAGLE to implement and integrate the Metadata Record Inspector for advanced curation and validation services.

At the time of writing (July 2014) the EAGLE infrastructure is under test for the collection (to be done over the next few months) of the first set of epigraphic objects (about 375.000 objects). This first round of collections will be useful to check the adequacy of the common metadata schema and to fine tune the collection meta-workflows. The aggregator will then be ready for the production phase, to reach the final goal of about 1.500.000 epigraphic objects.

EAGLE is also actively conducting a "recruitment campaign" to enlarge the initial group of epigraphic archives that are partners in EAGLE. There are many other cultural institutions inside and outside Europe that have precious epigraphic material, and EAGLE can offer them the possibility of making their content visible and available to a much wider audience. That would also be interesting for the EAGLE conceptual model and the common metadata schema, to see to what extent they could accommodate new types of epigraphic records. In any case, both of them are dynamic structures that could easily be extended with a minimal impact over the whole architecture, since only the mappings and the transformation workflows would need to be changed.

From the technical point of view, planned future extension of the infrastructure deal with the development of a monitoring component enabling the analysis and control of the content processed by workflows against required quality levels and metrics (e.g. metadata coverage and completeness, metadata field consistency, content volume over time, etc.).

Acknowledgements. This work is partly funded by the EU EAGLE Best Practice Network project: Grant Agreement CIP 325122, call CIP-ICT-PSP-2012-6.

References

1. Van Groningen, B.A.: Projetd'unification des systèmes de signes critiques. Chronique d'Égypte 7, 262–269 (1932)
2. http://sourceforge.net/p/epidoc/wiki/Home/
3. Bodard, G.: The Inscriptions of Aphrodisias as electronic publication: A user's perspective and a proposed paradigm. Digital medievalist (2008)
4. The EAGLE project, http://www.eagle-network.eu/
5. Europeana, http://www.europeana.eu
6. D-NET Software Toolkit, http://www.d-net.research-infrastructures.eu
7. OAI-PMH, http://www.openarchives.org/pmh/
8. SRW/CQL, http://www.loc.gov/standards/sru/cql/
9. Arachne, http://arachne.uni-koeln.de/
10. CIDOC-CRM, http://www.cidoc-crm.org
11. UbiEratLupa, http://www.ubi-erat-lupa.org/
12. The Cyprus Institute, http://www.cyi.ac.cy/starc/research-information/starc-ongoing-projects-ri/item/310-starc-akgdc-archaia-kipriaki-grammateia-digital-corpus.html
13. Trismegistos, http://www.trismegistos.org
14. The EAGLE mediawiki, http://www.eagle-network.eu/wiki/index.php/Main_Page
15. Casarosa, V., Manghi, P., Mannocci, A., Rivero Ruiz, E., Zoppi, F.: A Conceptual Model for Inscriptions: Harmonizing Digital Epigraphy Data Sources. In: EAGLE International Conference on Information Technologies for Epigraphy and Digital Cultural Heritage in the Ancient World, Paris, September 29-30 and October 1 (2014)
16. The EAGLE Aggregation Conceptual Model, http://goo.gl/hwmyve
17. Manghi, P., Mikulicic, M., Candela, L., Castelli, D., Pagano, P.: Realizing and Maintaining Aggregative Digital Library Systems: D-NET Software Toolkit and OAIster System. D-Lib Magazine 16(3/4) (2010)
18. DRIVER Project, http://www.driver-community.eu/
19. OpenAIRE Project, http://www.openaire.eu/
20. HOPE Project, http://www.peoplesheritage.eu
21. The EFG project, http://www.europeanfilmgateway.eu/
22. Manghi, P., Bardi, A., Zoppi, F.: Coping with interoperability and sustainability in cultural heritage aggregative data infrastructures. International Journal of Metadata, Semantics and Ontologies 9(2), 138–154 (2014)

23. Manghi, P., Artini, M., Atzori C., Bardi, A., Mannocci, A., La Bruzzo, S., Candela, L., Castelli, D., Pagano, P.: The D-NET Software Toolkit: A Framework for the Realization, Maintenance, and Operation of Aggregative Infrastructures, http://www.emeraldinsight.com/journals.htm?issn=0033-0337 (to appear)

24. EpiDoc, http://sourceforge.net/projects/epidoc/files/Example%20Stylesheets/

25. Europeana PMH, http://pro.europeana.eu/edm-documentation/

26. Amato, G., Falchi, F., Rabitti, F., Vadicamo, L.: Epigraphs Visual Recognition - A comparison of state-of-the-art object recognition approaches. In: EAGLE International Conference on Information Technologies for Epigraphy and Digital Cultural Heritage in the Ancient World, Paris, September 29-30 and October 1 (2014)

27. SOLR, http://lucene.apache.org/solr/

Information Extraction from Bibliography for Marker-Assisted Selection in Wheat

Claire Nédellec[1], Robert Bossy[1], Dialekti Valsamou[1],
Marion Ranoux[2], Wiktoria Golik[1], and Pierre Sourdille[2]

[1] INRA, unité UR1077 MIG (Mathématique, Informatique et Génome),
Domaine de Vilvert, 78 352 Jouy-en-Josas, France
[2] INRA, UMR1095 GDEC (Génétique, Diversité, Ecophysiologie des Céréales),
Domaine de Crouël, 5 chemin de Beaulieu, 63 039 Clermont-Ferrand cedex, France
`prénom.nom@jouy.inra.fr,`
`prénom.nom@clermont.inra.fr`

Abstract. Improvement of most animal and plant species of agronomical interest in the near future has become an international stake because of the increasing demand for feeding a growing world population and to mitigate the reduction of the industrial resources. The recent advent of genomic tools contributed to improve the discovery of linkage between molecular markers and genes that are involved in the control of traits of agronomical interest such as grain number or disease resistance. This information is mostly published as scientific papers but rarely available in databases. Here, we present a method aiming at automatically extract this information from the scientific literature and relying on a knowledge model of the target information and on the *WheatPhenotype* ontology that we developed for this purpose. The information extraction results were evaluated and integrated into the on-line semantic search engine *AlvisIR WheatMarker*.

Keywords: information extraction, corpus annotation, natural language processing, ontology building, biology, genetics.

1 Introduction

A large amount of work has been done in information extraction (IE) from scientific literature in biology during the past decade. Most of this research has been applied to the extraction of genetic regulations in the molecular biology field, such as protein and gene interactions. It has been popularized by shared tasks (LLL [1], BioCreative [2], BioNLP-ST [3]). Nowadays, the extraction of organism trait and phenotype mentions from papers encounters a growing interest [4,5]. This knowledge is critical in many domains notably agriculture and health and it is rarely available in databases. The phenotypes of plant varieties of agronomical interest are described in scientific papers with the genetic information used for the variety selection. Compared to genetic regulations, the extraction of this knowledge is challenging in IE. In the domain of wheat selection assisted by molecular markers, the knowledge to be

S. Closs et al. (Eds.): MTSR 2014, CCIS 478, pp. 301–313, 2014.

extracted and formalized belongs to various fields, *e.g.* genetics, physiology, plant environment, food processing. Its representation involves several n-ary relations and entities that are complex to identify in the texts. The terms that denote traits and phenotypes are very diverse and difficult to predict.

The main approach in relation extraction (RE) for biology uses supervised machine learning trained with reference annotated corpora. The annotation follows a schema that defines the type of relations and entities to be extracted. In this paper we describe how we formalized the knowledge of marker-assisted selection in wheat into a text annotation schema that is appropriate both for the annotation of the reference corpus by domain experts and for the automatic extraction and representation of the knowledge (section 3). Common methods for entity prediction include dictionary matching, supervised machine learning and term analysis. This paper presents a multi-strategy named entity recognition (NER) method that takes into account the diversity of the entity naming and the availability of nomenclatures (section 4). The lack of a controlled vocabulary on wheat phenotypes and traits led us to build a domain specific ontology. The results of the NER methods were evaluated with the reference corpus and used in a bibliographical semantic search engine (section 5).

2   Wheat Selection Assisted by Genetic Marker

Improvement of most animal and plant species of agronomical interest in the near future has become an international stake because of the increasing demand for feeding a growing world population and to mitigate the reduction of the industrial resources especially the oil. The new environmental constraints such as the reduction of inputs (water, fertilizers and pesticides) and of acreages involve the development of new breeding schemes that must be shorter and more powerful. This increase needs a significant improvement of the agronomical potential of the species through breeding. This is especially true for wheat, the most widely grown crop worldwide.

Until now, the conventional selection methods lead to maintain the yields just covering the current consumption. The recent advent of genomic tools contributed to improve linkage between molecular markers and genes of agronomical interest. This information must now be integrated in breeding programs and the aim is to move from genetic toward genomic selection. A large number of varieties and molecular markers have been developed these last ten years for the bread wheat (see [6] for a review). However, the most useful information has to be extracted from thousands of scientific articles among which only a few are relevant. In addition, within each interesting paper, only a small part deal with the linkage itself, they indicate the name of the closest marker, the gene itself and the protocol that is useful to reveal the appropriate molecular signal that can be used for marker-assisted selection (MAS). Much more than retrieving relevant papers, breeders need to access the information in a structured form.

Our information extraction goal is the extraction of relationships between entities that are molecular markers, genes, traits, phenotypes and varieties from published papers. Traits are defined as observable characters such as the resistance to a given disease. The phenotypes are the values of the traits, *e.g.* the resistance or the susceptibility to a disease. The alleles of the genes are the different versions of the genes leading to the genotype of the individual. They control the phenotypes. An allele is generally attributed to a molecular marker. The marker discriminates the different alleles of a same gene with the polymorphism of the DNA sequence. The molecular markers are used to select the varieties with a phenotype of agronomic interest. The linkage between molecular markers and genes we focused on are related to four main subjects with high economic impact, (1) biotic stress: resistance to diseases (*e.g.* rust, fusarium, septoria), resistance to pest (*e.g.* greenbug, Cecidomyides, Hessian fly); (2) abiotic stress (*e.g.* drought, soil salinity, temperature, lodging), (3) plant development (*e.g.* vernalization, flowering) and (4) bread quality (*e.g.* grain hardness, protein content).

A given knowledge may be expressed in the text of the papers in different ways as shown in example 1. In example 2, we can see that many entities and relations may occur in a single sentence. These features make the information extraction task difficult.

Example 1. The phenotype resistance to leaf rust diseases that is controlled by the gene *Lr34* is expressed by the two very different clauses:

a. *the gene* Lr34 *confers resistance to leaf rust* [..]
b. *[..] lines missing* Lr34 *allele are susceptible.*

In clause a., the gene *Lr34* is explicitly designated as controlling the resistance phenotype, whilst clause b. states the same fact in an indirect way: the genotype where the gene *Lr34* has been knockout makes the wheat variety susceptible to the disease. This means that the variety needs the gene *Lr34* to be resistant.

Example 2. [PMID 20002313]

*only two alleles, photoperiod insensitive (*Ppd-D1a *and* Ppd-B1a*) and*

*photoperiod sensitive (*Ppd-D1b *and* Ppd-B1b*), respectively, at each locus were known*

The four allele entities (*Ppd-D1a*, *Ppd-D1b*, *Ppd-B1a*, *Ppd-B1b*) and the two phenotype entities (*photoperiod insensitive* and *photoperiod insensitive*) are the argument of four instances of the *allele_expresses_phenotype* relationships.

Despite this complexity, the recent progress of RE in molecular biology as evaluated in shared tasks open up possibilities of large scale extraction of complex events in the wheat MAS domain.

3   Knowledge Model and Annotated Corpus

The source of information on the linkage between molecular markers and genes in wheat is diverse. We identified 1,229 scientific journals that published relevant papers. These references were obtained by querying Web of Science (WoS) with the *wheat, marker* and *gene* keywords. It yielded 3,170 references to scientific papers. Among the retrieved references, we selected 125 relevant journals according to their availability, their impact, their scope, their geographical area and the frequency of relevant publication. A corpus of 2,097 full-texts (*WheatMAS* corpus) was then obtained from the journal publishers that concentrate the target knowledge.

With the breeder experts, we built the MAS knowledge model for the representation of the relevant information of the text. The knowledge model contains 8 entity types and 14 n-ary relationships (10 binary relationships and 4 ternary relationships) that are shown in Figures 1a and 1b. The main entity types are marker, allele and gene, trait and phenotype and variety. *Type* represents the method used to identify the marker, *e.g.* AFLP, microsatellite, which is useful for the evaluation of its quality.

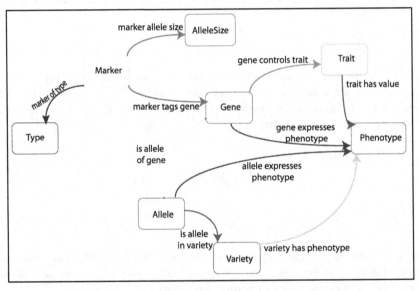

Fig. 1a. Binary relations of the knowledge model for wheat MAS

Binary relations may be used instead of ternary relations when an argument is missing. For instance, *marker_tags_gene* is used instead of *marker_tags_gene_in_variety* when the wheat variety is not mentioned in the text.

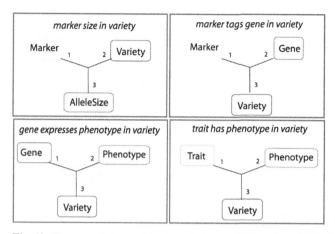

Fig. 1b. Ternary relations of the knowledge model for wheat MAS

Our RE method relies on the deep linguistic analysis and the supervised machine learning tools of the AlvisNLP pipeline [7]. The supervised machine learning method requires a training corpus of reference examples. For this purpose, we designed a corpus of 72 papers that were selected for their representativeness, most of them in *Theoretical and Applied Genetics, International Journal of Plant Breeding Research.* This journal publishes numerous manuscripts mentioning linkage between traits and molecular markers in wheat and is available on-line. 13 domain experts, mainly breeders and the GDEC authors of this paper annotated the corpus with the MAS knowledge model as annotation schema. To ensure effective and consistent annotation, we provided them with a guideline manual that describes the entities and the relations; it defines them and gives many examples that illustrate frequent and borderline cases. The annotation process follows the standard practice: double-blind annotation followed by adjudication. The text was automatically pre annotated by AlvisNLP with the entities that were frequent and easy to recognize in order to speed-up the manual annotation. The annotation editor AlvisAE [8] supported the whole process. The annotation campaign was defined by the annotation schema, the document collection and the two-step workflow. The 13 users were assigned a batch of documents to annotate and revise. We chose AlvisAE as annotation editor for its campaign specification tool and for its graphical user interface that was designed for non-computer scientists (Figure 2). The annotators were able to use it after one-day tutorial session. With AlvisAE the users annotated overlapping and discontinuous annotations. They also annotated co-references, which avoid the annotations of the repeated information.

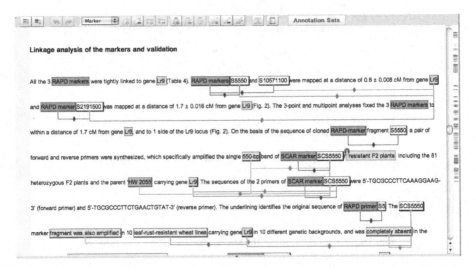

Fig. 2. The main screen of AlvisAE annotation editor. The entities are highlighted. The lines figure the relationships between the entities, for instance, the *maker tags the gene* relationship between S5550 and *Lr9* in the first line.

The double-blind annotation phase is achieved and the adjudication phase is ongoing. The annotators fully annotated the 293 sections in the 72 corpus papers that were relevant. Table 1 displays the distribution of the entity and relation annotations. The distribution reflects the importance of the different information for breeding. The gene, variety, trait, marker and marker type are the most frequent and critical. Conversely, the alleles are rarely named, which explains the low number of allele annotations.

Table 1. Number of manual annotations in the wheat MAS training corpus

Entities		Binary relations		Ternary relations	
Gene	1,826	marker_of_type	307	gene_expresses_phenotype_in_variety	103
Variety	1,284	gene_controls_trait	260	marker_size_in_variety	58
Marker	703	variety_has_phenotype	224	marker_tags_gene_in_variety	24
Type	508	marker_tags_gene	184	trait has phenotype in variety	24
Trait	603	allele_expresses_phenotype	107		**207**
Phenotype	403	is_allele_of_gene	107		
Allele	368	is_allele_in_variety	64		
AlleleSize	153	marker_alleleSize	55		
	5 848	trait has value	34		
			1 342		

It does not affect the extraction results since the allele name is not required for the extraction of the linkage between the marker and the phenotype.

4   Named Entity Recognition

We used two different methods for the recognition of the named entities. We distinguished the rigid designators [9] from the other names. They are proper names, numbers and acronyms. They denote genes, markers, marker identification methods, allele sizes and varieties. Conversely, the phenotype and trait names are subject to more variation.

4.1   Recognition of Proper Names and Acronyms

The NER method uses dictionaries such as gene and marker lists of the GrainGenes[1] database and hand-coded extraction patterns. The patterns identify typographic variations and perform word-sense disambiguation with the context of the target word. Disambiguation is particularly needed for the recognition of variety names that have frequent homonyms in the text, *e.g.* Leeds is cited both as a variety and a university. The quality of the method predictions has been evaluated with respect to the reference corpus. Table 2 displays the recall, precision and F_1 measures for an exact match and for a partial overlap between the predicted and the reference entities. F_1 is the harmonic mean of the precision and recall. The recognition of the names of the genes and markers is affected by homonymy: the marker of the gene is denoted by the same name as the gene. The reference annotations of markers and genes are mostly of good quality. Gain in prediction quality is to be found in the improvement of the disambiguation method and the gene name boundary identification. The performance of partial overlap in gene name recognition is 12 points over the exact match, which shows that the predicted gene name boundaries are often not correct.

Table 2. Quality of the named entity recognition

	Exact match			Partial overlap		
	Recall	Precision	F_1	Recall	Precision	F_1
Gene	0,61	0,49	0,54	0,73	0,61	0,66
Marker	0,58	0,65	0,61	0,59	0,66	0,62
Type	0,54	0,62	0,58	0,56	0,64	0,60
AlleleSize	0,39	0,49	0,43	0,46	0,50	0,48

The poor result of the recognition of the allele size is due to many errors in the reference corpus. Allele size names are numbers followed by *bp* (base pair) as *103 bp*. A close examination of the reference corpus revealed a high number of incorrect reference annotations, for instance *Ppd-D1a* designates an allele and not a size. Many annotated allele size represent an absence of the allele, for instance, *absence of PCR products*. An accurate correction of the reference corpus will allow a more significant evaluation of AlleleSize prediction quality.

---

[1] http://wheat.pw.usda.gov/GG2/

The examination of the experimental results of named entity recognition shows us clear directions for further improvement.

4.2   Recognition of Phenotypes and Traits

4.2.1   The *ToMap* Method

The recognition of the trait and phenotype terms cannot be efficiently achieved by the direct matching of dictionary entries with the text because of the high variability of the terms. Instead we used our ToMap method, previously named OntoMap [10]. ToMap requires a domain terminology and the results of a term extractor applied to the text. It matches the extracted terms with the terms of the terminology to determine which type of entity the extracted terms designate. The principle of the ToMap method is close to MetaMap method for the recognition of UMLS thesaurus terms in a corpus [11]. The matching relies on the similarity of the syntactic structures of the terms to be matched together. ToMap is applicable to any kind of text and terminology, being structured or not. ToMap has shown good results in the recognition of bacteria biotopes of the shared task *BioNLP-ST Bacteria Biotope* in 2011 and 2013 [12,13]. We used the term extractor BioYateA that is particularly well suited for this task because it provides the syntactic structure of the extracted terms and it extracts terms with prepositional phrases, e.g. *to crown rot* in *partial seedling resistance to crown rot* as described in [14].

4.2.2   The WheatPhenotype Ontology

We built an ontology dedicated to the description of phenotypes and traits in wheat called *WheatPhenotype*. The available terminologies and ontologies were not fully relevant to our IE purpose. The most suitable is the Trait Ontology[2] (TO), a controlled vocabulary that describes traits of plants of agronomic interest. It includes relevant traits such as disease resistance, development traits, but also many traits that are irrelevant to wheat selection (*e.g.* biochemical, molecular, anatomy and morphology) and some over general trait (*e.g.* plant aspect) that are not mentioned in wheat selection texts. Conversely, TO lacks many specific traits and synonyms in all categories. The resistance to fungal disease is a critical trait in wheat selection. Only 8 fungus resistance concepts relevant to the wheat are defined in TO; we identified 24 in the texts and databases. Moreover, in the scientific papers disease resistance is often described by the resistance to the pathogens that cause the disease, for instance, *resistance to fusarium head blight* is equivalent to *resistance to Fusarium graminearum* where *Fusarium graminearum* is one of the fungus species that causes *fusarium head blight*. TO does not record such information. Moreover many different names can be used for each fungus. For instance, *Microdochium nivale* that also causes *fusarium head blight* is also called *Fusarium nivale*. The listing of all pathogen names and acronyms for all wheat disease is needed for efficient information extraction. Another important information is bread-making quality since the selected

---

[2] http://archive.gramene.org/db/ontology/search?id=TO:0000387

varieties determines the quality of the flour for bread making (mechanical and sensorial properties).

The current version of the *WheatPhenotype* ontology defines 409 concepts with 361 synonyms. Its hierarchical structure comprises 9 levels. Figure 3 shows the main levels.

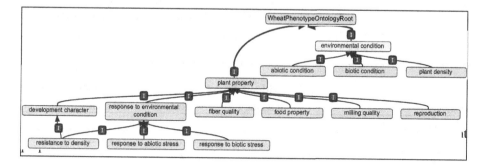

Fig. 3. The highest levels of the *WheatPhenotype* ontology

The abiotic factors represent the physico-chemical conditions of the plant development (water availability, temperature, wind force, soil composition). The properties of the plant are organized in six sub trees, the response to environmental factors, the development, the reproduction, the product processing and the quality of the product (fiber and food). All traits and phenotypes are considered, including the less studied (*e.g.* aluminum tolerance), but the response to biotic factors, in particular to fungal and bacterial pathogens, is the most developed. The *cause* relationship links *pathogens* to the corresponding infectious *diseases* defined in the biotic condition sub tree. The *WheatPhenotype* ontology will be made publicly available in Obo format after alignment to TO. The common concepts with TO will be explicitly identified by a cross reference as an xref property.

4.2.3 Experimental Results of Phenotype and Trait Prediction

We applied the ToMap method to the terms extracted by BioYateA from the training corpus by using the WheatPhenotype ontology. As already noticed for the allele size annotation, the quality of the trait and phenotype annotation of the reference corpus was not sufficient for a reliable evaluation of ToMap predictions. The on-going adjudication phase will detect these errors and correct them.

(1) A frequent error confuses genotypes with phenotypes and alleles. For instance, the term *wild type* denotes an organism, but it is frequently annotated as a phenotype or as an allele, *e.g. wild type alleles WB357* means the allele WB357 of the wild-type line.

(2) The confusion between the environmental factors and the phenotypes is also frequent, for instance *winter* is annotated as a phenotype by analogy with the phenotype *winter habit* that denotes the growth period of the variety.

(3) The phenotype value is also confused with the trait, for instance *ToxA sensitivity* is confused with *ToxA sensitive*.

To obtain a reliable experimental result, we manually validated the results of the method applied on the abstracts of a subset of 870 papers. The ToMap method classified 299 terms as denoting a phenotype or a trait among the terms extracted by BioYateA. The manual validation of the classified terms yielded a precision rate but not a recall rate for which a reference annotation is required. Table 3 details the experimental results for two versions of the method, without and with disambiguation.

Table 3. Precision of the phenotype and trait prediction

Category	Without disambiguation		With disambiguation	
	# terms	Rate	# terms	Rate
Positive	245	81%	212	95%
Correct and informative	227	76%	176	79%
Correct and general	18	6%	36	16%
Negative	54	19%	11	5%
Linguistic analysis error	5	1,7%	4	2%
ToMap error	16	5,4%	7	3%
ToMap setting error	33	11 %	0	0%

The first line gives a high precision rate of 81% that we divided into a correct and informative category (76%) and a correct but general category (6%). General terms are not useful for breeding but they are relevant for knowledge modeling. *Plant morphologic trait* is an example. A closer analysis of the false positive examples showed that a small number of the errors are due to linguistic preprocessing: word segmentation by the in-house tool SegMig and POS-tagging by TreeTagger [15]. Most of ToMap errors were due to an incorrect setting (11%). ToMap setting involves the setting of the list of term heads that are non-discriminant with respect to the named entity recognition goal. The list is dependent of the domain. The word *content* is an example of a non-discriminant head. It occurs in trait terms such as *Grain Protein Content* or *reduction in DON content*, but also in other terms, e.g. *polymorphism information content*. A better discrimination of terms with such heads was obtained by post-processing disambiguation hand-coded rules that used the words of the terms and their contexts. We also designed some domain specific rules to improve the boundary prediction by excluding irrelevant words such as *main* in the term *main growth habits*. As a result, the precision rate increased by 14 points to reach 95%. The total number of positive terms decreased from 245 to 212. Most of the 33 removed terms were not classified as negative, but merged with other terms as a result of the boundary correction (*main growth habits* and *growth habits* were counted as one instead of two in the previous setting).

These preliminary experiments are very promising yielding a precision rate of 95% in the prediction of traits and phenotypes for wheat selection. The reference manual annotations once consolidated will allow measuring the recall and F_1.

5   The *AlvisIR WheatMarker* Bibliographical Search Engine

The semantic search engine *AlvisIR WheatMarker* indexes the document collection of 2,097 scientific papers about the linkage between molecular markers and genes that will be used for information extraction. The search engine index includes all entities defined in the knowledge model. The trait and phenotype index was built with the WheatPhenotype ontology, which means that query terms may contain high-level concepts of the ontology that will be searched together with all specializations and synonyms.

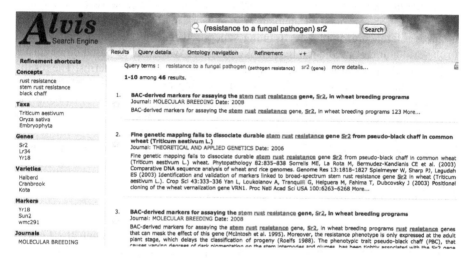

Fig. 4. Interface of the semantic search engine *AlvisIR WheatMarker*

Figure 4 shows the results of the query (*resistance to a fungal pathogen*) *sr2* that aims at retrieving papers about *sr2* involvement in any resistance to fungal pathogens. The snippets (short extracts) of the 46 relevant documents are displayed below the query. The relevant terms are highlighted in the same colors as the query terms, *sr2* gene in green, resistance to fungal pathogen in red. With its semantic capabilities, AlvisIR retrieves many different fungal pathogen resistances such as *stem rust resistance* as highlighted in the three first snippets. The left panel displays the facets, the most frequent index values in the answer set. The query can be refined by the selection of a facet. *AlvisIR WheatMarker* semantic search engine is publically available[3]. The current version of the search engine does not index the relations for which the information extraction methods are under development.

Once the marker information will be fully extracted, it will be indexed by the *AlvisIR WheatMarker* search engine. It will also be integrated in a public database interconnected with all relevant genetic information, physical map, the 4000 known markers and the available wheat chromosome sequences [16,17,18]. It is worth to

---

[3] http://bibliome.jouy.inra.fr/test/alvisir/FSOV/

note that ToMap not only extract phenotypes and traits from the papers but also normalize them with respect to the WheatPhenotype Ontology, enabling heterogeneous data integration.

6   Conclusion

The extraction of the available information on molecular marker published in scientific papers is a key issue for marker-assisted selection. It is particularly critical for wheat breeders that do not have access to this information in structured databases. We proposed a knowledge model that formalizes the knowledge needs in the form of an entity-relation schema. Our annotation framework involving a team of 13 breeders produces reference examples for training supervised machine learning methods and for the evaluation of prediction results. We proposed two methods based on linguistic analysis for the recognition of entities denoted by proper names and terms. The results evaluated on reference data yielded very encouraging results. The lack of structured vocabulary for extracting and normalizing phenotypes and traits led us to build the *WheatPhenotype* ontology. The prediction results and the *WheatPhenotype* ontology are used by the semantic search engine *AlvisIRWheatMarker* that index the full-text of the major papers of the domain. In the future, once consolidated, the reference wheat marker corpus will be made available to the community. It will be used for the training of the relation extraction methods. The overall approach will be then applied to other plants of agronomic interest, such as maize.

Acknowledgments. This work was partially funded by Oséo through the Quaero project and by FSOV through the SAM blé project. The authors thanks Jérôme Auzanneau (Agri-Obtention), Stéphane Boury (Caussade Semences), Emmanuelle Cariou-Pham (Arvalis), Clément Debiton (Unisigma), Noëmie Desmouceaux (Syngenta), Laure Duchalais (RAGT), Ellen Goudemand (Florimond Desprez), Pierre-Marie Le Roux (Secobra), Vanessa S. Windhausen (Saaten Union), Stephen Sunderwirth (Momont) for their participation to the annotation of the corpus.

References

1. Nédellec, C.: Learning Language in Logic – Genic Interaction Extraction Challenge. In: Proc 4th Learning Language in Logic Workshop (LLL 2005), pp. 31–37 (2005)
2. Hirschman, L., Yeh, A., Blaschke, C., Valencia, A.: Overview of BioCreAtIvE: critical assessment of information extraction for biology. BMC Bioinformatics 6(suppl. 1), S1 (2005)
3. Kim, J.D., Ohta, T., Pyysalo, S., Kano, Y., Tsujii, J.: Extracting bio-molecular events from literature – The BioNLP 2009 Shared Task. Computational Intelligence 27(4), 513–540 (2011)
4. Golik, W., et al.: ATOL: the multi-species livestock trait ontology. In: Dodero, J.M., Palomo-Duarte, M., Karampiperis, P. (eds.) MTSR 2012. CCIS, vol. 343, pp. 289–300. Springer, Heidelberg (2012)

5. Collier, N., Tran, M.-V., Le, H.-Q., Ha, Q.-T., Oellrich, A., et al.: Learning to Recognize Phenotype Candidates in the Auto-Immune Literature Using SVM Re-Ranking. PLoS One 8(10), e72965 (2013), doi:10.1371/journal.pone.0072965

6. Paux, E., Faure, S., Choulet, F., Roger, D., Gauthier, V., Martinant, J.-P., Sourdille, P., Balfourier, F., Lepaslier, M.-C., Brunel, D., Cakir, M., Gandon, B., Feuillet, C.: Insertion site based polymorphism markers open new perspectives for genome saturation and marker-assisted selection in wheat. Plant Biotechnol. J. (2009)

7. Nédellec, C., Nazarenko, A., Bossy, R.: Information Extraction. In: Staab, S., Studer, R. (eds.) Ontology Handbook, 2nd edn., pp. 663–686. Springer, Berlin (2009)

8. Papazian, F., Bossy, R., Nédellec, C.: AlvisAE: a collaborative Web text annotation editor for knowledge acquisition. In: Proc. 6th Linguistic Annotation Workshop (The LAW VI), pp. 149–152 (2012)

9. Kripke, S.: Naming and Necessity. Harvard University Press, Boston (1982)

10. Golik, W., Warnier, P., Nédellec, C.: Corpus-based extension of termino-ontology by linguistic analysis: a use case in biomedical event extraction. In: Proc. 9th Intl Conf. Terminology and Artificial Intelligence (TIA 2011), pp. 37–39 (2011)

11. Aronson, A.R., Lang, F.M.: An overview of MetaMap: historical perspective and recent advances. Journal of the American Medical Informatics Association 17(3), 229–236 (2010)

12. Ratkovic, Z., Golik, W., Warnier, P.: Event extraction of bacteria biotopes: a knowledge-intensive NLP-based approach. BMC Bioinformatics 13(suppl. 11), S8 (2012)

13. Bossy, R., Golik, W., Ratkovic, Z., Bessières, P., Nédellec, C.: BioNLP Shared Task 2013 – an overview of the bacteria biotope task. In: Proc BioNLP Shared Task 2013 Workshop 2013, pp. 74–82. Association for Computational Linguistics, ACL (2013)

14. Golik, W., Bossy, R., Ratkovic, Z., Nédellec, C.: Improving term extraction with linguistic analysis in the biomedical domain. In: Proceedings of the 14th International Conference on Intelligent Text Processing and Computational Linguistics (CICLing 2013), Samos, Greece (2013)

15. Schmid, H.: Probabilistic Part-of-Speech Tagging Using Decision Trees. In: Proceedings of International Conference on New Methods in Language Processing, Manchester, UK (1994)

16. Raats, D., Frenkel, Z., Krugman, T., Dodek, I., Sela, H., Simková, H., Magni, F., Cattonaro, F., Vautrin, S., Bergès, H., Wicker, T., Keller, B., Leroy, P., Philippe, R., Paux, E., Doležel, J., Feuillet, C., Korol, A., Fahima, T.: The physical map of wheat chromosome 1BS provides insights into its gene space organization and evolution. Genome Biol. 14(12), R138 (2013)

17. Choulet, F., Alberti, A., Theil, S., Glover, N., Barbe, V., et al.: Analysis of the wheat chromosome 3B reference sequence reveals structural and functional compartmentalization. Science 345 (2014), doi:10.1126/science.1249721

18. International Wheat Genome Sequencing Consortium (IWGSC) A chromosome-based draft sequence of the hexaploid bread wheat (Triticum aestivum) genome. Science 345 (2014), doi: 10.1126/science.1251788

SKOS Sources Transformations for Ontology Engineering: Agronomical Taxonomy Use Case

Fabien Amarger[1,2], Jean-Pierre Chanet[2], Ollivier Haemmerlé[1],
Nathalie Hernandez[1], and Catherine Roussey[2]

[1] IRIT, UMR 5505, UT2J, Département de Mathématiques-Informatique, 5 allées
Antonio Machado, F-31058 Toulouse Cedex, France
`firstname.lastname@univ-tlse2.fr`
[2] TSCF, Irstea de Clermont Ferrand, 9 av. Blaise Pascal CS 20085,
63172 Aubière, France
`firstname.lastname@irstea.fr`

Abstract. Sources like thesauri or taxonomies are already used as input in ontology development process. Some of them are also published on the LOD using the SKOS format. Reusing this type of sources to build an ontology is not an easy task. The ontology developer has to face different syntax and different modelling goals. We propose in this paper a new methodology to transform several non-ontological sources into a single ontology. We take into account: the redundancy of the knowledge extracted from sources in order to discover the consensual knowledge and Ontology Design Patterns (ODPs) to guide the transformation process. We have evaluated our methodology by creating an ontology on wheat taxonomy from three sources: Agrovoc thesaurus, TaxRef taxonomy, NCBI taxonomy.

Keywords: Ontology Development, Ontology Design Pattern, Non-Ontological Sources, SKOS, Trust, Agriculture.

1 Introduction

The French Ministry of Agriculture has launched the Ecophyto plan [1] in order to reduce drastically pesticide use. Ecophyto includes several monitoring systems of agricultural practices. One of those is based on alert bulletins that inform farmers of pest attacks on crops. Thus, farmers adapt their crop treatements based on these alerts. These bulletins are called "Bulletin de Santé du Végétal" (BSV) [2]. In order to follow the evolution of pest attacks over several decades, these bulletins need to be gathered, analysed and annotated. The first step to help the annotating process is to build a reference source on any organism that could appear in the fields (crop plant, crop auxiliary, crop aggressor). This reference source is stored as Knowledge Base (KB) in OWL format [3].

---

[1] `http://agriculture.gouv.fr/ecophyto`
[2] `http://agriculture.gouv.fr/ecophyto-BSV`
[3] `http://www.w3.org/TR/owl2-overview/`

S. Closs et al. (Eds.): MTSR 2014, CCIS 478, pp. 314–328, 2014.
© Springer International Publishing Switzerland 2014

In agriculture, many data are available in various electronic formats about crops: thesauri, databases... The next challenge is to make these data available to all stakeholders (farmers, agronomist researchers) so that they can use the data in decision support and analysis tools. Linked Open Data (LOD) is an opportunity to accelerate the sharing of data. Thus we want to publish on the LOD the annotations of alert bulletins.

In this paper we describe a method to build a Knowledge Base (an ontology populated with individuals) from various sources. Unfortunately, we cannot trust all the extracted knowledge with the same confidence, because some errors appear in some sources [17]. Thus we propose a new method based on redundancy and trust scores to filter trustable knowledge.

This paper is organised as follows: Section 2 presents a state of the art about ontology engineering and trust. Then our proposition is explained in section 3. Some experiments are presented and discussed in section 4. We conclude and present our future works in section 5.

2   State of the Art

2.1   Reusing Non-Ontological Sources

Most part of ontology engineering methods use non-ontological sources during knowledge extraction processes. We can cite for example the MethOntology [7], the method [20] of the Neon methodology [18] or the SMOL methodology [9]. In our work we focus only on ontology engineering methods using Knowledge Organisation System (KOS) like thesauri, taxonomies and classification schemes because they are the most current to describe and classify organisms. Many knowledge organisation systems share a similar structure, and are used in similar applications. KOS can be defined as a hierarchical organisation of normalised terms used to classify any real entities. Some of the KOS are available on the LOD using the Simple Knowledge Organisation System (SKOS) [4] format. The figure 1 presents a SKOS example which comes from the Agrovoc thesaurus. We studied ten methods able to create a knowledge base in OWL format using KOS [1]. These methods can be classified as manual, semi-automatic or automatic.

manual The more recent methods [14] [3] and [13] are manual methods. This can be explained by the difficulties to translate a KOS conceptual structure into a knowledge base, due to the fact that the semantics of the KOS structure do not imply any logical formalisation. Thus the KOS conceptual structure is ambiguous for a logical point of view. For example, the figure 1 contains two hierarchies using the *skos : broader* links. The left one defines different kinds of taxa (kingdom and phylum). The right one defines a taxonomy about plant organisms.

automatic In methods proposing some automatic processes, some of them follows the same strategy. They generate an *owl : class* for each normalised

---

[4] http://www.w3.org/TR/2009/REC-skos-reference-20090818/

term. Each hierarchical relation is transformed into an $owl : subClassOf$ relation. In this category we can cite [21,11,20,10,4]. The figure 2 illustrates the automatic transformation of the Agrovoc example of figure 1. Let us point out that some of the $owl : subClassOf$ relationships are false: A Phylum taxon is not a Kingdom one. To overcome this drawback, [20,11] includes a disambiguation process to validate the $owl : subClassOf$ relationship.

semi automatic Others proposed to associate a specific $owl : object\ property$ that can be the $owl : subClassOf$ one with the hierarchical relation of the KOS [17,19].

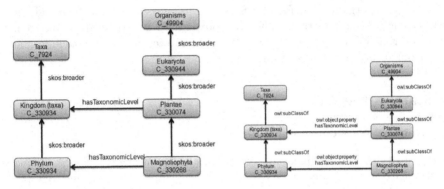

Fig. 1. example of agrovoc in SKOS format

Fig. 2. Automatic transformation of agrovoc example

All these methods show that the KOS transformation should be guided in order to build a valuable knowledge base. Thus we decided to reuse Ontology Design Patterns [8] to guide the transformation of a KOS. An Ontology Design Pattern (ODP) is defined as a modelling solution to a recurrent ontology design problem [8]. ODPs are normally generated by experienced ontology engineers, who submit them to online repositories[5]. These patterns are evaluated by the Ontology Engineering community and generally accepted as good practices.

2.2   Ontological Object Trust

Extracting ontological objects from various non-ontological sources with different qualities requires a consideration of trust on these objects. Several trust definitions in computer science and semantic web are presented in [2]. The one which corresponds the most to our purpose is:

"Trust of a party A to a party B for a service X is the measurable belief of A in that B behaves dependable for a specified period within a specified context (in relation to service X)."

---

[5] For instance, the repository at http://ontologydesignpatterns.org

Consider A as the user who wants to create a knowledge base, B as a source and X the extraction process. In this definition, trust is about a source B, with the extraction process X, which generates ontological objects with a trust score associated. This definition is very suitable for our purpose because they consider that a trust score is specific for a period, a context and a service. This corresponds to the fact that the trust on a source is variable depending on the objective of the project, the time and the source itself.

Using multiple sources to extract ontological objects leads to an aggregation of trust scores: Finding the same ontological object in several sources will increase the trust score of this object. As shown on [5] the aggregation of trust scores is more effective than classic approaches.

2.3   Synthesis

The method we propose can be seen as the combination of two Neon ontology engineering methods [18]: the one based on ODP [15] and the one based on non-ontological source transformations with NOR2O [20]. Note that in the SMOL methodology, the authors include a "knowledge structure construction" method in order to reorganise and harmonise the conceptual structures inherited from different sources. Moreover the Hepp method [11] includes an ODP to transform the KOS, because for 2 terms linked by a hierarchical relation, 4 $owl : classes$ and 3 $owl : subClasOf$ properties are build. Our method can be seen as a generalisation of [11] where different ODPs can be used depending of the domain of the ontology.

Moreover we take in consideration the consensus about each ontological object, to determine if we want to keep it or not. To do so, we use a trust score computed between all the sources used to extract ontological objects. As fas as we know, there is no ontology engineering method ables to transform KOS using consensus and ODPs. About consensus, we have to define a function to compute trust score and a way to aggregate them.

3   Our General Approach

Due to its completeness we selected the Neon methodology to build a KB. Neon proposes a set of nine methods for collaboratively building ontologies. Our ontology engineering method consists of adapting and merging two Neon methods.

Our method is composed of three processes detailed in next sections:

1 - **Source analysing:** During this process, the domain expert and the ontologist work together to select the most appropriate sources to build their KB. They inspect each source to evaluate its coverage and to have a broad idea if the source can be transformed to an KB or not.

2 - **Source Transformation** This process transforms each source into an KB in OWL format. It is based on Neon methods.

3 - KBs Merging This process builds the final KB based on all KBs extracted from sources. As far as we known, this process is not proposed in any ontology engineering method. Usually ontology engineering method uses several sources separately in order to enrich the KB in a incremental way. The merging process uses several KBs at the same time in order to extract consensual knowledge.

3.1 Source Transformation

The figure 3 present our "source transformation" process, which contains several other processes. The "module construction" is the Neon scenario 7 [8]. The scenario 7 proposes to build a module re-using Ontology Design Patterns (ODPs) and competency questions. We fully apply this method to build modules. The module is built once and is used for all the "source automatic transformation" processes. The "syntactic transformation" is an adaptation of the Neon scenario 2 [20]. The scenario 2 proposes to build a KB reusing non ontological source. We adapt this method to enrich modules previously build by scenario 7.

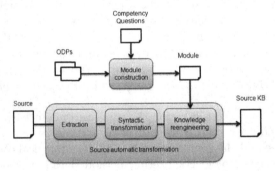

Fig. 3. Source transformation process

Module Construction. The current best practice to create an ontology is to reuse ODPs. We follow the method [8] in order to generate modules. An example of one of our modules is Agronomic Taxon [16] (c.f. appendix 6.1) which has been manually built for a specific task (representing organism scientific name using taxonomy). The module is composed of $owl : Classes$ and defines the set of $owl : Properties$ that may exist between them. It re-uses some ODPs coming from Neon project and two vocabularies already published on the LOD [16].

The Agronomic Taxon module models living organism taxonomy. All the taxon types wanted in our knowledge base are defined in the module as $owl : class$, child of the $neon : Taxon$ class. For example we only focus on the seven most known taxon types: kingdom, phylum, class, order, family, genus and species. The next process will use the sources to enrich automatically this module. The final KB should contains several taxa, individuals of the class $neon : Taxon$ that are used to describe organisms appearing in fields.

Source Automatic Transformation. As generally each non-ontological source follows some modelling principles and is implemented in a specific format. For example Agrovoc follows the modelling principles of multilingual thesaurus and is available in the SKOS format. The [20] [17] methods proposes transformation using patterns. The [20] method takes in account the modelling and implementation choices and applies the same transformation pattern on the source. The [17] method takes in account that the modelling choices may change over the same source and that the same pattern can not be applied on the whole source. We will take advantage on these two methods and apply transformation based on pattern.

As shown in Figure 3, we extract first from the source, the parts that seem to follow the same modelling principles and that meet our requirements. The previous "source analysing" process has defined that these parts exist in the source. Secondly we apply a syntactic transformation using [20] method and tools in order to have a file following the OWL syntax. The "knowledge engineering" activity produces a new owl file which is an enrichment of the module that is to say a KB. To do so, the module is mapped to the first owl file. The output is a set of mappings. Then the module is expanded using the owl file and following new pattern that re-engineered the owl file. Thus the new OWL axioms are compatibles with the module.

For example, if Agrovoc was selected during the "source analyzing" process. The experts decide that it is a good source to build a KB about plant taxonomy. They decide to work on the SKOS file of the Agrovoc thesaurus. Based on the module Agronomic Taxon, we will illustrate the "source automatic transformation" process. First we extract from Agrovoc all the data related to plant taxonomy (see figure 1), that is to say all the $skos : concepts$ under Taxa and under Plantae. Then we apply a transformation pattern based on thesaurus and SKOS format as presented in the section 2. We obtain an owl file like the figure 2. We first mapped manually the owl file to Agronomic Taxon module. The $owl : classes\ neon : Taxon$, $neon : Kingdom, neon : Phylum,$ and so one are mapped to $owl : class$ of Agrovoc file. Now we apply a re-engineering pattern (c.f. the appendix 6.3). This algorithm creates a new individual for each class representing a plant taxon. Using the $hasTaxonomicLevel$ link of Agrovoc the individual is typed by the corresponding rank type (Kingdom, Phylum and so one). Then the hierarchy between taxa is depicted using the $neon : hasHigherRank$ property of the Agronomic Taxon module. At the end of the re-engineered pattern the source KB contain the module plus new individuals as proposed in figure 4.

3.2   KBs Merging

The figure 5 shows that the merging of KBs previously built, named *Source KB*, is composed of three activities:

Mapping: this activity computes Alignments between all the *Source KBs*. Mapping activity identifies similar ontological objects contained in distinct *Source KBs*.

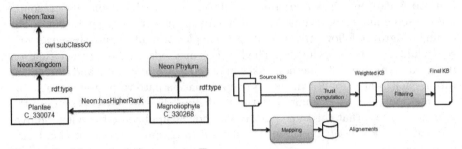

Fig. 4. Enrichment of Agronomic Taxon module using Agrovoc

Fig. 5. KB Engineering process

Trust computation: This activity identifies candidates and computes their trust score. A candidate contains a set of ontological objects that are found similar by the mapping activity.

Filtering: This activity filters candidates according to their trust score and add them in the final KB.

(1) Mapping Aligning KB_1 and KB_2 consists in computing all the mappings between objects of KB_1 and objects of KB_2. This is a large research area [6] and a lot of methods have been proposed and implemented in tools. We choose to use LogMap [12] because it can map any ontological objects, it obtains good results in OAEI Challenge[6] and its source code is available online[7] Let us define a mapping m as a triplet $< e_i, e_j, s_{ij} >$ such as:

$e_i \in KB_i$: is an ontological object belonging to KB_i ,
$e_j \in KB_j$: is another ontological object belonging to KB_j ($KB_j \neq KB_i$),
s_{ij}: is the similarity degree between e_i and e_j.

We define a function called $degree(e_i, e_j)$ from $KB_i \times KB_j$ to $[0, 1]$. Where $s_{ij} = degree(e_i, e_j)$ is the similarity score between e_i and e_j given by the mapping tool and 0 if there is no mapping.

(2) Trust Computation Due to space limitation of the article, we present two kinds of candidate, but more candidate types are taken in account in our method.

Individual Candidate (ic): Individuals are instances of classes. We define an individual candidate ic as a set of mappings that share common individuals. Each individual, belonging to a candidate, should belong to a distinct knowledge base.

---

[6] Ontology Alignment Evaluation Initiative -
http://oaei.ontologymatching.org/2013/
[7] https://code.google.com/p/logmap-matcher/.

Relation Candidate (rc):   the instances of property that links two individual
candidates. We define a relation candidate rc as a pair of individual candidates, such as there exist some instance of the same properties that link
components of individual candidates.

We define $dim(c)$ as the number of KBs involved in a candidate c.

Let consider the example in Figure 6 with three knowledge bases KB_1, KB_2
and KB_3. KB_1 and KB_3 contains two individuals a_i, b_i linked by the same
property p. The dash line represent mapping between individuals. There are two
individual candidates ic_1 and ic_2 and one relation candidate rc_1.

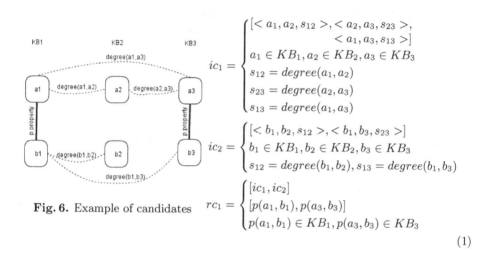

$$ic_1 = \begin{cases} [< a_1, a_2, s_{12} >, < a_2, a_3, s_{23} >, \\ \quad\quad\quad < a_1, a_3, s_{13} >] \\ a_1 \in KB_1, a_2 \in KB_2, a_3 \in KB_3 \\ s_{12} = degree(a_1, a_2) \\ s_{23} = degree(a_2, a_3) \\ s_{13} = degree(a_1, a_3) \end{cases}$$

$$ic_2 = \begin{cases} [< b_1, b_2, s_{12} >, < b_1, b_3, s_{23} >] \\ b_1 \in KB_1, b_2 \in KB_2, b_3 \in KB_3 \\ s_{12} = degree(b_1, b_2), s_{13} = degree(b_1, b_3) \end{cases}$$

Fig. 6. Example of candidates $$rc_1 = \begin{cases} [ic_1, ic_2] \\ [p(a_1, b_1), p(a_3, b_3)] \\ p(a_1, b_1) \in KB_1, p(a_3, b_3) \in KB_3 \end{cases}$$

$$(1)$$

In the example figure 6 $dim(ic_1) = 3$, $dim(ic_2) = 3$ and $dim(rc_1) = 2$.

Each candidate has a trust score to define how much we can trust this candidate. There are several way to compute this score. In the experiments we will
test several trust functions.

4   Experiments

The goal of our experiments is to test different functions to compute the trust
score. We want to determine which function obtain the best results. To do so,
we build a use case about wheat crops. We want to build a KB describing wheat
taxonomy.

4.1   Source Analysing Process

For the project of wheat taxonomy, our experts select the following sources:

Agrovoc[8]: a multilingual thesaurus with more than 40,000 terms,

TaxRef[9] a french taxonomic referential with 80,000 taxa created by the
"Muséeum national d'histoire naturelle",

NCBI Taxonomy[10]: a taxonomy created by the National Center for Biotech-
nology Information (NCBI) of the United States with 1,000,000 taxa.

We chose these three sources because of their complementarity. First NCBI
is the source with the most taxa. It is considered by experts to be the most
up-to-date source but this include potential errors and there are only few labels.
Alongside, Agrovoc contains labels in several languages with distinctions between
scientific labels and vernacular ones but less taxa than NCBI and with a quality
often criticized [17]. TaxRef overcomes this drawback and is considered as a
national reference in agronomic classification. But its number of taxa is limited
by the data verification process. Combining these three sources is very suitable
because we combine the taxa quantity (NCBI), with labels quantity (Agrovoc)
and the assurance of quality (TaxRef).

4.2 Source Transformation Process

We start the "source transformation" process by building a module about plant
classification (*Agronomic Taxon* [16], see appendix 6.1 for more details. From
each sources, we extract automatically subparts of the wheat taxonomic classification. We focus the extraction on the Triticum taxa. We create an OWL file
corresponding at the "syntactic transformation" of each source using NOR20
patterns. Then we define re-engineering patterns to extract instances of *neon :
Taxon* from the three different OWL files. For each individual we type them and
link them using the *neon : hasHigherRank* object property.

KBs Merging Process. For this process we reused LogMap tool for the mapping activity. Then we define several trust functions to compute trust score of
individual candidates and relation candidates. Then we apply a threshold empirically fixed at 0.6 to filter candidates. Thus a candidate becomes a component
of the final KB if its trust score is above 0.6 otherwise it is rejected.

Simple Trust Function. The simple way to extract consensual ontological
objects is to determine in how many KBs the candidate appears. We consider
that a candidate is consensual if it appears in at least two KBs. Otherwise
the candidate should not belong to the final KB. We defined a function called
$trust_{simple}$ to implement the simple consensus. $trust_{simple}$ is defined by the
following formula :

$$trust_{simple}(c) = \begin{cases} 1 & \text{if } dim(c) >= 2 \\ 0 & \text{if } dim(c) < 2 \end{cases} \qquad (2)$$

Degree Trust Function. We can also use the mapping degree (provided by
LogMap) to compute the trust score. We consider that a candidate with higher

mapping degrees implies more trust. For the degree consensus implementation there is a different formula for each kind of candidate.

The instance candidate trust function is defined by the formula:

$$trust_{degree}(ic) = \frac{\sum\limits_{i=1}^{dim(ic)} \sum\limits_{j=i+1}^{dim(ic)} degree(a_i, a_j)}{\frac{nb_{Sources}(nb_{Sources}-1)}{2}} \tag{3}$$

$$such\ as(a_i, a_j) \in ic$$

This function sum all mapping degree involved in the candidate. We normalised the result with the maximum number of individuals mappings possible in an individual candidate (We have 3 KBs thus we can have at most 3 mappings in an individual candidate). Here, $nb_{sources}$ is the total number of KBs involved on the merging process.

The relation candidate trust function is defined by the formula:

$$trust(rc) = \frac{dim(rc) + \frac{trust(ic1)+trust(ic2)}{2}}{nb_{Sources} + 1} \tag{4}$$

$$such\ as\ ic1 \in rc, ic2 \in rc$$

This formula takes in account the $dim(rc)$ and the average of trust scores of individual candidates, components of the relation candidate. We do so to simulate a mapping degree between object properties instances. Note that LogMap do not match object property instances. We normalised this result with the $nb_{Sources}$, which is the maximum value that $dim(rc)$ could be, plus 1, which is the maximum value that the average of the two ic trust score could be.

4.3 Experiment Set up

To build our Gold Standard KB in order to compare the output of the different KBs merging process, we ask to three agronomists to validate manually the three KBs, outputs of the "source transformation" process. We consider that an ontological object is validated by the experts if at least two experts validated it and the third one vote for the "don't know" option (more precision on the appendix 6.2). The baseline is composed of the union of all ontological objects validated by the experts. Two final KBs are generating using the different trust functions ($trust_{simple}$ and $trust_{degree}$). Precision, recall and f-measure are computing to evaluate the quality of the final KBs. The precision is the ratio between the number of ontological objects of the final KB validated by experts and the total number of ontological objects of the final KB. The recall is the ratio between the number of ontological objects validated by experts which appear on the final KB and the number of ontological objects validated by experts.

4.4 Results and Analyse

Table 1 presents our results. The column, called simple consensus, shows the results of the "KBs merging" process using the $trust_{simple}$ function. The column,

Table 1. Results

	Simple Consensus			Degree Consensus		
Candidate	Precision	Recall	F-Measure	Precision	Recall	F-Measure
Individual	0.91	0.66	0.77	1	0.59	0.74
Relation	0.41	0.48	0.45	0.44	0.4	0.4

called degree consensus, shows the results of the "KBs merging" process using the $trust_{degree}$ function. The fist line presents the results on individual candidates and the second line presents the results on relation candidates.

We can observe on the table 1 that the results are encouraging. All the individuals that our method is able to extract are valuable one (our individual candidate results obtain a high precision); But our method is not yet able to extract all the valuable ontological objects. The degree consensus approach worka little bit better than the simple consensus one. More over our approach is able to extract more individual, than links between individuals.

5   Conclusion and Future Works

In this article, we propose a method to transform several KOS into a knowledge base using Ontology Design Patterns and consensus. Our method estimate consensus by computing a trust score for each ontological object extracted. We determined which trust formula is the more suitable for our use case. This method helps the validation at the end of the process because some candidates could be validated (or rejected) automatically, by using different filtering thresholds.

We will focus our next works on the results filtering to answer to several problems we observed. First we want to implement the same approach to extract different type of ontological objects (labels, classes, ...). We should also improve the extraction of links between individuals. Then we have to face the problem of contradictions between candidates. Currently all candidates are considered and can be accepted, even if there is a conflict. To solve such conflicts, it could be possible to use the argumentation theory associated with the trust score to manage the candidate selection. We want also to work on another sub-domain than the plants taxonomy classification. We planned to work on the attacks from bio-aggressors using the module CultivatedPlant[11] with a database from the Arvalis[12].

Acknowledgements. We want to special thanks the three experts who helped us to validate our results by generating the gold standard:

Franck Jabot from Irstea Clermont-Ferrand, France
Jacques Le Gouis from INRA Clermont-Ferrand, France
Vincent Soulignac from Irstea Clermont-Ferrand, France

---

[11] https://sites.google.com/site/agriontology/home/irstea/cultivatedplant
[12] http://www.arvalis-infos.fr

References

1. Amarger, F., Roussey, C., Chanet, J.P., Haemmerlé, O., Hernandez, N.: Etat de l´art: Extraction d´information à partir de thésaurus pour générer une ontologie. In: INFORSID, pp. 29–44 (2013)
2. Artz, D., Gil, Y.: A survey of trust in computer science and the semantic web. In: Web Semantics: Science, Services and Agents on the World Wide Web, pp. 58–71 (2007)
3. Charlet, J., Declerck, G., Dhombres, F., Gayet, P., Miroux, P., Vandenbussche, P.Y.: Construire une ontologie médicale pour la recherche d'information: problématiques terminologiques et de modélisation. In: Ingénierie des Connaissances, pp. 33–48 (2012)
4. Chrisment, C., Haemmerlé, O., Hernandez, N., Mothe, J.: Méthodologie de transformation d'un thesaurus en une ontologie de domaine. In: Revue d'Intelligence Artificielle, pp. 7–37 (2008)
5. Downey, D., Etzioni, O., Soderland, S.: A probabilistic model of redundancy in information extraction. In: International Joint Conferences on Artificial Intelligence, pp. 1034–1041 (2005)
6. Euzenat, J., Shvaiko, P.: Ontology matching (2007)
7. Fernández-López, M., Gómez-Pérez, A., Juristo, N.: Methontology: from ontological art towards ontological engineering. In: American Asociation for Artificial Intelligence (1997)
8. Gangemi, A., Presutti, V.: Ontology Design Patterns. In: Handbook on Ontologies, pp. 221–243 (2009)
9. Gil, R., Martín-Bautista, M.: Smol: a systemic methodology for ontology learning from heterogeneous sources. Journal of Intelligent Information Systems, 415–455 (2014)
10. Hahn, U.: Turning informal thesauri into formal ontologies: a feasibility study on biomedical knowledge re-use. In: Comparative and Functional Genomics, pp. 94–97 (2003)
11. Hepp, M., De Bruijn, J.: GenTax: a generic methodology for deriving OWL and RDF-S ontologies from hierarchical classifications, thesauri, and inconsistent taxonomies. In: European Semantic Web Conference, pp. 129–144 (2007)
12. Jiménez-Ruiz, E., Grau, B.C., Zhou, Y., Horrocks, I.: Large-scale interactive ontology matching: Algorithms and implementation. In: European Conference on Artificial Intelligence, pp. 444–449 (2012)
13. Kless, D., Jansen, L., Lindenthal, J., Wiebensohn, J.: A method for re-engineering a thesaurus into an ontology. In: FOIS, p. 133 (2012)
14. Li, P., Li, Y.: On transformation from the thesaurus into domain ontology. In: Advanced Materials Research, pp. 2698–2704 (2013)
15. Presutti, V., Blomqvist, E., Daga, E., Gangemi, A.: Pattern-Based Ontology Design. In: Ontology Engineering in a Networked World, pp. 35–64. Springer (2012)
16. Roussey, C., Chanet, J.P., Cellier, V., Amarger, F.: Agronomic taxon. In: Workshop on Open Data, p. 5 (2013)
17. Soergel, D., Lauser, B., Liang, A., Fisseha, F., Keizer, J., Katz, S.: Reengineering thesauri for new applications: The AGROVOC example. Journal of Digital Information, 1–23 (2004)
18. Suárez-Figueroa, M.C., Gómez-Pérez, A., Motta, E., Gangemi, A.: Ontology engineering in a networked world (2012)

19. van Assem, M., Menken, M.R., Schreiber, G., Wielemaker, J., Wielinga, B.: A method for converting thesauri to RDF/OWL. In: McIlraith, S.A., Plexousakis, D., van Harmelen, F. (eds.) ISWC 2004. LNCS, vol. 3298, pp. 17–31. Springer, Heidelberg (2004)
20. Villazón-Terrazas, B., Suárez-Figueroa, M.C., Gómez-Pérez, A.: A pattern-based method for re-engineering non-ontological resources into ontologies. In: Int. J. Semantic Web Inf. Syst., pp. 27–63 (2010)
21. Wielinga, B., Schreiber, A.T., Wielemaker, J., Sandberg, J.A.C.: From thesaurus to ontology. In: International Conference on Knowledge Capture, pp. 194–201 (2001)

6   Appendix

6.1   AgronomicTaxon

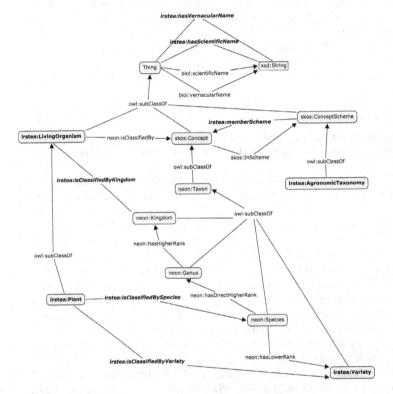

Fig. 7. AgronomicTaxon

6.2   Gold Standard

Experts Validation. To validate our approach, we asked to three domain experts to analyse the three knowledge bases extracted automatically from the three sources: Agrovoc, Taxref, NCBI. The experts have to determine which ontological objects are well represented and in the scope of the knowledge base.

An interface was implemented to let the experts validate the ontological objects. Here there was only instances of the *neon : Taxon* class. For each individual four questions were asked to the expert :

1. **Does the taxon belong to the domain?** first we ask if the element presented is really a taxon (an element of a taxonomy). Also we want to know if the taxon is in the scope of the KB that is to say (Triticum or Aegilops).

2. **Do the labels designate the same entity?**
   There are several labels available in KB (especially in Agrovoc) but sometimes some labels are inexact, because there are not synonym or they are not the exact translation (if the source contains multilingual labels).

3. **Is the taxon more specific than "anotherTaxon" ?**
   When we can extract a "hasHigherRank" relation between two taxa from the source, we want to validate this link. So we want to know if the first taxon is a specialisation of the second.

4. **Is the rank of the taxon "aTaxonType" ?**
   Sometimes there is information about the rank type of the taxon in the source. We want here to validate this extraction and define the type of the taxon. Is it a specie, a family, a gender, ... ?

At the end of the form, there is an input field to let the expert add a comment if the response was not obvious. We can see the validation interface on the figure 8.

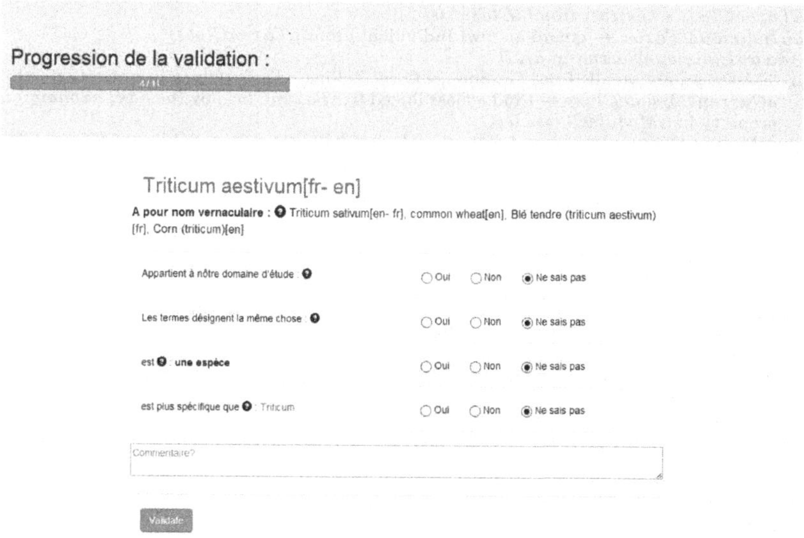

Fig. 8. Validation interface

This figure shows that for each question there are three available answer: Valid, Not Valid or Don't know.

The three experts have validated the owl : KBs (NCBI/Triticum, NBCI/Aegilops, Agrovoc/Triticum, Agrovoc/Aegilops, TaxRef/Triticum, TaxRef/Aegilops). At the end of the validation we have a list of ontological objects validated by the experts. We can then compare them with the candidates generated by the prototype.

Evaluation of the Consensus Intuition. To build our Gold Standard baseline, we first have to know if an agreement is possible between experts. To do so we computed a ratio between the number of experts and their number of validations. We consider that there is an agreement between experts when at least two experts validate the same ontological object and the third one select the *Don't know* option. We get a consensual ratio of **0.82**. We also computed the Fleiss Kappa score on the expert validations. Then we get the Fleiss Kappa of **0.69**. These two values show that the experts agree, most of the time, on the validation of the ontological objects. So we can use this consensus and use the experts validation as a gold standard to validate candidates.

6.3   Agrovoc Algorithm

Algorithm 1. Transformation Pattern : AGROVOC for AgronomicTaxon

---

$aModule$: the AgronomicTaxon module
$anOwlFile$: agrovoc transformed in owl using transformation pattern
$aModuleClassesList$: the classes of AgronomicTaxon module that are mapped to $anOwlFile$ (neon:Taxon, neon:Kingdom, neon:Phylum etc...)
aKB: the AgronomicTaxon module enriched by the data from agrovoc owl file
$aKB \leftarrow$ copy $(aModule)$;
$aClassLis() \leftarrow$ All subClasses of Plantae in $anOwlFile$
while $aClassList()$ is not empty **do**
    $aTaxonClass \leftarrow$ extract from($aClassList()$);
    $anIndividualTaxon \leftarrow$ create an Owl Individual From($aTaxonClass$)
    Add $anIndividualTaxon$ in aKB
    if Exist a property called $hasTaxonomicLevel$ linking $aTaxonClass$ in $anOwlFile$ **then**
        $aCurrentModuleClass \leftarrow$ Find a class linked to $aTaxonClass$ by the $hasTaxonomicLevel$ property in $aModuleClassList()$
        Add an $rdf:type$ property between $anIndividualTaxon$ and $aCurrentModuleClass$ in aKB
    else
        $aCurrentModuleClass \leftarrow neon:Taxon$
        Add an $rdf:type$ property between $anIndividualTaxon$ and $aCurrentModuleClass$ in aKB
    end if
end while
$anIndividualList() \leftarrow$ All $owl:individual$ type of $neon:Taxa$ in aKB
while $anIndividualList()$ is not empty **do**
    $aTaxonIndividual \leftarrow$ extractFrom($anIndividualList()$);
    $aTaxonClass \leftarrow$ Find a class equivalent to $aTaxonIndividual$ in $anOwlFile$
    if Exist a class subClass of $aTaxonClass$ in $anOwlFile$ **then**
        $aChildClass \leftarrow$ Find a class subClass of $aTaxonClass$ in $anOwlFile$
        $anotherTaxonIndividual \leftarrow$ Find an individual that is equivalent to $aChildClass$ in aKB

        Add a $neon$: $hasLowerRank$ object property between $aTaxonIndividual$ and $anotherTaxonIndividual$ in aKB
    end if
end while

Ontology-Based Model for Food Transformation Processes - Application to Winemaking

Aunur-Rofiq Muljarto[1,4], Jean-Michel Salmon[2], Pascal Neveu[1],
Brigitte Charnomordic[1], and Patrice Buche[3]

[1] MISTEA Joint Research Unit, UMR729, F-34060 Montpellier, France
aunur.muljarto@supagro.inra.fr
[2] Unite Expérimentale de Pech Rouge, UE0999, Pech Rouge, France
[3] IATE Joint Research Unit, UMR1208, F-34060 Montpellier, France
[4] Dept. of Agroindustrial Technology, Brawijaya University, Malang 65145, Indonesia

Abstract. This paper describes an ontology for modeling any food processing chain. It is intended for data and knowledge integration and sharing. The proposed ontology (Onto-FP) is built based on four main concepts: Product, Operation, Attribute and Observation. This ontology is able to represent food product transformations as well as temporal sequence of food processes. The Onto-FP can be easy integrated to other domains due to its consistencies with DOLCE ontology. We detail an application in the domain of winemaking and prove that it can be easy queried to answer questions related to data classification, food process itineraries and incomplete data identification.

Keywords: ontology-based model, data integration, food processing, winemaking.

1 Introduction

Researches on technological aspects in the field of food production have grown rapidly in recent years, mainly driven by consumer demands for food products that are safe, high quality and more sustainable [1]. The increasing complexity of technological aspects and the accumulation of heterogeneous data from research activities emerge new challenges related to data and knowledge organization, particularly to answer the following objectives. Firstly, providing researchers with a scientific tool for large scale data integration. It is important not only for presenting data in standard format, but the more important thing is, it will provide possibilities for further analysis by applying available knowledge [2]. Specific applications such as food traceability can only be achieved by applying data integration. Secondly, sharing data and knowledge between various stages of operations. Typically, data and knowledge are separated and reside on each section of food production chain. An expert on a particular section may not know the data and knowledge on the others. Therefore exchanging data and knowledge helps to coordinate the independent entities and increases efficiencies by greatly reducing redundancies [3]. Thirdly, providing feasible solution to address the

S. Closs et al. (Eds.): MTSR 2014, CCIS 478, pp. 329–343, 2014.
© Springer International Publishing Switzerland 2014

problem of incomplete data and information. By giving proper ways to work with incomplete data and information, it will increase the quality of the whole result [4].

Developing methods intended for decision support with those objectives is fairly complicated work due to the nature of data in the field of food production chain. Despite the large amount of data collected, there are issues that require further investigation. A first key issue is their various terms, data schemes and formats used. Most of the data collected relate to the product characteristic, process conditions and other influential factors which come from experiments. Experimental data are stored and conveyed in various formats with their own schemes, such as in simple text files, csv and excel work sheets, complex word documents, laboratory reports, image files, etc., [5]. A second issue concerns the heterogeneous sources of the data. In food production chain, data are scattered at several locations and come from a variety of stages such as from the cultivation, harvesting, transformation process, and distribution of products to consumers [6]. These two issues are major obstacles to be resolved, especially for the purpose of data integration and data sharing. A knowledge layer that acts as a backbone for data and knowledge integration should be provided to overcome these issues.

Recent studies show that the ontology-based model is a flexible solution for building that knowledge layer. Compared to the previous knowledge management methods, ontology-based approach has more advantages in acquisition and creation, integrating different data sources, and interoperability among different systems [7].

In this paper, we propose a food processing chain ontology (Onto-FP) to achieve the objectives mentioned before. This ontology focuses on transformation processes by taking into account their key characteristics, i.e., food product transformation, temporal factor of operations, and data organization. To our knowledge, our proposal is the first ontology-based model describing explicitly material transformation combined with a sequence of operations. This ontology was initially built for specific domain, i.e., winemaking. However, with the need to be applied to other similar food transformation process, this ontology has been further developed to be more generic.

This paper is organized as follows: Section 2 gives a brief state of the art on food domain ontologies and process design; Section 3 is dedicated to the proposed food production chain ontology that includes how the ontology building process was carried out, detail core elements and relationships; Section 4 provides a brief description how the Onto-FP can be integrated to an upper ontology, particularly the Dolce ontology; Section 5 demonstrates some practical uses of the proposed ontology in the domain of winemaking; Finally, in Section 6, conclusions are drawn and further works are outlined.

2   Related Works

2.1   Food Ontology

The need for ontologies has increased in food sectors due to the need of knowledge expression and sharing. Some works described the food world from a general point of view such as FOODS [8], which contains specifications of food ingredients, substances and nutrition facts. Contrary, the others developed ontologies for very specific food commodities, e.g., wine classification [9], potato [6], and fish production [10]. Another part of the food domain that recently attracts the attention of researchers is ontologies for food traceability. It is driven by a growing interest in developing systems for food supply chain. Some essential works in this domain have been carried out, such as The Food Track and Trace Ontology (FTTO) [11] and TraceALL [12].

The ontologies mentioned above have proven useful and can be applied to their domain. However there are some important things that have not been presented in those ontologies. Most of them describe the classification concepts and their relationships in the target domains, but how food product transformations and processes associated with the transformations as well as important factors such as temporal aspects of operations have not been widely studied.

2.2   Ontology-Based Model for Process Design

To date, an ontology related to food transformation processes has not been widely discussed. However, since food transformation processes are mainly derived from chemical processes, related works in the domain of chemical process design can be used to support this work.

A widely known ontology that currently become reference in the domain of chemical engineering is OntoCAPE [13]. It is a formal, heavyweight ontology. In this ontology, the design, construction, and operations of chemical plants are considered as the major engineering activities. Furthermore, OntoCAPE provides chemical engineering concepts needed for describing structural and phenomenological details of the chemical process. Based on this ontology, a framework for work process modeling in the chemical industries has been developed [14]. This framework comprises an iterative modeling procedure, an extensible modeling language for work processes (including temporal aspects of chemical operations), and software tools for its practical application.

3   Proposed Model

Food production chain is a complex system with many variations. Therefore, building an ontology that can be used to represent different food production chain is a challenging task. The ontology should be fairly generic to be easy to use. However, that ontology should also provide flexibility for different varieties of food production chain.

3.1   Ontology Building Process

To date, several methodologies related to the ontology development and maintenance have been proposed in the literature. [15] have discussed comprehensively
about the three most well known generic methodologies, i.e., TOVE (Toronto
Virtual Enterprise), Enterprise and Methontology. In the domain of agriculture,
[7] proposed a general method for the construction of agricultural ontology. The
main stages of this method are determination of ontology purpose and scope,
collection and analysis of domain information, key concepts and relationships
identification, formalization, confirmation an evolution, and ontology evolution.

Based on this development approach, the ontology building process of Onto-
FP has been done by a series of activities : (1) Defining ontology purpose and
scope through meetings with experts; (2) Knowledge acquisition by using various
techniques, such as brainstorming, interviewing with experts in the domain of
food processing, literature searching, etc; (3) Conceptualization by accurately
selected domain relevant concepts and relations according to the purpose; (4)
Formalization by using ontology language and semantic web technology (RDF,
RDFS, OWL DL, etc); (5) Confirmation and evaluation of ontology by using an
automatic reasoning tool provided by an ontology development tool (Protege)
in order to check its correctness and logical relationships between concepts.

3.2   Ontology Core Elements

Onto-FP is purposed mainly for providing researchers a framework for constructing their knowledge in semantic way. The domain is specified into food processing, where raw materials are processed into final products. It covers the wide
range of activities, started from harvesting, preparation, intermediate processes
and final processes.

Main Concepts. Four main classes have been defined to represent general
food transformation process, i.e., *Product, Operation, Attribute* and *Observation*.
Figure 1 shows the complete hierarchy of these classes. A short description for
each class is provided in the following paragraphs.

 – *Product*
   Product class represents an abstract model of the different types of food
   products. The product taxonomy used in the Product class is based on the
   product transformation stages. Thus, as shown in Figure 1, the second level
   of this class comprises *HarvestingProduct* that represents raw material entering particular food transformation process, *IntermediateProduct* represents
   semi or unfinished products, *FinishedProduct* is an abstract model of final
   products and *ServiceProduct* models all materials or products that are used
   by operations to transforms raw material or intermediate product during
   process flow.

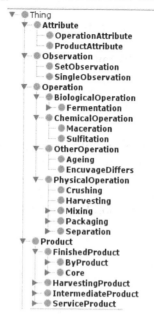

Fig. 1. Food processing domain hierarchy

- *Operation*
  Operation is class that conceptualizes the knowledge related to the process activities. The second level of this class corresponds to the general classification of operations including physical, chemical and biological operations (see Figure 1). The third level represents more specific operations widely known in the domain of food processing, such as fermentation, separation, mixing, maceration, crushing, etc. This level can be added depending on the needs of selected domain.
- *Attribute*
  Attribute class models all the characteristics of product or operation. The aim of this class is to store information about all features or qualities belonging to Product or Operation class. *ProductAttribute* is a class that represents all attributes of *Product* while *OperationAttribute* is used to model *Operation*'s attributes. For the purpose of generality, more specific attributes are defined as an instance of *ProductAttribute* or *OperationAttribute* rather than as a new class. For instance, volatile acidity as an attribute of finished wine is declared as an individual, not as a sub-class of ProductAttribute. By using this approach, this ontology becomes more stable and flexible enough to cope with the rapid changes on qualities used in product and operation, which commonly happen due to new innovations on sensors and observation methods.
- *Observation*
  The class of Observation is a conceptualization of an abstract model of activity where an instance of Attribute class is measured. Observation can be a single observation (*SingleObservation* class) that means one time only measurement or a set of observation (*SetObservation* class) where multiple

measurement to the particular attribute of product or operation are needed (see also in Figure 3). An instance of SetObservation will always have at least two SingleObservation instances. The class of SetObservation is very important to model a series of observations, such as fermentation temperature that is commonly measured not only once but several times in a given operation.

General Relations between Elements. Generally, relations among core elements can be grouped into four categories, relations between : (i) two or more products, (ii) products and operations, (iii) two or more operations and (iv) relations related to data observations. Figure 2 shows the first three general relations, while Figure 3 shows relationships between Observation, Product, Operation and Attribute.

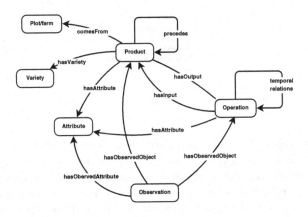

Fig. 2. General relationships between elements

– *Product transformation*

Product transformation is one of the key elements in food production. Raw materials are processed into intermediate products to subsequently be further processed into the finished products. In the domain of food processing, raw materials are crops that are harvested from farm. These products can be in different varieties. In most cases, varieties will determine what kind of operations that should be considered and what type of final products that may be produced. Therefore, the concept of variety is important (see Figure 2). There are two relations proposed concerning product transformation, i.e., product to product and product to operation relationships. The first relation aims to list all existing products and arrange them according to a particular sequence in a food transformation chain. Here, a transitive object property called *precedes* and its inverse *succeeds* is used to model this relation. The second relationship is inspired by the basic theory of material balances, where there are links between products as input, operations as processor, and other products as output. The object properties of *hasInput* and *hasOutput* are used to model this condition (see Figure 2). By using this representation, product changes due to a particular operation can always be identified.

– *Temporal relations of operations*

Temporal factors are important issues in food transformation processes. They become important considerations because they will affect the attributes of the raw materials, semi-finished products, as well as the final products. Representing temporal factors or dynamic aspects of a particular domain such as food transformation will help researchers or related actors to deal with problems of prediction, planning and data explanation [16]. Temporal relations also can be used to check the consistencies of the set of operations. Semantic temporal relations between operations can be described by the Ontology of Time for the Semantic Web proposed in [17]. This ontology relies on the interval representation of time developed by Allen [16]. Furthermore, this ontology has been refined and listed as W3C Working Draft since September 2006. According to this ontology, there are two subclass of *TemporalEntity*, i.e., *Instant* and *Interval*. "Intervals are, intuitively, things with extent and instants are, intuitively, point-like in that they have no interior points" [17]. Using this definition, it can be stated that Operation class is a subclass of Interval. Thus it will inherit the two important properties of Interval, i.e., *hasBeginning* and *hasEnd*. It can be also inferred that operations can use object properties of interval to represent semantic relation between operations. Table 1 shows all possible relations between two operations and corresponding examples.

Table 1. Temporal relations between operations

Relations	Inverse	Notation	Examples from winemaking
Before(A,B)	After(B,A)	$A < B$; $B > A$	Crushing occurs after destemming
Meets(A,B)	MetBy(B,A)	$A\ m\ B$; $B\ mi\ A$	Draining is started immediately after maceration
Overlaps(A,B)	OverlappedBy(B,A)	$A\ o\ B$: $B\ oi\ A$	Malolactic fermentation can be started before alcoholic fermentation is finished
Starts(A,B)	StartedBy(B,A)	$A\ s\ B$; $B\ si\ A$	Maceration is started when alcoholic fermentation started
Finishes(A,B)	FinishedBy(B,A)	$A\ f\ B$; $B\ fi\ A$	Sulfitation finished malolactic fermentation
During(A,B)	Contains(B,A)	$A\ d\ B$; $B\ di\ A$	Alcoholic fermentation occurs during maceration
Equal(A,B)		$A = B$; $B = A$	Extraction of ethanol is started and finished at the same time as alcoholic fermentation

– *Flexible data organization using attribute and observation*

Recording chronological changes in the products and operations during the process flow is very important. For the specific application of food traceability, data and information regarding product transformation are main sources for identifying potential causes if some problems arise. Therefore, data must be organized in such a way that represents the actual condition of the product or operation that has observed. Here, we proposed a simple approach based on natural relationships that occur between Product/Operation, Attribute, and Observation. Figure 3 shows how this approach is represented.

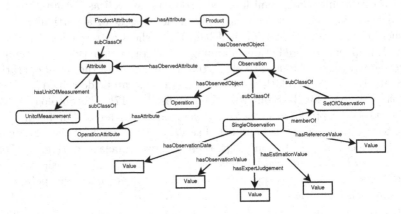

Fig. 3. Data organization using Product/Operation Attribute and Observation

The Observation class plays an important role to represent the attribute measurement process. An instance of single observation has always relations with an instance of product or operation through the object property of *hasObservedObject* as well as with an instance of product/operation's attribute using *hasObservedAttribute* object property. It is a natural representation where an observation is done on a particular attribute belonging to a given object (product or operation) at a specific time. Another important thing regarding observation is how various data types have to be represented. For a single observation result, data can be quantitative values provided by a sensor or based on estimation, or qualitative values based on expert judgments. Thus, as seen on Figure 3, object properties such as *hasObservationValue*, *hasEstimationValue*, and *hasExpertJudgment* are added to the single observation class.

4   Integration into an Upper Ontology

The Onto-FP was built initially for a specific domain (i.e., winemaking ontology). From the development perspective, it can be stated that it follows a bottom-up approach where the process started by defining the most specific concepts in the domain of winemaking. This approach results an ontology which is in accordance with the specific conditions of the domain being modeled. However, there is a possibility that this ontology will be difficult to be modified and integrated with ontologies developed for other domains [18]. Therefore, for the purpose of information and knowledge integration, it is necessary to do an analysis to show that the core concepts of the Onto-FP are consistent with an upper level ontology.

4.1   Upper Level Ontology

Upper level ontology can be defined as an ontology that contains very general concepts and relations from which more specific concepts and relations can be constructed [19]. This definition implicitly states that if a generalization is performed in ontologies from different domains, at some point there are the same concepts and relations across all domains. Some widely known upper ontologies are: Suggested Upper Merged Ontology (SUMO), Basic Formal Ontology (BFO), General Formal Ontology (GFO) and DOLCE [19].

This paper used DOLCE, a widely recognized and used upper level ontology, as reference. According to its authors, DOLCE is declared as an ontology of particulars, where particulars refer to instances which differs to universals that point to properties and relations [20]. The top-level categories of DOLCE and their relations are presented in Figure 4. According to this figure, there are four main classes of DOLCE, i.e., *Endurant, Perdurant, Quality* and *Abstract.* Endurants can be seen as "entities that are wholly present at any time they are present" while perdurants are "entities that happen in time" [20]. Qualities are the basic entities that can be observed or measured [20]. Abstract class refers to entities that do not have spatial nor temporal qualities, and they are not qualities themselves [20].

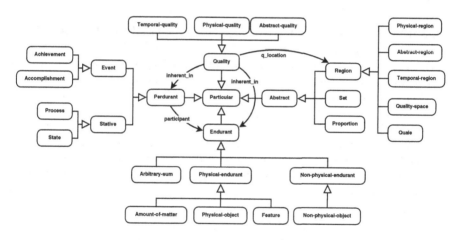

Fig. 4. Dolce main concepts

4.2   Structuring Onto-FP to the DOLCE Ontology

Structuring Onto-FP to DOLCE ontology consists of assignment of core concepts from the Onto-FP to the categories provided by DOLCE. The following paragraphs describe briefly relations between those concepts.

– *Product*

Product is a concept used to model all types of materials. This definition clearly expresses that Product is a physical entity. According to the definitions of DOLCE main concepts, Product can be categorized as an Endurant. More precisely, Product is a subclass of Physical-object (see Figure 4).

– *Operation*

Operation is a concept that represents process activities. It is an action that just extends in time by gathering different temporal parts. Every instance of Operation always has temporal parts, e.g. starting time, duration, end time, etc. From the DOLCE's point of view, this concept lies clearly under the Perdurant concept. Operation is close to the DOLCE's concept of Process which is a sub-subclass of Perdurant (see Figure 4). Another important thing here is the relation between endurants and perdurants called *participant* or *participation-in* as its inverse. This relation means that an endurant exists in time by participating in a perdurant [20]. This generic relation is comparable to the relations defined in Onto-FP, i.e., *hasInput* (inverse: *isInputOf*) and *hasOutput* (inverse: *isOutputOf*). An instance of Product exists by participating as an input (or output) of an instance of Operation. Thus *hasInput* and *hasOutput* can be declared as a specialization of participation-in relationship.

– *Attribute*

As defined before, Attribute is a class that models all the characteristics of Product or Operation. Using this definition, it can be directly revealed that Attribute is close to the DOLCE concept of Quality due to their similarity of meaning. Both of them are entities that can be observed. More precisely, Attribute could be considered as a subclass of Quality. In Onto-FP, Attribute is intended to represent physical qualities of Product or Operation. Therefore, the concept of Attribute is equal to the DOLCE concept of Physical-qualities. Additionally, from Figure 4, it can be seen that there is a relation between Quality and Endurant or Perdurant named *inherent-in*. This relation is identical to the relation of *hasAttribute* that link between Attribute and Product or Operation in Onto-FP (see Figure 3).

– *Observation*

Observation is a conceptualization of an activity where data or information from an instance of Attribute class is captured. Like Operation, Observation is an action that also has temporal parts. Therefore, it can be stated that Observation is a Perdurant.

5   Practical Use

In this section, three examples of the practical uses of this ontology will be presented. These three examples have been selected to represent common conditions found in winemaking. For the testing purposes, the Onto-FP has been populated using winemaking data collected from the *Unite Expérimentale de Pech Rouge*,

France from 2005 to 2008. These data contain observation results from the different stages of winemaking and are stored in more than 580 Microsoft Excel files.

5.1   Identifying Red Winemaking Data from the Other Types

The *Unite Expérimentale de Pech Rouge*, France produces different kind of wines. According to their color, it can be classified into red, white and rosé. The data observed from these three types of winemaking are stored together in the same file with similar scheme. Consequently, it is not easy to classify whether particular sets of data belong to red, white or rosé winemaking. Some guidance from experts are needed to check and verify them manually. Thus, it will take quite a lot of time to do this classification when the number of data increases. By using the ontology of food transformation process, this process can be done instantly by querying the data using specific criteria.

Lets take an example here. Suppose we want to select all sets of red winemaking data. The colors of wine are determined by the variety of grapes used and/or the processes used to make the wine. According to the experts, the easiest way to distinguish red winemaking to the other types is by checking the existence of *remontage* operation during alcoholic fermentation. *Rémontage* is the French term for the process of pulling out wine from underneath the cap of grape skins and then pumping it back over the cap in order to stimulate maceration. Therefore, the existence of a rémontage operation can be used as a criterion to filter related red winemaking data. The following lines is an example of SPARQL query for identifying red winemaking datasets.

Query 1.

```
SELECT * WHERE {
    ?WmDataset rdf:type own:Winemaking .
    ?WmDataset own:hasPart ?macName .
    ?macName rdf:type own:Maceration
    OPTIONAL {?remName own:during ?macName .
    ?remName rdf:type own:Remontage }
}
```

Query 1 shows simple SPARQL query using OPTIONAL statement to check if an instance of Rémontage (*remName*) exists during maceration operation (*macName*). If it is present then the instance name of rémontage will be displayed and the corresponding winemaking dataset (*wmDataset*) can be determined belongs to the red winemaking group. Figure 5 shows the result of this query.

5.2   Backward Tracking to Find Winemaking Itineraries by Given Wine Color Parameters

Color is one of the important characteristics of wines and probably the first attribute that affects consumer acceptance. The color of wines can be estimated

WmDataset	macName	remName
wm_0154	mc_0348	rm_0004
wm_0063	mc_0038	rm_0153
wm_0092	mc_0427	rm_0042
wm_0101	mc_0011	rm_0001
wm_0005	mc_0115	
wm_0106	mc_0061	

Fig. 5. Query results show the first four rows are winemaking datasets

by investigating their chemical composition which are related to color, such as anthocyanins, total phenolics and tannin. For researchers, the colors of wines are useful to find the relationships between wine color attributes and various factors such as grape varieties, selected processes, treatment during these processes, temporal factors, and other interesting studies. To describe these relationships, the first thing that should be known is the winemaking itineraries, which comprise all related products and operations to produce particular wines. Certain wines may be produced by using a single straight process flow, but the others may need the combined process flows. By using these itineraries, it will help researches for describing comprehensively all potential factors that affect to wine color attributes. This ontology provides mechanisms to do backward tracking by using transitive object properties mentioned before (*precedes*, *succeeds*, *hasInput*, *hasOutput* and temporal relations between operations). Query 2 shows an example how one of these object properties is used to find all previous operations.

Query 2.

```
SELECT  ?pa ?c WHERE {
    ?s own:hasObservedObject ?o .
    ?s own:hasObservedAttribute own:Anthocyanins .
    ?s own:hasObservationValue ?v .
    ?p own:hasOutput ?o .
    ?p own:after+ ?pa .
    ?pa rdf:type ?c
    FILTER (?v = 479.22)
}
```

Here, we want to find all operations that are used to produce a wine that has anthocyanins value of 479.22. The *after* temporal relation is used to find previous operation. Because it is a transitive object property, thus we can use one of SPARQL Property Path expressions, i.e., by adding operator "+". This operator allows to find a path of one or more occurrences of *after* object property. Figure 6 shows the result of this query.

5.3   Identifying Incomplete Data

Winemaking data contains large amounts of data collected from different sources. One of the conditions that normally occur on such data is that some parts of

Instance Name	Class Name
ag_0002	Ageing
sf_0002	Sulfitation
mf_0023	MalolacticFermentation
pr_0002	Pressing
dr_0250	Draining
af_0012	AlcoholicFermentation
cr_0228	Crushing
ds_0462	Destemming
hv_0025	Harvesting

Fig. 6. Set of operations for producing a particular wine with anthocyanins = 479.22

them are lost or unavailable [21]. These incomplete data will affect data analysis methods and the conclusions that can be drawn. Therefore, dealing with incomplete data is an integral part of research activities.

Unlike conventional database, RDF does not provide mechanism to store null value which is commonly used to represent incomplete data. RDF stores data in a triplestore which is a collection of triples rather than in a set of tables. Each triple contains flat data in the form of subject-predicate-object (S-P-O). This form has a basic consequence that all data should be known so that the triples can be built. According to this rule, the null value which is mostly used to represent that the value (data) is unknown or doesn't exist, does not fulfill the RDF standard form. Hence, null values will be disregarded because the triples cannot be generated. In conventional database, it is easy to query data using null values as a keyword, even without knowing the structure of data. But, to do that in a triplestore, it will be a bit tricky. Query 3 shows an example how to display all observation data and identify the existence of incomplete data.

Query 3.

```
SELECT DISTINCT ?obs ?obj  ?att ?val WHERE {
    ?obs rdf:type own:SingleObservation .
    ?obs own:hasObservedObject ?obj .
    ?obj rdf:type ?cob .
    ?obs own:hasObservedAttribute ?att .
    OPTIONAL {?obs ?h ?val .
        ?h rdfs:subPropertyOf own:hasInformation }
}
ORDER BY desc(?obj)
```

Again, here the OPTIONAL statement is used to check if a triplet that contains value exists (indicated by statement of "?obs ?h ?val"). If it is present, a complete triplet will be generated. Otherwise it will remain empty, which indicates incomplete data. Figure 7 shows the result of this query. There are two missing values found, i.e., values (*val*) of DO250 in the observations (*obs*) of so_0012 and so_0010.

obs	obj	att	val
so_0004	fw_0402	IPT	"45.90"^^<http://www.w3.org/2001/XMLSche
so_0003	fw_0402	Anthocyanins	"479.22"^^<http://www.w3.org/2001/XMLSch
so_0011	fw_0402	DO520	"6.414"^^<http://www.w3.org/2001/XMLSche
so_0007	fw_0114	IPT	"87.34"^^<http://www.w3.org/2001/XMLSche
so_0008	fw_0114	Anthocyanins	"463.44"^^<http://www.w3.org/2001/XMLSch
so_0012	fw_0114	DO520	
so_0002	fw_0031	IPT	"56.85"^^<http://www.w3.org/2001/XMLSche
so_0001	fw_0031	Anthocyanins	"674.53"^^<http://www.w3.org/2001/XMLSch
so_0010	fw_0031	DO520	
so_0005	fw_0003	Anthocyanins	"249.36"^^<http://www.w3.org/2001/XMLSch
so_0006	fw_0003	IPT	"35.92"^^<http://www.w3.org/2001/XMLSche
so_0009	fw_0003	DO520	"1.903"^^<http://www.w3.org/2001/XMLSche

Fig. 7. Query results for identifying incomplete data

6   Conclusion and Future Works

This paper presents an ontology-based model for food transformation process, the Onto-FP. The ontology is intended to be a knowledge layer that can be used by researchers for data and knowledge integration and sharing as well as for further analysis. The Onto-FP is based on four main concepts: Product, Operation, Attribute and Observation. Beside those main concepts, the key elements of this ontology are product transformation relationships, temporal sequence of operations and a flexible data organization. The Onto-FP has been qualitatively analyzed and proven to be consistent to DOLCE upper ontology, both on concepts and relationships. This ontology also has been tested in some potential uses, particularly in the domain of winemaking. It shows that this ontology can be easily queried to answer questions related to data classification, food process itineraries and incomplete data identification.

In the future, Onto-FP, which is general for the food domain, can be specialized and tested to different food products or even to a wider domain, i.e., bio-resources products. More concepts and relations in the food and related domains could be added in order to improve its adaptability. This ontology could be also completed by specific rules to represent expert knowledge in estimating incomplete data. Another interesting future work is an analysis of food process itineraries for two or more given characteristic of find products based on this ontology.

References

1. Lehmann, R.J., Reiche, R., Schiefer, G.: Future internet and the agri-food sector: State-of-the-art in literature and research. Computers and Electronics in Agriculture 89, 158–174 (2012)
2. Gardner, S.P.: Ontologies and semantic data integration. Drug Discovery Today 10, 1001–1007 (2005)

3. Chungoora, N., Young, R.I., Gunendran, G., Palmer, C., Usman, Z., Anjum, N.A., Cutting-Decelle, A.F., Harding, J.A., Case, K.: A model-driven ontology approach for manufacturing system interoperability and knowledge sharing. Computers in Industry 64, 392–401 (2013)
4. Graham, J.W.: Missing data analysis: making it work in the real world. Annual Review of Psychology 60, 549–576 (2009)
5. Zhang, J., Hunter, A., Zhou, Y.: A logic-reasoning based system to harness bioprocess experimental data and knowledge for design. Biochemical Engineering Journal 74, 127–135 (2013)
6. Haverkort, A.J., Top, J.L., Verdenius, F.: Organizing Data in Arable Farming: Towards an Ontology of Processing Potato. Potato Research 49, 177–201 (2007)
7. Zheng, Y.L., He, Q.Y., Qian, P., Li, Z.: Construction of the Ontology-Based Agricultural Knowledge Management System. Journal of Integrative Agriculture 11, 700–709 (2012)
8. Snae, C., Bruckner, M.: FOODS: A Food-Oriented Ontology-Driven System. In: 2nd IEEE International Conference on Digital Ecosystems and Technologies, pp. 168–176. Ieee (2008)
9. Graça, J., Mourao, M., Anunciação, O., Monteiro, P., Pinto, H.S., Loureiro, V.: Ontology building process: the wine domain. In: EVITA 2005 Proceedings, Vila Real, (i) (2005)
10. He, Q.Y., Zheng, Y.L., Xu, J.N.: Constructing the Ontology for Modeling the Fish Production in Pearl River Basin. Journal of Integrative Agriculture 11, 760–768 (2012)
11. Pizzuti, T., Mirabelli, G., Sanz-Bobi, M.A., Goméz-Gonzaléz, F.: Food Track & Trace ontology for helping the food traceability control. Journal of Food Engineering 120, 17–30 (2014)
12. Salampasis, M., Tektonidis, D., Kalogianni, E.P.: TraceALL: a semantic web framework for food traceability systems. Journal of Systems and Information Technology 14, 302–317 (2012)
13. Morbach, J., Yang, A., Marquardt, W.: OntoCAPEA large-scale ontology for chemical process engineering. Engineering Applications of Artificial Intelligence 20, 147–161 (2007)
14. Theißen, M., Hai, R., Marquardt, W.: A framework for work process modeling in the chemical industries. Computers & Chemical Engineering 35, 679–691 (2011)
15. Pinto, H.S., Martins, J.A.P.: Ontologies: How can They be Built? Knowledge and Information Systems 6, 441–464 (2004)
16. Allen, J.F., Ferguson, G.: Actions and Events in Interval Temporal Logic. Journal of Logic and Computation 4, 531–579 (1994)
17. Hobbs, J.R., Pan, F.: An ontology of time for the semantic web. ACM Transactions on Asian Language Information Processing 3, 66–85 (2004)
18. Batres, R., West, M., Leal, D., Price, D., Masaki, K., Shimada, Y., Fuchino, T., Naka, Y.: An upper ontology based on ISO 15926. Computers & Chemical Engineering 31, 519–534 (2007)
19. Mascardi, V., Cordì, V., Rosso, P.: A comparison of upper ontologies. In: WOA Conference, pp. 55–64 (2007)
20. Gangemi, A., Guarino, N., Masolo, C., Oltramari, A., Schneider, L.: Sweetening ontologies with DOLCE. In: Gómez-Pérez, A., Benjamins, V.R. (eds.) EKAW 2002. LNCS (LNAI), vol. 2473, pp. 166–181. Springer, Heidelberg (2002)
21. Cismondi, F., Fialho, A.S., Vieira, S.M., Reti, S.R., Sousa, J.A.M.C., Finkelstein, S.N.: Missing data in medical databases: impute, delete or classify? Artificial Intelligence in Medicine 58, 63–72 (2013)

A Food Packaging Use Case for Argumentation

Nouredine Tamani[1,4], Patricio Mosse[2], Madalina Croitoru[1,3,4],
Patrice Buche[1,2,4], and Valérie Guillard[2,3]

[1] INRIA, France
[2] IATE, INRA, France
[3] University Montpellier 2, France
[4] LIRMM, France

Abstract. Within the framework of the European project EcoBioCap (ECOefficient BIOdegradable Composite Advanced Packaging), aiming at conceiving the
next generation of food packagings, we introduce an argumentation-based tool
for management of conflicting viewpoints between preferences expressed by the
involved parties (food and packaging industries, health and waste management
authorities, consumers, etc.). In this paper we recall briefly the principles underlying the reasoning process, and we detail the main functionalities and the architecture of the argumentation tool covering the overall reasoning steps starting
from formal representation of text arguments and ending by extraction of justified
preferences. Finally, we detail its operational functioning through a real life case
study to determine the justifiable choices between recyclable, compostable and
biodegradable packaging materials based on stakeholders' arguments.

1 Introduction

Within the framework of the European project EcoBioCap (ECOefficient BIOdegradable Composite Advanced Packaging), we have designed a Decision Support System
(called DSS) whose objective is to select packaging materials according to possibly conflicting requirements expressed by the involved parties (food and packaging industries,
health authorities, consumers, waste management authority, etc.). The requirements and
user preferences are modeled by several ontological rules provided by the stakeholders
expressing their viewpoints and expertise.

The DSS software is made of two parts, as depicted in Figure 1:

1. a multi-criteria flexible querying process [2] which takes as inputs desired preferences associated with packaging characteristics (permeability, shape, dimensions,
   desired shelf life, ...) and retrieves from a packaging database a ranked list of the
   most relevant packagings.
2. an argumentation process which aims at aggregating several stakeholders (consumers, researchers, food industry, packaging industry, waste management policy,
   etc.) requirements expressed as simple textual arguments, to enrich the querying
   process by stakeholders' justified preferences. Each argument supports/opposes a
   choice justified by the fact that it either meets or not a requirement according to
   packaging aspects (biodegradability, recyclability, transparency, ...).

S. Closs et al. (Eds.): MTSR 2014, CCIS 478, pp. 344–358, 2014.

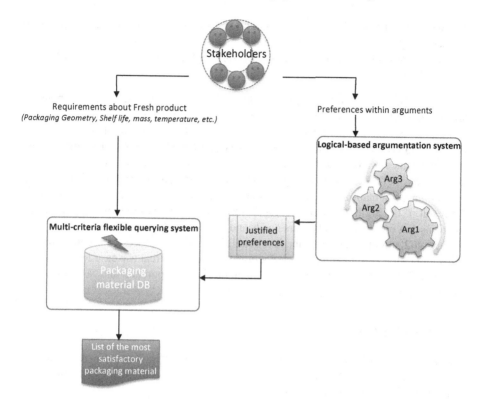

Fig. 1. Global insight of the DSS

Thus, our approach consists of two steps: (i) aggregating possibly conflicting preferences expressed by the involved stakeholders (ii) querying a database of packagings with the resulting aggregated preferences obtained at point (i). Indeed, packagings have to be selected according to several aspects or criteria (permeance, interaction with the packed food, end of life, etc.), highlighted by the expressed stakeholders' arguments.

In this paper we detail the implementation of the argumentation system. This module has as inputs stakeholders' arguments supporting or opposing a packaging choice which could be seen as preferences combined with their justifications, and returns consensual preferences which may be candidates to enrich the bipolar querying system. From the argumentation-based software standpoint, based on the recent survey of [8] and the web site *http://www.phil.cmu.edu/projects/argument_mapping/*, argumentation tools could be divided into the two following categories:

- Software for argument expression and modeling. These software such as Araucaria [6], Argunet [7] and DebateGraph (www.debategraph.org) allow the expression of arguments in a text format and manually formalizing them as logical implications made of hypothesis and conclusions. The user can after that save the arguments as an XML file.

– Software for extension computation (an extension is defined as a conflict-free subset of arguments defending themselves against attacks computed under a considered semantics [3]) over an argumentation graph given as input, like OVA-GEN
and ArguLab.

Despite the plethora of the software available in the field of argumentation, there are
few argumentation software implementing an argumentation process from argument expression to extensions computation, while providing users with several Graphical User
Interfaces to visualize the entire process. Unlike ArgTrust [4] in which the authors considered the uncertainty underlying the sources of the knowledge used in the argumentation framework for decision making, we introduce in this paper a real world application
based on argumentation reasoning and combining a querying process, which exploits
the result of the argumentation process as justified preferences expressing consensual
solutions that meet the stakeholders needs and requirements.

Section 2 summarizes the main functionalities of the tool. Section 3 details the architecture of the argumentation tool. Section 4 introduces a real use case for packaging
selection. Section 5 describes the implementation of the approach and Section 6 concludes the paper and sums up some future work.

2   User Requirements

We detail hereinafter the main functions of the argumentation system. After discussions and interviews with the project partners, we have identified some requirements
summarized in the following functionalities:

– *Formalize text arguments*: the argumentation system should provide users with a
user-friendly interface allowing them to express their arguments as text and then
formalizing them as concepts and rules. Here, a concept is either a *concrete* concept
defined over some attributes of the packaging material database for which values
(numerical, intervals or boolean) can also be specified, or an *abstract* concept which
is not related to any attribute in the database and only used in the reasoning process,
as illustrated in Example 1.

Example 1. The following text argument in favor of recyclable material *"Recyclable packagings are advised since they protect the environment according to the
life cycle analysis"* can be modeled by the following concepts and logical rules:
  • `RecyclablePack`: a concrete concept corresponding to recyclable packag-
    ing materials. It is defined over the boolean attribute *Recyclable* from the pack-
    aging materials database with the value `true`,
  • `ProtectEnvPack`: an abstract concept corresponding to packaging materi-
    als which protect the environment,
  • $RecyclablePack \Rightarrow ProtectEnvPack$ is a logical rule (implication) express-
    ing the fact that any recyclable packaging is a packaging which protects the
    environment,
  • $ProtectEnvPack \Rightarrow AcceptedPack$ is a logical rule expressing the fact that
    the decision of acceptance is attached to each packaging protecting the envi-
    ronment.

The system is also equipped with a function of import/export formalized arguments from/into an XML format. So, we can load already formatted concepts and rules directly in the system or obtain a local copy of the current project.

- *Process arguments*: the system should automatically compute the logical arguments obtained from the set of concepts and rules.

Example 2 (example of a logical argument). The text argument of Example 1 is automatically translated into a logical argument made of the following three steps of reasoning:

- Choice $C_1 = RecyclablePack$,
- By the rule "$RecyclablePack \Rightarrow ProtectEnvPack$" we get the conclusion: C_1 is $ProtectEnvPack$,
- By the rule "$ProtectEnvPack \Rightarrow AcceptedPack$" we get the final conclusion: C_1 is $AcceptedPack$.

The arguments can be gathered into pros and cons with regard to some packaging alternative characteristics. Once logical arguments are built, the system computes all conflicts or attacks among them and draws the corresponding argument graph.

Example 3 (example of conflict). The following argument *"recyclable packagings are not advised since they need to provide collect and treatment facilities, which could be very expensive"* is in conflict with the argument of Example 1.

- *Compute extensions*: an extension is a subset of non-conflicting arguments, which defined themselves against attacks, defined according to one semantics (admissible, preferred, grounded, stable, etc. see [3] for more details about semantics). The current version of the system implements different kinds of semantics. The user can compute one particular semantics or all the implemented semantics.
- *Enrich the bipolar querying*: based on the obtained extensions, the system extracts the criteria leading to either the rejection or the acceptance of some packaging types. These criteria and eventually associated values become predicates (conditions) which can be used latter as contraints or wishes to enrich the bipolar query which can be processed by the flexible querying system.

In addition to the above functions, the argumentation system must deal with interaction concerns such as:

- *multi-users*: the system must allow a real-time discussion among stakeholders. Every stakeholder has an account and a password. After logged in the system, a stakeholder can browse the current project, open one of them and join the discussion by adding or updating the expressed arguments.
- *persistence*: in the sense that the system saves in a database the ongoing or old projects (concept and rules) and already expressed concepts and rules and makes them available and accessible to the stakeholders to define quickly their own arguments.
- *informative*: the user can access to a log describing further details about the current state of the system including current users, complete description of logical arguments and conflicts.

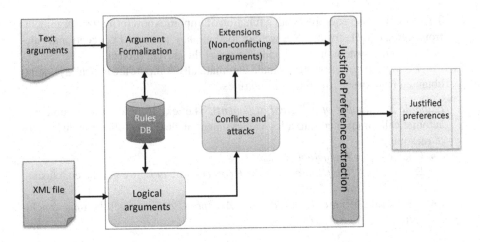

Fig. 2. The architecture of the argumentation system

- *configurable*: regarding to the amount of information the user can face during an argumentation session, the system can be run in either *expert* or *user* mode. The former allows to display all information about the process (argument graph, attack graph, conflicts, extensions, etc.) and the latter limits the information to the most relevant one (conflicts and extensions).

3   Architecture of the Argumentation System

As illustrated in Figure 2, the proposed argumentation system relies on 5 main modules, described below.

- *Argument formalization module*: this module implements a user-friendly interface for an interactive translation of text arguments into a formal representation made of concepts and rules (claims and hypothesis). The user has just to specify the part of the text argument corresponding to the claim and the part corresponding to the conclusion. Each part is modeled as a concept which could be either supported or not by the database. A graphical representation of the expressed rules is also built as the users formalize their text arguments. The formal representation obtained is finally saved in a database for a persistent storage allowing to reload argumentation projects without rebuilding all the arguments and to also reuse the already formatted rules in other projects.
- *Logical arguments*: this module receives as inputs the list of concepts and rules corresponding to text arguments. This list can be the result of the formalization module or given by the user as an XML file. As in [11,12] and by using a derivation process, this module builds all possible arguments according to the logical process defined in ASPIC/ASPIC+ logic-based argumentation frameworks [1,5]. This module also allows to export the argument list into an XML document.

- *Conflicts and attacks*: this module relies on the logical arguments built by the previous module. According to the negation operator, it detects all the conflicts among arguments and models them as attacks with respect to the definition of attacks introduced in [11,12]. The output of this module is an argumentation graph made of arguments (nodes) and attacks (edges).
- *Extensions*: an extension is a subset of non-conflicting (consistent) arguments which defend themselves from attacking arguments. The computation of extensions is made under one semantics (preferred, stable, grounded, eager, semi-stable, semi-stable, ideal) as defined in [3]. This module allows the computation of one or all semantics considered. We notice that theoretically we can get empty extensions under any semantics. This situation occurs when a user expresses at least one self-defeated argument, which is not attacked by any other argument, but attacks all the others. This kind of arguments are called contaminating arguments [13]. The current version of the system detects the rules leading to such arguments and discards them before performing the process of extension computation.
- *Extraction of the justified preferences*: the computation of extensions delivers one or several extensions. In the case of several extensions, the system lets the users selecting the most suitable one according to their objectives. The selected extension is then used to extract the preferences underlying the contained concepts. These preferences are translated into a list of couples $(attribut, value)$, where $attribute$ stands for a packaging attribute as defined in the packaging database schema of the flexible querying system part of the DSS, and $value$ is the preferred value expressed for the considered attribute. More details are provided in section 5.

4   Use Case

This section details a use case employed throughout the project and in this paper for exemplification reasons. We consider the following arguments expressed by the stakeholders obtained by interviews and surveys.

1. Packaging materials with low environmental impact are preferred, low environmental impact corresponds to carbon footprint of value $[0, 10]$ kg CO_2,
2. Waste management authority aims at collecting at least 75 % of recyclable packaging,
3. Consumers are unwilling to sort packaging cause of its extra taxe,
4. Life Cycle Analysis (LCA) results are not in favor of biodegradable and compostable materials,
5. Consumers are in favor of biodegradable material because they help to protect the environment,
6. Biodegradable materials could encourage people to throw their packaging in nature, causing visual pollution,
7. Micro-perforated packaging can increase the shelf life by about 20 days,

8. Multilayered byproduct made packagings allow a good permeance,

9. Biodegradable and compostable are expensive to product,

10. Consumers do not want pay an extra cost greater than 5% for a product packed with biodegradable or compostable packaging,

11. Recycling creates new jobs and encouraged by the waste management local administration.

Given the different concerns expressed by the experts, we have split the above arguments into several viewpoints. Focusing on a specific point of view or a concern helps experts to concentrate and to elicit knowledge. Such restriction is explained by (i) the huge number of arguments generated during the software testing phase, and (ii) the need for associating the packaging attributes with the argumentation process in its early stages. So, a viewpoint corresponds to one or several packaging attributes. In the current version of the system, argument splitting is made manually by the users when they express their arguments. In the above list of arguments, we can distinguish the following viewpoints:

- *end of life*: in this viewpoint, stakeholders (waste management authority, users, researchers) argue between biodegradability, compostability and recyclability of the packaging from their environmental effects. It contains arguments 1 to 6,
- *shelf life*: this viewpoint contains arguments 7 and 8, the choice is between multi-layered packagings or micro-perforated packagings,
- *economic*: this viewpoint deals with arguments expressed on the economic concerns such the extra cost of the final product, and the effect on employment. It contains arguments 9 to 11.

5   Implementation of the Approach

The implementation of the approach has been done in the context of the EcoBioCap DSS. A java GXT/GWT web interface was developed and a open version is accessible on *http://pfl.grignon.inra.fr/EcoBioCapProduction/*. Hereinafter, some user interfaces are displayed showing the obtained result in the case of the viewpoint "end of life". The main interface of the system is illustrated in Figure 3 which gives access to the functions of the **Logical-based argumentation system** in Figure 1 and detailed in Figure 2. It is divided into 5 zones. Zone 1 corresponds to the task bar implementing general functions applied on projects (create, load, close, refresh, export, etc.). Zone 2 lists the text arguments by stakeholders. Zone 3 displays the extracted concepts and rules from the text arguments, they are also listed by stakeholders. Zone 4 displays the graphical representation of the formalized concepts and arguments. Zone 5 is a notification area displaying the computed conflicts and extensions.

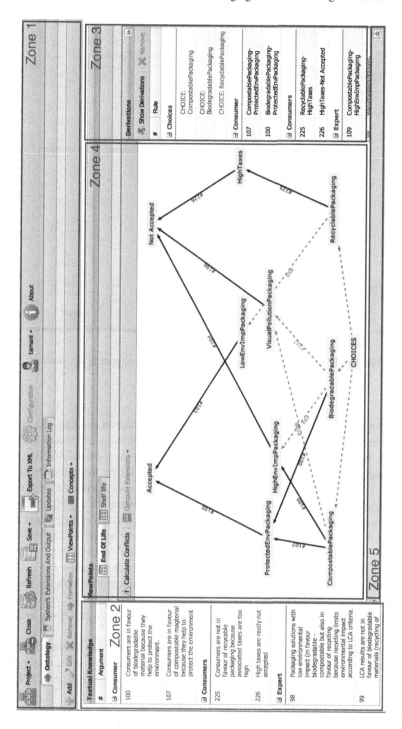

Fig. 3. Main interface of the argumentation system

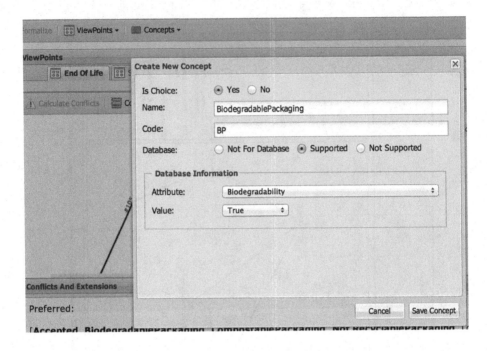

Fig. 4. Add a concept based on a defined attribute in the packaging database

After logging in, the user can create a new project, load an existing one or import a new project from an XML file. So, in the freely available version, stakeholder' arguments can be entered as (i) an XML file, by using the *import from XML* function, or (ii) text arguments to formalize then as concepts and rules by using a dedicated user interface (Figures 4, 5, 6 and 7) guiding and helping the user during all the process of formalization (implementing the **Argument Formalization** module in Figure 2). A new concept has a name and a short code, it can be defined as either a choice or not and can be related to a packaging attribute (as in Figure 4 for BiodegradablePackaging corresponding to packagings having the attribute Biodegradability = true in the packaging database), not related to any information in the database (as in Figure 5 for the concept HighTaxes), or can suggest a new attribute to enrich the packaging description in the database (as in Figure 6, concept HighEnvPackaging suggests the new attribute CarbonFootPrint, with the measure unit of $Kg\ CO_2\ eq.$ to describe packaging).

Figure 7 shows the formalizing interface in which a user can specify the already created concepts as premise or conclusion to form the rule underlying the text argument. The rule is then connected to a decision (accepted, not accepted). The rule and its decision can be specified either strict or defeasible.

Figure 8 illustrates the obtained ontology in the case of the viewpoint *end of life* in which stakeholders argued about biodegradability, recyclability and compostability. This ontology is the input of the **Logical Arguments** module in Figure 2.

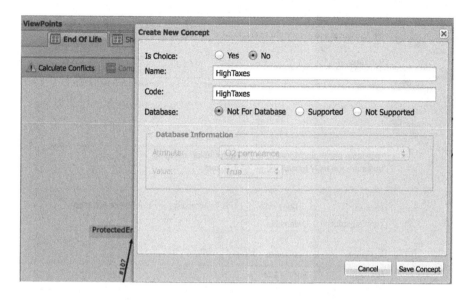

Fig. 5. Add a concept based which is not related to the database

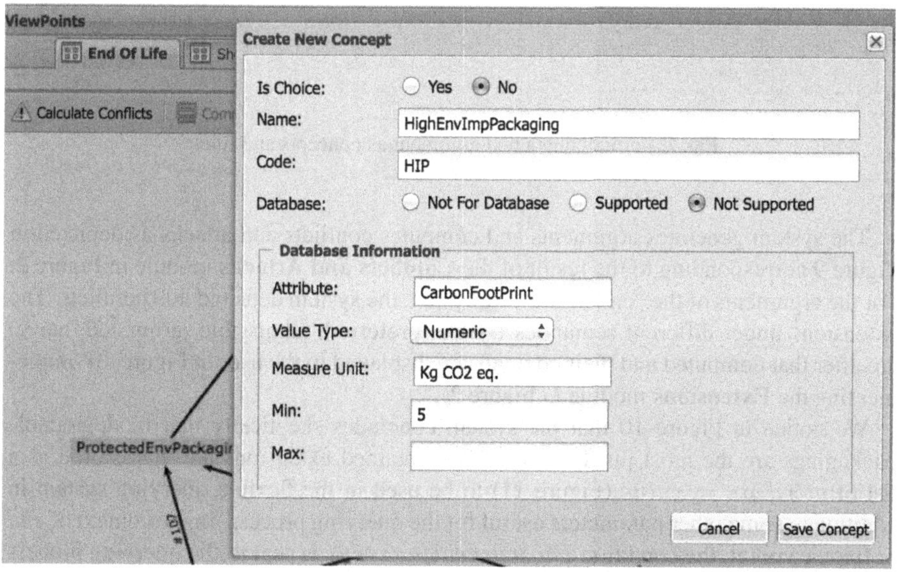

Fig. 6. Add a concept not currently supported in the packaging database but suggested for addition

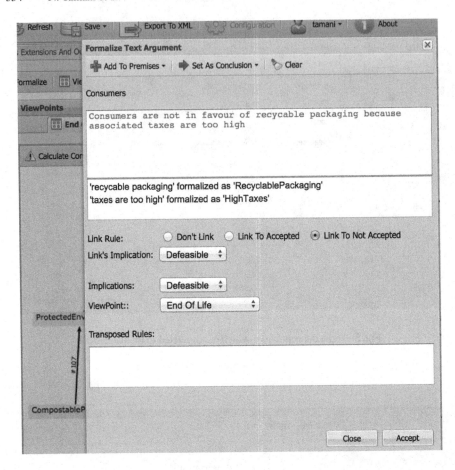

Fig. 7. Formalizing a text argument as concepts and rules

The system generates arguments and computes conflicts and attacks as depicted in Figure 9 corresponding to the result of the **Conflicts and Attacks** module in Figure 2. For the arguments of the "end of life" viewpoint, the system detected 409 conflicts. The extensions under different semantics (stable, preferred, admissible, grounded, naive) are after that computed and their contents are displayed to the user in Figure 10 (implementing the **Extensions** module in Figure 2).

We notice in Figure 10 that the system concludes skeptically that biodegradable packagings are the most justified ones. The obtained extensions are then stored as a list of $attribute = value$ (Figure 11) to be used in the flexible querying system in addition to some other parameters useful for the querying process. In the context of *end of life* viewpoint, the condition $Biodegradable = true$ is sent to the querying process to be used as a justified preference for packaging material selection.

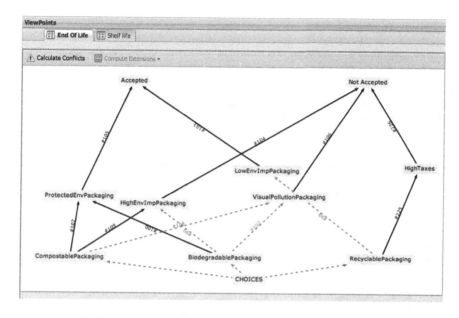

Fig. 8. Example of an ontology built upon the viewpoint *end of life*

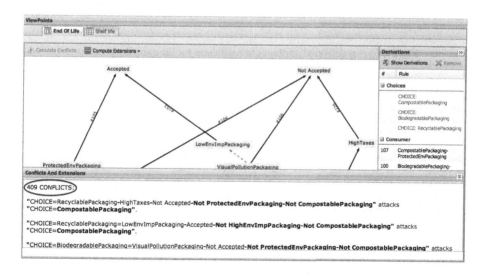

Fig. 9. Conflicts computed in the viewpoint *end of life*

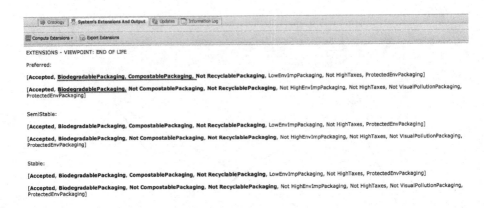

Fig. 10. Delivered extensions in the *end of life* viewpoint

Extension	ViewPoint	Concept	Attribute	Value 1	Value 2	Type	Type	Negated	Supported in DDBB
1	End Of Life	RecyclablePackaging	Recyclability	True	-	boolean	boolean	true	false
1	End Of Life	HighTaxes	TaxesLevel	True		boolean	boolean	true	false
1	End Of Life	ProtectedEnvPackaging	EnvImpact	30	50	percentage	percentage	false	false
1	End Of Life	BiodegradablePackaging	Biodegradability	True	-	boolean	boolean	false	true
1	End Of Life	CompostablePackaging	Compostability	True	-	boolean	boolean	false	false
1	End Of Life	LowEnvImpPackaging	EnvImpact	10	30	percentage	percentage	false	false
2	End Of Life	BiodegradablePackaging	Biodegradability	True	-	boolean	boolean	false	true
2	End Of Life	ProtectedEnvPackaging	EnvImpact	30	50	percentage	percentage	false	false
2	End Of Life	HighEnvImpPackaging	EnvImpact	50	70	percentage	percentage	true	false
2	End Of Life	CompostablePackaging	Compostability	True	-	boolean	boolean	true	false
2	End Of Life	HighTaxes	TaxesLevel	True		boolean	boolean	true	false
2	End Of Life	RecyclablePackaging	Recyclability	True	-	boolean	boolean	true	false
2	End Of Life	VisualPollutionPackaging	Pollution	True	-	boolean	boolean	true	false
3	Shelf life	BiodegradablePackaging	Biodegradability	True	-	boolean	boolean	false	true
3	Shelf life	MicroperforatedPackaging	MicroperforatedPack	True		boolean	boolean	false	false
3	Shelf life	ExtendShelfLifePackaging	NS	True		boolean	boolean	false	false

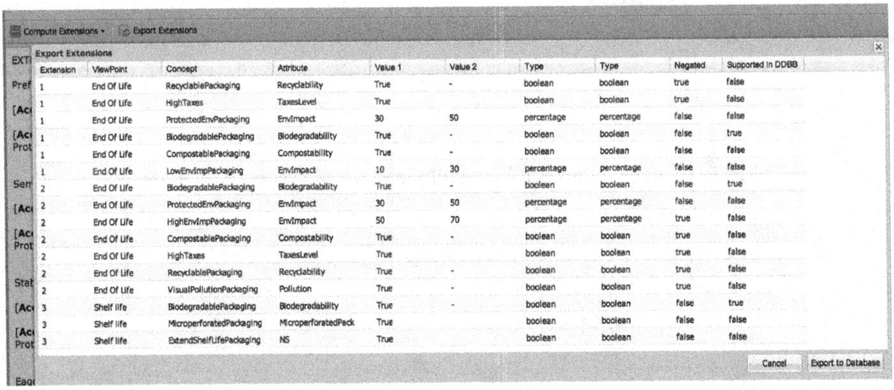

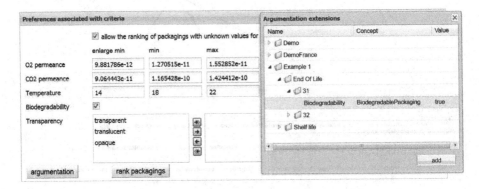

Fig. 11. Export delivered attributes to a database for the querying process

Fig. 12. Selecting the preferences associated with the *end of life* view point to complete the query with $Biodegradable = true$.

The user can actually select the extensions, previously translated into couples $attribute = value$, from the graphical user interface of the flexible multi-criteria querying system as displayed in Figure 12. Figure 13 finally displays the result after the execution of the multi-criteria querying which takes into account the aggregated preferences about biodegradability attribute. Four packagings are delivered and listed according to their relevance to the query preferences.

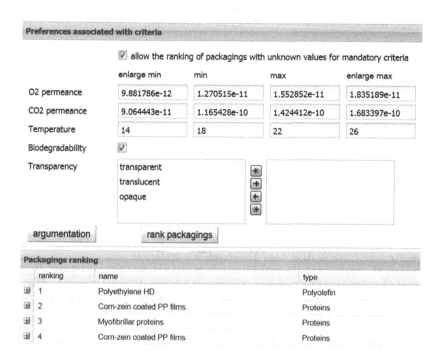

Preferences associated with criteria

☑ allow the ranking of packagings with unknown values for mandatory criteria

	enlarge min	min	max	enlarge max
O2 permeance	9.881786e-12	1.270515e-11	1.552852e-11	1.835189e-11
CO2 permeance	9.064443e-11	1.165428e-10	1.424412e-10	1.683397e-10
Temperature	14	18	22	26
Biodegradability	☑			
Transparency	transparent			
	translucent			
	opaque			

argumentation   rank packagings

Packagings ranking

ranking	name	type
⊞ 1	Polyethylene HD	Polyolefin
⊞ 2	Corn-zein coated PP films	Proteins
⊞ 3	Myofibrillar proteins	Proteins
⊞ 4	Corn-zein coated PP films	Proteins

Fig. 13. The final result after running the multi-criteria querying process.

6 Conclusion

We applied in this paper an argumentation approach on a real use case from the industry, based on a combination of an ASPIC argumentation system with a DLR-Lite specifications allowing stakeholders to express their preferences and providing the system with stable concepts and subsumptions of a domain. We have proposed an argumentation system in which each criterion (attribute or aspect) is considered as a viewpoint in which stakeholders express their arguments in homogenous way. Each viewpoint delivers extensions supporting or opposing certain choices according to one packaging aspect, which are then used in the querying process. The approach is finally implemented as freely accessible web application and a demonstration of the tool can also be provided. Some feedback obtained from test users point out the difficulties to consider a rule as either strict or defeasible and expressed the need to be able to specify a sort of importance encompassing the notions of strictness and defeasibility. So, one work in progress is to extend the proposed approach to fuzziness to make it possible to deal with vague and uncertain concepts and rules [10,9].

Acknowledgements. The research leading to these results has received funding from the European Community's seventh Framework Program (FP7/ 2007-2013) under the grant agreement n°FP7-265669-EcoBioCAP project. The authors would like to thank also the partners of the project for the help provided during the argument elicitation.

References

1. Amgoud, L., Bodenstaff, L., Caminada, M., McBurney, P., Parsons, S., Prakken, H., Veenen, J., Vreeswijk, G.: Final review and report on formal argumentation system.deliverable d2.6 aspic. Technical report (2006)
2. Destercke, S., Buche, P., Guillard, V.: A flexible bipolar querying approach with imprecise data and guaranteed results. Fuzzy Sets and Systems 169, 51–64 (2011)
3. Dung, P.M.: On the acceptability of arguments and its fundamental role in nonmonotonic reasoning, logic programming and n-persons games. Artificial Intelligence 77(2), 321–357 (1995)
4. Parsons, S., Sklar, E., Salvit, J., Wall, H., Li, Z.: Argtrust: decision making with information from sources of varying trustworthiness. In: Proceedings of the 2013 International Conference on Autonomous Agents and Multi-Agent Systems, pp. 1395–1396. International Foundation for Autonomous Agents and Multiagent Systems (2013)
5. Prakken, H.: An abstract framework for argumentation with structured arguments. Technical report, Department of Information and Computing Sciences. Utrecht University (2009)
6. Reed, C., Rowe, G.: Araucaria: Software for argument analysis, diagramming and representation. International Journal on Artificial Intelligence Tools 13(04), 961–979 (2004)
7. Schneider, D.C., Voigt, C., Betz, G.: Argunet- a software tool for collaborative argumentation analysis and research. In: 7th Workshop on Computational Models of Natural Argument (CMNA VII) (2007)
8. Schneider, J., Groza, T., Passant, A.: A review of argumentation for the social semantic web. Semantic Web 4(2), 159–218 (2013)
9. Tamani, N., Croitoru, M.: Fuzzy argumentation system for decision support. In: Laurent, A., Strauss, O., Bouchon-Meunier, B., Yager, R.R. (eds.) IPMU 2014, Part I. CCIS, vol. 442, pp. 77–86. Springer, Heidelberg (2014)
10. Tamani, N., Croitoru, M.: A quantitative preference-based structured argumentation system for decision support. In: Fuzz-IEEE, pp. 1408–1415 (2014)
11. Tamani, N., Croitoru, M., Buche, P.: A viewpoint approach to structured argumentation. In: Bramer, M., Petridis, M. (eds.) The Thirty-third SGAI International Conference on Innovative Techniques and Applications of Artificial Intelligence, pp. 265–271 (2013)
12. Tamani, N., Croitoru, M., Buche, P.: Conflicting viewpoint relational database querying: an argumentation approach. In: Scerri, L., Huhns, B. (eds.) Proceedings of the 13th International Conference on Autonomous Agents and Multiagent Systems (AAMAS 2014), pp. 1553–1554 (2014)
13. Wu, Y.: Between argument and conclusion. Argument-based approaches to discussion. Inference and Uncertainty. PhD thesis, Université du Luxembourg (2012)

Exploiting Textual Source Information
for Epidemiosurveillance

Elena Arsevska[1], Mathieu Roche[1], Renaud Lancelot[1],
Pascal Hendrikx[2], and Barbara Dufour[3]

[1] Cirad, Montpellier, France
[2] Anses, Paris, France
[3] EnvA, Maisons-Alfort, France

Abstract. In recent years as a complement to the traditional surveillance reporting systems there is a great interest in developing methodologies for early detection of potential health threats from unstructured text present on the Internet. In this context, we examined the relevance of the combination of expert knowledge and automatic term extraction in the creation of appropriate Internet search queries for the acquisition of disease outbreak news. We propose a measure that is the number of relevant disease outbreak news detected in function of the terms automatically extracted from a set of example Google and PubMED corpora. Due to the recent emergence we have used the African swine fever as a disease example.

Keywords: terminology extraction, internet disease surveillance.

1 Introduction

The new and exotic infectious diseases are an incising threat to countries due to globalization, movement of passengers, and international trade. With the traditional reporting schemes, often there are miss, delays or underreporting of disease outbreaks; leading to unawareness of countries about potential disease threats. As the Internet is a source of numerous and dynamic information, services need tools that could refine the search and detect the information of interest. Two important systems of the state-of-the-art, MediSys (Mantero *et al.* 2011) and Biocaster (Collier 2012) are based on a series of automatic steps to detect and acquire disease related news. The algorithms rely upon predefined templates, such keywords or patterns. Internet search queries have been proposed as inexpensive method to detect signals of diseases (ex. avian influenza) (Polgreen *et al.* 2008). In the face of many diseases and even more symptoms, the analysts face another challenge: How to identify appropriate queries for Internet disease surveillance? One option is to use the terms from existing thesaurus (e.g., MeSH). In this paper we present a new combined approach of selection of terms automatically extracted from relevant scientific and non-scientific corpora in order to identify most appropriate search queries for the detection of disease outbreak news on the Internet. As it is a recently emerging disease we use African swine fever (ASF) as a disease example.

S. Closs et al. (Eds.): MTSR 2014, CCIS 478, pp. 359–361, 2014.
© Springer International Publishing Switzerland 2014

2   How to Extract Relevant Information?

The methodology we propose consists of four stages: data acquisition, information retrieval, information extraction and information evaluation. Here we focus on the automatic term extraction and evaluation by domain experts in order to improve the relevance of the search queries for the detection of disease outbreak news on the Internet. For automatic extraction of terms from documents, we have used the BioTex tool which combines linguistic and statistic information adapted to biomedical domain (Lossio *et al.* 2014). More precisely, with Biotex (i) the list of syntactic structures of terms are learnt with relevant sources for our study (e.g., MeSH), and (ii) the relevant combination of information retrieval techniques (e.g. TF-IDF, OKAPI, and C-value measures). The aim of our work consists of weighting the terms extracted according to different sources of information. Therefore we propose a measure (see formula (1)) that privileges the terms extracted from the relevant sources and the high ranking obtained with Biotex.

$$w(t) = \sum \alpha_i \times \frac{1}{rank_{Si}(t)} \quad \text{with } \alpha_i \in [0,1] \text{ and } \sum \alpha_i = 1 \quad (1)$$

where t is the term, Si is the information from the Internet source, $rank_{Si}$ is the automatic Biotex rank of the term t from a source Si and where α_i is the weight attributed by experts to Si.

3   Experiments

Two principal sources of information were used in this work: Google and PubMED. The search queries were applied for the period from 01/01/2011 to 10/06/2014 on the 10th of June 2014. The Google corpus was acquired with the search query: "african swine fever outbreak" that resulted in 497 news. Only 123 HTML pages, reporting an ASF outbreak (place, time, animals affected, symptoms etc.) were considered as relevant to this work. The PubMED corpus was consisted of 232 abstracts that contained the term "african swine fever" in the title. Only 66 abstracts were selected as relevant to the epidemiology of ASF. 1200 terms were extracted and ranked from the Google and PubMED corpora. Domain experts identified 67 (5,6 %) terms from Google and 85 (7,1 %) from PubMED as relevant to describe an ASF case or outbreak, including acronyms and synonyms. According to this evaluation, the attributed weight (α_i) for Google was 0,4 and 0,6 for PubMED. For example the weight given to the term "asf outbreaks" based on the formula (1) was $(1/5)*0,6+(1/1034)*0,4 = 0,12$. This term used as a query enabled to identify 67 disease outbreak news not identified previously.

4   Conclusion and Future Work

Our work shows that both Google and PubMed could serve as sources of terms for Internet search queries (with PubMED giving 20% more relevant terms). We believe that search-term surveillance may represent an inexpensive way of performing supplemental disease surveillance. The use of search queries is not limited to ASF; it could also be used to monitor other infectious diseases or even symptoms (e.g., abortion, mortality). For this preliminary study, we limited our experiments to a small set of examples. In future we intend to test the relevance of a more precise set of terms or combinations thereof as Internet search queries.

Acknowledgements. This work was supported by the French Ministry of Agriculture, Food and Forestry and the French Agricultural Research Centre for International Development. We thank Sylvain Falala and David Chavernac for their technical support for this work.

References

1. Mantero, J., Belyaeva, E.E., Linge, J.P.: How to maximize event-based surveillance web-systems: the example of ECDC/JRC collaboration to improve the performance of MedISys. Publications Office of the European Union (2011)
2. Lossio Ventura, J.-A., Jonquet, C., Roche, M.: Teisseire, Towards a Mixed Approach to Extract Biomedical Terms from Text Corpus. Int. J. Knowl. Disc. Bioinfo. 4(1), 1–15 (2014)
3. Collier, N.: Uncovering text mining: A survey of current work on web-based epidemic intelligence. Glob. Public Health 7(7), 731–749 (2012)
4. Polgreen, P.M., Chen, Y., Pennock, D.M., Nelson, F.D.: Using Internet Searches for Influenza Surveillance. Clin. Infect. Dis. 47(11), 1443–1448 (2008)

Author Index